W9-CHU-505

UNHOLY SPIRITS

Other books by Gary North

Marx's Religion of Revolution, 1968
An Introduction to Christian Economics, 1973
Unconditional Surrender, 1981
Successful Investing in an Age of Envy, 1981
The Dominion Covenant: Genesis, 1982
Government by Emergency, 1983
The Last Train Out, 1983
Backward, Christian Soldiers?, 1984
75 Bible Questions Your Instructors Pray You Won't Ask, 1984
Coined Freedom: Gold in the Age of the Bureaucrats, 1984
Moses and Pharaoh: Dominion Religion Versus Power Religion, 1985
Negatrends, 1985
The Sinai Strategy: Economics and the Ten Commandments, 1986
Conspiracy: A Biblical View, 1986
Inherit the Earth, 1986
Honest Money, 1986
Dominion and Common Grace, 1986
Fighting Chance, 1986 [with Arthur Robinson]
Resurrection vs. Entropy, 1987
The Pirate Economy, 1987
Liberating Planet Earth, 1987
   (Spanish) *Teología de Liberación,* 1986

Books edited by Gary North

Foundations of Christian Scholarship, 1976
Tactics of Christian Resistance, 1983
The Theology of Christian Resistance, 1983
Editor, *Journal of Christian Reconstruction* (1974-1981)

UNHOLY SPIRITS

Occultism and
New Age Humanism

Gary North

Dominion Press
Ft. Worth, Texas

Copyright ©1986 by Gary North

All rights reserved. Written permission must be secured from the publisher to use or reproduce any part of this book, except for brief quotations in critical reviews or articles.

Published by Dominion Press
7112 Burns Street, Fort Worth, Texas 76118

Printed in the United States of America

ISBN 0-930462-02-5

This book is dedicated to
Bob Mumford

TABLE OF CONTENTS

INTRODUCTION

I hate to revise my books. The older the book is, the more I hate to revise it. I always feel compelled to read lots of books and articles that have been published in the interim that deal with the topic of the book in question. The longer the book has been out of print, the stronger my compulsion to read and revise extensively. So I tend not to re-release my older books. *Marx's Religion of Revolution* (1968) has been out of print for over a decade; *An Introduction to Christian Economics* (1973, with revisions through 1979) has been out of print for five years.

The original version of this book was written in 1974. It was published in early 1976 under the title *None Dare Call It Witchcraft*. It has been out of print since about 1979. It went through three printings, but then the original publisher, Arlington House, went bankrupt. While there has been a continuing trickle of inquiries about where to buy the book, I just did not have time to revise it. I have written and published about eight books since 1979, plus I completely reworked a ninth book into a new format, plus I have had to build up my newsletter business and the Institute for Christian Economics by launching about ten newsletters (and killing several as bad decisions). I have just not had the time to revise it thoroughly.

I have decided to compromise. I have made a few revisions in this book, but the text is very close to the original. I have added some chapters but have removed the original appendices by Rushdoony, Molnar, and Ketchen. These essays are still in print in *The Journal of Christian Reconstruction*, Vol. I, No. 2 (Winter, 1974): "Symposium on Satanism," which I edited. This journal is published by the Chalcedon Foundation, P.O. Box 158, Vallecito, California 95251.

Writing this Book

The original version had an odd history. In the summer of 1972, I was lecturing to a group of students at a conference sponsored by the Midwest office of the Intercollegiate Studies Institute (I.S.I.). I

1

discussed aspects of the relationship between religion and economics. I referred briefly to certain characteristics of the occult, and one student asked me if I planned to write a book on the topic. I replied, "Yes; I'll call it *None Dare Call It Witchcraft*." Gary Allen and Larry Abraham had just released their *None Dare Call It Conspiracy*, a title mimicking John Stormer's best-selling paperback, *None Dare Call It Treason* (1964). *None Dare* was a catchy title in those days.

Months later, I received a note from the student. "Have you written *None Dare Call It Witchcraft* yet?" Naturally, I hadn't. I hadn't even thought about the project. It was only a title invented on the spur of the moment. Besides, I was working for Leonard Read's Foundation for Economic Education (FEE), and Leonard, who was a dedicated free enterpriser publicly, was a dedicated socialist organizationally. When he hired me, he informed me (after I had arrived at FEE's headquarters in Irvington, New York) that I would have to turn over to FEE 100% of any money I earned "on the outside." There was not much incentive to produce. (Even the check I received for those I.S.I. lectures had to go to FEE, even though I gave them during my vacation. It has never ceased to astound me that Read could not understand that his socialist policy at FEE would depress staff output just as surely as socialism in the Kremlin does.) Nevertheless, I decided that since I had the title, maybe I should write the book. By that time, I knew I wouldn't be working for FEE forever, and the royalties (if any) would be handy when I left.

I inquired with Arlington House's Mitch Wright, a former seminary classmate (Westminster Seminary in Philadelphia), if he thought Arlington House would be interested. He said yes. So I signed a contract. (It was at that same meeting that I suggested that they publish the manuscript by Rushdoony that later became *The Politics of Pornography* and the history of the National Council of Churches by Gregg Singer that became *The Unholy Alliance*. It was a fruitful meeting.)

I did not really begin to write the book for another year, after I had left FEE. I wrote the bulk of it in 1974 and early 1975. In retrospect, I would not recommend that other people follow my lead without a special calling from God. Burying oneself in the literature of the occult may initially seem exhilarating, but eventually it becomes depressing. Only to the extent that an investigator is searching for connections between occult philosophy and occult practices, and in turn between occult philosophy and humanist philosophy, should the project even be considered. The goal should be to find contrasts, culturally and philosophically, between Christianity and occultism, and then to emphasize the positive ethical, intellectual, and cultural aspects of Christianity that necessarily reduce the influence of occultism when Christianity is put into widespread practice. A study of occult practices as such is a negative endeavor that cannot, in and of itself, do anything to reverse the drift into occultism. Such an investigation necessarily pushes the student too close to the borders of evil. Few people are ready for such an encounter.

I have seen serious investigators turn into quasi-occultists themselves. They began to believe what the occultists claimed for themselves and their religion just because the investigators saw that the occultists could, in fact, display supernatural powers in certain instances. The manifestations of occult power (which are all too real) blinded the investigators to the misrepresentations of the nature and source of such power. They became hypnotized by Satan's power religion because they were not grounded in God's ethics religion.

The book was published in early 1976. From start to finish, 1972-76, I went through three editors at Arlington House. The book sold moderately well, but set no records. It went through three printings. I have retitled it *Unholy Spirits: Occultism and New Age Humanism*. I had not used the term "New Age" in the original book, though I was familiar with the term. It has long been a common phrase in occult circles. The term is now well known in Christian circles,[1] so I have adopted it in this version.

The basic theme of the book is simple enough, and has not changed since I wrote it: the rise of occultism as a cultural force in the United States began around 1965, and paralleled the rise of the counter-culture and the breakdown of the older Establishment humanism, the "can-do" pragmatism which was apotheosized posthumously as Kennedy's "Camelot." Kennedy's death on November 22, 1963 was in fact the death rattle of the older rationalism. (Interestingly, the man who in our day best understood the devil and his kingdom, C. S. Lewis, also died that day, as did Aldous Huxley, grandson of Thomas Huxley, Darwin's first great promoter. Aldous

---

1. Constance Cumbey, *The Hidden Dangers of the Rainbow: The New Age Movement and Our Coming Age of Barbarism* (Shreveport, Louisiana: Huntington House, 1983); Dave Hunt, *Peace Prosperity and the Coming Holocaust: The New Age Movement in Prophecy* (Eugene, Oregon: Harvest House, 1983). Dave Hunt apparently hates commas almost as much as he hates New Age philosophy.

was a proponent of mysticism and drugs in the name of opening "the doors of perception.")

As I say in chapter nine, which deals with "flying saucers," it is my thesis that personal occult creatures whose goal is to confuse men, delude men, and keep them in a form of bondage, can do so by manifesting themselves in a form which is acceptable to men. When men are willing to believe in supernatural forces but not in God, then mankind is very close to the end—either the final battle, or at the very least, the end of the anti-Christian world of humanism. I think we face the latter.[2]

A Revival of Ancient Paganism

C. S. Lewis makes the observation in *The Abolition of Man* (1947) that occultism and humanism appeared in Western history at about the same time, during the Renaissance. Humanist philosophy and occultism were two sides of the same revival of paganism. Thus, he argued, occultism and humanistic rationalism are not enemies in principle but rather cooperating philosophies that are united against Christianity and Christian civilization. This is the theme of his great masterpiece, the novel *That Hideous Strength*. I read this book in the spring of 1964 as a class assignment at seminary, and it was by far the most important book anyone ever assigned me in any class I ever took. I also met David Ketchen at seminary, who had himself been involved in table-raising as a youth, and he introduced me to the writings of Kurt Koch, a European exorcist.

This two-fold background, both philosophical and practical, alerted me to the significance of occultism and its links with revolutionism, mysticism, and the quest for power. This understanding made it far easier for me to interpret the years of the counter-culture (1964-70), which began the following semester, when the student revolution broke out in the United States at the University of California at Berkeley. (I was enrolled at UCLA that semester, and transferred to UC Riverside in the spring of 1965.) That revolution shook the foundations of the older liberalism. It launched a series of "scientific revolutions" or "paradigm shifts" in every social science.[3]

---

2. David Chilton, *Paradise Restored: A Biblical Theology of Dominion* (Tyler, Texas: Reconstruction Press, 1985).

3. Gary North, "The Epistemological Crisis of American Universities," in North (ed.), *Foundations of Christian Scholarship: Essays in the Van Til Perspective* (Vallecito, California: Ross House, 1976).

Simultaneously, the appearance of occultism pointed to a revival of the same old Renaissance alliance. The new humanism and the new occultism of the late 1960's produced a new world view, which has in recent years begun to be identified as the New Age movement or New Age humanism. Such phenomena as "holistic healing," Eastern mysticism, "higher consciousness," monistic philosophy (the world is one: pantheism), magic, divine healing, astrology, and outright satanism began to multiply. The New Age philosophy proclaims the evolutionary development of man, the coming "leap of being" in which mankind will transcend its present creaturely limitations. This philosophy is in tune with Darwinian humanism, as well as with Marxism and other forms of revolutionism. It has cut across all ideological and age barriers; from 1965 on, little old ladies of both sexes mixed freely with bra-less young women and their unwashed male consorts. The conservative old ladies, however, were more likely to meet the younger hippie types at health food stores than at Vietnam peace marches; they were more likely to eat various grasses with them than smoke grasses with them.

At first, older humanists, both right wing and left wing, stood on the sidelines in astonished disbelief at the goings-on of the counter-culture. Men like Irving Howe (old liberalism) and Robert Nisbet (old conservativism) saw the campus antics as something fundamentally hostile to the concept of academic community and rational discourse. But steadily as the decade wore on, the counter-culture began to attract older campus liberals, in part because of their growing outrage at the Vietnam War. Why the delay in outrage? I think it was because the U.S. was perceived to be losing, especially after North Vietnam's suicidal Tet Offensive in February of 1968, and liberals generally get outraged at political systems that lose, or that fight "progressive" systems (for example, Nazism after June of 1941, when Hitler invaded the U.S.S.R.), as distinguished from political *candidates* who lose (especially Adlai Stevenson).

There was another important recruiting factor: their students were having a terrific time raising hell. (What they failed to perceive was that a small minority really *were* raising hell: occult powers.) Furthermore, the sexual revolution had begun; the protest movement opened up new possibilities for "rejuvenated youth" (and rejuvenated sex) to older liberals, especially non-tenured junior faculty members. Even a few conservatives made the switch; the most notable was Garry Wills, the former *National Review* columnist with a

Ph.D. in classics from Yale, who became a war protestor and nationally syndicated New Left columnist after 1965.

Six Years that Shook the World

Important events in the coming of the New Age revival of occultism were these: the assassination of President Kennedy on Nov. 22, 1963; the arrival ten weeks later of the Beatles to appear on the Ed Sullivan Show; the two military incidents (mostly mythical, as it later turned out) in the Gulf of Tonkin in July of 1964, and the Senate's resolution which gave the President the authority to escalate the war unilaterally; the Berkeley student protests (Free Speech Movement, FSM, led by Mario Savio) that began on September 15, the week before classes were to begin; the defeat of Goldwater by Johnson in November; the escalation of the war in Vietnam throughout early 1965; and the release of the Beatles' "Rubber Soul" album in 1965, which marked their transition from lighthearted boys singing "I want to hold your hand" to musical innovators and, as it turned out, musical revolutionaries. The counter-culture had arrived. So had occultism.

Not that "Rubber Soul" sounds very revolutionary in retrospect. Its very first song, "I've Just Seen a Face," has become more famous in American popular music as a bluegrass tune than as a rock number. The album seems almost harmless today. But the Beatles were innovators, and within a few months, the more creative and more threatening "Revolver" album appeared, with its haunting hymn of meaninglessness, "Eleanor Rigby," and its Eastern arrangements. George Harrison was learning to play the Indian sitar; he had only plucked a few notes on "Rubber Soul." Soon, they would introduce the Maharishi Mahesh Yogi to the West, and Transcendental Meditation took off.[4]

Nevertheless, "Rubber Soul" had served as the cultural wedge. I remember talking with a very bright, very liberal young man who had served as editor of the UC Riverside campus newspaper, and who by 1967 was already having second thoughts concerning the counter-culture. He told me the following: "When Rubber Soul first came out, we figured that if we could just get Johnson and Brezhnev

---

4. Jack Forem, *Transcendental Meditation: Maharishi Mahesh Yogi and the Science of Creative Intelligence* (New York: Dutton, 1974). What delights me most is that even in the title, Transcendental Meditation bears its all-important R with a circle around it: the sign of a registered trademark.

to sit down, smoke some marijuana; and listen to Rubber Soul a few times, they could work out the Cold War in one evening." That album was the Pied Piper leading the kids out of Hamlin to . . . where?

We also should note the short-lived attempt of California designer Rudi Gernreich to introduce topless fashions in the summer of 1964. The "topless bar" fad began. Carol Doda got her silicone implants and attracted nightly crowds of wide-eyed men in a San Francisco nightclub. Miniskirts appeared, and then micro-miniskirts. The counter-culture in women's fashions had arrived. The basic rule was this: women's clothing should show everything except good taste. It was clothing for well-endowed exhibitionists.

In racial matters, the Civil Rights Act was passed on July 3, 1964, just in time for the 4th of July holiday; thirteen days later, a race riot began in Harlem, New York, and thirteen months later, the Watts riot began, which was the beginning of the serious urban race riots that were to continue for three more years. Also in 1965: the beginning of the great dollar inflation.

The six-year period of chaos ended almost as rapidly as it had appeared. It seemed as though it might go on forever in 1968, but periods of social, moral, and cultural chaos never do. Bureaucracy (or something worse) always pulls things back together. Some things, not everything. There is never a *status quo ante*. Robespierre was replaced by Napoleon. Weimar Germany was replaced by Nazi Germany. Social orders have their limits, and Western Civilization had its limits. Toleration finally ran out, but only after many standards that previously had not been tolerated became acceptable.

A Bloody Culture

First, the counter-culture's culture ran into trouble — bloody trouble. In the second week of August, 1969, someone murdered actress Sharon Tate and her friends, and the next night murdered the LaBianca family. Los Angeles was shocked. When they found out who did it and why, the public *really* was shocked. But that was four months away. Miss Tate was the beautiful wife of Roman Polanski, the director of the financially successful occult movie, *Rosemary's Baby*. As the story unfolded, it turned out that drugs and kinky sex had been part of the partyings of Miss Tate and her late associates.

A week after the murders, the famous "Woodstock" rock festival in upstate New York marked the high water mark of the counter-culture. It was peace and love everywhere, and drugs and fornication: "Woodstock Nation," Mr. Yippie himself, Abbie Hoffman, later dubbed it — Abbie, of Chicago Seven fame, of *Steal This Book* fame, and much later, of drug pushing fame. On December 1, the story hit the papers: a jailed follower of Charles Manson's "dune buggy army" had admitted that she and others in the Manson clan had committed the Tate and LaBianca murders. The case was virtually solved, announced the Los Angeles Chief of Police, though he did not mention Manson that day. More of the gory details came out at the December 5 grand jury investigation, and were leaked to the press in time for the afternoon editions. The whole surrealistic story came out in the months that followed. Charles Manson, who was the friend of rock stars (including, as it later was revealed, several of the Beach Boys, who had actually recorded one of his songs), turned out to be a vicious con artist who used drugs, mysticism, occultism, Beatles' lyrics, Hermann Hesse's pop classic in Eastern mysticism, *Siddhartha*,[5] sexual debauchery, and other mind-altering techniques to create a dedicated little band of revolutionaries and murderers. The counter-culture began to look fearful to millions of people. The "let's all get high and read tarot cards" mystique had begun to fade. Things were going too far.

On December 6, the day after the grand jury hearings on Manson, the ill-fated, free-of-charge Rolling Stones rock concert took place at the Altamont Speedway near San Francisco, with 300,000 in attendance. "Woodstock West," it had been heralded. Someone (no one remembered afterward just who) had invited the Hell's Angels motorcycle club to serve as bodyguards. Throughout the day's performances by popular rock groups — Santana, Jefferson Airplane, etc. — the Angels' violence had intensified. Then, during the Stone's evening performance, a Hell's Angel killed a black man who had pulled a gun. It happened just after the Stones had begun to sing "Sympathy for the Devil." There had been a brief flurry of violence just as they started to sing. Mick Jagger stopped singing and tried to calm the crowd, remarking on-stage: "We always have something very funny happen when we start that number. . . ."[6] Funny peculiar, not funny amusing. Moments later, death intervened. The

---

5. Ed Sanders, *The Family: The Story of Charles Manson's Dune Buggy Attack Battalion* (New York: Dutton, 1971), p. 106.

6. Philip Norman, *Symphony for the Devil: The Rolling Stones Story* (New York: Linden Press/Simon & Schuster, 1984), p. 333.

knifing was recorded for posterity in the moving picture, "Gimme Shelter." The Stones' biographer summarized the film's conclusion well: "There, at last, was the crucial moment at Altamont in the red-spotlit dark, as Mick Jagger stood, helpless among the real demons his masquerade had summoned up."[7]

The performers did not know what had happened off-stage, so they finished the concert. The concert, in turn, finished the myth of the flower children and their happy music. A sanitized version of the event hit the papers the next morning, but by evening the grim details surfaced. Six weeks later, *Rolling Stone* magazine published a lengthy, damning essay on the affair. Sympathy for the devil was running low.

From Woodstock to Altamont: the hiatus lasted less than four months.

The next year, 1970, brought the death of the screaming, heroin-addicted sweetheart of the rock world, Janis Joplin, on October 3. (I remember well the explanation for her demise which was offered to me by one grief-stricken undergraduate: "The CIA got her.") Less than a month before, Jimi Hendrix, the black guitarist whose electric guitar was as noisy as Miss Joplin's singing, had died. Could the beat go on? (The following July, Jim Morrison, the lead singer of "The Doors," died mysteriously in France, but by then the counter-culture era was over.)

The Political Counter-Revolution

Second, 1970 also brought the long-awaited political reversal. The counter-culture's politics ran into trouble—again, bloody trouble. In early May, Richard Nixon gave a speech in which he admitted that the U.S. had begun an invasion of Cambodia. He justified the invasion and promised that it would help bring the war to a close. Student protests spread rapidly. A few days later, a protest at obscure Kent State University led to the shooting and deaths of several students by the Ohio National Guard. This event singlehandedly ended student protests around the world. Students vowed to be back in force the following semester, but when they returned, the campuses everywhere became astoundingly quiet, and have remained so for 15 years. The risks had gotten too high; the psychology of visible confrontation had ended. There was one more peace and

---

7. *Ibid.*, p. 338.

happiness rock concert, on the Isle of Wight in the English Channel, in August 1970. Then it was all over.

Economics on Campus

Third, the economic recession that was first revealed by the stock market in the summer of 1969 stretched into 1970 and then into 1971. The days of easy jobs for college graduates ended. Even more important for the campus, the 1964 prediction by New York University's president Allan Cartter came true: that in 1969, the boom in college hiring would end. It did. A glut of Ph.D.'s appeared, overnight. From the spring of 1969 until the present (and far into the foreseeable future), newly graduated Ph.D.'s in almost every field have not been able to get full-time college teaching jobs, let alone tenured positions. The non-tenured junior faculty members saw the handwriting on the wall, and there was no time left for love-ins with undergraduates — not during normal class hours, anyway, and not in groups.

It is now common for people in southern California who hold earned Ph.D.'s from major universities to take part-time jobs teaching nearly illiterate junior college students. For this they are paid $25 per classroom teaching hour. Deduct travel time, class preparation time (reviewing old class notes, reading the assigned textbook), exam-grading time (especially if the teacher gives essay exams), and the instructor discovers that he is working for about $6 per hour. So much for the value of the Ph.D. This is the financial return on an investment of the extra half decade to a decade of a person's youth that it takes to earn a Ph.D. This shift in market rewards ended the visible radicalism of the professors in the fall of 1970. It has never returned. "They ain't marchin' anymore."

We Can't Go Home Again

Many of the changes wrought philosophically and morally by the counter-culture are still with us. The New Age movement has become respectable and bureaucratized. The psychedelic baby did not exactly eat the cybernetic monster; it just grew up and bought an IBM PC. The hippies got haircuts, but a significant proportion of them have not abandoned their world view. The Weathermen went underground, but they still await a favorable time to begin terrorist attacks. LSD was out by 1970, but cocaine is in. Cocaine has become the preferred drug of stockbrokers everywhere. Standards have changed . . . for the worse.

In entertainment and popular literature, magic and witchcraft have fused with fantasy and science fiction to give us a whole new range of occult options: Dungeons and Dragons, wizardry, Conan the Barbarian, and an endless number of Saturday morning cartoon shows for children displaying the wonders of the occult. "Ghostbusters" was the biggest money-making movie in 1984. The Rolling Stones' facial lines are rapidly becoming middle-aged wrinkles, but they are still able to draw huge audiences all over the civilized world. Jumping Jack Flash is still jumping. The beat goes on.

The former youth culture also has lowered its standards, by raising the age limits of acceptable toleration. These days they don't trust anyone over 50; before, it was anyone over 30. And a job at Merrill Lynch doesn't look so bad any more, either, especially if the Dow Jones industrial average keeps going up. But will it? And if it doesn't, and the economy begins to unravel, what will our former flower children do? Even more to the point, what will the Weathermen do? We are sitting on top of a social volcano. It is inactive, not dead.

The Shattered Foundations

There have been significant changes since 1970. The Soviets have caught up with the West and have surpassed us in terms of armaments. Solzhenitsyn's *Gulag Archipelago* has at last brought reality into the thinking of the West's intellectuals concerning Soviet civilization. The U.S. economy has been through the inflation-recession wringer several times, and the rapidly escalating government and private debt load threatens Western economies everywhere. The New Deal welfare programs are geriatric and shuffling with the aged gait of the octagenarian. The Great Society's war on poverty is now known to have *increased* poverty.[8]

The self-confidence of the liberals is gone. The self-confidence of the economists has gone with it. France's Jean François Revel's remarkable book, *How Democracies Perish* (Doubleday, 1984), is an epitaph on modern democracy's inability to defend itself against dedicated, relentless Communist totalitarianism, and it has won rave reviews from Democrats everywhere. We are at the end of an era.

---

8. Charles Murray, *Losing Ground: American Social Policy, 1950-1980* (New York: Basic Books, 1984).

Simultaneously, the rise of the New Christian Right since 1979 has astounded political commentators. A major shift in the thinking of evangelicals is in progress. Younger charismatics and most of the independent Christian day schools are headed toward biblical law and away from the social and political policies of inaction that have been common in traditional, pietistic, dispensational circles since 1925. They are picketing against abortion clinics (legalized in 1973 by the U.S. Supreme Court, but not by God's supreme court). They are adopting ethics religion and abandoning the older escapist religion. The key word in this shift of perspective is "dominion." The secondary word is "resistance." Resistance to what? Secular humanism and its legal arm, the Federal government.

In contrast, Billy Graham, Wheaton College, Calvin College, *Christianity Today*, neo-evangelicalism, and the evangelical and Reformed seminaries seem to be headed toward liberation theology (an exception: Reformed Episcopal Seminary in Philadelphia). Old-line dispensational seminaries are desperately trying to stay out of the fight, and in doing so, they are becoming increasingly irrelevant. This split is affecting numerous old-line conservative denominations and para-church organizations. A Kuhn-like paradigm shift is underway. The older foundations are broken; new ones are being poured. New men are pouring them. It is a case of new wine in old wineskins. The old wineskins are screaming "foul!" as they feel the pressure from the bubbling liquid, but to no avail. They are about to burst.

Older evangelical intellectuals are now faced with what they regard as a dismaying choice: to line up with the practical prescriptions of the theocratic conservatives in the Christian Reconstruction movement, or to side with the socialistic liberation theologians, who are presently visibly pacifists but who threaten to become revolutionaries (as their spiritual forebears, the Anabaptists did, 1525-35). Either the new Puritans or the new Anabaptists. Either David Chilton[9] or Ronald Sider.[10] Either pro-legalized life or pro-legalized abortion.

The flagship of middle-aged Christian scholarship's fleet, the *Neutrality*, has been hit by several torpedoes, and is taking on water

---

9. David Chilton, *Productive Christians in an Age of Guilt-Manipulators: A Biblical Response to Ronald J. Sider* (3rd ed.; Tyler, Texas: Institute for Christian Economics, 1985).

10. Ronald J. Sider, *Rich Christians in an Age of Hunger: A Biblical Study* (2nd ed.; Downers Grove, Illinois: Inter-Varsity Press, 1984).

fast. The *Theistic Evolution*, a destroyer, has also suffered several direct hits. The *Keynes*, a cruiser, is in dry dock. This is a time that tries the souls of vaguely committed and risk-aversive scholars who teach in neo-evangelical colleges, meaning about 95% of the faculties.

Conclusion

Occultism surfaces as a cultural phenomenon at the end of civilizations. It came at the end of Rome, at least in its more debased forms. Classical civilization had always been affected by occultism, but generally a more restrained form predominated, except at the annual chaos festivals. The consistent occultism of the late Roman Empire overwhelmed the rational, confident aspects of older classical civilization and weakened it sufficiently so that only the Christians had sufficient authority and self-confidence to take over and rebuild its faltering institutions.[11] Occultism came at the end of the medieval world, not during it (contrary to popular opinion). It has now come at the end of Enlightenment humanism's civilization. While it always exists in the underground, such as during the French Revolution, it surfaces only when rationalism has lost its sense of destiny and its sense of power, and when humanists seek power from below.[12]

In the West, occultism has been a transitional phenomenon. It appears at the end of a civilization, and goes underground when the next phase begins to be built. It may become superficially civilized and absorbed into folklore and popular religion, but its more grotesque manifestations become illegal. If occultism is not at least partially suppressed, then no new civilization appears. Rural folk communities then replace the older civilization, and cultural cycles replace cultural progress.

In the West, Christianity drove late-Roman occultism underground, and established a new civilization. The late-medieval occultism of the Renaissance was challenged culturally by the Reformation, which steadily abandoned the few traces of occultism that had been present in early Lutheranism and early English Protestantism.[13] The rationalism of the Enlightenment partially infected Prot-

---

11. Charles Norris Cochrane, *Christianity and Classical Culture: A Study of Thought and Action from Augustus to Augustine* (2nd ed.; New York: Oxford University Press, [1944] 1957).

12. R. J. Rushdoony, "Power from Below," *Journal of Christian Reconstruction*, I (Winter, 1974).

13. Keith Thomas, *Religion and the Decline of Magic* (New York: Scribner's, 1971).

estantism, but the occultism of the Enlightenment went underground into the various secret societies and revolutionary groups that simmered throughout the nineteenth century.[14] Only since 1965 have we seen the revival of visible occultism.

This revival of occultism marks the end of an older rationalist civilization and points to the establishment of a new one: a self-conscious Christian civilization which is dominion-oriented. The only other possible contenders are Communism, which is the power religion of our era, and which is utterly bureaucratic, parasitic, and destructive, or New Age humanism, the major escapist religion, which is compromised by occultism and the theology of occultism. Neither can lead to a new civilization.

The new occultism is not at odds with the new humanism. It is only partially at odds with the older humanism. This is why the transition came overnight, 1964-65. This is why the political ideals of the New Left can be fairly described as radical extensions of the main political goals of the old Left. The solutions were the same: more taxes on the rich, more government jobs (especially for college graduates), more Federal spending on everything except national defense, more welfare for the poor (administered by college graduates), more sexual freedom (including abortions and homosexuality), more deficit spending for the sake of growth, and an end to the draft. Above all, an end to the draft. Nisbet called the older liberalism's program "liberalism and six percent." The New Left was simply more consistent, more radical, younger, and had fewer responsibilities—i.e., few children, 1965-70—than the old Left.

With this as background, the revised edition of my book on the occult becomes more useful. Some of these developments were not clear to me in 1976, especially the rise of the New Christian Right and its distinct though hesitant rediscovery of biblical law and optimism toward the future. The most important chapter is chapter ten, "Escape from Creaturehood," but you should read the whole book to find out why it is the most important chapter.

---

14. James Billington, *Fire in the Minds of Men: Origins of the Revolutionary Faith* (New York: Basic Books, 1980).

1

THE CRISIS OF WESTERN RATIONALISM

But faith is the substance of things hoped for, the evidence of things not seen.

Hebrews 11:1

So you believe in witches and warlocks, ghoulies and ghosties, and things, in the words of that old Scottish prayer, that go bump in the night.[1] Or perhaps you refuse to believe in such oddities. It might even be that you are simply curious about all the commotion, whether of the physical or intellectual variety. And because of your opinions, you have decided to read this book. The very fact that this book should exist in this, the final quarter of the remarkable twentieth century, itself is revelatory of the changes that have come upon us.

Why this new-found interest in the occult? What I argue in this book is that recent social changes are evidence of a looming crisis in the West. We have seen similar crises in the past, and each time they have appeared, they have without exception shaken the very foundations of Western Civilization. This book is therefore a study of what I regard as theological and social *pathology*, not simply a catalogue of curiosities. The stakes are very high—the highest that they have been since 1789.

Before you begin, let me point out that there are several themes in this book that continue to reappear. If you understand them from the beginning, the book will make a lot more sense to you as you read. Let me offer several of these themes. (You may detect others as you read it.)

1. The rise of occultism takes place at the end of civilizations,

---

1. From ghoulies and ghosties and long-leggety beasties and things that go bump in the night, Good Lord, deliver us!

and temporary outbreaks of occultism mark significant changes within the development of any given civilization.

2. Western civilization has experienced several outbreaks of occultism in the past, but has always suppressed them. Therefore, it has survived and flourished.

3. Western rationalism, which is now officially and self-consciously atheistic, is no longer able to maintain its resistance to occultism. This was also true during the Renaissance.

4. Humanism shares numerous presuppositions with traditional occultism. Thus, a significant and growing number of humanists have begun to drift into occult practices. They call themselves New Age humanists.

5. Christianity, not atheism, was the original philosophy which created Western science and technology. Thus, as the West has become increasingly atheistic and Darwinian, it has become vulnerable to anti-rational social philosophies and practices.

6. As New Age humanism becomes more widely believed, especially in tax-supported schools, the fruits of Western Civilization will be lost, and waves of violence and occultism will result: the "religion of revolution." (One historical example was Nazism, an occult social philosophy.)

7. The one alternative to occultism that can preserve both freedom and scientific progress is orthodox Christianity. If Christianity does not revive, and revive soon, then Western Civilization will be overrun by barbarians, both domestic and international.

8. Both Christianity and New Age humanism have a vision of a coming earthly millennium. Each group has representatives who offer rival views of what this millennium will look like, but the two basic viewpoints are incompatible.

9. The most significant doctrine which divides Christianity from all forms of humanism is the doctrine of sovereignty. Is God sovereign, or is man (the species) sovereign?

The Purpose of This Book

What I argue in this book is a very simple thesis: *ideas have consequences*. I argue that whenever the fundamental religious and philosophical presuppositions that have predominated during one era in history are abandoned, or at least become increasingly doubtful among the spiritual, moral, intellectual, and political leaders of that civilization, the result is predictable: *a transformation of that civilization.* Social and political revolutions follow religious and philosophical revolutions.

We have seen this take place in the history of Western Civilization at least four times: 1) when classical civilization broke down and was replaced by early Christianity; 2) when the Platonic early Middle Ages were replaced by the Aristotelian later Middle Ages; 3) when the Reformation replaced late medieval Roman Catholic civilization — a revolution which was preceded by and paralleled by the revival of Roman paganism during the Renaissance (especially in the Italian city states); 4) in the modern transformation, which commenced with Darwin, spread to modern physics in the 1920's, and was culminated by the rise of the New Age movement after 1964. These transformations were all-encompassing. No area of thought and culture was immune.

This chapter may be confusing to some readers. It is a brief survey of some of the most important themes (and battles) in Western philosophy. Why is this survey necessary in a popular book on magic? Several reasons. First, before we discuss the reality (or unreality) of the world of the occult, we need to understand that men have long differed over the question, "What is reality?" This raises the question, "Can we define reality?" If so, "Then who is *we*?" Why don't men agree about their conclusions concerning the nature of reality? In short: *What can men know, and how can they know it?*

Second, we need to account for the revival of occultism in our day. When occultism has revived in history after a period of being either legally suppressed or at least under cultural restrictions, we have seen major challenges to civilization. We are now facing an occult revival. Are we facing a collapse of our civilization? More to the point, if we can understand how this occult revival has come about — why the older rationalism began to retreat after 1964 — we can also begin to answer questions about how we, as Christians, can begin to reshape the civilization that will follow the disintegrating rationalistic culture of the West. In short, in order to provide valid *answers*, we need to understand the fundamental *questions*.

Warning: this book is not designed to be a source of excitement, or titillation, or weird experiences. It is designed to be part of a training program for Christian reconstruction. I am not playing games. I am not inviting people to play games. I am calling people into a war — a war which is rapidly escalating, and which, if God-fearing men refuse to fight, the West is going to lose. Thus, I am interested in recruiting people who are willing to become dedicated trained troops, comparable to those who marched into Canaan under Joshua. I am interested in recruiting officers. This book is a manual for Officers Candidate School. It requires a degree of self-discipline to read it. Those who are unwilling to "do their homework" as they read about the rise of New Age occultism should avoid the whole topic. Dabbling in the occult, even intellectually, is not recommended. It is like visiting a free fire zone between armies. Go there only if you have a good reason. Inform yourself about occultism only if you intend to do something about it. A battlefield is no place for civilians.

The Evidence of a Looming Crisis

Prior to the mid-1960's, you could have looked in vain for more than a few scattered new books on occult phenomena. Not that such titles were not in print, but they were usually produced by peculiar groups, probably located either in southern California, New York, or London, such as the Theosophical Society, the Lucis [originally Lucifer] Trust, and many others. But the typical local bookstore, let alone a campus bookstore, would seldom stock such titles. Some owner of a used book shop might have admitted to a friend that occult books were a sizable part of his trade, but his friends never asked. There were heavily footnoted anthropological studies of "primitive" magic and witchcraft, written from the perspective of an officially neutral academic observer. There were histories of folklore and magic (these were often imports from England), and a good number of these titles were reprints of studies produced no later than 1935. Only the stodgy old Mystic Arts Book Club, of New Hyde Park, New York, actively advertised its hardback University Books titles, and these, too, were mostly reprints of carefully researched books, though not necessarily skeptical, that had been produced half a century earlier. The dearth of books, especially paperback books, dealing with occultism, magic, witchcraft, and paranormal science reflected the climate of opinion of the day. There were few potential buyers of such books, it was thought (probably correctly), in the United States, and even fewer writers.

Almost overnight, the picture changed. One of the most radical discontinuities ever recorded in American culture took place. There was no one cause and no single zone of American life—also, West European life—untouched by the multiple dislocations of 1964-70. In music obviously, but also in clothing, deportment, entertainment in general, sexual roles (especially among the young), theology, church liturgy, academic curricula, politics, economics: change was accelerating at a tremendous rate.

To illustrate my point, try to imagine a history of the 1960's that would not include a section on the Beatles. It would not be too difficult to write a history of the preceding fifty years, decade by decade, without mentioning popular music, except insofar as it was in some way preparatory for the Beatles (Elvis Presley, for example). Their impact, as cultural wedges, was enormous. The climate of opinion was transformed.

The Collapse of Traditional Rationalism

Someone who was not on a university campus throughout the 1960's can scarcely imagine the extent of the change in outlook, especially among students and the younger faculty members. The Vietnam war helped to crystalize the new opposition to traditional political liberalism, but far more was involved than politics. The whole university structure was under fire: administration, tenure, the methodology of the academic disciplines, dormitory life, dating standards, everything. Anyone who had graduated in 1963 or even 1964 would hardly have recognized his alma mater in 1967.

A pair of articles in *The Saturday Evening Post*, itself a casualty of the 1960's, illustrates the nature of the change. The first one, published in May of 1964, announced the following facts concerning the University of California, Berkeley, America's most prestigious state-supported university (second, then as now, only to Harvard in the evaluations of the nation's academic establishment): "The larger campuses, Berkeley especially, are smug in their conviction that they already provide the best university education possible. They believe no important reforms are necessary." The President of the University of California, Clark Kerr, the man who coined that monstrous and absolutely accurate term, "multiversity," was trying to produce quality mass education. "With his talent for achieving a consensus, the chances are that he will succeed. If he fails, the future will look bleak not only for his own university but for all higher education in America." You would be hard-pressed to find a more prophetic statement in the annals of popular journalism, for Kerr did indeed fail to gain consensus, and so did his bureaucratic counterparts on the nation's prestigious university campuses. The fabric of education was torn to shreds institutionally, and a decade later, the leading educational theorists were still in shock. Ironically, the original article had been called, "The Exploding University of California." The author had been speaking of size, but the phrase was really appropriate just one semester later.

The second article, "I Am a U. C. Student: Do Not Fold, Bend or Mutilate," appeared two years later (June 18, 1966). No longer was Berkeley the smug center of institutional conservatism, the place where "no important reforms are necessary." All that was long gone. "Berkeley is surely the leader. It is the most serious and committed to change. Berkeley is, as they say, 'out of sight.' It is the model of the rebellious enclave within the affluence of mid-century America." Shortly thereafter, Clark Kerr was dismissed by the Board of Regents of the University. He left with his sense of humor, disappearing from the public's hostile eye with this final occupational epitaph: "I am leaving this job just as I entered it: fired with enthusiasm."

Yet this was not the final act for Berkeley. Again it would serve as a model, for after 1970 a new series of weird phenomena appeared: pseudo-Eastern mystics, outright occultism and witchcraft, and the Jesus (Freaks) People. There was also a revival of fraternities and sororities, which had fallen on hard times, 1965-70. There was a shift from hard drugs to marijuana and cheap wine, and an almost total *internalization of concern* — personal salvation, grade point average, professional training, grad school. The Old Grad, class of '63, would have been more comfortable on campus in 1973 had he returned to his alma mater.

Pessimism and Social Disorder

Nevertheless, there had been a subtle psychological shift: the optimism of technocratic liberalism, so fundamental to university life from 1945-64, had become subdued. The older optimism concerning the benefits of liberal arts training, the possibilities of future employment, the hope of social transformation, and the self-confidence of the earlier era had been smashed by the futility of Cold War liberal rhetoric and the equally futile radical campus protests. Joe College, after 1970, became known as a drudge, a grind, a very dull lad. And he has had some very strange extracurricular habits and out-of-class-room philosophies. Strangest of all is the fact that Joe may well be majoring in some aspect of witchcraft. Which campus do you suppose granted the first bachelor's degree in witchcraft? Of course: Berkeley.

What America and the Western world discovered in the period 1965-70 was the fact that witchcraft and parallel occult phenomena emerge from the cultural underground and become popular and even influential social factors during times of rapid and unfamiliar social change. They are products of that change initially, and then they become contributing causes. This was the case from the first century A.D. through the fourth, as the Roman Empire peaked and then disintegrated. Eastern cults infiltrated the life of Romans throughout the Empire. A millennium later, the great outbreak of witchcraft and witchcraft trials, from the fourteenth century through the late seventeenth, was also a time of historically unparalleled change, especially intellectual change. Magic was not a prominent feature of the early Middle Ages, or "Dark Ages" (500-1000 A.D.).[2] The concern with witchcraft began to increase in the later Middle Ages, especially in the fourteenth century,[3] accompanied by increasing church reform and increasing heresy,[4] increasing wealth as a result of urbanization and trade, and increasing social disruptions and mob violence,[5] and the most devastating force of all, *Pasteurella pestis*, a bacterium which lives in the stomach of a flea that is carried by rats, a flea whose bite transmits bubonic plague to humans. Between 1348 and 1350, between one-quarter and one-third of the population of Europe died, especially in port cities that were close to the ships that carried black rats.[6] This brought great psychological ter-

---

2. Mark Wyndham, "Gnostic Dualism and the Origins of the Medieval Definition of Witchcraft," *Journal of Christian Reconstruction*, I (Winter, 1974).

3. Jeffrey Burton Russell, *Witchcraft in the Middle Ages* (Ithaca, New York: Cornell University Press, 1972).

4. Jeffrey Burton Russell, *Dissent and Reform in the Early Middle Ages* (Berkeley: University of California Press, 1965). Russell's focus is on the eleventh and twelfth centuries.

5. Norman Cohn, *The Pursuit of the Millennium: Revolutionary Millenarians and Mystical Anarchists of the Middle Ages* (rev. ed.; New York: Oxford University Press, 1970).

6. For a popular introduction, see Philip Ziegler, *The Black Death* (New York: John Day, 1969).

ror and pessimism to Europe, which was reflected in European art.[7] It was a century of enormous social change and confusion.[8] Occultism and magic escalated during the Renaissance (1400-1600), and it was the intellectual leadership that dabbled in it.[9]

Western civilization from the fifteenth[10] to the late nineteenth century is generally categorized as optimistic and progressive. This optimism was manifest from the end of the seventeenth century as a result of the scientific and intellectual achievement of Sir Isaac Newton. It seemed as though Newtonian scientific techniques would at last bring to mankind dominion over the external world. This optimistic faith increased and became universal throughout the eighteenth and nineteenth centuries. Even though there were implicit elements of pessimism in original Darwinism and original Freudianism,[11] a fact recognized as such by a few scholars from the beginning, pessimism was not part of the popular culture, including the only slightly less faddish culture of the intellectuals. Both Darwin[12] and Freud[13] were revised in the early twentieth century by their more optimistic humanist disciples. World War I no doubt shattered much of Europe's already fading optimism,[14] and the advent of the Nazis and fascists shook men's confidence in their present and their past. But America, the victor, had not yet tasted defeat; defeat had not yet produced cynicism and pessimism. The intellectual underground of existential despair had not yet become a part of America's outlook; at best, this underground stream was a footnote or two in monographs in philosophy or psychological pathology. Until 1965.

On November 22, 1963, Lee Harvey Oswald's bullet made a martyr of the world's primary media hero—a hero literally created

---

7. J. Huizinga, *The Waning of the Middle Ages* (New York: Anchor, [1924] n.d.), chaps. 1, 2.

8. Barbara Tuchman, *A Distant Mirror: The Calamitous 14th Century* (New York: Knopf, 1978).

9. Frances Yates, *Giordano Bruno and the Hermetic Tradition* (New York: Vintage, [1964] 1969).

10. F. R. H. Du Boulay, *An Age of Ambition: English Society in the Late Middle Ages* (New York: Viking, 1970).

11. On the pessimism of Freud's original psychological system, see R. J. Rushdoony, *Freud* (Philadelphia: Presbyterian & Reformed, 1965), pp. 45-52.

12. Gary North, "From Cosmic Purposelessness to Humanistic Sovereignty," in North, *The Dominion Covenant: Genesis* (Tyler, Texas: Institute for Christian Economics, 1982), Appendix A.

13. Rushdoony, *Freud*, pp. 52-68.

14. H. Stuart Hughes, *Consciousness and Society: The Reorientation of European Social Thought, 1890-1930* (New York: Vintage, 1958).

by the media and the sycophant intellectuals who surrounded Kennedy — and brought to an end the hero's dynasty of rhetoric, cutting down a man whose programs, like the technocratic liberalism he promulgated, were mostly form without substance. Lyndon Johnson's skillfully and ruthlessly imposed legislative substance — the final culmination of the old Progressive optimism — soon turned to dust in the mouths of his followers. The Vietnam war, the race riots, and the deficit-induced price inflation broke the spirit of the age. Johnson could not be re-elected in 1968, just four years after he was elected President. No one can read the devastating vitriol of David Halberstam's popular history of the Vietnam war and the Eastern Establishment which promoted it and lost it, *The Best and the Brightest* (1972), and not recognize the end of not only a political era but of a state of mind.

My thesis: John F. Kennedy was an unimpressive President in terms of the legislation he was able to push through Congress during his three years of power, but in a very real sense, it was his death which symbolically closed an intellectual age: *from Newton to Kennedy.* There was a brief transitional gap for ten weeks. Then the Beatles landed in New York.

The Crisis of Secular Faith

On the campus, the new Bible for campus intellectuals after 1964 was Thomas Kuhn's *The Structure of Scientific Revolutions* (1962). Kuhn, a physicist and historian of the history of science, introduced a thesis which, though not really novel in the humanities, was a blockbuster in the natural sciences. The history of science, he argued, is the history of scientific breakthroughs. Not just new variations on an older theme, not simply a progression upward from fact to fact, testing everything along the path of scientific progress, but real revolutions. In these breakthroughs, the older men in an academic discipline or guild resist the new position. The new outlook does not conform to the accepted paradigm, that is, the older, established, *accepted* way of viewing the world. The establishment insists that different sorts of questions are supposed to be asked, using different methods of inquiry, looking at different facts, and producing different conclusions. The young innovators ignore them, and in a true scientific revolution, replace them.

The newcomers, who are very often skilled amateurs, or professionals working in self-imposed (or guild-imposed) isolation, or

younger men who find that the old ways of investigating specific phenomena — disturbing phenomena — are no longer sufficient, are the
sources of the scientific revolution. In short, the old guard is seldom
converted; it simply dies off. *Science moves in discontinuous leaps:* breakthrough, guild battle, retirement or death of the resistors, and a new
era of painstaking research and even drudgery — "normal science" —
in terms of the new paradigm. In other words, scientists are not
neutral investigators, neutrality is a myth, and there is no real standard of truth or universally accepted methods of verification.
Epistemological relativism, long understood by the best of the scientists, began to filter down to the undergraduates.

All of this was at least implied in modern, post-Newtonian
twentieth-century physics. Social scientists had vaguely known that
guilds operate in this fashion, that "all truth is really relative." Historians such as Carl Becker and Charles A. Beard had been saying
so for decades, as had Karl Mannheim, whose *Ideology and Utopia*
(1936) had served a few serious scholars as a kind of Bible of relativism. But the old orthodoxy had still prevailed in 1963. There might
be a nod of the head, a kind of academic genuflect, to the idea of
epistemological relativism, and then it was back to the business at
hand, namely, the transformation of the whole world in terms of rationalistic, liberal humanism. After 1964, however, everyone was
reading Kuhn; it was assigned reading in education classes, sociology of knowledge classes, philosophy seminars, and history.
Whether the natural scientists, who tend to neglect and even resent
inquiries into just how it is possible for them to know what is going
on "out there" beyond the visible world, grasped what Kuhn was saying, is problematical. The undergraduates in sociology did, and sociology, as an academic discipline, will never be the same.[15]

The Counter-Culture

Once the old orthodoxy of rational neutrality and rational investigators was shattered by Kuhn, Vietnam, marijuana, LSD, Eastern
philosophy, and all the rest of the cultural acids of the day, the barrier to really strange phenomena was gone. It was no longer possible
to argue, *a priori*, that occult phenomena have no existence. Students
were experimenting with everything else; they could also experiment
with occultism. If anything, the philosophy of mysticism, East and

---

15. Robert Nisbet, "Radicalism as Therapy," *Encounter* (March 1972).

West, blended in quite well with many aspects of the cosmology of the occult.

The official ideology of the campus had long been Kantian, and Kant's philosophy was a philosophy of radical *criticism*.[16] Unfortunately for Kant and his spiritual heirs, the students of the mid-1960's took criticism seriously, turning the intellectual searchlight on Kantian rationalism — a rationalism which Kant had deliberately constructed as a final antidote to dogmatism. Yet it was his system which proved to be too dogmatic for certain elements of the cultural revolution. The students had learned their lessons well. Their unwillingness to take seriously parts of the old orthodoxy — the technocratic, optimistic, secular parts — led a vocal minority into new paths, which in fact are very ancient paths. Clark Kerr had never known what a *real* multiversity is; it was to consume him as thoroughly as the mythical Freudian Oedipus was devoured by his children.

The counter-culture was a strange brew, an attempted fusion of high technology and mysticism, power and escape, activism and passive contemplation. A *Newsweek* interview (Feb. 6, 1967) with the leader of a San Francisco-based secret society called the Psychedelic Rangers revealed this dualistic aspect of the movement. The motto of the Rangers was: "The psychedelic baby eats the cybernetic monster." By this, the spokesman explained, they expected the LSD-drug culture to sweep over the technological civilization of the West. It was a vision somewhat like Aldous Huxley's in *Brave New World*. People will be liberated from their everyday lives by chemical escape. The Rangers expected both internal freedom and the high per capita wealth of mass-produced capitalism. His vision of the coming new era was comprehensive: "That doesn't mean back to savagery. It doesn't mean we're going to tear down all the computer systems. It's only a question of the mind being tuned enough, so it's involved in making things better. And this will result in a civilization that is super-beautiful. We're out to build an electric Tibet." *Electric Tibet:* here was the long-heralded solution to the dualism of post-Kantian thought: the fusion of the phenomenal realm of science and the noumenal realm of freedom. Problem: Who will be running the computers? In what mental state? Toward whose goals?

The Dualism of Humanist Speculation

We now come to the most difficult section of this book. The reason why serious readers need to understand this section is because of

---

16. Immanuel Kant, *Critique of Pure Reason*, trans. Norman Kemp Smith (New York: St. Martin's, [1929] 1965), section B xxxiv, pp. 31-32.

the overall thesis of this book: that the rise of New Age humanism and the revival of occultism since 1965 really does constitute a break with over three centuries of Western Civilization. This break represents a threat to the continued existence of Western culture. It is a battle for the minds and souls of men. Anyone who does not understand why this challenge is significant, and also what preceded it, will not be able to deal successfully with the challenge. (Nevertheless, you can still understand most of this book even if you skip the remainder of this chapter. If you get too confused or bogged down, just go on to chapter two.)

There are certain features of humanist philosophy that have made our atheistic rationalist culture especially vulnerable to occultism. This vulnerability was not apparent to many in 1963, but it has grown more obvious since then. We need to answer this question: *What was it in Western thought and culture that weakened the West's resistance to the occult revival?* Occultism always simmers under the surface of culture. The war between good and evil, God and Satan, always goes on until the day of judgment. But why an occult revival *now*? Why the rise of occultism in the final third of the twentieth century? Why not before? Why not later?

To answer this, we need to know about a series of crises and contradictions in the history of Western philosophy. Because of the breakdown in the self-confidence of humanist rationalists, we are witnessing the revival of occultism. We need to know what these weaknesses were, and why Christianity offers a valid alternative that will not capitulate to the New Age magicians.

Reformation and Renaissance

The Reformation of the early sixteenth century and the Renaissance of the fifteenth century through the sixteenth century paralleled each other in certain areas, but diverged in two fundamental respects: the attitude toward the *Christian religion*, and the attitude toward *time*. This is not the place to go into great detail, but on the whole, we can accurately summarize the differences between the two rival civilizations as the difference between the idea of a world governed by God (a *providential* universe) and one governed by fate or chance or political power (an *impersonal* universe). There were certain elements of magic and the occult in the Reformation, but these steadily were abandoned;[17] not so in the Renaissance, which was a

---

17. Keith Thomas, *Religion and the Decline of Magic* (New York: Scribner's, 1971).

self-conscious imitation of Roman civilization, including the "mysteries" of occultism.

Equally important for subsequent Western history was the fact that the Reformation was based on a *linear* view of history, while the Renaissance was based on a *cyclical* view of history. It was the linear view rather than the cyclical view which produced Western science and applied technology.[18] Modern science was the product originally of a providential, orderly world view, one which affirmed man's place in the universe as a subordinate to God whose task is to subdue the earth by means of biblical law. The hermetic or Renaissance view of man was based on a fusion of magic and power, especially political power. Man would be saved by knowledge, including occult knowledge, and by the application of this knowledge to political affairs. *Salvation by knowledge*, especially secret or elitist knowledge, is the ancient heresy of *gnosticism*. It is the underlying faith of both power religion (politics) and escapist religion (mysticism).[19] It was the increasing acceptability of this gnostic doctrine of salvation which steadily undermined the Christian roots of the modern world. It culminated in the occult revival after 1964.

The Hypnotic Lure of Mathematics

The seventeenth century produced a new world view based on Cartesian rationalism and Newtonian science. René Descartes [day-CART] was a rationalist and probably heretical, but as a Frenchman, he feared the Roman Catholic Church, so he kept his theological views to himself. Isaac Newton, on the contrary, was an outspoken providentialist. Both systems rested on the foundation of applied mathematics. The previous century had brought the startling conclusions of Copernicus and Kepler concerning the heliocentric nature of the solar system. They had helped to created interest in mathematics as a tool of comprehension, in opposition to the assertion of orthodox Aristotelian philosophy that mathematics is not central. In a very real sense, Copernicus and Kepler had returned to Plato, Pythagoras, and the Neo-Platonists, who also saw mathematics as important.[20]

---

18. Stanley L. Jaki, *The Road of Science and the Ways to God* (University of Chicago Press, 1978), chaps. 2-6; Jaki, *Science and Creation: From eternal cycles to an oscillating universe* (Edinburgh: Scottish Academic Press, 1974).

19. Gary North, *Moses and Pharaoh: Dominion Religion vs. Power Religion* (Tyler, Texas: Institute for Christian Economics, 1985), Introduction.

20. E. A. Burtt, *The Metaphysical Foundations of Modern Physical Science* (Garden City, New York: Anchor, [1926] 1954), pp. 52-56.

The neo-pagan mysticism and sun worship of Kepler, however, did not accompany the spread of his mathematical world view.

The success of Descartes, who had experienced an ecstatic illumination in 1619 which had informed him that mathematics is the sole key for unlocking the secrets of nature, and then the even greater success of Newton at the end of the century, had elevated mathematical logic to a position of pre-eminence.[21] The capacity of mathematics to describe the regularities of certain natural and physical processes convinced many philosophers, most notably Hobbes, that mathematics is a universal tool which could be used to create a science of man and society.

Blinded by the dazzling success of Newton in physics and astronomy, a success which was vastly greater than the crude measuring devices of his era could record, men hesitated to inquire into the apparent absurdity of Newtonian science. Why should mathematical reasoning, an abstract mental skill and even art, be found to correspond to the mechanical processes of the observed world? Why should such a mind-matter link exist? As the Nobel-prize winning physicist Eugene Wigner has put it, such a finding is utterly unreasonable.[22] But the correlation exists.

The Christian knows why the correlation exists. It exists because man is made in the image of God. Man has been assigned the task of exercising dominion over the earth as God's lawful subordinate (Genesis 1:27-28). Because God exhaustively and perfectly understands His creation, men are able analogously (though not perfectly and exhaustively) to understand the creation. The creation is not lawless, for it was created by an orderly Creator who sustains it by His providential sovereignty. In short, ours is a *personal* universe. We are persons made in God's image, so we can understand our world. The world was not a product of random events, nor are our minds the product of random evolution. The world was created by God. Mathematics, too, is God-given, and can be understood and defended only as a product of a Creator God.[23] Thus, there can be and is a correspondence between the logic of mathematics and the operations of the external world.

---

21. *Ibid.*, p. 105.

22. Eugene Wigner, "The Unreasonable Effectiveness of Mathematics in the Natural Sciences," *Communications on Pure and Applied Mathematics*, XIII (1960), pp. 1-14.

23. Vern S. Poythress, "A Biblical View of Mathematics," in Gary North (ed.), *Foundations of Christian Scholarship: Essays in the Van Til Perspective* (Vallecito, California: Ross House, 1976).

The atheist rejects this explanation. Thus, the correlation between mathematics and the natural world is unexplainable and ultimately unreasonable for him. Nevertheless, without faith in this correlation, modern science becomes impossible. Cartesian and Newtonian science rests on this correlation between mind and matter. Because this correlation between mind and matter exists, the atheistic followers of Descartes and Newton immediately faced a fearful intellectual problem: *What becomes of the free will of "autonomous" man in an impersonal, mathematically deterministic universe?* In a world of cosmic impersonalism and determinism, what becomes of the human *mind?* Is man's mind simply a ghost in the cosmic machine? Doesn't the very certainty of mathematical logic spell the end of human freedom, since man is undoubtedly a part of this universe? Is man ultimately a machine?

The Hypnotic Lure of Greek Philosophy

These questions, or ones analogous to them, have been with man from the beginning. Men ask themselves this question: How can we make sense of a constantly changing world? Answer: only by means of fixed standards of measurement or comparison. This raises another question: Where do these fixed standards come from? And another: How do these fixed standards interrelate with the flux of life? For thousands of years, men have grappled with these questions.

The ancient Greek philosophers struggled with these dualisms — structure vs. change, law vs chaos, determinism vs. freedom — in terms of the so-called *form/matter* framework. The world was understood as the product of eternal conflict: abstract (but real) metaphysical forms partially subduing raw, chaotic matter.[24] Another variation of this approach had matter imitating form. The ultimate form was understood as monistic in nature, the ultimate One. *Out of one came many,* that is, diversity. (This is a basic theme of the New Age movement today. It is also the basic theme of Eastern mysticism and ancient pagan occultism.)

As to which had priority, abstract fixed form or fluctuating matter, Greek philosophers differed. How the two were linked together, or how one or the other was not swallowed up by the other, or how it is possible to compare infinite quantities of raw matter or the neces-

---

24. Herman Dooyeweerd, *In the Twilight of Western Thought: Studies in the Pretended Autonomy of Philosophical Thought* (Philadelphia: Presbyterian & Reformed, 1960), pp. 39-42.

sarily infinite number of abstract forms, no one was sure. The inability of classical philosophers to reconcile this fundamental dualism led to the disintegration of classical culture. Eastern mystery cults spread over the Hellenistic and Roman worlds. Total impersonal Fate battled with total impersonal Chance for control of the universe. Astrology flourished, was banned, and still flourished; chaos cults were everywhere. Men could no longer make sense out of their world. Christianity replaced classicism's fragmented culture.[25] But the lure of Greek philosophical speculation — the logic of the hypothetically autonomous human mind — was nearly irresistible to Christian philosophical apologists. They incorporated aspects of Greek wisdom, and therefore Greek dualism, into their defenses of the orthodox faith. The result was intellectual schizophrenia — philosophical syncretism. Christian philosophers attempted to combine irreconcilable systems: Greek philosophy and biblical revelation.

Thus was born the so-called *nature/grace* framework. The truths of autonomous human reason, whether Platonic (as in the early Middle Ages), Neo-Platonic and mystical (same era), or Aristotelian (late Middle Ages), were understood as autonomous truths. These autonomous truths were believed to require the grace of God's revelation to complement and extend them, but they are independent (autonomous) truths nonetheless. Nature (meaning philosophical speculation) and grace (theology) were to be reconciled by means of a synthesis of Christian theology and Greek (Aristotelian) philosophy. Late medieval scholasticism, the great attempted synthesis, was finalized by Thomas Aquinas (d. 1276).[26] This scholastic synthesis was effectively challenged within a century.

Dualism: Logic vs. Faith

In the fourteenth century, the synthesis was attacked from two sides. William of Ockham is deservedly famous for the assertion of "Ockham's razor," a hypothesis that complex explanations that attempt to describe any natural process should be abandoned whenever a "simple" explanation suffices. He and his followers used this hypothesis to shave grace out of the universe. If logic or observation accurately describe a particular event, then men must not appeal to

---

25. Charles Norris Cochrane, *Christianity and Classical Culture: Studies in Thought and Action from Augustus to Augustine* (2nd ed.; New York: Oxford University Press, [1944] 1957).

26. *Ibid.*, pp. 44-45.

God or angels to explain it. Natural reason is therefore sufficient to understand the world. (Modern scientists use a variation of Ockham's razor to deny the existence of supernatural phenomena.) Grace informs us of nothing indispensable concerning nature and its processes.

On the other side of the debate, Thomas Bradwardine dismissed reason as a tool of comprehending God's revelation. Personal experience, not endless chains of logical reasoning, is the heart of true religion. Bradwardine thereby granted Ockham the use of his famous razor, but only in the observable natural world. Bradwardine ceded to Ockham's razor all the intellectual territory that its users could clear in the forest of existence. A dualism between faith and reason was therefore established by "treaty" between Ockham and Bradwardine. The "natural" world was announced to be autonomous and not supernatural—the very meaning of "natural."

Ockham's system led to this conclusion: the Bible, or theology based on the Bible, cannot challenge the "facts" and speculations of philosophy (and science). Bradwardine's response was that philosophy therefore cannot challenge the truths of theology. The problem for society is this: men *appear* to be able to live without theology, but they cannot live without logic, meaning an understanding of cause and effect in the world around them. So theology went from the queen of the sciences to second best. This "treaty" between Ockham and Bradwardine spelled the doom of medieval philosophy. Unless it can be shown that theology does govern both the form (operating principles) of philosophy and the content (details and issues) of philosophy, theology becomes progressively irrelevant. (The dependence of philosophy on the Bible is what Cornelius Van Til has attempted to demonstrate in this century, and this is what neither contemporary philosophers nor theologians, as defenders of Ockham's autonomous razor, will admit.) Thus, the debate between Ockham and Bradwardine was important. The same debate goes on today.

Prof. Gordon Leff's assessment of the battle between the two positions not only throws light on the breakdown of the medieval philosophical synthesis, but it also reveals a great deal about similar disputes between contemporary scientists and rationalists on the one hand, and religionists or mystics on the other. In fact, the whole question of *what constitutes valid evidence for an investigation of the supernatural* has not advanced much beyond this fourteenth-century debate. Each side dares not acknowledge the *exclusive and universal* legitimacy of the other's methods of investigation and interpretation. They are *mutually exclusive approaches*. The debate still rages, especially with respect to the question of occultism. For this reason, I need to quote Leff at some length. "The importance of the disputes between Bradwardine and his opponents lies in the change wrought upon scholasticism. Each side, in starting from either faith or reason to the exclusion of the other, made them virtually separate pursuits. Since Ockham and his followers refused to see the supernatural through the natural, they put faith beyond reason's bounds. Because Bradwardine allowed reason no autonomy it lost any validity, and faith became the only law. This meant that, on the one hand, reason, philosophy and science tended to become autonomous disciplines without reference to theology; while, on the other, faith and theology became increasingly a regime for worship, independent of ratiocination. The effect of this break was plain to see: for philosophy and reason it meant the virtual self-sufficiency preached by the Averroists;[27] it could choose to discuss man in its own terms without much more than a passing reference to God. At the hands of Ockham and his followers, it recognized no more than a nominal obligation to be at the disposal of faith, while in its attention only to practical knowledge it in fact rejected such a role. On the part of theology, the effect of this division was no less far-reaching: through the withdrawal of reason's support, faith came increasingly to rely upon dogmatic assertion and personal experience."[28]

Grace could progressively be ignored in Ockham's rationalism. "To follow the natural laws of the skeptics," argues Leff, "could only mean that grace was questioned, for its existence was too intangible to be asserted." When Ockham asserted the authority of reason, he inevitably pushed God out of rationalism's universe. The voice of authority is unashamedly man's.

The rationalist's hostility to supernaturalism led, understandably, to a reformulation of the old Greek form/matter dualism. Ockham and the nominalists denied any reality to overarching metaphysical forms. Such forms were understood as simply being linguistic

---

27. Averroës, a twelfth-century Arabic scholar, was an Aristotelian, and his writings were extremely influential in the West during the revival of Aristotle's philosophy. He held a dualistic position with respect to the truths of faith and the truths of reason. Unlike Aquinas, he believed that a philosophical truth can be theologically false, and vice versa. Philosophy is the way of highest truth, he argued.

28. Gordon Leff, *Bradwardine and the Pelagians* (Cambridge, England: Cambridge University Press, 1957), p. 19.

conventions. Reality inheres in the particulars. But there were problems with this perspective. What about nature itself? What binds nature's actions into a coherent unity? Is nature lawless? Is nature a capricious threat to man, a whirling mass of particulars that strikes out randomly to thwart the plans of men? How can men control nature if they have no access to hypothetical forms that themselves impose structure on matter? Man is a slave to nature unless he can find a means of binding down nature to serve his purposes. Nature stands as a threat to man's power and therefore man's freedom and autonomy. How, then, can man take dominion over nature in order to regain his freedom and power?

The answer of Copernicus, Kepler, Descartes, and the Newtonians was clear enough: man must discover the mathematical laws that somehow are inherent to all of nature's processes. The *quest for the knowledge of natural laws* was therefore a *quest for power and freedom.* Though Kepler was a pagan worshipper of the sun, as well as an astrologer,[29] and Newton regarded himself as an accomplished student of biblical prophecy, nevertheless their intellectual legacy, at least in retrospect, was the veneration of the quest for natural laws, that is, mathematical laws to be applied to an essentially mechanistic universe.

The Loss of Freedom

On first glance, this new world view would seem to provide man with an escape from the tensions of dualism. Instead, the most baffling dualism of all was introduced, the *nature/freedom* antinomy (contradiction). If man gains power over nature by subduing all of nature to mechanistically applied laws, then what becomes of man himself? Man is a product of nature. To the extent that we understand nature, we must use law as a guide. But is man simply another effect in an endless chain of cause and effect? Are man's deepest thoughts nothing more than the products of certain chemical reactions in the physical brain? Is man actually determined entirely by the mechanistic laws of nature? Is his sense of freedom and personal moral responsibility a delusion? Can the laws of nature be applied to society, as Thomas Hobbes believed, thereby enabling a supreme monarch-scientist to construct a political system in which all events would be as predictable as the movement of the stars above?

---

29. Burtt, *Metaphysical Foundations,* pp. 58, 63n.

By gaining control over his universe by means of logic, experiment, and mathematics, man simultaneously reduces his own zones of contingency — chance — and increasingly contingency was viewed as the last refuge of freedom from mechanistic law. Man's quest for freedom through autonomous power turned in upon itself. It led to the enslavement of nature, but also of man himself, who is (so far as he can be known by himself) nothing more than a natural phenomenon.[30]

Descartes' resolution of the antinomy, writes Burtt, was to hypothesize the existence of an indeterminately huge material world — a giant mathematical machine — which was correlative to another world of unextended, thinking subjects. "But the Cartesian answer," concludes Burtt, "raises an enormous problem, how to account for the interrelation of these diverse entities. If each of the two substances exists in absolute independence of the other, how do motions of extended things produce unextended sensations, and how is it that the clear conceptions or categories of unextended mind are valid of the *res extensa*? How is it that that which is unextended can know, and, knowing, achieve purposes in an extended universe?"[31]

What is the link between mind and matter? Does matter control mind, thereby erasing human freedom, or does mind control matter as an independent creative agency, thereby denying the fundamental principle of Cartesian science, namely, the universal rule of mechanistic law in all physical extension? Does mechanical law destroy man's freedom, or does man's autonomy — necessarily defined as *outside* the cause-and-effect chain of natural succession — threaten the universal rule of the natural law of cause and effect? There is no answer that the philosophy of autonomous man can provide, yet the question demands an answer.[32] The history of modern philosophy can be fairly described as a history of men's failure to come up with an acceptable answer to the problem of reconciling autonomous man's freedom in a world of deterministic cause and effect.[33]

In our day, this failure can be seen in the rise of New Age philosophy and the rise of occultism. To understand how this came about, we need to look at two key philosophers, David Hume and Immanuel Kant (KAHNT).

---

30. Louis I. Bredvold, *The Brave New World of the Enlightenment* (Ann Arbor: University of Michigan Press, 1961).

31. Burtt, p. 121.

32. Dooyeweerd, *Twilight*, pp. 46-52.

33. Dooyeweerd, *A New Critique of Theoretical Thought*, 4 vols. (Philadelphia: Presbyterian & Reformed, 1953-58).

The Loss of Confidence

David Hume, in the middle of the eighteenth century, provided the classic answer of the skeptic: natural law really does not exist as a force independent of man's mind. Natural law is nothing more than the agreement among men that certain actions follow necessarily from prior actions. Cause-and-effect relationships, in other words, are nothing but *conventions*. The sensation of pain when I thrust my finger into boiling water may have no relation to that water. I may experience pain each time, but experience is not the same as rigorous mechanical law. We simply call certain events effects of prior events (the causes). Nominalism, that is, the denial of the existence of metaphysical forms which order nature, had grown to maturity in the philosophy of Hume. Whirl once again became king, despite the fact that men naively think that the laws or conventions of their minds relate in some way to a hypothetically lawful universe out there beyond our senses. Law becomes convention. As a result, confidence turns into skepticism.

Men do not normally choose universal skepticism, but Hume's arguments seemed to make it impossible to avoid such a choice. Hume's arguments were useful in refuting dogmatic theology, so his skepticism could be used against eighteenth-century Christianity, but the price paid for this anti-Christian weapon soon proved to be too high. Such was the conclusion of the philosopher who still stands as *the* philosopher of the modern world, Immanuel Kant.

Hume's ideas, Kant later wrote, awoke him from his dogmatic slumbers, but the decade of his conversion to Humean skepticism (1763-72) led him to search for certainty, and certainty clearly was not to be found in the contingent rules of human experience. On that, Hume and Kant were in agreement. First comes dogmatism, then skepticism, and finally, Kant said, truly critical certainty. "Scepticism is thus a resting-place for human reason, where it can reflect upon its dogmatic wanderings and make survey of the region in which it finds itself, so that for the future it may be able to choose its path with more certainty. But it is no dwelling-place for permanent settlement. Such can be obtained only through perfect certainty in our knowledge, alike of the objects themselves and of the limits within which all our knowledge of objects is enclosed."[34] To find *a priori* certainty, Kant concluded, men must be humble. They must

---

34. Immanuel Kant, *Critique of Pure Reason*, A 761 (B 789), p. 607.

limit their questions to those that can be answered by the combination of sense data (experience) as interpreted by the universal, fixed categories of human thought.

This Kantian humility is bogus. It is the humility of self-proclaimed autonomous man. It is the humility of the man who says: "The visible, scientific world is capable of being discovered and molded by man's mind and man's activities as a rational species, and nothing that man is incapable of understanding scientifically is relevant in the external world." But if this is true, *then how can man's morality be autonomous from scientific cause and effect, and yet also be connected to the realm of rational human action?* In other words, how can man's personality be preserved in a world of strict cause and effect? What happens to human freedom in such a world?

Rationalism vs. Irrationalism

The foundation of regularities of nature is not inherent in nature itself, Kant argued. It is in the *a priori* categories of the human mind. Nothing can be known without sense data, but without the categories of human thought to assemble the data into coherent wholes, experience tells us nothing. There is therefore no way of knowing anything beyond our senses *as categorized and ordered* by the concepts of the autonomous mind. "Thus the order and regularity in the appearances, which we entitle *nature*, we ourselves introduce. We could never find them in appearances, had not we ourselves, or the nature of our mind, originally set them there."[35] The human understanding, he concluded, is "the *faculty of rules*."[36]

It is therefore man's autonomous mind which creates that entity which we know as nature. The "stuff out there," that is, the so-called "things in themselves," must be forever unknown and unknowable to us. We can only know nature through our own *a priori* categories of reason. *Man's mind legislates the laws of nature!* "Thus the understanding is something more than a power of formulating rules through comparison of appearances; it is itself the lawgiver of nature. Save through it, nature, that is, synthetic unity of the manifold of appearances according to rules, would not exist at all. . . ."[37] *Man is the ultimate creator of his own reality.* Man is autonomous. In this there is certainty of knowledge. This is the so-called "humility" of Kantian philosophy.

---

35. *Ibid.*, A 125, p. 147.
36. *Ibid.*, A 126, p. 147.
37. *Ibid.*, A 126-27, p. 148.

How do men make moral decisions in this world? If the *a priori* categories of logic are universal, then in what does our moral freedom consist? Furthermore, how do men know for certain that the "stuff out there" is not personal, active, and independently powerful? God, "things in themselves," morality, the transcendental human ego, freedom, and contingency are assigned by Kant to an impotent and logically unknowable realm of *noumenal* reality. The *phenomenal* realm is the only one we can ever know logically — the world of interpreted sense data. In short, the noumenal realm of freedom and moral choice, as well as the world of God, demons, angels, and "stuff out there," is nothing more than a hypothetical *limiting concept*, that is, an intellectual device to avoid answering the fundamental questions that autonomous human reason has found itself unable to answer.

C. S. Lewis' Warning

Men live by ideas, and no idea in man's history produced more evil than this one: *the sovereignty of man.* It is humanism's chief presupposition. Man, the god. Man, the predestinator. Man, the central planner. Man, the director of the evolutionary process. Man, the maker and shaker of things on earth and in the heavens. As Karl Marx's partner, Frederick Engels, put it over a century ago, "man no longer merely proposes, but also disposes."[38] But most important of all is this promise: *Man, the savior of Man.*

This vision is inescapably religious. The impulse lying behind it is religious. Some have called it the religion of secular humanism. Others have called it the will to power (Nietzsche). But no one has described its implications better than C. S. Lewis. "What we call man's power is, in reality, a power possessed by some men which they may, or may not, allow other men to profit by. . . . From this point of view, what we call Man's power over Nature turns out to be a power exercised by some men over other men with Nature as its instrument. . . . Man's conquest of Nature, if the dreams of some scientific planners are realized, means the rule of a few hundreds of men over billions upon billions of men. Each new power won *by* man is a power *over* man as well. Each advance leaves him weaker as well as stronger. In every victory, besides being the general who triumphs, he is also the prisoner who follows the triumphal car. . . . For the power of Man to make himself what he pleases means, as we have

---

38. Frederick Engels, *Herr Eugen Dühring's Revolution in Science* [*Anti-Dühring*] (London: Lawrence & Wishart, [1877-78] 1934), p. 348.

seen, the power of some men to make other men what *they* please."[39]

But there is something missing in Lewis' analysis. Must all progress necessarily lead to elitist power over others? If so, we have a problem. If we proclaim the moral legitimacy of progress, and therefore the legitimacy of increasing man's power over his environment (power such as we possess with modern medicine), how are we to restrain the rise of power-drunk elites? Must we too become tyrants, just because we believe in historical progress? Progress, after all, is not the product of cultural impotence. It involves the use of power. To avoid becoming tyrants, must we give up the idea of progress (as many in this century have done), and call for a retreat into mysticism? Are we to abandon the struggle against moral and social evil, in order to sit peacefully and contemplate our navels (or wait for the Rapture)? Are we culturally beaten before we start? In short, can we keep our own *vision of victory* — and every successful group in history always has possessed such a vision — from becoming just another stepping stone in the advance of political tyranny?

The answer is "yes, we can." But to achieve progress without tyranny, we must elevate *ethics* over power. This is what is missing from Lewis' summary (or at least missing from my summary of Lewis). We must recognize that in a cosmically personal universe, there are perpetually binding moral rules. These rules are ethical. They should remind us that all *autonomous* (self-made) power corrupts, and absolute autonomous power (in the hands of sinful creatures, meaning all of us) corrupts absolutely.

This does not mean that all power is evil. It is always necessary for righteous men to possess power if they are to reconstruct a civilization that has been run by evil men who possess raw power. The issue is ethics, not power as such. It depends on which ethical system a society adopts. Some ethical systems are evil. Marxism is a case in point. The question is: *which ethical system should men adopt*? One which elevates man and man's goals, or one which elevates God and therefore limits man's power? In short, will men choose the religion of God or the religion of humanism? Will they choose the dominion religion or the power religion?

Van Til's Rejection of Humanism

Cornelius Van Til, a twentieth-century Christian philosopher and theologian, has argued throughout his career that Kant's philos-

---

39. C. S. Lewis, *The Abolition of Man* (New York: Macmillan, [1947], 1967), pp. 68, 69, 70, 71.

ophy is the touchstone of all modern thought. Van Til's analysis is central to the thesis of this book, namely, that the current revival of occultism and witchcraft represents a throwback to the paganism of the pre-Christian world. Furthermore, it is my thesis that *modern secular humanism is not only powerless intellectually to call a halt to the occult revival, but that it is in fact one of the primary causes of the revival.* Without Van Til's guidance, I probably would never have come to this conclusion.

Van Til makes it clear that the epistemological dualism of modern philosophy — rationalism vs. irrationalism — is inherent in all forms of autonomous philosophical speculation. From the day that Adam tried to test the word of God concerning his destiny, man has attempted to find some voice of authority other than God. By locating their preferred voice of authority outside of God's revelation, both verbal and natural, men thereby create for themselves a series of unsolvable intellectual dilemmas. The most important principle of apostate man is therefore the principle of his own *autonomy*. Wherever his preferred voice of authority may be located, it is not supposed to violate the principle of human autonomy.

Inescapably, man must have some principle of authority. Van Til's arguments in this regard are vitally important for any consideration of the rules of scientific evidence. We come now to the longest quotation in this book, and by far the most important one. It boils down to this: we need *a sovereign authority independent of ourselves* in order to know anything truly, since we can never know everything exhaustively. In short, we need the God of the Bible. If we reject Him, we shall drown in an ocean of "chance" facts. *Chance and endlessly moving time will swallow up meaning and law.* Eternal randomness will become king of the universe. The Christian asserts, "Better God's eternal plan and ultimate sovereignty than chance," while the humanist asserts, "Better ultimate randomness and meaninglessness than the God of the Bible." This has been humanism's answer to the God of the Bible since Adam and Eve, and surely since the Greek philosophers. But as Van Til points out, an *acceleration of irrationalism* has taken place in Western philosophy, especially since Kant. As "autonomous" man has become more consistent with his own presuppositions, he has become more irrational.

It is my contention that it was the triumph of irrationalism in humanist philosophy in the early decades of the twentieth century which led to the rise of occultism in the final third of the century. It is the revolt against nineteenth-century popular scientific (Newtonian) rationalism which has also led to the New Age movement. Men want neither deterministic scientific law nor random chance to rule over them. They also do not want God to rule over them. This leaves only one other major candidate for sovereign ruler, who in fact has always been the only alternative: Satan.

Spend five minutes or so carefully studying this quotation from Van Til, and the logical tricks of modern (or ancient) atheistic humanism will never be a threat to you again. Pay particular attention to his concept of the "secret treaty" between rationalism and irrationalism — a treaty against God. (For added readability, I have broken his three original paragraphs into seven.) Once you have Van Til's analysis "under your belt," the rest of this book will be easy. Remember the key question men have asked: How do we make sense out of the ceaseless change in life? The answer: by means of some sort of authority. The question then is: *which authority?* And when we decide on such an authority, how can we be sure that it will overcome that ancient force of nature, *chance?*

First there is the need for authority that grows out of the existence of the endless multiplicity of factual material. Time rolls its ceaseless course. It pours out upon us an endless stream of facts. And the stream is really endless on the non-Christian basis.

For those who do not believe that all that happens in time happens because of the plan of God, the activity of time is like to that, or rather is identical with that, of Chance. Thus the ocean of facts has no bottom and no shore.

It is this conception of the ultimacy of time and of pure factuality on which modern philosophy, particularly since the days of Kant, has laid such great stress. And it is because of the general recognition of the ultimacy of chance that the rationalism of the sort that Descartes, Spinoza and Leibniz represented, is out of date. It has become customary to speak of post-Kantian philosophy as irrationalistic.

It has been said that Kant limited reason so as to make room for faith. Hence there are those who are willing to grant that man's emotions or his will can get in touch with such aspects of reality as are not accessible to the intellect. The intellect, it is said, is not the only, and in religious matters not even the primary, instrument with which men come into contact with what is ultimate in human experience. There is the world of the moral imperative, of aesthetic appreciation, of the religious a priori as well as the world of science. There is in short the world of "mystery" into which the prophet or genius of feeling or of will may lead us.

It is of the greatest import to note that the natural man need not in the least object to the kind of authority that is involved in the idea of irrationalism. And that chiefly for two reasons. In the first place, the irrationalism of our day is the direct lineal descendant of the rationalism of previous days. The idea of pure chance has been inherent in every form of non-Christian thought in the past. It is the only logical alternative to the position of Christianity, according to which the plan of God is back of all. Both Plato and Aristotle were compelled to make room for it in their maturest thought. The pure "non-being" of the earliest rationalism of Greece was but the suppressed "otherness" of the final philosophy of Plato. So too the idea of pure factuality or pure chance as ultimate is but the idea of "otherness" made explicit. Given the non-Christian assumption with respect to man's autonomy, the idea of chance has equal rights with the idea of logic.

In the second place, modern irrationalism has not in the least encroached upon the domain of the intellect as the natural man thinks of it. Irrationalism has merely taken possession of that which the intellect, by its own admission, cannot in any case control. Irrationalism has a secret treaty with rationalism by which the former cedes to the latter so much of its territory as the latter can at any given time find the forces to control. Kant's realm of the noumenal has, as it were, agreed to yield so much of its area to the phenomenal, as the intellect by its newest weapons can manage to keep in control. Moreover, by the same treaty irrationalism has promised to keep out of its own territory any form of authority that might be objectionable to the autonomous intellect.

The very idea of pure factuality or chance is the best guarantee that no true authority, such as that of God as the Creator and Judge of men, will ever confront man. If we compare the realm of the phenomenal as it has been ordered by the autonomous intellect to a clearing in a large forest, we may compare the realm of the noumenal to that part of the same forest which has not yet been laid under cultivation by the intellect. The realm of mystery is on this basis simply the realm of that which is not yet known.[40]

This "secret treaty" between the scientific phenomenal realm and the personalistic noumenal realm has one major purpose: *to shove God out of the universe*.

Heisenberg and Indeterminacy

This treaty is breaking down in our era. The "not yet known"—pure randomness—has today reasserted itself with a vengeance in modern science and philosophy. Heisenberg's scientific principle of indeterminacy in physics is first cousin to psychological and philo-

---

40. Cornelius Van Til, *The Defense of the Faith* (rev. ed.; Philadelphia: Presbyterian & Reformed, 1963), pp. 124-26.

sophical existentialism. German physicist Werner Heisenberg in 1927 announced an important finding of modern physics, the *uncertainty principle*. "This principle, which is derivable from wave mechanics, says that, irrespective of technical errors of measurement, it is *fundamentally impossible* to describe the motion of a particle with unlimited precision. We may specify the position of a particle with increasing precision, but in so doing we introduce uncertainty into its motion, in particular into its momentum. Conversely, we may observe the momentum with increasing precision, but then we introduce uncertainties into its position."[41] This observation about the limits of observation in the world of subatomic physics led to another disconcerting discovery: the light wave which enables the scientist to observe phenomena itself upsets the observation (or makes observation impossible) at the level of subatomic physics. The positions between electrons are far smaller than the smallest light wave, so the light serves as a kind of blanket which covers up what is going on. If smaller gamma rays could ever be employed in a "microscope," these would strike the electrons and "kick" them, thereby changing their momentum. In short, *the observer interferes with the observed.* "A quantitative analysis of this argument shows that beyond any instrumental errors there is, as stated by the uncertainty principle, a residual uncertainty in these observations."[42]

The great success of Newtonian mechanics, based, as we have seen, on observations of gross matter, gave rise to the conviction that there is a strict cause-and-effect relation in natural processes—that, in other words, a certain body placed in a certain situation will move in a certain way. An identical body placed in the same situation will move in identically the same way. But this seems not to work with atomic particles. A stream of electrons, all identical,[43] passing through the same crystal will not all emerge in the same direction. (But there is a most probable direction.) . . . A corollary of the causal relations of classical science is determinism: the belief that, if the position and motion of all particles of a system are known, the future of the system will be completely in accord with the laws of science. Such a mechanistic philosophy was given great impetus in the eighteenth century by the successes of Newtonian mechanics in describing and predicting the motions of both terrestrial and celestial objects. The great advances of the nineteenth century only strengthened this view, and it was confidently expected

---

41. G. S. Christiansen and Paul H. Garrett, *Structure and Change: An Introduction to the Science of Matter* (San Francisco: Freeman, 1960), p. 558.

42. *Ibid.*, p. 559.

43. But how can we verify this "identicality"?

by many that ultimately all responses (including human) would be perfectly described by the laws of science. The uncertainty principle denies that this ultimate goal can ever be reached. The principle does not say that the deterministic view is wrong; but it does say that we are fundamentally unable to fulfill the initial condition. There is no way of exactly observing both the position and the motion of particles.

These arguments do not disprove a causal deterministic philosophy. What they do say is that there is no way for observational science to prove that the philosophy is ultimately true; and proponents of such a philosophy must therefore look elsewhere for proof of their position.[44]

The random event in nature, by way of quantum mechanics, is presently intruding into every nook and cranny of man's formerly trustworthy Newtonian universe. The physicists have begun to teach their fellow physical scientists of the wonders of the irrational.[45] And with indeterminacy has come relativism and the loss of faith in wholly objective, totally neutral scientific observation.[46]

The rational clearing in the irrational forest, once thought to be almost entirely devoid of trees—just a few unexplained (but unquestionably somehow explainable in principle) *chance facts*—has been found to be covered with a thick underbrush of the scientifically unexplained and the innately unexplainable. The underbrush of the unexplained is now so tall in places that it threatens to cover up rationalism's clearing. Worse: this underbrush, unlike the more conventional trees, keeps breaking rationalism's sharpest tools. Nothing can cut this underbrush away. It has gotten completely out of hand: quantum mechanics, Freudian and Jungian psychology, paranormal science, existential philosophy, irrational modern art, Eastern mysticism, New Age messianic visions, and most threatening of all, a revival of orthodox Christianity. The result has been increasing despair about rational man's ability to make his own autonomous sense of this world, and therefore despair over his inability to control it. The supposedly orderly universe of the nineteenth century has

---

44. *Idem.*

45. Fritjof Capra, *The Tao of Physics: An Exploration of the Parallels Between Modern Physics and Eastern Mysticism* (2nd ed.; Boulder, Colorado: Shambala, 1983).

46. A brilliant attempt by a Roman Catholic scientist and historian of science, Father Stanley Jaki, to call into question this modern skepticism by scientists, and to provide justification for belief in an objective universe, is his book, *The Road of Science and the Ways to God* (Chicago: University of Chicago Press, 1978). Its weakness is its commitment to a scholastic natural theology based on "being" rather than a Protestant approach based on the covenant and God's six-day creation.

been found to be a massive delusion.

The breakdown of the secret treaty between rationalism and irrationalism has also brought a hole in the philosophical defenses against occultism and demons.

To Catch a Ghost

Clearly, old-fashioned Kantian men believed that they could safely forget about a God who reveals Himself in the Bible and in history, or demons that grant power to their human subordinates. Men must forget about discovering any earthly manifestations of the supernatural. "Supernatural" is defined as *not influencing the natural*. Such a view, however, leads to a whole series of problems — problems that have led, especially since 1965, to a revival of occultism and the abandonment of Kantian rationalism.

A hundred years ago, the line which separated the ranks of the credulous, some of them respected scientists (*before* they began publicly to hunt ghosts), from the ranks of the professional skeptics, was fairly clearly drawn. The rationalists had spent the nineteenth century trying to squeeze the last traces of God out of the universe, and Darwinism was understood to have accomplished the task. There would be no more elements of meaning or directionality in the universe, except that which man would supply. The last traces of "final causation," or ultimate directionality in the processes of biological evolution, had been replaced with random biological adaptation to randomly changing environments over whatever quantity of time was deemed sufficient to give random change sufficient elbow room to bring our world into existence. The God of orthodox Christianity had supposedly lost His last remaining toehold on the phenomenal realm. From now on, God would have to content himself with dabbling with the noumenal — a safe enough place for Him, really, since nothing in the noumenal realm is able to influence the phenomenal (except, illogically enough, autonomous man and his man-centered morality). The noumenal, the "something-in-itself," was chained up by mechanical Newtonian law, forever impotent to invade the realm of the logical.

But then late-nineteenth-century ghost hunters and table rappers began to break the treaty. Serious British investigators — even respected scientists — created the Society for Psychical Research in 1882. Their stated goal was to study such phenomena — *phenomena?!*

—as mental telepathy, hypnotism, and apparitions.[47] They were talking as though they might be willing to allow certain aspects of Kant's noumenal "something-in-itself" to creep across the treaty's boundary markers. While such odd phenomena were believed to be wholly explainable by rational laws, given enough study, the desire of the spiritualists to relate these odd phenomena to affairs of the noumenal realm—phenomena who have somehow dropped in for a chat from the noumenal realm—was quite properly understood by the rationalists as a violation of the post-Kantian secret treaty. The unknown is supposed to *stay* unknown until modern science has an acceptable way to explain it; any time the unknown becomes known, it is supposed to become completely subject to the comprehensive *a priori* laws of the autonomous human mind. That is the rule, the rationalists insist. No exceptions.

No faithful nineteenth-century Kantian rationalist ever believed that the unknown was actually *invading* the realm of the known and disrupting its deterministic operations. What he resented was the obstinacy of the ghost hunters in clinging to their fantasy that there *could* conceivably be such an invasion. To acknowledge the possibility of such an invasion was tantamount—indeed, identical—to saying that there is a crucial flaw in the only philosophical tool which the humanist possesses which can be used to keep God locked out of the phenomenal realm. A defect in this tool means that the crack in the wall between the phenomenal realm of scientific and comprehensive knowledge and the *presently* unknown might allow God to sneak back in to control the destiny of the universe and to judge it on the final day. If any force has impact in our world, it just has to be a phenomenal force, that is, a force that operates in terms of rigorous scientific law, even if we have not yet discovered that law.

Rationalism's mutual defense treaty with irrationalism against God was being ignored by the spiritists. Their denial rankled the minds of naive Newtonian rationalists. The naive Newtonians did not understood that Newton had personally rested his case for a coherent universe on God's providence, and that when Kant destroyed men's faith in Newton's providentialism, he thereby in principle destroyed the foundation of predictable science. If God does not hold the universe together, then who does? Man? Man's mind? The *a priori* categories of man's mind? What a feeble founda-

47. Nandor Fodor, *Encyclopaedia of Psychic Science* (New Hyde Park, New York: University Books, 1966), pp. 350-51.

tion! By the late nineteenth century, that foundation had begun to reveal cracks, and these cracks continued to multiply. But the naive Newtonians systematically ignored these cracks. They continued to argue that rationalism, and only rationalism, can explain the visible events in nature.

Van Til has used the following analogy. A fisherman claims that his net can catch every fish in the sea. His friend is skeptical of his claim, but he goes along to see. The fisherman tosses his net into the water, pulls in several fish, but several more slip through the net and swim to freedom. "Look there," says his friend. "Your net didn't catch those fish." "Nonsense," replies the fisherman. "Those aren't fish. *What my net doesn't catch isn't fish.*"

What those fish were for the fisherman, so are all the bits of evidence for supernatural powers for the cosmologies of the rationalists. "No supernatural forces are allowed into the realm of phenomena," they shout. "The net of scientific observation screens out all noumenal effects, since cause and effect is strictly phenomenal. If there is an effect, it has to be phenomenally produced. By definition." In short, "What our net won't catch isn't fish."

Psychical Research

In 1882, scholars in Britain who were interested in pursuing "noumenal-phenomenal relationships" by means of scientific procedures founded the Society for Psychical Research. Initially, several were avowedly spiritualists, but they steadily left the Society. Some members were quite famous as men of science, including William James, Sir Oliver Lodge, Sir William Crookes, and Henry Sidgwick, the first president of the SPR, and, much later, Sigmund Freud. Some members, like Frank Podmore, were skeptics who were nonetheless interested in examining the data.

The organization was always regarded with suspicion and consternation by orthodox rationalists and scientists. Opponents were of the opinion that such phenomena, being phenomena in the Kantian sense, were simply phenomena. Such data were of little interest as phenomena; only as signs of noumenal or supernatural influence could they have any significance, and that possibility was denied by the very canons of scientific investigation. Thus, even the prestige of Alfred Russel Wallace, the co-discoverer with Darwin of the principle of evolution by means of natural selection, did not impress orthodox scientists, including Darwin himself, when Wallace became a convinced spiritualist. What Prof. Irvine wrote of Darwin, he could have written about most rationalistic scientists of the late nineteenth century: "The supernatural interfered with the aesthetic symmetry of his ideas. The Deity had become an epistemological inconvenience."[48]

Students of Witchcraft

One of the last representatives of this naively confident older humanism who still writes on the topic of witchcraft with real authority is Rossel Hope Robbins. He was still teaching on university campuses in the late 1960's. His important book, *The Encyclopedia of Witchcraft and Demonology* (1959), announces in no-nonsense terms his presuppositions regarding the witchcraft phenomena of the late Middle Ages: "I have selected what I conclude to be the most significant for the total picture of witchcraft presented here: a colossal fraud and delusion, impossible because the 'crime' of witchcraft was an impossible crime. The present entries could have been doubled or trebled, but the reader would not necessarily be that much richer or wiser." Indeed, when one begins with a religiously held conviction that a particular kind of phenomenon is impossible, every last bit of evidence offered to the contrary will be reinterpreted (or ignored) in order to force it into another mosaic of interpretation — hallucination, torture, self-delusion, desire for notoriety, etc. Robbins is only echoing sixteenth-century skeptics, such as Johann Weyer, a Protestant physician, who blamed the confessions of witches on their confusion. He was not alone in his opinion. Robbins lists several pages of the titles of tracts dealing with witchcraft from the early modern period, and half a dozen were skeptical. Robbins writes in the same tradition of the two great historians of witchcraft in the last century, both totally skeptical: Joseph Hansen and Henry C. Lea. They deny any supernatural reality to the witchcraft phenomena for the same reason that they deny a personal God who manifests Himself in human time: *the natural realm is ours and ours alone, by definition.*

At the other end of the spectrum are the totally credulous. Montague Summers is the classic example of a scholarly historian of the occult — witchcraft, vampires, werewolves — who believed almost every word in every document charging these crimes against certain individuals. Looking at the same documents that Lea and Hansen

---

48. William Irvine, *Apes, Angels and Victorians: The Story of Darwin, Huxley, and Evolution* (New York: McGraw-Hill, 1959), p. 113.

examined, he concluded the opposite: witchcraft is real, not just as a social pathology, but as an example of supernatural power. But there have always been other kinds of credulous "searchers" of occult mysteries, and they are all too often taken in either by charlatans or truly sinister characters, i.e., those figures described by the Bible as "having a form of godliness, but denying the power thereof" (II Tim. 3:5). The totally credulous are these people's victims. "For of this sort are they which creep into houses, and lead captive silly women laden with sins, led away with divers lusts, ever learning, and never able to come to the knowledge of the truth" (II Tim. 3:6-7). These are the seance ladies, the yoga ladies, the Mystical Church of Cosmic Vibrations ladies. They are the only too willing victims of the swamies, gurus, mahatmas, healers, mumblers, and holy men, many of whom seem to have been chosen by God in miraculous visions delivered to them near an off-ramp of the Hollywood Freeway.

Conclusion

The increasing quantity and improved quality of the evidence of demonic and paranormal phenomena have become obvious to millions of American and European citizens in the last two decades. As younger scholars, themselves the product of the higher education systems, delve into avenues once closed by academic definition, there will be an even larger stream of data. It is unlikely that the data, in and of themselves, will convert present skeptics to full-blown occult believers. A few skeptics will experience something like religious conversion, as their interpretive frameworks are overloaded by the new data, and finally one new piece triggers a kind of short-circuiting effect in the rationalist interpretive scheme, but these events are rare.

What seems far more likely is that the skeptics, as the torch-bearers of a now-dying optimistic, technocratic rationalism, will simply retire or die off. It may take two generations, but the hole in the dike since 1965 has only grown larger. What the serious investigator has to do now is to find *an alternative framework to the old skepticism*—a new paradigm or interpretive scheme which can handle the supernatural data that are now being released into the modern world. There is only one which will work, the one which humanists have rejected for four centuries: Christianity.

The proper approach must combine confidence and humility. Confidence in one's basic interpretive framework is mandatory for serious intellectual investigation; it is the first step in any scientific or historical enquiry. Yet at the same time, the researcher must be humble. The data can fool him, especially data provided by "true believers," confidence men, and serious but overenthusiastic researchers on the fringes of orthodox science. The data may be of "phenomenal" rather than "noumenal" origin; it may be a question of simply not having enough data or not having discovered some new set of rules that can deal with these perplexing data. But in some cases, the data will truly reflect their supernatural origin. The question which faces each man who encounters such data should therefore be: What should I do about my encounter with the supernatural? And if you are not a Christian, and therefore not the beneficiary of special protection, the answer is twofold: 1) run; 2) repent and be converted.

2

THE BIBLICAL FRAMEWORK OF INTERPRETATION

. . . for Satan himself is transformed into an angel of light.
II Corinthians 11:14

We live in terms of presuppositions. We cannot know everything exhaustively, so we use ideas, stories, and principles to "sort out" the "facts" and eliminate the "irrelevant." What is irrelevant is sometimes referred to as *noise*. We need principles of interpretation to differentiate "signal" from "noise." The myths, ideas, and principles of a particular civilization determine what sorts of facts are, in fact, relevant, or are, in principle, relevant. Every society (or subgroup) necessarily operates as follows: what is not *in principle* relevant is discarded as not being *in fact* relevant. We prefer familiar myths and familiar stories to difficult facts that undermine our confidence in our myths. It is too painful to rethink our myths, for that would involve rethinking all of our facts, too. So we ignore painful facts.

My favorite example of a reigning myth in U.S. history is the story of Mrs. O'Leary's cow. This cow supposedly kicked over a lantern in a Chicago barn on the night of October 8, 1871, and the resulting fire burned down the city. A popular movie was made about this terrible event. Every schoolchild in my generation has heard of Mrs. O'Leary's cow. It is a charming story, and while nobody could really prove it, nobody had to. It was just a story, and so everyone decided it was all right to believe it. The truth has never been put into the textbooks. That truth is too painful.

On October 8, 1871, a mysterious giant fireball struck the Midwest. There had been drought for three months. The prairie was like a tinderbox. At 9:30 P.M., the fireball struck. All over the Midwest, fires broke out. In Wisconsin, 1,500 people died in a 400 square mile area. As many as 750 died immediately by the suffocating cloud that descended with the fireball. Nine towns in four counties were burned

50

to the ground.[1] A surviving eyewitness of the destruction of Peshtigo reported: "In one awful instant a great flame shot up in the western heavens, and in countless fiery tongues struck downward in the town like a red-hot bolt. A deafening roar, mingled with blasts of electric flame, filled the air and paralyzed every soul in the place. There was no beginning to the work of ruin; the flaming whirlwind swirled in an instant through the town. All heard the first inexplicable roar, some aver that the earth shook, while a few avow that the heavens opened and the fire rained down from above. The tornado was but momentary, but was succeeded by maelstroms of fire, smoke, cinders and red-hot sand that blistered flesh."[2]

The fires continued to burn in some places for two months.[3] In Indiana, Illinois, and Iowa, no lives were lost, but crops were destroyed. In Minnesota, the flames came close to St. Paul, and 50 people died, but the towns were spared. South Dakota experienced fires that night. But the great Chicago fire gets all the publicity.

There was indeed a fire in O'Leary's barn, but it was put out. Then another fire was reported in St. Paul's Church, two blocks north. It, too, was checked. Then another broke out, and another, and the conflagration spread. There were also oddities about these fires. "Reporters told of buildings, far beyond the line of fire, that burst into flames simultaneously from the interior 'as if a regiment of incendiaries were at work. What latent power enkindled the inside of these advanced buildings while externally they were untouched?' And there were references to a 'food for fire in the air, something mysterious as yet and unexplainable. Whether it is atmospheric or electric is yet to be determined.' "[4] The flames melted stone and displayed fantastic color patterns of red, blue, and green. It left nothing unburned. Six-story structures were destroyed in five minutes. Several hundred tons of pig iron near the river bank and 200 feet from the nearest building were melted into one massive lump.

Fires also appeared in the Sierras, the Rocky mountains, in the Alleghenies, and in the Red River region.[5] Tornados hit Ontario

---

1. Vincent H. Gaddis, *Mysterious Fires and Lights* (New York: Dell, 1967), p. 58.

2. *Ibid.*, p. 59. He cites Ben Kartman and Leonard Brown, *Disaster* (New York: Pellegrini and Cudahy, 1948).

3. *Ibid.*, p. 61.

4. *Ibid.*, p. 63. The author cites Herbert Ashbury, *Gem of the Prairie* (New York: Knopf, 1940), p. 87.

5. *Ibid.*, citing James W. Sheahan and George P. Upson, *History of the Great Conflagration* (Chicago and Philadelphia: Union Publishing Co., 1872), p. 392. These men were associate editors of *The Chicago Daily Tribune*.

and Nova Scotia in Canada.

Explanations? Nothing fits. So the history textbooks remain silent.

Spontaneous Human Combustion

They are also silent concerning another kind of mysterious fire. If 1871 was a big year for prairie fires, 1938 was a spectacular year for people fires. Here is one representative account. On September 20, 1938, a woman was dancing on a crowded dance floor in Clemsford, England. Without warning, she burst into flames. Not her clothing — her body. Her flesh emitted blue flames, indicating tremendous heat, as she crumpled to the floor. Her escort and others tried to put out the flames, but it was hopeless. Within a few minutes, there was nothing left of her except a few ashes. There was no longer any trace of a human being. Coroner Leslie Beccles announced: "In all my experience, I've never come across any case as mysterious as this."

He would not have been able to make this statement had he been coroner at England's Norfolk Broads the previous July 30. On that day, a woman, her husband, and her children were paddling in a small boat when she suddenly caught fire. She was rapidly reduced to a mound of ashes before the horrified eyes of her family, yet the boat was undamaged and the other occupants were unaffected by the heat. Eric Frank Russell, the British novelist, discovered newspaper accounts of 19 victims of these fires in Britain in 1938.[6]

This, for want of an explanation, is simply classified as spontaneous human combustion, or SHC. It has existed in the medical literature of all European nations for over two hundred years. The earliest example appears in *Acta Medica & Philosophica Hafniensia* (1673). Today, almost no medical experts are willing to admit its existence, despite over one hundred cases recorded during the last century. Lester Adelson, pathologist to the coroner of Cuyahoga County, Ohio in the early 1950's, desperately hoped that some logical explanation of SHC would be found, but he knew of no likely candidate. He did define the problem in the March-April 1952 issue of Northwestern University's *Journal of Criminal Law, Criminology and Police Science:* "Spontaneous human combustion is that phenomenon wherein the body takes fire without an outside source of heat and is

6. *Ibid.*, p. 190.

rapidly reduced to a handful of greasy ashes. Paradoxically, inanimate objects nearby escape relatively unharmed." So much for definitions.

Specialists in forensic medicine are the scientists who are most likely to encounter the phenomenon. Desperate police officials cannot explain these phenomena, so they expect the local coroner to take the responsibility. The specialists prefer to decline the honor. They would really prefer to deny the phenomena. In 1861, J. L. Casper dismissed the whole thing in his *Handbook of the Practice of Forensic Medicine*. His language is all too familiar to anyone who has researched any aspect of paranormal science. The odd phenomena tend to stay the same, and so do the scientific reasons for rejecting the evidence. "It is sad to think that in an earnest scientific work, in this year of grace 1861, we must still treat of the fable of 'spontaneous combustion.' . . . the very proofs of whose existence rest on the testimony of people who are perfectly untrustworthy nonprofessionals."[7]

The phenomenon has been around for a long time. The description does not change very much. Here is a summary account by one French researcher, published in the *Texas Register* (Nov. 7, 1835):

Spontaneous combustion commences by a bluish flame being seen to extend itself, by little and little, with an extreme rapidity, over all the parts of the body affected. This always persists until the parts are blackened, and generally until they are burned to a cinder. Many times attempts have been made to extinguish this flame with water, but without success. When the parts are touched a fattish matter attaches itself to the finger, and still continues to burn. At the same time a disagreeable smell, having analogy to burnt horn, spreads itself through the apartment.

A thick smoke escapes from the body and attaches itself to the furniture, in the form of a sweat, unctious to the touch. In many cases the combustion is arrested only when the flesh has been reduced to a cinder and the bones to powder. Commonly the feet and a portion of the head are not burned. When the combustion is finished an incinerated mass remains, which is difficult to believe can be the whole of the body. All this may happen in a space of an hour and a half. It is rather uncommon for the furniture around it to take fire; sometimes even the clothes are not injured.[8]

The "Fortean" (disciples of that curious investigator of the curious, Charles Fort) periodical *Pursuit* publishes accounts of odd facts that conventional scientists refuse to deal with. Ivan T. Sanderson

---

7. Quoted by Larry Arnold, "Human Fireballs," *Science Digest* (Oct. 1981), p. 90.
8. *Mysterious Fires and Lights*, p. 187.

was Charles Fort's most famous and cogent disciple. In Appendix A of his book, *Investigating the Unexplained* (Prentice-Hall, 1972), he printed fine-print pages of SHC accounts, from the seventeenth century until 1969. It is reprinted in the Fall, 1976 issue of *Pursuit*, in an essay by Larry Arnold, "The Flaming Fate of Dr. John Irving Bentley," a victim of SHC in 1966.

I first came across a reference to the phenomenon in an English class in the spring of 1960. We had been assigned the ghastly task of reading *Wieland*, a ghostly late-eighteenth-century novel by America's first novelist, Charles Brockden Brown. He kills off the father of the hero in the first chapter by means of fireball-SHC phenomena. This phenomenon did not register on me until four years later, when I read about SHC in a *True Magazine* story, "The Baffling Burning Death" (May 1964). In 1960, I was uninterested in occultism; in the spring of 1964, David Ketchen, a seminary classmate of mine, had told me of his early encounters with table-raising, and he had introduced me to the writings of the European exorcist, Kurt Koch. (Years later, I had Ketchen write his story for the second issue of *The Journal of Christian Reconstruction*, and I included it as Appendix B of the original edition of *None Dare Call It Witchcraft*.) Other examples of SHC in literature can be found in Charles Dickens' *Bleak House*, who discusses it in his preface, and in Herman Melville's *Redburn*.

December, 1956, Honolulu: Mrs. Virginia Caget dashed into the room next to hers in an apartment house that was occupied by a seventy-eight-year-old invalid man, Young Sik Kim. He was on fire in an overstuffed chair. Blue flames shot out of his body, making it impossible for her to approach him. When firemen arrived fifteen minutes later, the victim and his chair no longer existed, except for his undamaged feet, still propped on his wheelchair, unmoved. Had he felt no pain? There are numerous cases in the literature that indicate precisely this.

According to Professor Wilton Krogman, a physical anthropologist at the University of Pennsylvania, it takes eight hours in a crematorium at temperatures of 2,000 degrees Fahrenheit to reduce a body to bones. To turn the bones to ash, temperatures of over 3,000 degrees are required. Krogman has made a study of the records of a hundred modern cases of SHC, and still he has no explanation of how a body can catch fire in this way and how so few objects around it are harmed.

July 1, 1952, St. Petersburg, Florida: Mrs. Mary Reeser, a sixty-seven-year-old widow, was visiting in her room with her neighbor, Mrs. P. M. Carpenter. When she left her that evening, Mrs. Reeser was seated in her armchair by the window, dressed in a rayon nightgown, slippers, and a housecoat, and was smoking a cigarette. The next morning, a Western Union messenger failed to raise her by knocking at her door to deliver a telegram. Concerned about her normally light-sleeping neighbor, Mrs. Carpenter started to open the door. The brass doorknob was hot. She cried out, and two house painters ran to see what was wrong. Together they broke into the house. Although both windows were open, the room was hot. In front of an open window were some ashes; a chair, an end table, and Mrs. Reeser. All that remained of her were a few pieces of charred backbone, a shrunken skull the size of an orange, and a wholly untouched left foot, still in its slipper. Her room was generally unaffected, except for some melted wax candles and melted plastic fixtures. From four feet above the floor was the soot. The clock had stopped at 4:20 A.M., but when plugged into an unmelted wall outlet, it started running again. There were no embers and no smell of smoke. Mrs. Reeser had weighed 175 pounds the night before; now only ten pounds remained.

The FBI was called in. The case received lots of publicity locally. Result: no explanation. Professor Krogman happened to be visiting friends nearby and volunteered to study the case. His conclusion: spontaneous human combustion. But he had never seen a head shrunken by fire. The skull should have exploded, not shrunk. Said Krogman: "Never have I seen a skull so shrunken or a body so completely consumed by heat. This is contrary to normal experience and I regard it as the most amazing thing I've ever seen. As I review it, the short hairs on my neck bristle with vague fear. Were I living in the Middle Ages, I'd mutter something like 'black magic!'"

Not living in the Middle Ages, he can only mutter "spontaneous human combustion." But what comfort is that? The phenomenon exists. It exists in the twentieth century. People want explanations for phenomena; if they are denied explanations, they prefer to ignore the phenomena. This is why the major news services refuse to pick up stories like the death of Mary Reeser—or did in 1952. In earlier days, when medical men could still hope to find an explanation, the phenomenon of SHC was still discussed and reported.

Adelson wrote only a few months before the Reeser case: "The most noteworthy feature of the entire topic is the prolonged acceptance of those phenomena by educated scientific men when chemistry, physics, and biology should long have effectively relegated them to the status of spontaneous generation, witchcraft, necromancy, and black magic." Spontaneous generation is old hat; spontaneous human combustion, on the other hand, is supposed to say something. But his point is well taken: the phenomenon should indeed be relegated to the realm of witchcraft, necromancy, and black magic.

Black magic? Surely such things are not possible. Black magicians, perhaps, somewhere in tribal societies not yet blessed with television and stereophonic cassettes, but not in the modern world. Yet SHC is possible — frighteningly possible. It is the most spectacular of a whole class of impossible yet actual events, which are conveniently described as *paranormal phenomena*. Prior to the mid-1960's, investigations of such phenomena were conducted only by kooks — kooks being defined as those kinds of people who investigate paranormal phenomena. Kooks like William James, Sigmund Freud, and Carl Jung, for example. Kooks like Alfred Russel Wallace, the co-discoverer (with Darwin) of the principle of evolution through random variation and natural selection. Kooks like Sir Oliver Lodge, Sir Arthur Conan Doyle, and the members of the British and American Societies for Psychical Research. And, frankly, a lot of certifiable kooks. But since the mid-1960's, a vast new market for books on the occult and paranormal phenomena has developed, and interest in research into the paranormal has been kindled in at least untenured junior faculty members of major universities.

But what of black magic? What of the demonic? Do these worlds really exist? Or are they just catch phrases, like paranormal, extrasensory perception, and spontaneous human combustion — handy classification devices for the presently unknown? Is there any relationship, other than purely psychological or sociological, between the simultaneous rise of interest in the paranormal and the rise of interest in the occult?

The question has validity, especially at temperatures of 3,000 degrees Fahrenheit that do not burn curtains, wheelchairs, and slippers.

The Growing Literature of Occultism

There is such an immense and growing quantity of information available on occultism, written from so many different viewpoints, that investigators are likely to give up in despair. How is it possible to assimilate all of this material? Obviously, it is not possible, any more than it is possible to assimilate all the economic data or chemical data or any other kind of data that might present itself to a serious researcher. The quest for exhaustive knowledge is illegitimate. Men are creatures with creaturely limitations. That they are not God, with God's comprehensive and authoritative knowledge of all factuality, should not disturb men. Yet the ideal of exhaustive knowledge has placed modern scientific man on an endless treadmill, a kind of modern quest for the holy grail (itself a magical image). Man thinks that if he does not know everything exhaustively, he cannot know anything confidently. On the presuppositions of the pretended autonomy of human thought, this is precisely the case. Since any fact in the universe can conceivably influence any other fact, in order to know any fact truly, a man must understand all facts exhaustively. Yet no man or society can know all the facts of the universe exhaustively. So, then, where can we go to inform ourselves of the eternally valid principles of interpretation for the facts of the occult realm? I go to the Bible.

The Bible teaches man humility, but it also teaches man confidence: humility *before* God and confidence *under* God that the earth can be mastered by man to the *glory of* God. God, as the creator and sustainer of all facts, provides man with the necessary framework of interpretation that enables man to know facts accurately enough to accomplish his assigned tasks. The key is the interpretive framework rather than the quantity of raw data. In fact, facts are never "raw"; they are always interpreted facts, since they exist in terms of God's sovereign plan. There is no brute factuality; there is only God-ordained factuality. Therefore, man can have confidence in his intellectual labors if he subordinates his investigative labors to the interpretive framework provided to him in biblical revelation. Because of the existence of revelation, man need not know every fact — in this case, facts about occultism — in order to have accurate knowledge concerning the world. More time spent in study, more facts, better facts, and more attention paid to literary style no doubt would improve people's knowledge of occult phenomena, but as limited creatures, we can still have confidence that we do have a sufficient grasp of the topic in spite of the fact that we can never have perfect grasp of all phenomena. Not even Satan himself has perfect grasp of occult phenomena, so we need not despair. Satan should, however. The most important passages in the Bible concerning occultism are not those that refer to angels, demons, visions, magic, and witchcraft. The truly crucial passages are those that tell us about God and His relation to the creation, for it is God who is central, not Satan and his host. The universe is *theocentric*. If men would acknowledge this fact and conform their activities to it, there would be no necessity of dwelling on biblical passages dealing with occult phenomena. It is because men consistently suppress their knowledge of the truth that the revelation to man concerning occult phenomena takes on new importance.

After a while, an observant student of the occult arts in history begins to detect recurring themes in occult literature. Occultism is the outworking of a series of philosophical and ultimately religious presuppositions about the nature of man, the world, and law. It is a *system*, however disjointed and even self-contradictory the records may be. Like any system of thought and life, it has basic presuppositions. These presuppositions are the heart of the revival of occultism in our era. The miracles, the oddities, the visions, the unexplained — and in terms of post-Kantian philosophy, unexplainable — phenomena get the attention of the newspaper reporters and the thrill-seekers, but oddities, like the poor, have always been with us. The more important problem is this one: Why have these phenomena reappeared and multiplied so astoundingly in the final third of this supposedly rational century? The answer lies in the *philosophy* of occultism, which is almost a mirror image of biblical revelation, but which is in conformity with contemporary humanism on point after fundamental point. To understand the occult revival, it is mandatory that we understand orthodox Christianity and its presuppositions. It is impossible to understand Christianity without grasping the significance of certain doctrines: creation, the fall, the incarnation, and the final judgment.

Creation

This is the starting point, both philosophically and revelationally. The Bible opens with this announcement: "In the beginning God created the heaven and the earth" (Gen. 1:1). By the fiat and absolutely authoritative command of God's word, all that exists was created out of nothing—*creation ex nihilo*. Matter-energy was not co-extensive and co-eternal with God, as Aristotle taught (*Physics*, VIII) and as the pagan cosmologies of the ancient world taught. God did not bring the world into existence by struggling with some ultimate chaotic matter in order to produce order. God commanded the light, and there was light (Gen. 1:3). We cannot explain this fiat act, nor do we need to. Neither can questions concerning origins be answered by the followers of Kant, whose system was created by Kant in order to call a halt to the asking of such unanswerable questions, nor can they be answered by the Marxians, since Marx explicitly prohibited the asking of questions concerning origins.[9] All we know is what we are told by the One who was there at the time.

Because God created the universe, there is a permanent, unbridgeable gap between the ultimate being of God and the derivative being of creatures. There is a Creator-creature distinction. Though men are made in the image of God (Gen. 1:27), they do not partake of God's being. They are like God, but they are not of the same substance as God. There is no more fundamental doctrine than this one. Significantly, in every form of occultism this principle is denied, sometimes implicitly and usually explicitly. Satan's old temptation to man hinges on his denial and man's denial of the Creator-creature distinction. "For thou, LORD art high above all the earth: thou art exalted far above all gods" (Ps. 97:9). He is not some impersonal force, but a sovereign, totally personal God: "For thus saith the high and lofty One that inhabiteth eternity, whose name is Holy; I dwell in the high and holy place, with him also that is of a contrite and humble spirit, to revive the spirit of the humble, and to revive the heart of the contrite ones" (Isa. 57:15). God is not an evolved man: "For my thoughts are not your thoughts, neither are your ways my ways, saith the LORD. For as the heavens are higher than the earth, so are my ways higher than your ways, and my thoughts than your thoughts" (Isa. 55:8-9). Close to the man with the contrite heart, yet infinitely removed from the rebellious creature: here is the God of creation.

Because God created the universe by the power of His word, He also *sustains* it. This is the doctrine of *providence*, the corollary of the doctrine of creation. All things come to pass within the overall plan

---

9. Karl Marx, "Private Property and Communism," *Economic and Philosophic Manuscripts of 1844* (New York: International Publishers, 1964), pp. 144-45.

of God (Isa. 45:5-12), despite the fact that He is not responsible for sin. This is also a humanly unanswerable antinomy, and the apostle Paul specifically called attention to it, and then denied that man, the creature, has any right to answer it (Rom. 9:19-22). It is an antinomy in every existing philosophical system, for all systems fragment on the antinomy of free will and predestination, personal responsibility and unbendable cause-and-effect law. The Christian system presents a God who is sovereign and man who is responsible. All other existing systems, as Van Til has demonstrated so well, rest on the presupposition of a chance universe: chance out of chance returning unto chance. But there is no zone of ultimate contingency that can serve man as a "neutral safety zone" for the testing of God's word. There are no zones of existence outside His control. "The king's heart is in the hand of the LORD, as the rivers of water: he turneth it whithersoever he will" (Prov. 21:1). Similarly, "A man's heart deviseth his way: but the LORD directeth his steps" (Prov. 16:9). The theme of the heavenly potter and his earthly clay — out of which man was created — appears in both the Old and the New Testaments. "O house of Israel, cannot I do with you as this potter? saith the LORD. Behold, as the clay is in the potter's hand, so are ye in mine hand, O house of Israel" (Jer. 18:6). It is this image that Paul uses in establishing the doctrine of the sovereignty of God (Rom. 9:20-21).

In direct contrast to the biblical view of man and God, the occult systems, from the magical sects of the East to the gnostics of the early church period, and from there unto today's preachers of the cosmic evolution and irresistible karma, one theme stands out: *monism*. There is no Creator-creature distinction. We are all gods in the making. Out of One has proceeded the many, and back into One are the many travelling. Eastern mystics, philosophical Hegelians, and followers of the overrated Teilhard de Chardin are all agreed on the reality of ultimate monism. It is such a convenient doctrine, for it denies any eternal separation of God and His creation, and therefore it denies any eternal separation of saved and lost. It denies any ultimate distinction between good and evil, past and present, structure and change.

In the revival of mysticism, which is invariably monistic, whether Eastern or Western, the popular culture has produced many documents that aid the cause, but one of the most successful is Hermann Hesse's pseudo-Eastern book, *Siddhartha*. Published in 1951, in the late 1960's it became a touchstone among members of the counter-culture who were still willing and able to read. (For the illiterates, 1973 brought the movie.) Its message: all is one. The last three paragraphs of the book bring this point home graphically. Govinda, Siddhartha's (Buddha's) friend, stares into Siddhartha's face, and he sees a series of pictures in a vision. Lives appear before him, all different but really all the same: an infant, a fish, a murderer, lovers, crocodiles, elephants, oxen, gods, and, of course, Siddhartha's face, unifying all of these scenes into a harmonious unity in a peaceful smile. "Govinda bowed low. Uncontrollable tears trickled down his old face. He was overwhelmed by a feeling of great love, of the most humble veneration. He bowed low, right down to the ground, in front of the man sitting there motionless, whose smile reminded him of everything that he had ever loved in his life, of everything that had ever been of value and holy in his life."[10] So ends *Siddhartha*. Should we be surprised that it was this book, among one or two others, which Charles Manson permitted his "Family" to read at the Spahn Ranch, as they crept into the night to steal and finally to murder?[11] For in terms of monism, everything is valuable and holy in life or death, for there is no death, as Manson was fond of telling everyone, including the prosecuting attorney at his trial. Monism is the philosophy of nihilism, however disguised it may be.

The other non-Christian philosophy is *dualism*: good and evil are in eternal tension, and neither can triumph. It undergirded many of the medieval revolutionary sects that turned, in some instances, to magic and occultism. It argues that God is not sovereign, for He did not actually create all things; the evil god created matter and is sovereign over it. Like monism, this philosophy leads to an attempt to escape the control of matter over the soul, either by radical asceticism or a radical immersion in perversion (to deny matter's relevance).

What both monism and dualism have in common is the denial of the sovereignty of a personal God, for in neither system is there a Creator-creature distinction. Each leads to rampant immorality, and each leads to a dismissal of earthly affairs and earthly responsibility. The result in each case is moral nihilism.

The Fall

The rebellion of man against the explicit command of God was an *ethical* rebellion. The fall of man was ethical rather than metaphy-

---

10. Hermann Hesse, *Siddhartha* (New York: New Classics, 1951), p. 153.
11. Ed Sanders, *The Family* (New York: Dutton, 1971), p. 106.

sical. It involved his whole being, body and soul, and the curse of
God in response to this rebellion penalized both body and soul, including man's mind. Nevertheless, the Fall itself was not a metaphysical "fall from Being." It was not some lack in man's being which led
to his downfall; it was willful rebellion. The curse of God on man involved the creation in which man was now to labor (Gen. 3:15-17);
his world would now be a world of scarcity. But it was not a flawed
environment that was man's downfall, although Adam blamed Eve,
and Eve blamed the serpent, and they all, by implication, blamed
God for their plight. The Fall was *ethical*, and therefore the restoration
has to be ethical—not a "leap of being" by mystical means, nor by environmental manipulation, such as through Marxist revolution.[12]

The restoration of man and the creation is promised (Isa. 65, 66;
Rom. 8; I Cor. 15). This is the work of God in calling His people unto
Him (John 17). Restoration is not to be achieved by "secret wisdom"
through initiation into "mysteries." The words of Jesus in the Sermon on the Mount forbade secret wisdom to His followers. It thereby forbade mystical secret societies. "Ye are the light of the world. A
city that is set on an hill cannot be hid. Neither do men light a candle, and put it under a bushel, but on a candlestick; and it giveth
light unto all that are in the house. Let your light so shine before
men, that they may see your good works, and glorify your Father
which is in heaven" (Matt. 5:14-15). Restoration, both ethically and
externally, stems from the grace of God—another doctrine anathema both to the modern world and to occult philosophy. Restoration is not the product of men's neutral reason, nor is it the product
of their own unaided, self-initiated works (Eph. 2:8-9).

The Incarnation

The message of the first chapter of the Gospel of John is quite
straightforward: God Himself walked this earth in human flesh during a specific period of human history. He appeared in time and on
earth, one person in two natures: perfect humanity and full divinity,
but without confusion of these two natures. The promise given to the
people of God is that each man, while retaining his own personality,
will be conformed to the image of Jesus Christ on the final day
(I Cor. 15:42-50). In short, redeemed man does not become divine; he

---

12. Gary North, *Marx's Religion of Revolution: The Doctrine of Creative Destruction*
(Nutley, New Jersey: Craig Press, 1968).

finally attains perfect humanity, but not divinity. The Divine once became a man, and only once. Because of Christ's atoning work on the cross — a judicial act of sacrifice which satisfied God's own standards of justice — some men can be saved (John 17; Rom. 5). But no man can become God. The attempt to become God, or a part of God's being, is wholly illegitimate and constitutes the essence of rebellion. The Creator-creature distinction is everlasting.

The doctrine of the incarnation asserts that God took on flesh. The doctrine of monism asserts that out of God flesh and matter appeared, and eventually they must return to (or into) God. Monism implies that God is somehow incomplete. This is the specific teaching of Hegel, for example. We are needed to complete God's being and to restore Him to his pre-temporal wholeness. Man is therefore a part of the process of God's salvation. God is saved by man. It is man's efforts to be reunited with God that are crucial in the process of time. The emphasis of monism, while officially theistic, is nonetheless humanistic. A very fine example of just this kind of reasoning is found in a fragment of the writings of Meister Eckhart (1260-1328), the German mystic. Heretical to the core, Eckhart's monism led him into the wildest kinds of philosophical rambling. Yet he was consistent in his presentation of the theology of monism, as indicated by the following passage: "God's divinity comes of my humility, and this may be demonstrated as follows. It is God's peculiar property to give; but he cannot give unless something is prepared to receive his gifts. If, then, I prepare by my humility to receive what he gives, by my humility I make God a giver. Since it is his nature to give, I am merely giving God what is already his own. It is like a rich man who wants to be a giver but must first find a taker, since without a taker he cannot be a giver; for the taker, in taking, makes the rich man a giver. Similarly, if God is to be a giver, he must first find a taker, but no one may be a taker of God's gifts except by his humility. Therefore, if God is to exercise his divine property by his gifts, he well may need my humility; for apart from humility he can give me nothing — without it I am not prepared to receive his gift. That is why it is true that by humility I give divinity to God."[13]

Where this approach to "humility" is present, either in the explicit thinking or implicit presuppositions of would-be autonomous man, the resistance to occultism is socially and culturally close to

---

13. *Meister Eckhart*, trans. Raymond Bernard Blakney (New York: Harper & Row, 1941), pp. 233-34.

zero. While Ph.D.'s in philosophy may not succumb to the temptation of dabbling in the supernatural as a means of climbing up the scale of universal being, the average person who hears such speculation and takes it seriously, especially when it comes from some mystical guru or charismatic leader, will have no intellectual foundation to help him to resist. The steps to personal transcendence — the promised "leap of being" — are only too often little more than intellectualized magic. The quest for *metaphysical transcendence* rather than ethical transformation and repentance is a major source of the impetus to occultism. Occult exercises are too often the means of the promised self-transcendence.

Final Judgment

The doctrine of the last judgment is clearly a part of the orthodox Christian tradition. The Bible presents it as a time of reward (I Cor. 3:11-15) and punishment (Luke 12:47-48). It leads to an eternal separation between saved and lost (Luke 16:19-31). It is a once and for all event (Rev. 20). In short, "it is appointed unto men once to die, but after this the judgment: So Christ was once offered to bear the sins of many; and unto them that look for him shall he appear the second time without sin unto salvation" (Heb. 9:27-28).

The significance of this doctrine with respect to the philosophy of occultism is its *absolute denial of reincarnation*. Eastern monism, both Hindu and Mahayana Buddhist, as well as most of the Western forms of occult transcendentalism, holds specifically to the doctrine of *karma*. One's deeds have an inescapable effect on one's destiny in this life and in the next. Endless cycles of birth and death are required for men (or their impersonal souls) in order to shed the effect of matter before they are reintegrated into the One of timeless perfection. It is a theology without grace; men's actions, over vast eons of time, heal their former metaphysical condition. The polluting contact with matter must be washed away by deeds of ascetic withdrawal from or ascetic immersion in matter. Judgment is temporary, though extended in possibly millions of cycles. Life is in balance, though ultimately it is a progressive balance which leads all living things back into the impersonal perfection of the timeless Void. The judgment on men's evil deeds is impersonal and in the long run, however long the run may be, it must end. The personal judgment of a personal God on men who have but a few years of life on earth is denied; the knowledge of it is actively suppressed in the minds of men (Rom. 1:18-22). By theorizing on the almost infinite extension of time in which men are "imprisoned," the theologians of karma think they have imprisoned God and His judgment. The motive of all evolutionary thinking, whether Darwinist or karmist, is the same: to escape the wrath of God by pushing the creation and the judgment out of this world and the next. It is also the motive of post-Kantian humanism, including Hegelianism and Marxism.

Prohibitions on Occultism

Because men do not accept the validity of the preceding biblical doctrines, they are susceptible to occult forces. The people of Israel were protected from occultism by the revelation of God concerning Himself and His relationship to the creation, as well as by His promise of ultimate restoration. But the doctrines alone were not sufficient to preserve the people from the idolatry of the pagan cultures which surrounded them. Explicit prohibitions were placed on citizens of Israel against dabbling in the occult arts. These arts were well known. The most comprehensive prohibition appears in Deuteronomy 18:10-12, but there are numerous other outright prohibitions and warnings against the consequences of occult experimentation.

> Witchcraft (sorcery) — Ex. 22:18
> Necromancy-Spiritualism — Lev. 19:31; 20:6; Deut. 18:11
> Astrology — Isa. 47:13
> False prophecy
>   inaccurate — Deut. 18:20-22; cf. I John 4:1
>   idolatrous — Deut. 13:1-3
> Divination — Deut. 18:10
>   arrows — Ezk. 21:21
>   livers — Ezk. 21:21
>   images — Ezk. 21:21
> Fire walking — Deut. 18:10
> Omens — Jer. 10:2
> Wizardry (secret knowledge?) — Deut. 18:11
> Charms (snakes) — Jer. 8:17
> Enchantment (spells) — Isa. 47:9-12
> Times (lucky days?) — Lev. 19:26

The term translated "witch" by the King James Version is more accurately rendered "sorcerer." The influence of Walt Disney's witch in the animated movie, "Snow White," while terrifying to young children, is amusing to adults. To a great extent, this is the traditional image of the witch: broomstick, black hat, black cat near at hand. It is as old as the medieval witchcraft trials. Popular culture, since 1965, has updated the witch: she is cute Samantha of "Bewitched" fame, with her middle-class home in middle-class America. (This, by the way, is a far more accurate picture of the modern witch.) She wiggles her nose and — poof! — all the morning dishes are washed, dried, and put away. She was immensely popular, even more than her nearest rival, Jeannie, who lived in a bottle in the mid-1960's, cleaning house for an astronaut — the fusion of scientific expertise and magic. So cute, both of them. And so very temporary. By 1970 the public was watching television programs that delved into the evil and powerful side of magic. In 1974, "Kolchak: The Night Stalker" combined the public's taste for private detective shows with its seemingly unquenchable thirst for occult themes. In Kolchak's world, there are killers loose on the streets who possess supernatural powers. Here, at last, is the biblical witch.

The Septuagint, a Greek translation of the Old Testament in the second century, B.C., substituted *pharmakeia* for the Hebrew word for sorceress in Exodus 22:18, from which we derive our word "pharmacy." The witch of the classical world was an expert in potions. More accurately, he or she was known as a *poisoner.* Throughout the Middle Ages, men were fearful of suspected witches, in part because of this reputation. They could be dangerous.

The prohibition on occult practices was basic to the preservation of covenantal faithfulness to God. Other gods were false gods, and sacrifice to them was spiritually deadly and even literally deadly. The worshippers of Moloch (Molech, Milcom) made their sons and daughters pass through the fire as a form of sacrifice-testing (II Ki. 23:10). Basic to the worship of pagan antiquity was the creation of a divine state which rested on a theology of continuity, that is, the denial of the Creator-creature distinction. The state could take the lives of its children as sacrifice to the god of the state. The prohibitions on occult worship were not only a means of protecting people's lives from perverse practices morally but also a means of restricting the power of a political order theoretically unbounded by the restraint of limited men. Rushdoony has commented on what he calls the "Moloch state": "While relatively little is known of Moloch, much more is known of the concept of divine kingship, the king as god, and the god as king, as the divine-human link between heaven and earth. The god-king represented man on a higher scale, man ascended, and the worship of such a god, i.e., of such a *Baal*, was the assertion of the *continuity* of heaven and earth. It was the belief that all being was one being, and the god therefore was an ascended man on that scale of being. The power manifested in the political order was thus a manifestation or apprehension and seizure of divine power. It represented the triumph of a man and of his people. Moloch worship was thus a political religion. . . . Moloch worship was thus state worship. The state was the true and ultimate order, and religion was a department of the state. The state claimed *total jurisdiction* over man; it was therefore entitled to *total sacrifice*."[14]

A revival of occultism in our day, or in the era of the Renaissance, can and must bring with it a revival of the politics of ancient paganism. A state which claims total jurisdiction is demonic. It cannot provide law and order, but only order, and that order is man-centered and oppressive. It was this development which the Hebrew prohibitions on occultism were intended to prevent: the rise of the total state. Increasingly, this is what the modern world faces, for both secular, rational humanism and occult humanism deny that there is any voice of authority outside of man who cares for man. Secular humanists may wish to manipulate the world through state power, and occult humanists may wish to manipulate the powers of the "beyond" for their own benefit, but the quest for power leads to the construction of a massive instrument of power. That instrument is the modern state. It is the planning state, the forecasting state, the macroeconomically programmed state. Rushdoony is quite correct: "The Moloch state simply represents the supreme effort of man to command the future, to predestine the world, and to be as God. Lesser efforts, divination, spirit-questing, magic, and witchcraft, are equally anathema to God. All represent efforts to have the future on other than God's terms, to have a future apart from and in defiance of God. They are assertions that the world is not of God but of brute factuality, and that man can somehow master the world and the future by going directly to the raw materials thereof."[15] The supposed death or nonexistence of the God of creation is in fact the death of human freedom and human personality.

---

14. R. J. Rushdoony, *The Institutes of Biblical Law* (Nutley, New Jersey: Craig Press, 1973), p. 32.
15. *Ibid.*, p. 35.

Angels and Demons

There are about 300 references in the Bible to "angel, angels," and about 120 to "devil, devils." In contrast, there are some 600 references to "evil" and perhaps 800 to "sin, sinner, sinneth" and their variations. The overwhelming emphasis on ethical deviation and rebellion is characteristic of the Bible's message. It does not ignore the operations of supernatural agencies, but the concern of both Testaments is with sin and repentance, not exorcism.

What is an angel? Both the Hebrew and the Greek words that are translated as "angel" can also be translated as "messenger." There are times when the more conventional usage is preferred, such as in Job 1:14: "And there came a messenger unto Job. . . ." We find instances where the Hebrew word is applied to a prophet (Hag. 1:13; Mal. 3:1) or to a priest (Mal. 2:7). Paul refers to his "thorn in the flesh," which seems to have been a physical ailment or infirmity (II Cor. 12:9-10)—as "the messenger [angel] of Satan" (II Cor. 12:7). These, however, seem to be infrequent. Normally, the term refers to a supernatural being of some kind.

An angel is a spirit, whether a clean one serving as a messenger of God (Heb. 1:14) or an evil one (I Sam. 18:10; Matt. 8:16). They manifest themselves as men on occasion. Joshua was confronted by one whom he took as a man; it turned out to be the captain of the Lord's host (Josh. 5:13-14). The angels who appeared at the tomb from which Jesus had risen were angels (John 20:12), yet were perceived as men (Luke 24:4). The Book of Hebrews warns us: "Let brotherly love continue. Be not forgetful to entertain strangers: for thereby some have entertained angels unawares" (Heb. 13:1, 2). This was what happened to Lot; angels, seen as men, came to warn him about the impending destruction of Sodom (Gen. 19).

There are a lot of them. "Ten thousand times ten thousand" is Daniel's phrase (Dan. 7:10), indicating a massive host. The New Testament uses the terms "multitude" (Luke 2:13) and "innumerable" (Heb. 12:22). One famous Old Testament incident illustrates the invisible company of angels. Elisha's servant, fearful about the army of Syrians that had encompassed the city in which he and his master were staying, was comforted in a unique manner by Elisha: "And he answered, Fear not: for they that be with us are more than they that be with them. And Elisha prayed, and said, LORD, I pray thee, open his eyes, that he may see. And the LORD opened the eyes of the young man; and he saw: and, behold, the mountain was full of horses and chariots of fire round about Elisha. And when they came down to him, Elisha prayed unto the LORD, and said, Smite this people, I pray thee, with blindness. And he smote them with blindness according to the word of Elisha" (II Ki. 6:16-18). Blindness among the enemies was also the method of freeing Lot from Sodom (Gen. 19:11). It was not that the angels used their chariots of fire or great numbers in order to impede the plans of the Syrian army, but their presence was meant to assure Elisha of his own safety.

One of the difficulties in describing various kinds of angels is that the biblical writers would see them in visions, and they themselves were well aware of the non-literal nature of some segments of these visions — the candlesticks of the Book of Revelation, for example, or even the great chain which binds Satan (Rev. 20:1). The idea of chains and spirits may make fine reading in Dickens' *A Christmas Carol*, but this should not be confused with the spiritual nature of God's bondage of demons. Therefore, Daniel's description of the cherubim — four-faced creatures, part beast and part human, with four wings — may reflect only God's means of revealing the majesty and power of His angels (Ezk. 10:10-21). John's vision of the seraphim is analogous: four beasts — "like a" lion, calf, man, and eagle, each with six wings — crying "Holy, holy, holy, Lord God almighty" (Rev. 4:7-8). When children, or adults for that matter, sing the hymn, "Holy, Holy, Holy," they probably do not spend a lot of time thinking about the original source of the lyrics. These could conceivably be the permanent shapes of these various angels, but in the references to their appearances before men (outside of visions), they take less shocking shapes. Obviously, one would be unlikely to entertain these visionary angels unawares.

There are some Old Testament references that indicate that God takes the form of men-angels from time to time. These revelations of himself are usually called theophanies. We are told that God walked in the garden of Eden (Gen. 3:8), that He appeared in human form before Abraham at Mamre (Gen. 18:1-2, 22), and that He wrestled through the night with Jacob, afterward providing him with his new name, Israel (Gen. 32:24-28). The most famous theophany in the Bible, the appearance of God before Moses in a burning bush, actually states that "the angel of the LORD appeared unto him in a flame of fire out of the midst of a bush" (Ex. 3:2), yet the voice clearly claimed to be God (3:14; cf. Ex. 23:21). Christ specifically stated that "No man hath seen God at any time; the only begotten Son, which is in the bosom of the Father, he hath declared him" (John 1:18). These theophanies would seem to have been manifestations of the Second Person of the Trinity—not Jesus Christ as the *incarnate* Son, but pre-incarnate revelations. The importance that the writer of the Book of Hebrews places on Melchisedec, who was both priest and king of Salem (Gen. 14:18), and who was without "father, without mother, without descent, having neither beginning of days, nor end of life; but made like unto the Son of God; abideth a priest continually" (Heb. 7:3), should indicate that Melchisedec was a theophany of God. The centrality of the themes of priesthood and sacrifice in the Book of Hebrews—Christ's sacrifice as *the* sacrifice that satisfies God's standards of justice—leaves no doubt as to the importance of Melchisedec for Christian theology. He was no mere man. No ordinary angel is ever compared to the Son of God, either.

The function of angels is multiple. They are messengers of God, although it is unclear how this task operates in post-Apostolic times. They are eventually to serve as agents of divine judgment (Matt. 13:41-42; Rev. 6-10). Despite the fact that, in terms of power, men are "a little lower than the angels" (Ps. 8:5), men are nevertheless to serve someday as judges of the angels (I Cor. 6:3). As creatures, they are fellowservants of God with men (Rev. 19:10), and therefore they are not to be worshipped (Col. 2:18). It should be clear that since the closing of the biblical canon, angelic demonstrations of power have either been subdued or else attributed by men to other factors, either natural law or the direct intervention of God. Demons, frankly, make better copy.

Demons are fallen angels, both ethically and geographically. Christ announced: "I beheld Satan as lightning fall from heaven" (Luke 10:18). The twelfth chapter of Revelation, which is not so difficult a passage as some expositors would make it, affirms that a "dragon" stood before a "woman" about to give birth "for to devour her child as soon as it was born. And she brought forth a man child, who was to rule all nations with a rod of iron: and her child was caught up unto God, and to his throne" (Rev. 12:4b-5). There should be no doubt concerning the identity of a child who was caught up to heaven and to God's throne.

And there was war in heaven: Michael and his angels fought against the dragon; and the dragon fought and his angels, And prevailed not; neither was their place found any more in heaven. And the great dragon was cast out, that old serpent, called the Devil, and Satan, which deceiveth the whole world: he was cast out into the earth, and his angels were cast out with him. And I heard a loud voice saying in heaven, Now is come salvation, and strength, and the kingdom of our God, and the power of his Christ; for the accuser of our brethren is cast down, which accused them before our God day and night. And they overcame him by the blood of the Lamb, and by the word of their testimony; and they loved not their lives unto death. Therefore rejoice, ye heavens, and ye that dwell in them. Woe to the inhabitants of the earth and of the sea! for the devil is come down unto you, having great wrath, because he knoweth that he hath but a short time (Rev. 12:7-12).

The Book of Job indicates the nature of Satan's accusing tongue. After the crucifixion of Christ, that tongue could no longer be wagged before the throne of God. The brethren overcame him, with the cooperation of Michael and the angels, through the blood of the lamb. This was an historical event. It did not take place in some misty pre-Adamic period, nor did it take place in Old Testament times.[16] The ethical rebellion did take place, obviously, before the Fall of man, although we are never told just when. (My own *guess* is that it was on the morning of the seventh day, since God pronounced his blessing upon creation on the sixth day, and Satan is certainly a created being. But this is mere speculation.)

The results of that ethical rebellion have been applied steadily to Satan and his host over time. The religion of Christianity, like that of orthodox Judaism, is a religion of time. Understandably, the essence of Satan's religion is a denial of time, for time seals his doom and is an ever-present reminder to him that he has been vanquished and will ultimately suffer total, eternal defeat (Matt. 25:41; Rev. 20:14). Time must either be denied as being real or else be extended infinitely in each direction, thereby denying the final judgment. Again and again, we find in occult speculation, whether Eastern or Western, ancient or modern, a denial of the reality of *linear, bounded* time — the uniquely Western tradition which was first presented in its

---

16. The passage usually cited to show that the event was prior to New Testament times is Isaiah 14:12-15. This interpretation is as old as the early church fathers. But the Hebrew word translated "Lucifer" merely meant "morning star" or "bright star," and its position in a passage dealing with the coming destruction of Babylon indicates that, at best, it is only analogous to Satan's fall. Verse 16 clearly refers to "the man that made the earth to tremble. . . ." Cf. J. A. Alexander, *Commentary on the Prophecies of Isaiah* (Grand Rapids: Zondervan, [1865] 1974), pp. 295-98.

developed form in Augustine's *City of God*. Demons are "unclean spirits" (Matt. 10:1), "evil spirits" (Acts 19:11-12). They are, in short, *unholy spirits*. They are rebels who, according to Jude 6, "kept not their first estate, but left their own habitation," and we are told that God has now "reserved [them] in everlasting chains under darkness unto the judgment of the great day." This does not mean, by any stretch of the imagination, that they are impotent today; it simply means that they are more limited now than they were before Christ's own era. They no longer can deceive the nations as before, for the gospel is no longer confined to a barren strip of land in Palestine (Rev. 20:3). As followers of Satan, their power today is limited (II Pet. 2:4). Hell, prepared for them so long ago (Matt. 25:41), is their abode. And after hell has fulfilled its purpose, the lake of fire will receive them (Rev. 20:14).

They are not impotent, however. They have the power to control the actions of ethically rebellious men and to influence or harass the saints of God on earth. This is taught explicitly throughout the New Testament, but especially graphically in the Gospel of Mark: 1:32; 5:1-6; and 16:17. Jesus specifically stated that one of the signs — indeed, *the* sign — of the advent of His kingdom was His ability to cast out demons "by the Spirit [finger] of God" (Matt. 12:28 [Spirit]; Luke 11:20 [finger]). Perhaps the most graphic of all biblical passages dealing with exorcism is in Mark's Gospel:

And one of the multitude answered and said, Master, I have brought unto thee my son, which hath a dumb spirit; And wheresoever he taketh him, he teareth him: and he foameth, and gnasheth with his teeth, and pineth away: and I spake to thy disciples that they should cast him out; and they could not. He answereth him, and saith, O faithless generation, how long shall I be with you? how long shall I suffer you? bring him unto me. And they brought him unto him: and when he saw him, straightaway the spirit tare him; and he fell on the ground, and wallowed foaming. And he asked his father, How long is it ago since this came unto him? And he said, Of a child. And ofttimes it hath cast him into the fire, and into the waters, to destroy him: but if thou canst do any thing, have compassion on us, and help us. Jesus said unto him, If thou canst believe, all things are possible to him that believeth. And straightaway the father of the child cried out, and said with tears, Lord, I believe; help thou mine unbelief. When Jesus saw that the people came running together, he rebuked the foul spirit, saying unto him, Thou dumb and deaf spirit, I charge thee, come out of him, and enter no more into him. And the spirit cried, and rent him sore, and came out of him: and he was as one dead; insomuch that many said, He is dead.

But Jesus took him by the hand, and lifted him up; and he arose. And when he was come into the house, his disciples asked him privately, Why could not we cast him out? And he said unto them, This kind can come forth by nothing [else], but by prayer and fasting (Mark 9:17-29).

It took prayer, fasting, and faith in God's healing grace on the part of the father to cure the boy. Even with Jesus commanding the demon, the boy was still injured as it left his body. The disciples had been able to do nothing.

But for a really difficult exorcism, consider the pathetic sons of Sceva: "Then certain of the vagabond Jews, exorcists, took upon them to call over them which had evil spirits the name of the Lord Jesus, saying, We adjure you by Jesus whom Paul preacheth. And there were seven sons of one Sceva, a Jew, and chief of the priests, which did so. And the evil spirit answered and said, Jesus I know, and Paul I know; but who are ye? And the man in whom the evil spirit was leaped on them, and overcame them, and prevailed against them, so that they fled out of that house naked and wounded" (Acts 19:13-16).

Exorcism is no game. It is practiced by the spiritual sons of Sceva, and sometimes the exorcisms seem successful, but the price of these exorcisms is high, if not to the exorcist, then for the one who has been exorcised. As Jesus warned concerning the works of a faith not grounded in Him: "When the unclean spirit is gone out of a man, he walketh through dry places, seeking rest; and finding none, he saith, I will return unto my house whence I came out. And when he cometh, he findeth it swept and garnished. Then goeth he, and taketh to him seven other spirits more wicked than himself; and they enter in, and dwell there: and the last state of that man is worse than the first" (Luke 11:24-26). The illustration was meant to warn men concerning the nature of true faith, but it was based on a concrete example of a temporarily successful exorcism.

Conclusion

The testimony of the Bible is that occult phenomena are real. They are the products of acting beings who are normally invisible to man. They possess great power. Their activities are not limited to the manipulation of external phenomena. If anything, their activities in the spiritual, that is, moral and ethical realm, are vastly more important, especially in a Christian or Christian-influenced secular culture which does not acknowledge occult phenomena. While

Christian men need not fear the visible activities of demons so much as they should fear temptations to sin, they should nonetheless be aware of the existence of occult phenomena and occult philosophy. To be ignorant of such matters — matters that matter in the realm of matter — is to be unarmed in an era of increasing demonic activity.

3

PARANORMAL SCIENCE SINCE 1960

We have largely evicted superstition from the physical universe, which used to be the dumping ground of the miraculous. . . . But we have great ground to rejoice that science is now advancing into this domain more rapidly than ever before, and that the last few years have seen more progress than the century that preceded. The mysteries of our psychic being are bound ere long to be cleared up. Every one of these ghostly phenomena will be brought under the domain of law. The present recrudescence here of ancient faiths in the supernatural is very interesting as a psychic atavism, as the last flashing up of old psychoses soon to become extinct.

G. Stanley Hall (1910)[1]

Science no longer holds any absolute truths. Even the discipline of physics, whose laws once went unchallenged, has had to submit to the indignity of an Uncertainty Principle. In this climate of disbelief, we have begun to doubt even fundamental propositions, and the old distinction between natural and supernatural has become meaningless. I find this tremendously exciting.

Lyall Watson (1973)[2]

The official position of the vast bulk of scientists in the academic world as recently as 1959 was far closer to G. Stanley Hall's presentation of the "facts" than Lyall Watson's. Indeed, the majority of tenured physical and biological scientists today would probably prefer to be categorized as followers of Hall. But the naive confidence of Hall, writing as he did prior to the discovery of the principle of indeterminacy by Werner Heisenberg and prior to the development of

---

1. G. Stanley Hall, "Introduction," Amy Tanner, *Studies in Spiritism* (New York: Appleton, 1910), p. xxxii.
2. Lyall Watson, *Supernature: A Natural History of the Supernatural* (Garden City, New York: Anchor Press/Doubleday, 1973), Introduction, p. ix.

quantum mechanics, is decidedly out of style today. While only a tiny handful of scientists would go as far as Watson has gone in his book *Supernature* or Capra in his book *The Tao of Physics* (1983), most scientists nevertheless would acknowledge the validity of Watson's epistemological position: relativism has invaded physics.

The older faculty members may still cling to the literary fashions of nineteenth-century science, but if pressed in a debate, they would have to admit that the theoretical world on which nineteenth-century rationalistic optimism was based is no longer a valid intellectual option. The Newtonian universe may have conformed to mathematical law down to the atom itself, but with the discovery of subatomic particles, a revolution was born in the minds of men. The crack in the intellectual dike, while originally no wider than an electron (indeterminate as it was with respect to velocity and location simultaneously), allowed the collapse of the dam of scientific confidence. The world of G. Stanley Hall was engulfed at its foundations, and the structures have begun to slide noticeably.

Yet at bottom the two positions are not that different. If Hall and Watson could be interviewed together, they would regard each other as either superstitious (Hall regarding Watson) or naive (Watson regarding Hall). But both would be firmly committed to a concept of *a universe that is open to anything but the God of the Bible*. Whatever oddities nature may bring before us to examine, it is always nature that brings them, for nature alone has produced them. Hall would prefer to interpret these oddities within the framework of universal laws — universally comprehensible by the universally rational mind. Watson would prefer to bring a degree of what he would call "mystery" into the universe. The noumenal realm should be given its due, not in the sense that it is somehow personal — no demons or personal God "out there" to mess around with the processes of the phenomenal realm — but in the sense that the random and the ultimately incomprehensible event must be acknowledged as basic to the structure of the universe.

In this sense, Hall was really pre-Kantian in his perspective. His was the confident world of Descartes, with its mathematical laws comprehending and sustaining everything. Watson is the modern figure, far more self-conscious epistemologically. Nevertheless, both Hall and Watson would refuse to give an inch or a proton's worth of influence to any cause which was itself not produced by the processes of autonomous nature. Hall's approach would be to deny the ultimate "oddness" of any oddity; Watson would affirm the ultimate "oddness" of all phenomena; but neither would open his universe to the unnatural—the truly supernatural.

Watson, however, realizes that Hall's world is too narrow to encompass oddities that must be explained in order to affirm the autonomy of nature, so he has broadened the legitimate definition of the natural: "The supernatural is usually defined as that which is not explicable by the known forces of nature. Supernature knows no bounds. . . . Supernature is nature with all its flavors intact, waiting to be tested. I offer it as a logical extension of the present state of science, as a solution to some of the problems with which traditional science cannot cope, and as an analgesic to modern man."[3] In his definition of what constitutes the science of supernature, Watson sets forth the case for paranormal science.

Michel Gauquelin's Astounding Discoveries

Watson thinks that perhaps the French investigator Michel Gauquelin may be onto something. Gauquelin studied the birth times of famous Frenchmen, and he found a statistical correlation between French scientists and medical men with the *astronomical* position of Mars. Soldiers, it seems, are mostly Jupiters, as are politicians. But what does all this mean? Were the samples too small? Does "astrology" apply only to *French* soldiers, politicians, and scientists? Have these relationships been eternal? Watson, being an enthusiastic paranormal scientist, categorically states that Gauquelin's work "shows, beyond reasonable doubt, that the position of planets means something—the position, and not the planets themselves. We still have to decide whether the planets are acting directly on us or whether their position is merely symbolic of some much larger cosmic pattern of energy of which they, and we, are just a small part."[4]

Before examining the conclusions concerning astrology that Watson draws from Gauquelin's discoveries, we need first to examine in detail what he has discovered. They are remarkable discoveries. They hold up to rigorous testing. But what must be understood from the beginning is that they are not astrological in nature. They are *astronomical*. But at present, they are unexplainable.

---

3. *Ibid.* p. xi.

4. *Ibid.*, p. 57. Cf. H. J. Eysenck and D. K. B. Nias, *Astrology: Science or Superstition?* (London: Temple Smith, 1982).

Most of us who read about Gauquelin's supposed discoveries may be initially skeptical. Yet of all the "astrological" findings ever offered to the world, his are unquestionably the most difficult to disprove. He is a trained statistician, and he has devoted decades to exceedingly thorough research of local birth records. So thorough has his research been that the various conventional and orthodox scientific organizations that devote time and money to debunking pro-occult experiments have steadfastly refused to criticize Gauquelin. The American Humanist Association, publishers of *The Humanist*, has even suppressed the results of their own study which corroborated his findings. So did the Belgian Committee Para.[5] The Humanist Association had promised to publish the results no matter what, but when they came out positive, the Association insisted on another group of tests.[6] It is the same old game: only negative results are deemed scientific.

Gauquelin earned a doctorate in psychology at the Sorbonne in Paris. He also did extensive work in statistics. He had been interested in astrology as a youth, but he became increasingly skeptical as he began to investigate such claims as "professional soldiers are often born under Aires or Scorpio, and rarely under Cancer." He found no statistical support for such generalities. But he continued his detailed studies of birth records.[7] What he did discover was the oddity that famous people from various occupations, such as acting and medicine, are more often than statistically random likely to have been born when the planets were in particular positions.[8]

His first investigation involved 576 members of the French Academy of Medicine. He selected physicians who had attained distinction. He used objective criteria for this initial selection. He discovered that eminent doctors tended to be born when Mars and Saturn had just risen or had just passed midheaven.[9] We are speaking here of the actual planets in relation to the earth's horizon, not astrological charts. He divided the heaven into 12 sectors, so that at the point of birth, 16.7% of those born will be in any given planetary sector. More than 16.7% of the famous members of a given profession are born under the sectors of Mars or Saturn, either rising or just

5. The Committee for the Scientific Investigation of Alleged Paranormal Phenomena.

6. Eysenck and Nias, *Astrology*, pp. 196-200.

7. *Ibid.*, p. 182.

8. *Ibid.*, p. 183.

9. *Ibid.*, p. 184.

beyond the culmination overhead.

He collected a random sample of births from the general population covering the same period of births as the doctors. They were born according to normal statistical distribution: Mars or Saturn had no "advantage" over the other planets. Then he studied another 508 doctors who had produced important research. Again, Mars and Saturn were over-represented. But what is oddest of all, the results of his investigations only apply to famous members of any given occupation.

Two examples may suffice. First, Gauquelin looked at the distinction between arts and science that has long been recognized in education. He contrasted 5,100 successful artists with 3,647 successful scientists, and found that Saturn was the planet that best differentiated these two groups . . . . [T]he scientists tended to have been born when this planet had just risen or had just passed the midheaven. In contrast, the artists were significantly less likely to have been born at these times; they showed a distinct tendency to avoid being born "under" Saturn. Similarly contrasting results were obtained when certain other groups were compared, such as soldiers and musicians. In the case of musicians specialising in military music, their results tended to fall mid-way between the soldiers and the other musicians!

The second example concerns Mars, which has long been recognized as the symbol of the god of war. Gauquelin looked to see if this planet occupied the critical zones (just past the rising point and just past midheaven) in the charts of 3,438 military leaders. It did, with 680 cases in these zones instead of the expected 590. Moreover, Jupiter was even more apparent, with 703 cases instead of an expected 572.[10]

He ran control group tests on ordinary scientists and soldiers, and he found no abnormal correlations. Then he studied the birth dates and times of war heroes who had been injured seriously, and whose military careers were cut short. The same pattern appeared that marked the successful career officers. As Eysenck and Nias comment: "This was a crucial finding, because it suggested that the relationship was not with destiny but with the character or personality that makes for success."[11]

In subsequent studies, they discovered that personality was related to the planets, not occupation; it was because certain personality traits are associated with successful occupations that leaders in

10. *Ibid.*, pp. 185-86.
11. *Ibid.*, p. 187.

these fields tend to be linked to a particular planet.[12] Understand, these results were produced by "blind assessment" statistical tests; the psychologist was not informed of the "astrological" predictions in advance. She simply rated the personalities of famous people by biographical data available publicly; the correlations predicted by Gauquelin were kept secret from her until after the experiment was over.

Gauquelin then examined an assertion by Kepler that the children of parents born under one zodiacal sign tend to be born under that same sign. He found that there is no correlation with zodiacal signs, but there is with the planetary position. A study of 15,000 couples and their children produced this odd fact: if one or both parents had been born under a particular planetary configuration, there was a statistically significant tendency for their children to be born "under" this particular planet. This effect is most marked by the Moon, Venus, and Mars, followed by Jupiter and Saturn.[13] This works with ordinary people, not just the famous.[14] This correspondence between child and parent applies about equally to father and mother.[15]

Eysenck's conclusion is totally humanistic: "A child tends to be born under a particular planet if one of the parents, either mother or father, was also born at that time. This finding that the father has such a role can only mean that it is the child, and not the mother who initiates the birth process." There are other possibilities: God controls the birth process, or an angel (in the Bible, angels in general are associated with planets in general). But clearly not the mother. If both father and mother were born under the same planet, there was double the likelihood of the child being born under it.[16]

Then Gauquelin went farther. He compared the correlations with two groups, those born naturally, and those born by induced birth, including drugs. He found that the planetary effect applied only to the "natural birth" group.[17]

Furthermore, if there was geomagnetic activity on the day of birth, the children were even more likely to share a parent's planet.

So Gauquelin ran two more tests. Each sample group contained 15,000 couples. (Notice that he chose larger samples, not smaller, in

---

12. *Ibid.*, p. 189.
13. *Ibid.*, p. 191.
14. *Ibid.*, p. 192.
15. *Ibid.*, p. 194.
16. *Idem.*
17. *Idem.*

order to reduce any statistical anomalies.) The results were the same: induced vs. natural birth, two parents under one planet doubling the chances of the child's birth under that planet, the geomagnetic effect, and the independence of the sex of the parent.[18]

Can any other scientist duplicate any aspect of his results? Yes. Will anyone else admit this? Not so far. The Belgian Para Committee is a case in question.

After fifteen years' perusal, having found no serious errors in Gauquelin's methods and calculations, they decided to supervise a replication, choosing famous sportsmen for this purpose. Earlier, as we have seen, Gauquelin had found that relative to both a control group of ordinary sportsmen and theoretical expectation, Mars tended to be in one of the critical zones at the birth of 1,553 sports champions. This study was repeated for a new group of 535 sports champions from France and Belgium. In the original study, 21.4 per cent of the champions were born in one of the two critical sectors, while in the replication the proportion was 22.2 per cent. (Chance expectation in both cases is 16.7 per cent.) The odds against this result occurring by chance were now several millions to one.

In spite of this apparently very successful replication, the Committee Para was not convinced. In a short statement published in 1976, they suggested that the results could be due to an artefact, saying, 'The Committee Para cannot accept the conclusions of the research of M. Gauquelin based on hypotheses in which the committee has found inexactitudes.'[19]

In short, what our net doesn't catch isn't fish. What our presuppositions do not allow cannot be true. End of report. This, in spite of the fact that the control group of ordinary sportsmen came very close to the normal distribution of 16.7%.[20] *The Humanist* also refused to publish a study by Gauquelin which produced similarly "disturbing" conclusions, despite the fact that they had hired a university statistician to design the test, and despite the fact that they had agreed to publish the results, no matter what the findings. He studied 303 champions, and compared them with 16,756 people born in the same regions at about the same time. The Mars effect was manifest for 22% of the champions, and was not for the control group.[21] And what was the response of *The Humanist*? No deal. We want

---

18. *Ibid.*, p. 195.
19. *Ibid.*, pp. 196-97.
20. *Ibid.*, p. 198.
21. *Ibid.*, p. 198.

another test! (The joke was on Gaquelin; he actually had believed that *The Humanist* plays fair, and that his study of 17,000 charts would pay off. Silly man.) A committee ran the next test. Because the birth times are not recorded in many U.S. birth records, the study was poorly designed. The sample size of those whose birth times were available was too small. When the results of this small sample proved positive anyway (20.3%), the committee dumped in more names, this time of substandard sportsmen. When this group finally produced negative results, the committee announced its negative conclusion.[22] This is how the game of orthodox science is played.

As we have seen, Michel Gauquelin is no simple-minded astrologer. He opposes what he calls "pop astrology."[23] His findings have scientific validity. He makes no claim to be able to predict the future. He rejects traditional astrology. Nevertheless, Watson praises Gauquelin's limited but scientifically rigorous findings, and then proceeds in his discussion of traditional, simple-minded astrology, as if this were in some way related scientifically to the observable lunar and solar rhythms of our world. "Supernature knows no bounds." Anything can conceivably be related to anything or everything. In other words, to cite the phrase so dear to the hearts of the occultists and magicians of the so-called rationalistic Renaissance: *As above, so below.* This was the theological and cosmological foundation of all magic and astrology from the beginning. It is Watson's creed. "Matter, mind, and magic are all one in the cosmos," he states.[24]

New Age Science

Although the science of the occult or odd phenomena had been limping along since at least the 1880's, it experienced the beginning of a massive revival about 1965. So massive has this revival been in terms of the *methods* of experimental science that a whole new literature has developed. While the practitioners of paranormal science are still few in number, the impact that this tiny band is having on the way in which the general public views its world is nothing short of astounding. Establishment scientists, most of whom at any stage in history are essentially skilled technicians who pursue incredibly narrow and almost arcane avenues of investigation, are ill-equipped to

---

22. *Ibid.*, p. 199.
23. Michel Gauquelin, *Cosmic Influences on Human Behavior* (New York: Stein and Day, 1973), p. 27.
24. *Supernature*, p. 284.

meet the charges and assertions of these younger and often amateur-
ish scientists of the paranormal. The latter are writing easily understood paperback books for the millions, and the millions are buying
them.

The average reader is not much interested in bickering footnotes;
what he wants is something novel, something to tickle his imagination. Paranormal science fits the bill perfectly. The public is convinced, and not without good reason, that for the affairs of life, including the oddities of life, the razor-sharp intellectual tools of professional scientists are so specialized and precise that they are unfit
for anything other than academic hairsplitting. The modern readers
of paperback science are only too similar to the residents of Athens
in the days of Christ: educated and bored, with a lot of time on their
hands. "For all the Athenians and strangers which were there spent
their time in nothing else, but either to tell, or to hear some new
thing" (Acts 17:21).

Anomalies in Nature

Many of the anomalies that Watson presents in his study really
do seem to be the products of nature. (Nature in this sense being independent of supernatural secondary causality, though not independent of the *sustaining* hand of a personal God.) God's universe is
far more extensive than the canons of nineteenth-century scientific
theory. For example, oysters studied by biologist Frank Brown display some amazing properties. Collected by Brown from their home
beds in the Long Island South off Connecticut, they were able to
maintain their patterns of opening and closing with the tides, even
when shipped to his laboratory in Evanston, Illinois. But these patterns persisted for only fourteen days. On the fifteenth day, they
began to deviate from the original patterns — simultaneously. Watson
summarizes: "Brown calculated the difference between the old
rhythm and the new one and discovered that the oysters now opened
up at the time the tide would have flooded Evanston — had the town
been on the shore and not perched on the bank of a Great Lake 580
feet above sea level."[25] Furthermore, they persisted in their new
rhythm in the dark and under seemingly fixed control conditions.
Brown then discovered that their movements generally corre-
sponded to the position of the moon, opening when the moon was di-

---

25. *Ibid.*, p. 23.

rectly overhead Evanston. "This was the first piece of scientific evidence to show that even an organism living away from the ocean tides could be influenced by the passage of the moon."[26]

Watson goes on to record other well-known animal responses that are influenced by lunar rhythms: the running (spawning) of the California grunion fish, the movement of a particular variety of worms, and May flies. Even rainfall has been found to be abnormally heavy just after full and new moons, and *Science*, a prestigious establishment periodical, has published the data on this unexplained statistical phenomenon.[27] In addition to lunar rhythms, there are solar rhythms. We are learning that sun spots may influence some aspects of the earth's weather. They also may influence earthquakes. Changes in human blood serum have been attributed to sun-spot activity.[28] Even the speed of chemical reactions, says Giorgio Piccardi, the director of the Institute for Physical Chemistry in Florence, Italy, is influenced by sun spots. Watson summarizes his experiments with bismuth oxychloride (a colloid), which forms a cloudy precipitate when poured into distilled water. Three times a day he and his assistants carried out this simple test, until they had 200,000 separate results. Sure enough, over a ten-year period they found that the reaction took place more rapidly during sun-spot activity.[29] (Here is a typical test procedure of orthodox science.) These tests have been replicated by other scientists throughout the world.[30]

What is mind-boggling to the average reader, assuming he pays much attention to what he is reading, is not that sun spots have some kind of influence over bismuth oxychloride, but that any highly placed scientist would conduct a decade-long experiment of this nature. What if — perish the thought — the results had been negative? Ten years, a ton of bismuth oxychloride, and a zillion gallons of distilled water — right down the proverbial drain. And the positive nature of the experiment has fascinated only parapsychologists and scientists of the odd, themselves highly suspect in the eyes of orthodox scientists. Finally, there is the question of financing. "Who cares?" is too easy. "Who paid?" is more to the point. Even more as-

---

26. *Idem.*
27. *Ibid.*, p. 27.
28. *Ibid.*, pp. 52-53.
29. The effect was inhibited when the solution was shielded by a copper screen, for whatever that is worth: Eysenck and Nias, *Astrology*, p. 137.
30. *Idem.*

tounding, someone financed other scholars in their successful attempts to imitate Piccardi's discovery.

Watson includes these curious facts in his second chapter. All well and good, but after the long, slow curve comes the fast break: "Astrology is based upon the fundamental premise that celestial phenomena affect life and events here on earth. No scientist, and certainly no biologist familiar with the latest work on weather and natural rhythms, can deny that this premise is proved."[31] We have now leaped from oysters to astrology, for in Watson's universe, both have the same foundation: the premise of celestial-terrestrial relationships. But, to put it bluntly, the moon ain't the North Star, and the stars and galaxies making up the perceived constellations have got nothing to do with the astrological signs of lions and crabs and twins.

By taking up the old creeds of Renaissance magic, Watson has placed them into post-Kantian methodological boxes. Randomness has replaced demons in his cosmology, but the goal is still much the same. A new age lies before us, an age of human power: "So we have arrived at the moment of control with a new and growing consciousness both of the enormity of the task and the breadth of our own ability to cope with it. In this situation two things stand out above all others; one is that our greatest strength lies in unity with all of Supernature here on earth, and the other is that this unity could give us the impetus we need to transcend the system altogether. Supernature could become something really supernatural."[32]

With this call to power and self-transcendence — metaphysically, a "leap of being" — Watson ends his book and sets before us the most ancient of man's heresies: to be as God. Man shall control his own destiny, ultimately merging with the cosmos in a new evolution. It is this goal that unites Chaldean astrologers, Hindu mystics, the paranormal scientists, the evolutionary philosophers and scientists, and the magicians: to be as God, by means of evolutionary leaps. Above all, it demands the *exercise of power.* Man is a part of a closed universe; there is no higher court of appeal. And as C. S. Lewis has warned, when we hear talk about the possibility of man's taking control of mankind, watch out: some men are about to try to take control of all others.

---

31. *Ibid.*, p. 55.
32. *Ibid.*, p. 315.

New Age Evolution

The theme which unites Darwinian scientific humanists, occultists, New Age mystics, and virtually all other contemporary anti-Christian movements, is the doctrine of evolution, and more specifically, the doctrine of *man, the director of evolutionary processes*. Watson's summary is representative: "This is Supernature, and man sits at the center of its web, tugging at the strands that interest him, following some through to useful conclusions and snapping others in his impatience. Man is the spearhead of evolution, vital, creative, and immensely talented, but still young enough to wreak havoc in the first flush of enthusiasm. Hopefully this period of awkward adolescence is coming to an end as he begins to realize that he cannot possibly survive alone, that the web of Supernature is supported by the combined strength of a vast number of individually fragile fragments, that life on earth is united into what amounts to a single superorganism, and that this in turn is only part of the cosmic community."[33]

In short, "ye shall be as God." Man is the director of cosmic evolution, yet autonomous from God. He is a cooperator in the creation, yet not higher than the creation. The cosmos is one, but it is also autonomous. The impersonal forces of evolution have anointed man as king of creation, but these forces, being autonomous, therefore give man his license of autonomy from God. This is pure humanism, and it is also pure satanism. It is the common gospel of twentieth-century philosophy.[34]

Because of this common philosophy, modern secular humanists have been unable to counter successfully the mysticism and occultism represented by a book such as *Supernature*. Secular humanists no doubt feel uncomfortable with Watson. They do not think much of astrology. But they think a lot less of the Bible. They much prefer Watson's New Age humanism to the doctrine of the sovereignty of God, or the doctrine of creation out of nothing. Secular humanists are therefore allies of the New Age mystics. So, it turns out, are the ultimate secular humanists, the Communists of the Soviet Union.

---

33. *Ibid.*, pp. 313-14.

34. Gary North, *The Dominion Covenant: Genesis* (Tyler, Texas: Institute for Christian Economics, 1982), Appendix A: "From Cosmic Impersonalism to Humanistic Sovereignty."

Soviet Experiments

If G. Stanley Hall had ever heard about the existence of the book by Sheila Ostrander and Lynn Schroeder, *Psychic Discoveries Behind the Iron Curtain* (1970), he would never have believed a word of it. [35] If Joseph Stalin had ever heard of it, he would have had a copy translated; within six weeks, the book would no longer have been true. This book, by 1975, had become the Bible of paranormal science, although it is written in a journalistic fashion by nonscientists. It went through five printings as a hardback in 1970, and by mid-1974 had gone through ten printings as a paperback. To say that it was a bestseller does not do it justice. Watson cites its reports over and over in his own best-selling book. The book fully deserves its wide circulation, for it tells the story of impossibilities within an impossibility — paranormal studies financed by the most rationalistic political empire in the history of man.

Stalin had prohibited investigations into the occult (although certain forms of telepathy, oddly enough, were not completely banished as scientific facts). Yet within a decade of his death, the Soviet Union's scientific community began to be hit with a series of mini-revivals. Upper-echelon members of the scientific establishment began to examine phenomena that had previously been banned as not only nonexistent but un-Marxist. Here, in the most thoroughly rationalistic and bureaucratized state in man's history, was a scientific guild that was permitting the study of what scientists throughout the world had long called occultism. Yet such studies were being made in the name of Marxism-Leninism, that is, materialism. The Soviets were slowly discovering Supernature. By the late 1960's, scientists in the Iron Curtain nations had become the most heavily subsidized paranormal scientists in the world. Though no scientist would have wanted or dared to admit it, total rationalism was steadily being fused with supernaturalism, that is, the old irrationalism.

What kinds of phenomena are under investigation? Mind over matter (telekinesis), telepathy, and extrasensory perception (the Western phrase given to the unknown and the theoretically impossible). Sight without eyes. Hypnosis-induced reincarnation. Precognition. Bioplasmic bodies (auras). Prophecy and astrology. From the late 1950's, when hardly a word of such research could filter into any

---

35. Sheila Ostrander and Lynn Schroeder, *Psychic Discoveries Behind the Iron Curtain* (New York: Bantam, 1970).

official Soviet publication (and that means any legal Soviet publication), to the very early 1960's, old-fashioned scientific orthodoxy
reigned supreme. By 1965, as in the United States, the dam had
broken. The scientists of the Soviet Union were tentatively being
offered a whole new world to explore. Soviet scientists, bit by bit,
began to make their peace with the hitherto banned data of the occult. No doubt such a shift in scientific opinion was easier for Soviet
scientists than it has been for Americans: the state paid them to
change their minds, and in the Soviet Union the discovery of eternal
truths inside previously prohibited facts is a familiar process. The re-
vision of encyclopedias in the Soviet Union is literally a way of life.

Telekineses and Telepathy

In 1959, reports hit the USSR (but not the USA) that the U.S.
Navy had been experimenting with telepathy. The submarine *Nautilus* had supposedly been trying ESP techniques (or magic, or not-
yet-knownness) as a means of communication between underwater
points, something thought to be impossible by presently known
scientific techniques. Leopold Vasiliev, a highly respected Soviet
physiologist (who had for years been running a highly secret laboratory for parapsychological research), warned fellow scientists that
the USSR should not fall behind the USA in the field of paranormal
science. He stated himself forthrightly: "The discovery of the energy
underlying ESP will be equivalent to the discovery of atomic
energy."[36] Like any well-salaried employee of a messianic state, Vasiliev saw his opportunity and he took it. Call attention to the national
enemy (the United States), point to a secret new discovery that holds
out the promise of almost unlimited power, and make certain that
the authorities bankroll it, since it just happens to be one's own area
of expertise. In the United States, this technique is called "grants-
manship." Vasiliev got what he wanted: access to research money
and, perhaps even more important, access to the hitherto closed
pages of the academic journals. A special ESP laboratory was established under his direction at Leningrad University.

By far the most prominent human subject of Soviet research into
telekinesis — mind over matter — has been "Nelya Mikhailova" (Nina
Kulagina), a Leningrad housewife of peasant background. Over forty
top Soviet scientists have tested her abilities. After two to four hours

36. *Ibid.*, p. 7.

of intense concentration, Nelya can perform the following wonders (sometimes): spin a compass needle from several feet away (a terrific talent, especially when you're lost); move various objects around a table — or off; separate the yolk from the white of an egg that is suspended in a saline solution, and then put them back together. All of these activities produce intense physiological reactions in Nelya, including a heart pulsating as fast as 240 beats per minute. A measurable magnetic force field is created by her during these experiments — focused on the object of her concentration. These experiments have been conducted under rigorous test conditions and recorded on film. There are no known explanations.[37]

One of the key signs of occult powers as distinguished from remarkable but natural powers is the *repeatability factor.* Like virtually all psychics, Nelya never knows for certain if her powers are going to appear. Unlike American establishment scientists, who dimly grasp the significance of repeatability, the Soviet scientists who are involved in paranormal scientific research put up with the seemingly random display of these experimental oddities. American scientists dismiss such phenomena as being unreal, which they assuredly are not, or as purely random events needing no explanation, which they certainly do need. But this basic skepticism has kept most of them away from the dark paths of occult power.

The Soviets, demonic to the core in their official materialism, have now embarked on an equally demonic journey into the realms of power that are anything but materialistic. Screwtape, the mythical demon of C. S. Lewis' *Screwtape Letters*, is having his devilish wish come true behind the Iron Curtain. Writing to his nephew, the neophyte demon Wormwood, Screwtape sets forth basic policy: "Our policy, for the moment, is to conceal ourselves. Of course this has not always been so. We are really faced with a cruel dilemma. When the humans disbelieve in our existence we lose all the pleasing results of direct terrorism, and we make no magicians. On the other hand, when they believe in us, we cannot make them materialists and skeptics. At least, not yet. I have great hopes that we shall learn in due time how to emotionalise and mythologise their science to such an extent that what is, in effect, a belief in us (though not under that name) will creep in while the human mind remains closed to belief in the Enemy. The 'Life Force,' the worship of sex, and some aspects of Psychoanalysis may here prove useful. If once we can pro-

---

37. *Ibid.*, pp. 67-76.

duce our perfect work—the Materialist Magician, the man, not using, but veritably worshipping, what he vaguely calls 'Forces' while denying the existence of 'spirits'—then the end of the war will be in sight."[38]

It is hardly surprising that outside the Iron Curtain countries, the scientists who are most deeply involved in the study of the paranormal are psychologists: *parapsychologists*. Many of them are deeply Freudian or Jungian. Indeed, Freud himself began investigating psychic phenomena at the end of his career, and Jung built much of his analytic structure around occult themes and powers. But the Soviets are officially materialists; they have no time for such bourgeois theories as found in Freudian psychology, a fact which undoubtedly has made their psychological research far more concrete. What the Soviets are after, purely and simply, is power.

Take telepathy. Telepathic experimentation never died out in the USSR, but since 1965, there has been a renewed interest in telepathic phenomena. The most famous telepaths in the USSR are Karl Nikolaiev, an actor, and Yuri Kamensky, a biophysicist. They send wireless messages without any form of apparatus. Mental messages, both visual and numerical. Emotional messages, in which one emotional experience is transmitted from one to the other over many miles. Kamensky is the "sender." These experiments are rigidly controlled by scientists who, initially, are often quite skeptical of the whole operation. For example, objects are placed randomly in sealed boxes, and the boxes are then opened randomly by Kamensky. Kamensky then focuses his attention on the contents of the particular box. Then, 1,500 miles away, Nikolaiev records his mental impressions of what the object is. He is correct in an astonishing number of cases. Electrodes attached to Nikolaiev's head recorded the moment of his response to the "message" each time Kamensky "sent" one. By comparing the times in each laboratory, scientists found that Nikolaiev received his messages within a matter of seconds after they had been sent—or at least the responses on the charts indicated a brief delay. These experiments, which were conducted from 1966 on, were fully approved by the Soviet academic guild. Yet the 1956 *Soviet Encyclopedia* had announced: "Telepathy is an antisocial, idealistic fiction about man's supernatural power to perceive phenomena which, considering the time and the place, cannot be perceived."[39]

---

38. C. S. Lewis, *The Screwtape Letters* (New York: Macmillan, [1943] 1969), Letter VII, pp. 32-33.

39. Ostrander & Schroeder, *Psychic Discoveries*, p. 20.

The most revealing fact about the Nikolaiev-Kamensky researches is the following footnote. The authorities, in characteristically Soviet fashion, had secretly employed a third telepath to monitor the experiments from his apartment. The psychic, Victor Milodan, was able to pick up three of the five images sent by Kamensky on one occasion, and in all five cases knew exactly when the messages had been sent.[40] There are experiments, in the Soviet view, and then there are *the* experiments. (If there are ever enough telepaths running around, the Soviets will pay Western firms a mountain of money — borrowed from the Export-Import Bank at below-market rates, of course — to develop jamming devices for telepathic communications.)

From the 1920's onward, the Soviets had experimented with a combination of telekinesis and telepathy. Vasiliev had been one of these scientists. Dr. K. I. Platonov had demonstrated in the mid-1920's that he could put a dancing woman into a trance-like sleep merely by concentrating on her from across the dance floor. The woman had been involved in a series of experiments in hypnosis conducted by Platonov. Here, in fact, was the very essence of Soviet social theory in action: mind over mind. As the authors remark: "The ability to put people to sleep and wake them up telepathically from a distance of a few yards to over a thousand miles became the most thoroughly tested and perfected contribution of the Soviets to international parapsychology. It is *the* Soviet experiment."[41] Vasiliev found that the ability to transmit telepathic directions to a human receiver is not affected in any known way by any known screening device, including lead capsules and Faraday cages. (This fact of noninterference will be discussed later in relation to the transmission of mental images to a Polaroid camera.) One estimate of the number of people who can be affected by such mental transmissions is four percent.[42]

The goal, needless to say, is *control*: the whole man must be put under the domination of the modern scientific state. "In the main, what the Soviets are probably seeking in their exploration of ESP's effect on consciousness is control in a more generalized, everyday, pervasive sense. You hear the word *control* often in the USSR, not as a political concept, but in its comparatively upbeat, scientific meaning. As a Moscow scientist told us, 'Science has learned to control outer nature to the great benefit of mankind. Now we are trying to

40. *Ibid.*, pp. 130-34.
41. *Ibid.*, p. 101.
42. *Ibid.*, p. 110.

learn the laws governing inner nature. Just as an understanding of outer nature allowed us, for example, to generate electricity to light huge cities, so the ability to control the untapped resources of man should bring equally amazing benefits.' "[43]

Sight Without Eyes

There is a phenomenon known throughout the world that baffles every scientist who has ever investigated it — not many, to be sure. Certain individuals who are totally blind, sometimes from birth, have developed the ability to perceive distinctions among colors and even to read letters printed on a page. From time to time, the popular press reports these cases, though usually with considerable skepticism or confusion. An American Pentecostal evangelist, Ronald Coyne, upon removing his glass eye and covering his seeing eye with a handkerchief that is then sealed with adhesive tape, has the ability to read from materials selected by the public. The phenomenon appears to be genuine in his case. He says he is a healer, and in 1969 he healed his way into a Cadillac El Dorado.[44] The public likes a good show, and if an evangelist can mix religion with a visible miracle like eyeless sight, the folks will part with those twenty-dollar bills, even if they are relatively poor people.

In the Soviet Union, the bureaucracy parts with the equivalent of thousand-dollar bills. Rosa Kuleshova, a blind young woman living in the Ural mountain town of Nizhiniy Tagil, found in the early 1960's that she could perceive colors in her fingers. The news of her ability spread like wildfire. She was taken to Moscow laboratories to be studied. She performed. She became a celebrity. The great eyeless sight fad was born. Blind students all over the USSR began training themselves, just as Rosa said she had done for six years. Like Rosa, some were found who could perceive lights shined on their hands, color by color. Colors feel differently, apparently. Some learned to read letters. But Rosa's fame destroyed her. She gave demonstrations of her powers, and finally they left her. Over the long run, her power to see with her hands could not be repeated.[45]

This sort of power fascinates Americans who dabble in the occult or who at least read a lot about it. *Probe* magazine, which was published in the mid-1970's, featured an article, "Eyeless Sight," in its

43. *Ibid.*, p. 115.
44. Riverside, Calif. *Press-Enterprise* (March 29, 1969).
45. Ostrander & Schroeder, *Psychic Discoveries*, ch. 11.

September 1975 issue. There is no doubt that the phenomenon exists. There is also no doubt that it has nothing to do with unassisted human skills.

Reincarnation by Hypnosis

Dr. Vladimir Raikov, a Moscow psychologist, has developed a truly innovative system of art training. He takes zero-talent students, hypnotizes them, tells them in their trances that they are famous artists of the past, and then wakes them. In case after impossible case, they begin to display hitherto unknown artistic capacities. They do not become master artists, but people who had been hard-pressed to draw stick figures have become commercial (pardon the bourgeois phrase) artists. As always, Raikov is searching for the "unknown laws" that govern these artistic transformations that literally create talented people out of average citizens. These techniques have also been used to produce mathematical abilities in otherwise dull students.

If true, the following bit of historical revisionism is a shocker. Raikov claims that Sergei Rachmaninoff had been hypnotized by a Dr. Dahl during a period of depression. For years after the performance in St. Petersburg of his First Symphony, which had received catcalls, he had been unable to compose. Dahl put him under hypnosis, trained him in autosuggestion, and let him loose on his music. The Piano Concerto No. 2 in C Minor was the first result. Rachmaninoff later claimed that whole passages of music would simply come upon him. The phenomenon may be related to the dream-induced musical creations of Wagner and Tchaikovsky.[47]

Hypnosis is hoped to become a tool for the unlocking of hidden talents. The problem is, however, the *source* of such talents. Where, exactly, had they been hidden for so long? And why does hypnosis bring them out? Hypnosis — a phenomenon which has led, time and again, to other manifestations of paranormal powers — is not yet understood by any investigator, yet it is used increasingly by psychologists all over the world. It releases "untapped forces." Indeed, and at times untrapped forces.

Water Dowsing

The age-old practice of water dowsing (also metal dowsing, missing-object dowsing, etc.) is being revived in the Soviet Union.

---

46. *Ibid.*, pp. 156-57.
47. Thelma Moss, *The Probability of the Impossible* (Los Angeles: Tarcher; distributed by Hawthorne Books, New York, 1974), p. 228.

Of course, it really never has been absent from either side of the Iron Curtain. There is an American Society of Dowsers which meets annually.[48] The U.S. Army, like the Red Army, employs dowsers for various purposes. In Vietnam, they were used to ferret out underground Viet Cong bunkers.[49] Few and far between are the American municipal water companies that do not (secretly) employ a dowser or two. But in the USSR, scientists are beginning to take them seriously. Men like America's Henry Gross, who once "dowsed" for water on Bermuda from his home in Maine (using a map of Bermuda) and found the only underground fresh-water sources discovered in the island's history, are not ridiculed.[50] (The pendulum, a phenomenon related to dowsing, is also receiving new attention.) Naturally, the phenomenon had to be renamed. Its translation from the Russian is "Biophysical Effects Method." (In France, it is called "radiaesthenia.") Scientists have been able to conclude that this force is not electrical, although physiological changes in the dowsers can be measured when they walk over a so-called dowsing area. (In a series of Swiss experiments, curious scientists discovered that certain plants and trees will not grow in a dowsing zone, nor will mice sleep in one.)

Like American dowsers, Soviet scientists assert that the revolving rods can answer questions concerning the depth of the water or mineral deposits, or the size of the deposits: one revolution equals so many meters, and so forth. Yet all of this is argued in terms of the standards of materialistic science. No magic here.

Pavlita Boxes

Years ago a Czechoslovakian manager of a textile factory, Robert Pavlita, developed a patent for a new manufacturing process. The royalties made it possible for him to do research that nobody else would finance. He rummaged through hundreds of ancient Czechoslovakian manuscripts, which Czech authorities today refuse to cite directly. Out of designs described in these unnamed manuscripts (alchemical manuscripts, in all likelihood), he came up with designs for dozens of peculiarly shaped metal boxes. Various moving parts ro-

48. *New York Times* (Sept. 12, 1971).

49. Reported by *New York Times'* Hanson W. Baldwin; reprinted in Martin Ebon (ed.) *The Psychic Reader* (New York: New American Library, 1970), pp. 51-53.

50. Kenneth Roberts, *Henry Gross and His Dowsing Rod* (New York: Pyramid Books, [1951] 1969), chaps. 13, 18.

tate in these boxes. There is a problem, however. They are not attached to any known source of power. Pavlita stares at them, and the devices inside the boxes begin to move. He can walk away, and they keep right on rotating. They are receptacles of human energy — tiny generators. Many of them are useless, but some offer intriguing promises. Sealed bottles of dye-filled water are purified in twelve hours by energy radiated by a Pavlita generator. Furthermore, analysis revealed that the actual molecular structure of the now-pure water had been altered: the two hydrogen atoms were spread farther apart.[51]

One generator has operated independently for as long as three days. This one supposedly speeds up plant growth. Another one is psychic. This experiment, by the way, is repeatable. Five ESP cards are laid out in front of the generator's pointer. In another room a "sender" concentrates on a similar set of five cards. Turning up one card at a time, he concentrates. The pointer on the machine slowly points to the comparable card. According to Czech scientists, the machine never misses. Never.

Although films of these generators exist, few Western scientists have been allowed to see them. As of 1970, they were skeptical. But why should Czech state officials pour money into the projects? Was Pavlita nothing more than a hoaxer, trying to fool his American visitors who were going to write a book on psychic discoveries behind the Iron Curtain? In any case, the fact that the authorities openly admit that such generators exist indicates that there is substance to the claims made for them. Not necessarily scientific substance, however.

Pyramid Occultism

If Pavlita's boxes can be dismissed as some sort of elaborate practical joke, what can be done with the discovery of another Czech inventor, Karl Dyrbal? Dyrbal found that by making a scale model of the great Cheops Pyramid, placing a used razor blade one-third of the way to the apex (where the pharaoh's chamber would have been, had there been a scale model of the pharaoh), putting the edges of the blade on an east-west axis, and waiting for a week, the dull blade gets sharp. Placed there every night, it never gets dull. Well, almost never, but a cheaply made Iron Curtain country blade — as all such are — can be used for 240 shaves. The experiment is repeatable to a fault.[52] If

---

51. Ostrander & Schroeder, *Psychic Discoveries*, p. 384.
52. Max Toth and Greg Nelson, *Pyramid Power* (New York: Freeway Press, 1974), ch. 8.

you don't think so, write to the president of Gillette. (He knows but won't say.)

The Cheops Pyramid has fascinated both historians and occultists for generations. Herodotus was duly impressed. So are all the rest of us. How could such structures have been built in the middle of a desert? Something like 2.5 million massive blocks of stone, some weighing perhaps twenty tons, each averaging 2.5 tons, were used to build the Cheops structure.[53] There are no traces of carbon on the inner walls. How did the workers and priests light the interiors? What instruments could have been used during the so-called bronze age to form perfectly measured blocks? How did they level the massive site to a deviation of only half an inch? Questions like these go on and on, to the total confusion of the theorists, who are themselves hard-pressed to manufacture hypotheses as rapidly as the Egyptians constructed the pyramids.

The pyramids had religious significance architecturally. Like the great tower described in Genesis 11, they were built to be staircases to heaven. The 267th pyramid text of the Fifth and Sixth Dynasties reads: "A staircase to heaven is laid for him [the pharaoh], so that he may mount up to heaven thereby."[54] The theological significance should be obvious: man, by means of his own powers, shall attain divinity, or near divinity. This was explicitly the teaching of Egyptian religion concerning the pharaoh, himself the descendant of the sun god.

Occultists and cultists have, for over a century, devoted great efforts to interpreting the significance of Cheops' dimensions. It seems that in both inches and centimeters, it is possible to see important historical events foretold in the "key" dimensions of the Cheops Pyramid. A whole prophetic literature has grown up around these three-dimensional studies. I choose not to go into detail here, but I can report that prophecies based on these dimensions, if properly interpreted, have achieved extraordinarily high correlation rates, but only so long as the fulfillments of the possible predictions are investigated *retroactively*. (Years ago I read a similar study, written by a pyramid skeptic, of the Washington Monument.)

The most important figure in the revival of pyramid occultism, apart from Dyrbal, is a French occultist, Antoine Bovis. Bovis, after

---

53. Charles F. Pfeiffer and Harold F. Vos, *Wycliffe Historical Geography of Bible Lands* (Chicago: Moody Press, 1967), p. 68.

54. Toth & Nelson, *Pyramid Power*, pp. 97-99.

consulting a pendulum, was led to visit the Cheops Pyramid. He was permitted a rare overnight visit. While inside the pyramid, he noticed that animals that had died — rodents, cats — had been placed in trash cans, yet after considerable periods of time these carcasses did not decay. Supposedly he had been told of this phenomenon in a vision or revelation he received while consulting with the pendulum. This feature of the pyramid was apparently confined to the pharaoh's chamber, exactly where Dyrbal was later to place his razor blade (after reading about Bovis's discovery). Bovis returned to France, and he constructed a scale model. Sure enough, organic matter is preserved for long periods of time. No refrigeration is needed.[55]

The most striking fact of these reports is the repeatability of the phenomena. Dyrbal had to wait for years for the Czech government to grant him his patent. He had to show that the razor-repairing effect is truly scientific. Dyrbal's theory is incomprehensible: the shape of the pyramid creates certain resonating effects that somehow dehumidify the water molecules in the blades' steel structure. Anyway, in 1959, patent number 91304 on the pyramid was issued. You can buy models throughout the Western world. (If I were you, I wouldn't, as this book will make clear later on.)

More obviously occult psychological effects are produced by the pyramid shape. Some firms make "pyramid tents" that are used for personal meditation. By placing one's head close to the apex (not too hard in a small tent), the meditating mystic sometimes achieves a "higher consciousness."[56] Furthermore, one company now offers a kind of prayer kit (magic kit) built around the pyramid. Prayers or requests are written on certain colored sheets of paper, with colors matching the type of request. The paper is placed inside the pyramid (made of cardboard), and a chant is made over it. After incubating for an unspecified time, the paper is removed and burned, in order to "liberate" the wish. Rewards, according to specifications, are supposed to follow.[57] People who are the products of the rationalistic American public school system are buying these devices.

Some people report tingling sensations in their fingers when they raise them close to the apex inside a pyramid tent. This is strikingly parallel to the tingling sensations in the fingers reported by table-

---

55. *Ibid.*, pp. 150-52. Cf. Peter Tompkins and Christopher Bird, *The Secret Life of Plants* (New York: Avon, 1974), pp. 310-11.

56. *Ibid.*, pp. 159-60.

57. *Ibid.*, pp. 160-62.

raisers just before the table activates (or is activated). Furthermore, dowsing rods respond to the pyramid shape.

The danger with pyramid occultism, as with so many other forms of occult phenomena, is the simultaneous curiosity and semi-scientific nature of the phenomena. After all, a lot of people do shave with blades sharpened, day after day, by these devices. Yet the devices are not normal. They seem safe, yet there is an air of mystery about them. The fruitless quest for accurate prophecies may have kept cultists off the streets for a century, but the recently revived curiosity in pyramid shapes may prove to be another irrational wedge in the door of rational culture. The Egyptian magicians and designers must have known of the occult properties of the pyramid. They certainly knew of its architectural symbolism. But the sorcerer's apprentices of today, blithely sharpening their razor blades or preserving hunks of meat, are too naive. They do not understand the relationship between symbols and demonic power.

Kirlian Photography

One of the most familiar of the doctrines among psychics, theosophists, occultists, and healers is the doctrine of the "aura." This second body, also called the astral body, supposedly surrounds each human being. At death, the astral body departs; ghosts and spirits are often believed to be manifestations of the astral bodies of the dead. It is believed that some gifted or highly trained individuals can experience out-of-body travel — astral projection — by means of the human aura. (In the movie *The Other* the grandmother of a little boy, who himself later becomes a murderer, first trains him in astral projection. Much of the space in Carlos Castaneda's books on Yaqui Indian sorcery is devoted to astral projection.)

All of this speculation concerning the astral body might have remained confined to curious metaphysical societies had it not been for a Russian technician, Semyon Davidovich Kirlian. In the late 1930's, Kirlian happened to witness a demonstration of a device used in electrotherapy. It emitted a high-frequency spark when its electrode came close to the patient's skin. Kirlian wondered whether it would be possible to photograph the person's skin by means of the light emitted by the spark. He began to experiment with a machine that he constructed. He placed a photographic plate between the electrode and his arm. Sure enough, he got a picture. He also received a serious burn. Undaunted, he continued his experiments.

Eventually he began to produce a series of astounding photographs. They revealed thousands of fiery lights, like miniature flames, shooting from the palms of his hands. Leaves and other types of organic matter also displayed the fireworks, although a cut of drying leaf projected weaker and fewer lights. Early in the 1950's, word about his photographs spread to scientific circles. One visitor brought what appeared to be two identical leaves to be photographed. After struggling throughout the night with picture after picture, Kirlian admitted that he was unable to produce identical pictures; one leaf seemed duller than the other. The visitor, the chairman of a Soviet scientific research institute, was elated. One leaf was known to be diseased, for the plant from which it had been plucked had been deliberately contaminated. Yet no known diagnostic process was then available to warn botanists of the inevitable fate of the plant in question. Kirlian's photograph had diagnosed the illness in advance of any other means available.

One of the fascinating aspects of Kirlian photography is that the experiments are repeatable. Dr. Thelma Moss, an assistant professor at UCLA and a medical psychologist attached to the Neuropsychiatric Institute of that university, has been a leading figure (though few tenured Ph.D.'s are following) in parapsychology, and has used Kirlian photography as a primary tool of her research. Her book, *The Probability of the Impossible* (1974), is perhaps the best written and most intelligent introduction to the field of paranormal science that exists. It was published by J. P. Tarcher, a Los Angeles publishing firm that specializes in New Age books. It was Tarcher that published Marilyn Ferguson's best-selling New Age handbook, *The Aquarian Conspiracy* (1980).

Dr. Moss has discovered that people under different emotional conditions will produce different Kirlian photos: different colored lights, different intensities, etc. Sickness also affects the results. One professional hypnotist (mesmerist) who employs "magnetic passes" has made such passes over leaves. Subsequent photographs of the "magnetized" leaves reveal brighter beads of light. Even more curious are the photos of the fingertips of a psychic healer and his patient. Prior to the "healing" (or whatever it is), the healer's prints are brighter than after the healing, and the patient's fingertips display the reverse effect. Furthermore, one pathologist at the cross-town University of Southern California has been photographing rats in double-blind studies (the experimenters do not know which are which during the experiments). Tumorous rats produce photographic images that are visibly different from those produced by healthy ones.[58] No one knows why.

Most remarkably, one Soviet surgeon who had studied acupuncture in China in the 1940's examined photographs of hands made with Kirlian techniques. He noticed that certain points of the hand emitted brighter lights. These bright points coincided with the traditional acupuncture points for the hand. The surgeon, M. K. Gaikin, returned to Leningrad from his visit with the Kirlians and constructed, with the help of an engineer, a pen-light device that can be used in locating the acupuncture points. The "tobiscope" is now being used by Soviet researchers. Thus, two odd phenomena, the photographs and the ancient techniques of acupuncture, have been linked scientifically.[59] Why such links are possible, or why either phenomenon should exist at all, no one is sure.

What has not been incorporated into the Kirlian system is the occult theory of the astral body. Yet it seems odd that a leaf can be sliced into two sections and, under the Kirlian high-frequency flash of electric light, a "phantom" image of the cut-off section of that leaf appears on the photograph. In any case, the existence of this photographic technique, though still disparaged and/or ignored by most American scientists, has opened up several new avenues of research, and some of them most certainly border on the paranormal. The problem now is to find whether the border line skirts simply the "not yet known" or the truly occult. The links with faith healing indicate the latter, while the link to acupuncture or leaf diagnosis seems to indicate the former.

The chief problem is not technological; it is that those doing the research (such as Dr. Moss) do not acknowledge the distinction between the occult and the "not yet known." Thus, an insatiably curious public may be subjected in the future to another wedge of the occult into a rationalistic world. The book-buying public, unlike the establishment scientists, is no longer content to wrap each new phenomenon in the swaddling clothes of Kantian phenomenal rationalism. The time-honored formula of the scientific guild — to ignore and dismiss anything that seems not to fit the inherited (and steadily weakening) rationalistic methodology — does not impress millions of those who are buying the paperback books. To that extent, they are

---

58. Moss, *Probability*, pp. 58-59.
59. Ostrander & Schroeder, *Psychic Discoveries*, pp. 226-31.

increasingly at the mercy of the unenthusiastic and untenured experimenters — untenured either by their scientific guilds or by the guild of the magicians. The sorcerer's apprentices are now loose in the land.

The Vegetarian's Nightmare: Talking Plants

The fertility religions of the ancient world, like many of the "primitive" cultures of today, were animistic. It was believed that each field, or each species of plant, or even each individual plant, possessed its own personal spirit. Very often this spirit was understood as being malevolent and had to be placated ritually to ensure agricultural productivity. It has always been the mark of a culture that is essentially the product of Christian orthodoxy, with its trinitarian personalism instead of polytheistic personalism, that animism fades away, at best surviving in the ritual practices of folklore. It may persist in rural areas that have been only marginally influenced by Christian orthodoxy, but generally animism lives a furtive, underground existence in a Christian culture. But whenever the influence of Christianity recedes, animism is likely to appear.

The Secret Life of Plants (1973), by Peter Tomkins (a pyramid cultist) and Christopher Bird, became an immense bestseller. Over a million paperbacks were issued in the fall of 1974. More than any other book available in English, this one is the cultural wedge for a revival of animism. It dresses up the animist religion in scientific garb, but there can be little doubt that the book's basic premise is animistic.

In the final chapter, "Findhorn and the Garden of Eden," the authors describe a family of outright mediums (not media, surely) and animists who have converted a dreary section of the Scottish seacoast into a "garden of Eden," in the authors' words. They have used organic gardening techniques, coupled with huge doses of mysticism and spiritualism, to transform the land. There, in the inhospitable north of Scotland, a group of mystics planted a half acre garden. It grew. It grew as no other garden anywhere nearby had ever grown. They grew 40-pound cabbages (weight, not price). They grew dozens of fruits and vegetables. When did all this lush growth begin to sprout? In 1964, the same year that all kinds of occult plants began to sprout, all over the Western world.

One of the "gardeners," who asserts that the spirits gave her the name Divina, "had managed to get into direct contact with the devas or angelic creatures who control the nature spirits that are said by clairvoyants to be everywhere at work nurturing plant life."[60] This perspective, needless to say, is pure animism. "Divina contributed detailed descriptions of the messages she said she received directly from the devas, of which she described whole hierarchies responsible for every fruit and vegetable, for every flower and weed."[61] (In *Silent Spring*, Rachel Carson informed us that our insecticides are killing off the robins, but she neglected to tell us that we may also be interfering with the Intercosmical Association of Devas and Wood Spirits Union.)

There was a theology undergirding all this growth. There almost always is: radiations, vibrations, and most important, man, the new god. "Man appeared to have the role of a demigod; by cooperating with nature he might find no limit to what could be achieved on this planet."[62]

What was not known to me at the time I wrote the earlier version of this book was that Findhorn, the little Scottish town where the big tomatoes grow, has become perhaps the most important single exporter of New Age occultism. Constance Cumbey calls it the Vatican City of the New Age movement.[63] It was founded in 1962. "Esoteric lore, from Tibetan Buddhism through UFOlogy, was actively pursued by the Findhorn initiates and would-be initiates." And to think: it all started with gardening. But, then again, as the residents of Findhorn seem to understand, so did Satan's temptation of Eve.

Scientific Experiments

The "scientific" interest in talking plants seems to have begun with Cleve Backster. Back in 1966, Mr. Backster, an internationally famous polygraph (lie detector) expert, hooked up one of his plants to a polygraph device. He noticed that the device recorded significant responses whenever he directed a mental threat toward the plant, such as burning one of its leaves. In a now-famous and frequently cited experiment—frequently cited in paranormal science books, that is—Backster placed brine shrimp on plates, which in

---

60. Tompkins & Bird, *Secret Life*, p. 381.
61. *Ibid.*, p. 382.
62. *Ibid.*, p. 379.
63. Constance Cumbey, *The Hidden Dangers of the Rainbow: The New Age Movement and Our Coming Age of Barbarism* (Shreveport, Louisiana: Huntington House, 1983), p. 51.

turn would dump them into boiling water on a random basis. The machines connected to several plants under control conditions recorded statistically significant responses to the death of brine shrimp —five to one above what random responses would have been. The more limited conclusion would seem to be that plants react to the death of brine shrimp. The more comprehensive conclusion is the one authors of bestselling paranormal science books prefer: plants can read your mind. (*The Secret Life of Plants, Supernature* and *Psychic Discoveries Behind the Iron Curtain* all spell emotional trouble for the complacent vegetarians of the world—just the kind of people who might read and believe these books.)[64]

Two other serious sets of tests have been conducted, one set by Pearl Weinberger and Mary Measures at the University of Ottawa, and the other by Mrs. Dorothy Retallack and her instructor at Colorado Women's College (formerly Temple Buell College, formerly Colorado Woman's College). The Ottawa experiments indicated that some seedlings respond to certain audio frequencies (for example, 5,000 cps, or hertz) by growing more rapidly than would otherwise be statistically normal. Tests are being conducted in a number of laboratories to confirm or refute this thesis.

The Retallack experiments are less rigorous and therefore much more interesting. She has found that some plants—corn, petunias, squash, and marigolds—grow away from loudspeakers that blare hard-rock music, and grow in the direction of speakers playing Bach. They are apparently neutral toward country-western and folk music.[65] (Bluegrass—the music, that is—was not tested. Presumably, the plants, if they have any music taste at all, will fall over their tendrils trying to get closer to Earl Scruggs.)

The idea of talking and thinking plants is recent, but the notion of sentient plants goes back to the turn of the century. India's great biological scientist, Sir Jagadis Chandra Bose, conducted decades of research into the response of plants to electrical and other stimulations. He found that chloroformed plants could sometimes be transplanted under conditions that were usually fatal to them. By developing extremely sensitive measuring instruments, he discovered that responses characteristic of animal tissues are found in plant tissues.[66]

---

64. Orthodox scientists have criticized Backster's experiments for being unrepeatable.

65. Tompkins & Bird, *Secret Life*, ch. 10.

66. *Ibid.*, p. 104.

His scholarly papers were suppressed, time after time, by the Royal Society, although the Linnean Society was willing to publish some of them. Too much carbon dioxide, he found, affected plants the way that too much liquor affects men: they swayed, passed out, and finally revived.[67] One instrument, the crescograph, measured incredibly minute growth rates among plants, and Bose claimed that by merely touching a plant it is possible to retard its growth rate in some cases.[68]

The authors quite properly identify what Bose's work involved: "an amalgamation of the wisdom of the ancient East with the precise scientific techniques and language of the modern West."[69] This is one of the most important of all occult goals: the fusion of rationalism and irrationalism, of mysticism with science. It is, in the words of C. S. Lewis' fictional demon Screwtape, the goal of discovering the materialist magician: the man who believes in occult forces and scientific power, but not in God. When he appears, "the end of the war will be in sight."[70]

In the 1920's, at the time Bose was continuing his researches, Soviet scientist Alexander Gurwitsch conducted a series of experiments with the roots of onions. He thought it possible that some form of energy linked onion plants. He built an apparatus that exposed portions of the roots of two onions to each other by means of a glass tube. After three hours of exposure, he said he was able to detect significant increases (twenty-five percent) in the growth rate of the exposed section of the "receiving" onion's root.[71] He tried yeast as a receiver. It increased its growth rate by thirty percent.[72] Several European studies claimed to have duplicated Gurwitsch's findings, but the American Academy of Sciences denied finding any change in growth rates. Gurwitsch was forgotten.

Half a century later, Soviet scientists revived Gurwitsch's discredited theory. At the Institute of Automation and Electrometry, scientists placed identical tissue cultures into hermetically sealed vessels separated by a wall of glass and then introduced a lethal virus into one chamber. The second colony was unaffected. But when quartz was substituted for glass, the second colony died. Then they used

---

67. *Ibid.*, p. 108.
68. *Ibid.*, p. 112.
69. *Ibid.*, p. 91.
70. C. S. Lewis, *The Screwtape Letters*, ch. 7, p. 33.
71. Ostrander & Schroeder, *Psychic Discoveries*, p. 69.
72. *Ibid.*, p. 412.

chemical poisons and radiation to kill off a colony. The second colony died. Perhaps ultraviolet rays are the answer, since glass will not carry them. This was Gurvitch's theory. Apparently ultraviolet rays can carry information between cells.[73]

Still, apart from Backster's experiments, plants have not yet been shown to think. They may react in ways that establishment scientists prefer not to admit, but thought is a different kettle of fish — or brine shrimp. *The Secret Life of Plants* spends a chapter on the uncanny career of Luther Burbank, but only in the final paragraphs do the authors reveal that Burbank talked to plants in order to create "a vibration of love." The sources of these revelations are peculiar, however: Manly P. Hall, a Southern California esoteric-mystic philosopher, and Paramhansa Yogananda, the founder of the Self-Realization Fellowship. Even if Burbank did talk to his plants, his successes as a plant breeder are not proof that they answered him. If something *did* answer him, was it a plant?

Hypnotizing Plants

This is not to say that there is no evidence of some very peculiar events associated with the talking-plant theory. Marcel Vogel, a research chemist, read about Backster's experiments, threw the article away, and then returned to retrieve it a few days later. He decided to begin his own research. He is a genius inventor, having specialized in liquid crystals, magnetics, and computer applications. He has developed several patented concepts. He was teaching an evening training course for IBM. When he introduced some experiments for testing the response of plants, only he among the people in the classroom could duplicate Backster's results. "Vogel wondered why he alone seemed to be successful." The next few sentences of *Secret Life* give the answer, although the authors seem not to realize this: "As a boy, he had been interested in anything which might explain the workings of the human mind. After dipping into books on magic, spiritualism, and hypnotic technique, he had given stage demonstrations as a teenage hypnotist."[74] Here is the key that unlocks many of the doors in paranormal science: a prior series of experiences in occultism by the experimenter or subject.

Vogel asked a "spiritually gifted friend," Vivian Wiley, to conduct an experiment. Each morning she was to think friendly thoughts

73. Tompkins & Bird, *Secret Life*, pp. 212-13.
74. *Ibid.*, pp. 33-34.

toward one plant and no thoughts toward the other. One was told mentally that it would live; the other was ignored. Within a month, the ignored plant was dying. Vogel duplicated this feat with plants of his own. By hooking up philodendrons to various machines, he found that he could produce responses on the machine's recording devices—"in the plant" supposedly—by directing friendly thoughts toward them.

Vogel had discovered early in his career that by "relaxing his mind," he could visualize activities in the behavior of liquid crystals under a microscope that his professional colleagues could not see. He refers to this phenomenon as his "higher sensory awareness."[75] He had trained himself in this state of higher consciousness. Later he became aware of his own unique position in his experiments with plants. Again and again, manifestations of paranormal science are found to be intimately linked to the experimenter—so strongly linked, in fact, that the odd phenomena do not occur when he is not present. As the authors state: "It became clearer to Vogel that a certain focused state of consciousness on his part seemed to become an integral and balancing part of the circuitry required to monitor his plants. A plant could be awakened from somnolence to sensitivity by his giving up his normally conscious state and focusing a seemingly extra-conscious part of his mind on the exact notion that the plant be happy and feel loved, that it be blessed with healthy growth. In this way, man and plant seemed to interact, and, as a unit, pick up sensations from events, or third parties, which became recordable through the plant. . . . Asked to describe the process in detail, Vogel said that first he quiets the sensory responses of his body organs, then he becomes aware of an energetic relationship between the plant and himself. When a state of balance between the bioelectrical potential of both the plant and himself is achieved, the plant is no longer sensitive to noise, temperature, the normal electrical fields surrounding it, or other plants. It responds only to Vogel, who has effectively tuned himself to it— or perhaps simply hypnotizes it."[76]

Problem: How is anything—even a plant—"simply hypnotized"? Just because the phenomenon of hypnosis is so widespread, scientists and laymen alike tend to dismiss it as another of those daily miracles associated with the mind of man. But to appeal to hypnosis as an explanation for paranormal phenomena is to evade the question

---

75. *Ibid.*, p. 35.
76. *Ibid.*, pp. 37-38.

of paranormal phenomena, for hypnosis is one of the most intriguing and least explainable of all paranormal phenomena. As has been remarked by students of demonic possession, hypnosis permits men to respond in ways that "primitive" observers would instantly recognize as demonically induced. Furthermore, continued experiments with hypnosis can lead to possession itself. The very principle of hypnosis — subjection to the suggestions of another person, and the implied rejection of responsibility for the subject's actions — is the principle of demonic possession. How, then, does Vogel "hypnotize" his plants? By what kind of power?

Non-Union Working Plants

Another "plant communicator" is Pierre Paul Sauvin of West Paterson, New Jersey. A confessed medium and a minister of the Psychic Science Temple of Metaphysics (the name tells all!), Sauvin also tinkers with Rube Goldberg plant communication devices. He would call them on his home telephone from a secret phone strapped to his leg (which he also used to communicate from his desk at his job with ITT to various editors, since he was moonlighting as a technical writer). He then monitored their responses. He could communicate with them mentally by putting himself into a light hypnotic trance. He would give himself a light electrical shock at work, and miles away at his home, the plants would respond — or at least the recording equipment to which they were attached would respond.

Finally, he put the plants to work. He hooked them up to his garage door opener, and when he approached the door from the outside, he had only to signal them mentally to open it up. This way, the garage was burglarproof, or at least safer. He thinks that a "plant man" could control the flight of an airplane by means of plant communications. (I have this mental impression of being strapped in my seat in a Boeing 747 at 35,000 feet when a recorded voice comes over the loudspeaker: "Welcome aboard. This is your philodendron speaking. My co-pilot this morning is a petunia.") Or plants could be used as screening devices at airports to detect emotionally disturbed people who might be hijackers.[77] (My guess is that if word gets out that plants are flying the planes, the odds are very strong that anyone doing much flying will probably be emotionally disturbed.) Nevertheless, despite all the nonsense, the fact does exist that plants

---

77. *Ibid.*, ch. 3.

can be used as intermediaries in producing certain electrical-mechanical responses.

Animism

Paranormal science does raise questions that should be answered. Unfortunately, establishment science is not equipped even to acknowledge that the data or the questions really exist. If the issues raised by Sir Jagadis C. Bose could not be handled by orthodox science, then the issues raised by Backster, Vogel, and Sauvin are far too difficult.

The key fact of *The Secret Life of Plants* is that the vast bulk of the reported cases of odd plant phenomena have been recorded by occultists, mystics, and others whose "sympathetic attitude" toward both the plants and the experiments made it possible for the peculiar reactions to take place. With the possible exceptions of Backster's lie detectors and the experiments with sound, virtually all of the reported experiments are admitted to be repeatable only by those who are "sympathetic." This is a distinct case of borderline science in action. The premise of modern experimental science — repeatability — is violated.

But there is more of the occult than meets the eye of some of the anti-establishment experimenters. The possibility of *animism* — demonic interference in the experiments — is never acknowledged, either by the orthodox scientists (who conveniently dismiss all signs of the abnormal) or by the parascientists (who do not want hostile, supernatural forces to interfere in *their* sympathetic creativity). There is a whole new zone of research for Christian scientists to clarify — disentangling long ignored patterns of God's creation from the activity of demons. The non-Christian investigators are powerless to sort out facts from theory when demons tinker with the meters.

Psychic Photography

The occult phenomenon of psychic photography is seldom (if ever) discussed in popular photographic magazines, yet the phenomenon has existed for over a century. First encountered by Boston engraver William Mumler in the middle of the nineteenth century, it was pursued rigorously by the British parapsychologist F. W. Warrick in his book, *Experiments in Psychics* (1939). A photograph, sometimes taken by nonpsychic Mumler, but more often taken by or with the cooperation of an occultist, produces strange additions on the negatives. These may merely be streaks of light for which there is no mechanical explanation. There may be what appear to be double-exposed images superimposed on the negative. Perhaps most peculiar of all are "ghost" images, which usually are small reproductions of existing photographs of deceased subjects. Sometimes these images are of famous persons, while other times they are photo reproductions of snapshots of dead relatives of the subject being photographed. These images can appear on films produced by a Polaroid Land camera under test conditions. These weird images can also be found on supposedly unexposed sheets of film that have never been put into a camera. The psychic photographer can actually transfer mental images to sealed, fresh film packs. One of the most proficient of these medium-mentalists is John Myers.

John Myers is a wealthy industrialist who picked up his talent for psychic photography after a visit with Emma Deane, the medium whose work had been basic to Warrick's *Experiments in Psychics*. He has performed his feats of occult skill under numerous conditions, including an appearance on the old *PM East* television show in 1961. Several of his photographs are reprinted in Hans Holzer's book, *Psychic Photography* (1970). Packs of photographic paper are purchased by the experimenter from any store. Myers concentrates his attention on the film for a few minutes, announces that the test is finished, and the film is then developed. Symbols may appear, such as a cross or a tombstone; human faces sometimes appear. Myers is unable to predict in advance just what will appear, but he is aware when the psychic process is finished.

Another successful psychic photographer is Dr. Andrew Von Salza, a West Coast physician. In March 1966, he visited the Holzers in New York City, where he took a photograph of Mrs. Holzer, using a Polaroid camera, model 103. Mrs. Holzer's image appeared quite normally, but next to her in the frame was a vague ghostly impression of a painting of Russia's Catherine the Great, suspended in midair. When Holzer had a reproduction of this picture made, it turned out poorly. Nevertheless, he sent a copy to Von Salza. The latter immediately "felt led" to re-photograph the copy. This time he obtained a print with "Catherine" quite clear. He sent back two reproductions of this new picture to Holzer.

To check on this strange procedure, Holzer visited Von Salza in May 1966. The physician repeated the process. He aimed his Polaroid camera at the copy Holzer had sent him, and out of his camera popped another picture of Mrs. Holzer and "Catherine," only this time "Catherine" had extended her arm, as if she were offering a crown to Mrs. Holzer. Unknown to Dr. Von Salza at the time, Mrs. Holzer is a sixth-generation descendant of Catherine the Great. (The "Catherine" in the photographs appears as a painting.)

Holzer had met Von Salza a year earlier. He visited the physician's home, along with several other guests, to witness a demonstration. Von Salza set up a Polaroid camera in his living room and photographed the assembled group several times. Each time, the resulting photographs included strange and highly extraneous images. The images appeared above the group. Faces, apparently photographs, of unknown people, plus one each of President Kennedy and John D. Rockefeller, Sr., were suspended above the heads of the guests. Kennedy's image also appeared in another 1966 photograph taken by Von Salza, only this time it was accompanied by an image of Abraham Lincoln. (This one looks suspiciously like a put-up job by the Democratic National Committee, but I am ever the skeptic — of politics, not of ghosts.) Another Von Salza snapshot looks like one of those montage efforts popular in the late 1960's, with dozens of faces, including Marilyn Monroe's and Lee Harvey Oswald's, plastered all over the frame.

Anyone who is looking for an explanation of all this in the realm of physical science is doomed to be disappointed. On the other hand, anyone who is looking for an explanation of the famous Turin shroud, which has a picture of a face (Jesus?) on it, would be well advised to pursue this avenue as a likely explanation. Psychic (demonic) photography would explain why it is that as photographers photograph pictures of the shroud, and then pictures of the pictures, rather than the shroud itself, the face's image gets clearer. This is contrary to known physics. A later copy is never as faithful as an earlier copy, *if we are discussing the realm of physics*. The realm of demonic photography is not tightly governed by the laws of physics.

Mrs. Florence Sternfels, another medium and clairvoyant, had the ability of going into a trance and imprinting her image — blurred — on an X-ray plate placed inside a shielded box that had been placed beneath her foot. It took about one hour of trance to accomplish this feat. (Frankly, back in 1952 when this event occurred, it would have been much simpler, faster, and clearer to have used a Brownie Hawkeye!) Another series of photographs snapped with black flashbulbs and infrared film show her in a trance. An "ectoplasm" outline of a small dog can be seen emerging from her lower abdomen.

The most famous mental photographer of all, however, is a semi-alcoholic former elevator operator, Ted Serios. Serios' case was made famous by Dr. Jule Eisenbud, a psychologist and parapsychologist.[78]

---

78. Jule Eisenbud, M.D., *The World of Ted Serios* (New York: Pocket Books, 1968).

For years, Eisenbud had despaired of finding psychic phenomena that would be subject to that criterion of criteria in modern science, repeatable experiments. It is the nonrepetitive nature of most paranormal phenomena that plagues those researchers who are trying to bridge the gap between paranormal science and normal science. Either the subjects or the experimenters "somehow" influence the outcome of the experiments — a fact which, in and of itself, ought to cause more intelligent responses from orthodox scientists than the usual cry of "fraud!" Eisenbud himself was highly skeptical when informed of Serios' abilities, even though there had been published material concerning them.

What the scientific community says it wants are some experimental tests like those conducted by J. B. Rhine, formerly of Duke University, or those devised by European parapsychologists. But Eisenbud was well aware of the fact that orthodox scientists, even when allowed to devise such tests and monitor them, invariably assert that some loose end must have been overlooked, and that the experiment was without value. They assert this, it should be mentioned, only when there is positive evidence that paranormal phenomena have been recorded. One of the only truly repeatable paranormal subjects, Pavel Stepanic, the Czech psychic who loves ESP card experiments, has been studied by numerous orthodox scientists, and the startling results have even filtered into the orthodox journals, but it has not been enough to crack the wall of epistemological skepticism. Stepanic once made a sensational run of 2,000 guesses involving cards that were black on one side and white on the other. The cards having been placed in opaque envelopes on a random basis, Stepanic was able to guess which side was up in 1,114 cases. Odds against: one billion to one. He has performed again and again before scientists who devised the tests. No fraud has been unearthed.[79] The guild's reaction is silence.

Eisenbud hoped Ted Serios would be his Pavel Stepanic, only a far more spectacular Stepanic. On several occasions, Serios demonstrated his most peculiar ability. He would work himself up for several hours, usually with a good quantity of liquor, and then pick up a Polaroid camera. Covering the lens with his "gismo" — a tube covered with black tape, which was carefully examined by observers on countless occasions — Serios would trip the shutter. Out would come

---

79. Ostrander & Schroeder, *Psychic Discoveries*, ch. 15.

a picture, usually of some building. But if there was ever a nonrepeatable, Serios was the man. When invited to perform before scientists, sometimes he would go on a binge, or leave town. Other times, especially under the scrutiny of a large group of scientists, he could produce only "whities" — perfectly white frames — which did not impress his witnesses, although obtaining such pictures from a Polaroid with its lens covered is quite impossible. Still, he did perform well on some occasions, as over one hundred photographs in Eisenbud's book demonstrate.

Serios' background is revealing. He had developed his ability under the prodding of an amateur hypnotist during his stint as an elevator operator in Chicago. The hypnotist, also an employee of the hotel, was convinced that hypnotism might give Serios the ability to project his "astral body" in a search for treasure. Serios now claims that a "spirit guide" named "Jean Laffite" met him and took him on several journeys. But "Laffite" made fewer and fewer contacts, became increasingly transparent, and finally told Serios to strike out on his own. Serios told Eisenbud that he did locate a few hiding places of valuables, but too late: someone else was digging them up. Serios' partner then wondered if Serios could "photograph his visions." He bought Serios a roll-film camera to try out. Serios was skeptical, but he did project a few thoughts at it, and when the film was returned, there were images on a few of the frames. Serios then bought himself a Polaroid and began practicing. His images were a bit blurred, but recognizable in many instances.[80]

(Significantly, Pavel Stepanic was also introduced to his ESP abilities — or the abilities were introduced to him — by means of hypnotism. Stepanic is the product of a highly successful trainer of psychics, Dr. Milan Ryzl, who defected to the West in the late 1960's. Hypnotism was Ryzl's primary tool in developing psychics. There is more to hypnotism than meets the eye of modern observers.)

Eisenbud's book has been one of the most popular in the library of parapsychology, and Serios' case is quoted again and again in the literature. Strange as Serios' abilities may be, even stranger are Eisenbud's explanations of them. When he begins to deal with paranormal phenomena, Eisenbud retreats into the language and concepts of Freudian psychology, and the radical humanism of Freud's position colors the entire analysis. The small segment of the academic

---

80. Eisenbud, *Serios*, p. 313.

community that concerns itself with paranormal phenomena from a "rigorously scientific" point of view subjects its methodology to theories even more incredible than the paranormal events it claims to deal with.

What was the source of the mental pictures? Ted's subconscious mind, of course.[81] And why not? What is the subconscious mind, if not the bottomless pit of the unsolved riddles of the mind itself? Being bottomless, it can certainly hold a few psychic pictures produced by Ted Serios. We do not know the mechanism of such tricks, or where to look to uncover it, or how to shield it in some totally rigorous experiment. No known shield can impede the phenomena; whether Ted is inside the Faraday cage or the camera, the pictures still are transmitted. What Freudian psychology tells us, however, is that the source of these phenomena *must* be in Ted's mind. They cannot possibly be demonic, since there is no such thing as the demonic. Demonic beings are the product of sick minds. When a ghost persists, then the psychiatrist's "psychotherapy was not completely successful, and that, as is so often the case, residual conflict material remains to be teased out to the light and worked through: . . ."[82]

Eisenbud's humanism is common to parapsychology. It is the link to orthodox science. In discussing automatic writing, where relaxed persons holding a pencil produce writings that often are in a foreign language unknown (consciously, of course) to the writer, or sometimes reveal information unknown to the writer, Dr. Thelma Moss, good humanist that she is, explains: "Generally such persons are deluded into the belief that the writing is coming from some outside source, whether divine or demonic, when in all likelihood it is coming from a barely subliminal region of the mind."[83] Parapsychology, by definition, must focus on man alone, asserts Eisenbud. "What is unique about the data of psychical research is that only they suggest that man has in fact within him vast untapped powers that hitherto have been accorded him only in the magic world of the primitive, in the secret fantasies of childhood, and in fairy tales and legend."[84] Parapsychology is *the* legitimate science of man because it ascribes so much *power* to man.

Why, then, should establishment science, itself so thoroughly hu-

---

81. *Ibid.*, p. 266.
82. *Ibid.*, p. 334.
83. Moss, *Probability*, p. 129.
84. Eisenbud, *Serios*, p. 313.

manistic, resist the findings of parapsychology? In good Freudian fashion, Eisenbud blames that old standby, the mother-child relationship. Modern scientism, being mechanistic, is a product of men's guilt. Men always hated their mothers. The all-powerful mother, not the father, was the threat to man's autonomy. To suppress guilt feelings, men construct for themselves a universe that eliminates responsibility because it substitutes impersonal, mechanistic forces for human choice. Thus, parapsychology is a threat to scientific orthodoxy.[85] It threatens to dredge up the *personal* side of science, such as the subconscious mind's ability to project images. Man's "dark and sinister side," as Eisenbud calls it, is being brought into view by parapsychology. Man's *mind* has power independent of machines — or at least the subconscious mind does. Orthodox mechanistic science is repelled by such a notion. "It is hardly to be wondered that it automatically sees anything faintly suggestive of the power of thought as superstitious nonsense to be rejected firmly and out of hand."[86]

It seems likely that other reasons are also involved in orthodoxy's rejection of parapsychology, or at least of the data of parapsychology. Scientists see only too clearly that phenomena like these are not explainable in terms of any known view of man, and there is the scent of the supernatural in the air. Furthermore, while there is a mechanistic tradition in all modern science, a point made clear half a century ago in E. A. Burtt's *Metaphysical Foundations of Modern Physical Science,* there has always been a "personalist-indeterminist" strain in scientific orthodoxy. Eisenbud and the other paranormal scientists are trying to enlarge the field of science to include more of the "not yet known," but their colleagues are convinced that *this* kind of "not yet known" is just too close to the demonism that was only too well known three centuries ago.

Eisenbud's summary of the knee-jerk reaction of establishment science to the troubling data of parapsychology is illuminating: "Science, like a well-behaved compulsive neurotic, is committed to following out blindly a conspiracy of denial and rejection that is bred into its very marrow. As a result anthropologists automatically take it for granted that the stories and legends of the occult they have been collecting these many years from their primitive informants have no basis whatever in fact. Psychiatrists and psychologists, for

---

85. *Ibid.*, p. 319.
86. *Ibid.*, p. 322.

their part, just as automatically assume that accounts they may hear of alleged telepathic incidents or dreams from their informants must be due to malobservation or purely chance coincidence, and unhesitatingly write off anyone manifesting an interest in the subject as suffering from a regressive need for the miraculous."[87]

But what of Ted Serios? Why should he be able to accomplish these feats of psychic photography, while the rest of us have to rely on light meters, viewfinders, and other physical baggage? Eisenbud has an answer straight out of Kant's *Critique of Pure Reason*—so Kantian that he outdoes Kant himself. Extrasensory perception, telepathy, mental photographs, and other such phenomena stem from an excess reservoir of mental power. The bulk of this *mental reservoir of power* is in use on a full-time basis. Where is it used? *It is holding up the universe!*

Actually the primitive himself had a clue to the mystery in his sense of oneness with nature but, what with his not being an analytically minded fellow, it may not have occurred to him to do the "power auditing" that might have led to the insight I am leading up to. This is, of course, that the latent mental power which all of us possess goes into sustaining—and is thus manifest in—all the natural processes that we see around us, from the growth of the lowliest seed to the movements of the heavenly bodies. It might thus be put down under the heading of "general maintenance." . . . If the curious reader would like to know, however, what would happen if the rest of us were to withdraw our power from the universe at large, all I can suggest is a simple so-called thought experiment which he can either do for himself or take my word for, as I have done it many times and can tell him exactly what will happen: the universe collapses and in fact vanishes, like the image on a television screen when the current is shut off, putting an end at once to the controversies of the cosmologists, who simply disappear in the general confusion.[88]

Unquestionably, this is as powerful a statement of radical humanism as one is likely to encounter. Both the world of regularity and the world of Ted Serios are the same world, for they are supported by the human mind, although different parts of the mind. "According to this point of view then, the question of what keeps the universe running—the question of who or what is in the back of the Big Store—admits of an answer that is not only sublimely simple but in principle unassailable: just look for the throne behind the

---

87. *Ibid.*, p. 323.
88. *Ibid.*, pp. 326, 327.

power."[89] It is man who sits on that throne. All of post-Kantian science affirms this theory of the universe, but Eisenbud has stated it more forthrightly than most others are willing to do. Man is the creator and sustainer of his universe. And from time to time, certain gifted men dip into the humanistic reservoir of power to perform what many men call magic.

Primitive man's theory makes a lot more sense: demons, not parapsychological power-dipping, are the source of the phenomena.[90]

Precognition

Jeanne Dixon aside, what can be said about scientific studies concerning men's ability to forecast future events? This has been the goal of man for thousands of years. The fact that the Bulgarian government has put their Jeanne Dixon, Vanga Dimitrova, on the state payroll (collecting a fee from her dozens of daily callers) is indicative of the shift of opinion behind the Iron Curtain. Also indicative is the fact that the Czechoslovakian government finances the astrological research of Dr. Eugen Jonas, who claims to be able to forecast by means of a mother's astrological sign when she can conceive, what sex the child will be (ninety-eight percent accuracy claimed), whether the woman is even pregnant, and what sex the now-conceived child is (eighty-seven percent accuracy claimed).[91] But the interest shown by American scientists is far more limited. Nevertheless, some interesting tests have been devised, and some even more interesting results obtained. Some subjects not only guess the present order of cards in a pack, but actually predict the order that will occur *after the deck is shuffled*. Consider Wayne Sage's description of one classic and utterly unexplainable (by Newtonian science) experiment:

89. *Ibid.*, p. 329.

90. James ("The Amazing") Randi, a professional magician and full-time debunker of paranormal "frauds," that is, anyone who can perform seemingly impossible feats without sleight of hand, has asserted that he can duplicate all of Serios' "tricks." This is the standard rebuttal of all professional magicians. However, when challenged to match Serios' skills under controlled conditions, Randi has consistently begged off: Curtis Fuller, "Dr. Jule Eisenbud vs. the Amazing Randi," Fate (Aug. 1974), pp. 65-74. Randi is the author of a book supposedly debunking all of Uri Geller's key-bending, mind-reading stunts: *The Magic of Uri Geller* (New York: Ballantine, 1975). The book was ecstatically praised by establishment scientists.

91. Ostrander & Schroeder, *Astrological Birth Control* (Englewood Cliffs, New Jersey: Prentice-Hall, 1972).

Perhaps the most ardent of all current psychic research is that which is out to find a new guinea pig for its studies — that is, one other than man. The pioneering work in this area was carried out by French psychologists Pierre Duval and Evelyn Montredon. One mouse at a time was placed in a cage with a wired floor. Electric current was then directed randomly to different sections of the cage in order to deliver a shock whenever the mouse happened to be in the wrong place at the wrong time. When random jumps of some mice were analyzed they were found to have consistently avoided the spot where the next shock was aimed, despite the fact that there was no consistent pattern to the shocks. . . . But the ultimate along these lines must be the test devised by psychologist Helmut Schmidt for his pet cat. This otherwise quite ordinary curl-up-at-the-hearth-type feline was locked in a cold building with a heat lamp wired to come on intermittently through the night. The number of times the light would switch on was completely randomized by the electrical apparatus, as was the length of time the light would stay on each time it lit. Naturally, the cat wanted the lamp on to provide warmth, and fantastically enough, did seem able to affect its workings. The light repeatedly came on more often and stayed on for longer periods of time when the cat was in the room than when the cat was not present.[92]

Lyall Watson reports on a study by an American mathematician, William Cox, that sought to discover whether people somehow avoid trains that have accidents. He selected a station and took information concerning the number of passengers who rode the train during each of the seven days preceding an accident, as well as the fourteenth, twenty-first, and twenty-eighth days before. The data covered a seven-year period. On days that were marred by an accident, there were always fewer passengers than statistically normal. The difference between the predicted number of passengers, using statistical methods, and the actual number was so great that the odds against it were one hundred to one.[93]

Over and over, the question of the reality of such events hinges on the comparison of chance or random events and those that are supposedly abnormal and therefore evidence of ESP, precognition, or whatever. This is the required methodology of modern science, since modern science rests on the hypothesis of the existence of a world formed by chance and developed by the processes of Darwinian evolution, that is, chance-induced change. Yet in the midst of

---

92. Wayne Sage, "ESP and the Psychology Establishment," *Human Behavior* (Sept./Oct. 1972), p. 58.
93. Watson, *Supernature*, p. 72.

random change there is stability: the laws of probability. Random changes operate, says modern science, by the fixed laws of probability. These are the test of coherence in any series of events. It is a rigged test, however.

Paranormal science experimenters have found that statistical probability is a one-way street within conventional scientific circles. It is allowed to screen out paranormal phenomena, converting them into random events within a normal distribution. When these paranormal patterns persist, establishment scientists either blame the experiment's control procedures or, in a last-ditch effort to sweep their universe clear of noumenal influences, appeal to luck — good old lady luck. (You can lead an establishment scientist to a significant deviation, but you can't make him swallow the paranormal camel.) As one commentator summarizes the situation: "All scientific insight rests on some reasonably invariant relationship. The structure of an experiment must be such that when A is done in the lab, B occurs. Psychic research seemed to hypothesize that, when all known factors are controlled, any score deviating from chance would be by definition due to ESP — which continued to mean telepathy to parapsychologists, luck to critics."[94]

Every time a parapsychologist discovers a significant deviation from normal events, he is tempted to think that he has shown that the prevailing scientific world view is flawed, and that evidence of its flawed nature now exists. "Meaningless lucky event," reply the establishment critics. In short, "Results based solely on odds against chance could simply not be accepted as definitive proof; they had to be confirmed in turn by a repeatable laboratory experiment under controlled conditions which would show that a signal had traveled from one point outside the mind of a human being to some point within. No such experiment had ever been accomplished."[95] The scientific guild still prefers to have something concrete to measure, even when, in Heisenberg's indeterminate world, the very act of measurement distorts the experiment's results. The protection of phenomenal science is the highest priority of the establishment scientist; this is the very essence of establishment science.

This is why no such measured experiment *could* be devised and still remain paranormal; as soon as some "signal" is discovered, if such a signal exists, then it immediately becomes absorbed into the

---

94. Sage, "ESP," p. 57.
95. *Ibid.*, pp. 57-58.

realm of the scientifically normal. This would please most parapsychologists — the ones most concerned about scientific respectability — but not all of them. The critics' complaints about the lack of scientific rigor in paranormal experiments are acts of religious devotion. We see a priesthood defending the crucial dogmas of the received faith. But this requirement of absolute precision in relativism's random world is an act of hypocrisy. The mind-matter link is so insecure in modern philosophy and modern psychology that any such rigorous experimental demand placed upon the methodology of parapsychology is wholly hypocritical, since the hypothesized links in psychology are equally unproven and probably unprovable. The mysterious relationship between "stimulus" and "response" is still as baffling and divisive an issue among scientists as it was a century ago. The age-old question, "What do we know, and how can we know it?" still remains unanswered by the non-Christian scientific establishment.

The Religion of Statistics

What we have in the division between paranormal and normal science is not a failure to communicate. What we have is not a semantic problem. What we have is a religious debate that is based upon fundamentally opposed presuppositions concerning the nature of reality and man's place in it.

When orthodox scientists keep appealing to statistics, they always mean those statistics which confirm their hypotheses. After all, if their view of reality is correct, then statistical results *must* conform to it, since the laws of statistics are by definition controlled by the reality principle, that is, the logic of the phenomenal world. Thus, concludes Wayne Sage: "As intriguing as such findings may be, however, the fact remains that after 40 years of such work, nothing has been 'proven.' Statistics for deviations from a theoretical probability can always be rejected out of hand, and generally are by the scientific community at large. In the words of Rhine himself: 'To say that it [parapsychology] is properly a branch of psychology . . . is to idealize psychology. There is no field of science that now recognizes, even as a possibility, the kind of reality to which the evidence of parapsychology offers support."[96] And if the secular parapsychologist suspects that anyone is using his research's findings to support any truly occult or demonic source of the "causes" of the paranormal

---

96. *Ibid.*, p. 58.

responses, he too will line up behind the banner of Kantian science to keep such nonsense out of *his* universe.

That Sage should quote J. B. Rhine is not surprising. It was J. B. Rhine more than anyone else who created the academic subdiscipline of parapsychology. In the early 1930's, this young psychologist shocked the academic world with his findings, and that world has not yet forgiven him. From the mid-1930's to the mid-1960's, Rhine conducted his research at Duke University. He now heads his own Foundation for Research into the Nature of Man.

For decades the academic guild has cried fraud whenever a new finding emerged from Rhine's lab, but Rhine patiently went about tightening the controls and producing more paranormal results. It was never enough. "Other psychologists began to demand tighter controls, often tighter than they themselves were using in their own labs."[97] The response of the guild to Rhine's stimuli has been predictable. After four decades of findings, about ten percent believe in parapsychology, ten percent reject it outright, and eighty percent still prefer to suspend judgment and avoid conflict. These guild statistics have not changed significantly since the 1930's.[98]

It is not a question of tests and controls and footnotes; it is a conflict over presuppositions, a debate as to how one legitimately *interprets* the results. There is only one way for the parapsychologists to triumph: win the younger men and wait for the older establishment men to die off. Concludes Sage: "In the final analysis, perhaps we were wrong to think that ESP ever would, or could be proved to exist. . . . Which is to say that perhaps with ESP, as with religion and the occult, either you believe it or you don't — which is to say that whether or not ESP is now or ever has been or ever will be proved depends on what one is prepared to accept as proof. What parapsychology has given us during its relatively short life is only data to worry over in the manner of Caesar worrying over the ides of March. It is within the nature of such predictions that when they prove accurate, we know no more about how our soothsayers knew — or whether they knew — than we did before they spoke. That which is supernatural requires belief, not proof, simply because it is supernatural. And if we have run short on beliefs these days, it seems we might just as profitably search out new ones with our more traditional divining rods and Ouija boards as with statistical analy-

---

97. *Ibid.*, p. 57.
98. *Ibid.*, p. 59.

ses. At least divining rods and Ouija boards are known to work—a certain small percentage of the time."[99]

Sage is trying to stay within the standards of contemporary science's post-Heisenberg relativism. That relativism is constantly being subjected to new pressures from the findings of paranormal science. Rhine's successor at Duke, Helmut Schmidt (whose cat seems to be able to control the random flashing of light bulbs), has devised several experiments that are so radically random in their foundations that any deviation has to indicate the presence of psychic phenomena. Professor Schmidt is a physicist, not a psychologist, and he has turned to atomic physics to demonstrate "psi" phenomena. Subjects were asked to predict which of four lamps would flash next, and out of over 63,000 trials, their results were so positive that the odds against chance occurrence were two billion to one.[100]

In another experiment, Schmidt built a random number generator that was hooked to a display panel. The generator produced random sequences of two numbers that were determined "by a simple quantum process (the decay of radioactive strontium-90 nuclei)." A circle of lights would flash either clockwise or counterclockwise. Subjects had to predict which way the lights would flash. In 256 runs of 128 jumps in the lights, fifteen subjects scored hits on a thousand-to-one level of probability.[101] These experiments, according to Arthur Koestler, have made far more impact on orthodox scientists than Rhine's card-guessing studies ever did. His apparatus has removed their ability to charge fraud. His reports have been published in conservative establishment scientific journals. With the acceptance of the American Society of Parapsychology into membership by the American Academy for the Advancement of Science, the mid-1970's witnessed a major breakthrough.

Nevertheless, parapsychology, and especially the branch experimenting with psychokinesis (mind over matter), is still on the fringes of orthodox science. Telepathy is one thing; mind over matter is another. Extrasensory *perception* may find a way into orthodoxy by sliding through the tiny cracks of Werner Heisenberg's uncertainty principle. But this principle works only in subatomic physics. The law of large numbers is supposed to cancel out the randomness of nature. The deviations have to cancel out, orthodoxy asserts.

---

99. *Idem.*
100. Arthur Koestler, *The Roots of Coincidence* (New York: Vintage, 1973), p. 44.
101. *Ibid.*, p. 45.

Koestler writes: "I am unaware of any serious attempt at a physical-istic explanation of how a mental effort could influence the motions of rolling dice. . . . You cannot influence the progress of a macro-scopic body like a rolling die, by microphysical particles or wavicles of imaginary mass. Thus the law of large numbers, which lends such authority to the evidence for ESP, is at the same time the main obsta-cle to any physicalistic explanation of PK."[102]

Orthodox science is at an apparent dead end. The subatomic holes of randomness through which ESP has crept into the thinking of a mi-nority of orthodox scientists is simply not large enough to allow PK.[103] If PK is to be demonstrated, then the law of large numbers must be overthrown, yet it is this law that supports the "ESP-ness" of billion-to-one deviations from randomness in long series of experiments. The parapsychologist needs this law to "prove" ESP, yet needs to violate it to "prove" PK. He is caught in a methodological contradiction.

Nevertheless parapsychologists go right on investigating, steadily beating down the foundations of modern rationalism. Science, the most majestic edifice ever built by the philosophy of hypothetically au-tonomous man and his lawful mind, is being chipped away by men like Schmidt and Rhine—all in the name of a "broader" science, a "new, improved science." Orthodox scientists, unlike parapsycholo-gists, know what is involved. They instinctively grasp the enormous threat posed by paranormal "science." Something more than mere Heisenberg indeterminism is invading the halls of rationalism. Some-thing sinister and threatening to the very presuppositions of Western rationalism lies behind those dice-throwing experiments. In horror, the majority of orthodox scientists turn their backs on the data, pre-ferring to ignore unpleasant facts or denounce them after a cursory examination of the data. But such efforts seldom last more than a generation, once faith in a paradigm has faded. Parapsychologists are laying siege to Western science in the name of open-mindedness.

What is happening is quite simple: demons are beginning to affect the experiments.

Conclusion

If a serious Christian is to make sense of all this, where should he begin? If he wants to become a scientist, or even an amateur investi-gator, where should he begin? After all, it is the oddities of nature

---

102. *Ibid.*, pp. 80-81.
103. Psychokineses, or "mind over matter."

that first attract those geniuses who launch scientific revolutions. Just because a book is published by Tarcher does not automatically mean that it was written by an occultist. The best example is Rupert Sheldrake's *New Science of Life*, published by Tarcher, a Christian's devastating critique of certain long-suppressed biological experiments that point to the fraud of Darwinian explanations of the development of new species.[104]

Anomalies need not be occult. They need not be scientific, either. The Christian investigator should ask several questions before making a preliminary judgment for or against the validity of some observed phenomenon:

1. Were there witnesses?
2. Are their accounts coherent on the surface?
3. Have there been further investigations?
4. Have the new investigators offered plausible alternative explanations?
5. If it is an experiment, can it be duplicated by people who do not share the innovator's theology and/or theory?
6. Is the explanation of the phenomenon exclusively connected to New Age or evolutionary theory?
7. Have the defenders remained exclusively technical in their research for over a decade, or did they subsequently adopt New Age principles?

The criterion of repeatability is very high on the list. If only "true believers" can duplicate the results, then the possibility of occult power lying behind the phenomena is increased. If the phenomena can only be duplicated under special conditions that have nothing to do with cleanliness, or an electronically shielded environment (i.e., inside a Faraday cage), or other technical restriction, then they are suspect. The division of labor principle is basic to science. Open experiments openly reported (once patents have been applied for) is the principle of science. It is basic to the history of scientific progress in the West. The difference between alchemy and chemistry can be found here: the secret experiment performed by the spiritual initiate of a secret society vs. the repeatable, open experiment performed by a guild member whose skills were developed in an institution or set-

---

104. Rupert Sheldrake, *A New Science of Life: The Hypothesis of Formative Causation* (Los Angeles: J. P. Tarcher, 1981).

ting to which all people may apply, and which operates under open competitive rules. Scientific guilds may resemble secret societies, but they are subject to scientific criticism, and they go through public revolutions from time to time. What they do is not "hid under a basket."

In the case of people who possess unique powers, can these powers be explained as highly developed skills?

1. Do other people possess similar abilities?
2. Is there some common religious or philosophical thread linking those who possess it?
3. Did these abilities appear overnight?
4. Were the circumstances of this overnight appearance linked to New Age or occult training?
5. Can these abilities be transferred to others without respect to initiation or profession of faith?
6. Can the program of training be successfully adopted by people of many religious backgrounds or professions of faith?
7. Do these abilities involve the possession of special knowledge or power that are manifested only intermittently? Under what conditions?
8. Is there any legitimate biblical-spiritual reason for these powers to be limited to a handful of possessors?

As in the case of science, the normal operating biblical principle of institutional life is the division of labor (I Cor. 12). Unique gifts are occasionally given to people, but only in a corporate setting, under the discipline of the church, and for the edification and benefit of the church as a corporate body. Why should some gift to an individual be given by God? If this unique gift — prophecy, healing, special knowledge, unique power — is not straightforwardly brought to the service of the institutional church in its legally corporate status, then it is highly suspect. It does not meet the criterion of the division of labor. If the manifestation of the gift is outside the normal corporate guidelines that are established for the church in the Bible, then the gift is guilty until proven innocent. If it is given only in the dark, or only in a special physical environment (location), or only to people who are part of an inner circle other than the eldership, then it is guilty until proven innocent.

4

THE WORLD OF A SORCERER

I've told you already, only a crackpot would undertake the task of becoming a man of knowledge of his own accord. A sober-headed man has to be tricked into doing it.

don Juan Matus

In the summer of 1960, a 35-year-old graduate student in anthropology at UCLA, Carlos Castaneda, was investigating the use and effects of psychedelic plants. He intended to write a master's thesis on the subject. The general public knew very little about such substances in 1960, apart from marijuana and hard drugs. Information on mescaline and other plant derivatives was usually confined to little-read monographs such as J. S. Slotkin's *The Peyote Religion* (1956). From time to time the news media picked up a story, but not often.

Probably the most publicized early incident in Southern California took place in the fall of 1958, when a University of Redlands freshman, Richard Lanham, walked into his dorm room to find his roommate sitting on the edge of the top bunk. The student fell forward to the floor. Lanham called for assistance; the young man was found to be dead. He had been experimenting with psychedelic substances. The university, a Baptist institution, was embarrassed, and promptly put a blackout on all further information on the strange death, including a prohibition on Lanham's speaking with the press.

Incidents such as this were temporarily sensational, but they were not sufficient to catch the public's notoriously short attention span. This was the period when Timothy Leary, an untenured psychology professor at Harvard, was conducting experiments quietly on the effects of psychedelic drugs, but news of this work had not yet hit East Coast sophisticates, let alone denizens of the primitive West Coast. A few people may have read Aldous Huxley's *Doors of Perception* (1954), the account of his own limited mescaline experiments, but it all seemed too esoteric — the pastime of the idle educated. The LSD counter-culture was half a decade away.

Castaneda knew something about the use of peyote in the religious practices of the Indian tribes of the American Southwest. In a town close to the Mexican border, he managed to obtain an introduction to an elderly Yaqui Indian, Juan Matus (the Yaqui equivalent of "John Smith"[1]) who is called don Juan by Castaneda. For some reason — a very specific reason, the old man confessed years later — he took an interest in Castaneda. He allowed him to visit him at his house in the desert. As it turned out, don Juan was a *brujo* — a sorcerer. The old man had been drawn to Castaneda because he said it had been revealed to him that the younger man would make an excellent initiate into the secret wisdom. The revelation was quite correct; Castaneda has written seven provocative books telling of his dozen years of off-and-on initiation:

The Teachings of Don Juan: A Yaqui Way of Knowledge (1968)
A Separate Reality: Further Conversations with Don Juan (1971)
Journey to Ixtlan: The Lessons of Don Juan (1972)
Tales of Power (1974)
The Second Ring of Power (1977)
The Eagle's Gift (1981)
The Fire from Within (1984)

Unless Castaneda is exposed as a total fraud, these books are likely to become classics — not classics in Yaqui magic, but classics in their capacity as primary-source documents of the American counter-culture of the mid-1970's. Are they fraudulent? Some reviewers have said so, though not a majority of them. The first book got through the editorial screening process of the academically proper University of California Press, while the third was accepted as a doctoral dissertation at UCLA.[2] Furthermore, by the time *Ixtlan* was accepted as a dissertation, Castaneda had become a best-selling author and a cult figure of the youthful drug subculture. His committee was not interested in taking unnecessary chances, yet they gave him his Ph.D. Professional anthropologists believed that it rang true. As primary-source documents of the mind and world of the

---

1. *Time Magazine*, 1973, reprinted in Daniel C. Noel (ed.), *Seeing Castaneda: Reactions to the "Don Juan" Writings of Carlos Castaneda* (New York: Putnam's, 1976), p. 94.
2. *Ibid.*, p. 100.

primitive sorcerer, the first four are incomparable. A careful reviewer may suspect that a lot of the incidents and discussions in these books are mythical, but they are nonetheless accurate representations of the occult world of sorcery. Certainly, his doctoral committee believed that they were.

The popularity of the first four books in the early 1970's was enormous. The three subsequent books at least had a substantial market, which is why Simon and Schuster continued to publish them. Between the time that Castaneda first began his studies of the old man (1960) and the time of the first book's publication (1968), an intellectual revolution occurred in both the academic world and the public at large. His books were gobbled up; two different sets of paperbacks were released. The first four became best-sellers.

They are difficult to classify. They are written in the form of a series of conversations and flashbacks. Castaneda is a superb storyteller. The reconstruction of the conversations is imaginative, although Castaneda's copious note-taking became a source of amusement for don Juan and another sorcerer, don Genaro. In fact, they were convinced that this fixation on writing was itself useful in Castaneda's initiation: writing, as a distinctly rational form of activity, would serve as a sort of talisman to shield him from the magic-charged universe into which he was to enter. Time and again, when demonic forces came close, don Juan insisted that he write and keep on writing. It is likely, then, that the basic perspective of the old sorcerer is preserved intact in at least the first three volumes.

The popularity of these books also raises another question. Did the reading public suddenly find itself sympathetic to an ancient world-and-life view, or is that ancient perspective fundamentally modern anyway, involving no great shift of perspective on the part of the readers? Castaneda's description of don Juan's perception of reality is no doubt colored by his own modern education, but in the later books, as Castaneda's perspective is more and more that of don Juan, the books become more explicitly epistemological in tone. The "Yaqui way of knowing," so-called, is really only revealed in the fourth book, *Tales of Power*. The earlier studies were more along the lines of a UCLA graduate student's interpretation of a Yaqui way of knowing. Yet in the fourth volume, when Castaneda's initiation is completed, don Juan's mind is revealed for what it is: dualistic to the core and strangely modern in its primitive animism. (Whether it was "Yaqui" is questionable; scholarly critics have pointed out the Yaqui

Indians are not peyote users, and that there is nothing in Castaneda's books that ties the old man's world view to anything explicitly Yaqui.)[3]

A dualism between rationalism and irrationalism, phenomenal and noumenal, undergirds don Juan's epistemology. This is modern man's philosophy, too. But the break with modernism comes with the old man's doctrine that two literal beings inhabit the human body, the *tonal* and the *nagual*, which correspond to the rational and the irrational in man's mind. It is not simply that man's mind is dualistic, don Juan finally reveals; the secret of Yaqui sorcery is that there really are two separate *beings* involved. This was the theme of another extremely popular book and film in the mid-1970's, Thomas Tryon's *The Other*, a ghost story about a murderous little boy who had mastered occult techniques quite similar to those presented by Castaneda in his fourth volume.

The world of the sorcerer is radically different from the world of the pre-1965 Western rationalist. As the West has continued to abandon the moral and religious foundations of its rationalistic heritage — a personal God of order who has created a lawful universe that reflects His orderly nature and who has made men in His image with rational minds corresponding to the laws of nature — we have found ourselves confronted with a new paradigm of the world. Forces and possibilities that had once been rejected as preposterous by Western rationalists are now given consideration by a growing number of scholars and a very wide popular audience.

Nevertheless, as I argue in this chapter, the intellectual presuppositions of the old Indian, as expressed by his younger initiate — though not *that* young; he was born in 1925, *Time* discovered in 1973[4] — in some ways are very similar to post-Kantian rationalism. This is why the older humanism was unable to call a halt intellectually to neither the spread of fascist irrationalism in the 1930's, nor the spread of occultism in the late 1960's. Below the thin surface of Western rationalism there has always lurked an implicit sea of irrationalism. This has been Cornelius Van Til's voluminously docu-

---

3. Duke University's Weston La Barre, an anthropologist and author of a book, *The Peyote Cult*, argued in 1971 in an unpublished review of *A Separate Reality* that "it is even unclear to what degree Don Juan was Yaqui in culture." *Seeing Castaneda*, p. 41. This review was commissioned and paid for by *The New York Times Book Review*, but it was never published. Subsequent reviews in the *Times* were favorable, which is indicative of the shift in perception among intellectuals.

4. *Seeing Castaneda*, p. 103.

mented assertion from the 1920's onward, and the rise of occultism after 1964 testified to the accuracy of his analysis.

Don Juan, a very ancient man living in a very ancient universe, was able to convert Castaneda from the inherited rationalism of the university. In doing so, he found a man with a distinctly Western skill, namely, the ability to write, who could offer don Juan's interpretation of his animistic universe as a possible alternative to the West's view. The revival of interest in sorcery made possible the presentation of the world of the sorcerer. *We cannot have the magician's power apart from the magician's universe.* (In retrospect, it is both amusing and depressing to recall those heady days of 1975, when tens of thousands of youthful turned-on marijuana smokers were reading Castaneda's books to achieve mystical illumination, completely unaware that he was a 50-year-old anthropology professor.)

The Quest for Power

As Castaneda was to learn only in later years (and Castaneda's adoring drug-ingesting readers also learned too late), recommending psychedelic drugs was a device used by don Juan to disrupt the initiate's perception of reality. This was fundamental in the process of initiation. *The transfer of power to Castaneda could not be accomplished apart from shattering his Western view of reality.* Drugs were the vehicle. Don Juan admitted that on several occasions he had lied to Castaneda, including the time he insisted that drugs were necessary to cross the barrier into the sorcerer's world. Drugs were not absolutely necessary to this transition, but they were certainly an efficient tool in promoting the initial breakthrough.

The key was the attainment of a new perception, or as Castaneda calls it, the attainment of *states of nonordinary reality*. It could also be termed altered consciousness or higher consciousness. Yet very early in his training, don Juan informed him that these states are not to be sought after for their own sake. The ultimate goal is always *power*; knowledge, whether ordinary or occult, is simply a means to power. But the magician's power must be sought through altered consciousness. This is the heart and soul of witchcraft. "Don Juan believed the states of nonordinary reality to be the only form of pragmatic learning and the only means of acquiring power. He conveyed the impression that other parts of his teachings were incidental to the acquisition of power. This point of view permeated don Juan's attitude toward everything not directly connected with the states of nonordinary reality."[5] Knowledge for its own sake is a product of Western rationalism; the old sorcerer would have none of it. "Power rests on the kind of knowledge one holds," he insisted. "What is the sense of knowing things that are useless?"[6]

C. S. Lewis on Power

This concern with power is one of the important links between the mind of the sorcerer and the mind of the Western rationalist. C. S. Lewis' novel *That Hideous Strength* rests on the possibility of collaboration between modernism and magic, since both are power-hungry by nature. Lewis observed that the great age of magic was unleashed, not by the medieval world, but by the rationalistic Renaissance. There was relatively little magic during the Middle Ages. "For the wise men of old the cardinal problem had been how to conform the soul to reality, and the solution had been knowledge, self-discipline and virtue. For magic and applied science alike the problem is how to subdue reality to the wishes of men: the solution is a technique; and both, in the practice of this technique, are ready to do things hitherto regarded as disgusting and impious — such as digging up and mutilating the dead."[7] This speculation was confirmed conclusively by Miss Frances Yates' book, *Giordano Bruno and the Hermetic Tradition* (1964), an exhaustive study of a rationalist-magician of the Renaissance. The Renaissance was animistic and pagan to the core, despite its surface rationalism.

Whenever the question of power is raised, another problem immediately asserts itself: Who is controlling what? C. S. Lewis faced this problem more forthrightly than don Juan did. When man begins to take control of nature, with nature regarded as a means to human ends, "Nature turns out to be a power exercised by some men over other men with Nature as its instrument."[8] When it comes to power, "Man is as much the patient or subject as the possessor, since he is the target both for bombs and for propaganda."[9] If man is seen as nothing more than a product of evolutionary natural forces, then the means by which nature is controlled must simultaneously

---

5. Carlos Castaneda, *The Teachings of Don Juan: A Yaqui Way of Knowledge* (New York: Pocket Books, 1974), p. 21. Originally published by the University of California Press, 1968.

6. *Ibid.*, p. 24.

7. C. S. Lewis, *The Abolition of Man* (New York: Macmillan, [1947] 1965), p. 88.

8. *Ibid.*, p. 69.

9. *Ibid.*, p. 68.

pose a threat to the freedom of other men. Men seek power over nature in order to assert their freedom from nature's caprices, yet in doing so they see their own freedom from other men and institutions slipping away. This is so-called nature/freedom antinomy, and it is one of the crucial problems, philosophically and politically, of the modern world. Lewis writes: "Man's conquest of Nature, if the dreams of some scientific planners are realized, means the rule of a few hundreds of men over billions upon billions of men. There neither is nor can be any simple increase of power on Man's side. Each new power won *by* man is a power *over* man as well. Each advance leaves him weaker as well as stronger. In every victory, besides being the general who triumphs, he is also the prisoner who follows the triumphal car."[10]

In short, "For the power of Man to make himself what he pleases means, as we have seen, the power of some men to make other men what *they* please."[11] But what or who controls the scientific planners? This is the crucial question regarding the exercise of power, whether magical or technocratic. If all is ultimately technique (in science) or ritual (in magic), there can be neither ethical good nor ethical evil. There can only be successful or unsuccessful manipulations. If vast evolutionary forces control our thought processes, then Nature, with a capital N, reasserts its domination over mankind through the power of materialistically determined scientists. But if men are not determined, then the transmission belt of scientific technique is slashed. This is the major philosophical problem of modern thought.

Don Juan sensed the dilemma of power. Power, he said, is personal. "It commands you and yet it obeys you."[12] Or, with respect to human choice: "When we think we decide, all we're doing is acknowledging that something beyond our understanding has set up the frame of our so-called decision, and all we do is acquiesce."[13] But in what does the magician acquiesce? He has no answer, any more than the scientist in his self-proclaimed intellectual autonomy has an answer. Given the presuppositions of modern science, Lewis finds the only answer open to the consistent scientist: "Nature, untrammeled by values, rules the Conditioners and, through them, all humanity. Man's conquest of Nature turns out, in the moment of its

10. *Ibid.*, p. 71.
11. *Idem.*
12. Castaneda, *Journey to Ixtlan* (New York: Pocket Books, [1972] 1974), p. 122.
13. Castaneda, *Tales of Power* (New York: Simon & Schuster, 1974), p. 243.

consummation, to be Nature's conquest of Man. Every victory we seemed to win has led us, step by step, to this conclusion. All Nature's apparent reverses have been but tactical withdrawals. We thought we were beating her back when she was luring us on. What looked to us like hands held up in surrender was really the opening of arms to enfold us for ever."[14] Lewis is quite correct: "The wresting of powers *from* Nature is also the surrendering of things *to* Nature. . . . It is the magician's bargain: give up our soul, get power in return."[15]

The West's Lawful Universe

The triumph of Western rationalism came from the faith that men of the seventeenth and eighteenth centuries had in a lawful universe. The source of this faith was the Christian doctrine of creation. The earth is to be subdued to the glory of God, not as a foreign and impersonal thing, as Professor Lynn White has erroneously maintained, but as a part of God's own handiwork. Men are responsible as stewards.[16] The doctrine of creation, when coupled with the doctrines of the cultural mandate and of Christian stewardship, led to the idea of applied science and technology.[17]

The secularization of this vision, with man established as the sovereign over nature, no doubt shifted the older perspective, but the idea of law was equally crucial. Man was to accomplish his dominion through the discovery of physical laws. But Darwin's breakthrough shattered the confidence in orderly law. Random variation became lord of the universe. Man was placed in a desperate situation; failure to compete successfully meant literal extinction. The

---

14. Lewis, *Abolition of Man*, p. 80.

15. *Ibid.*, p. 83.

16. Lynn White, Jr., "The Historical Roots of Our Ecological Crisis," *Science* (March 10, 1967). This widely quoted essay has been ably refuted by R. V. Young, "Christianity and Ecology," *National Review* (Dec. 20, 1974). See my remarks: Gary North, *The Dominion Covenant: Genesis* (Tyler, Texas: Institute for Christian Economics, 1982), pp. 33-36.

17. Stanley Jaki, *Science and Creation: From eternal cycles to an oscillating universe* (Edinburgh: Scottish Academic Press, 1974); Jaki, *The Road of Science and the Ways to God* (University of Chicago Press, 1978); Robert K. Merton, *Social Theory and Social Structure* (rev. ed.; New York: Free Press of Glencoe, [1957] 1962), ch. XVIII: "Puritanism, Pietism, and Science"; Charles Dykes, "Medieval Speculation, Puritanism, and Modern Science," *Journal of Christian Reconstruction*, VI (Summer, 1979); E. L. Hebden Taylor, "The Role of Puritan-Calvinism in the Rise of Modern Science," *ibid.* This journal is published by the Chalcedon Foundation, P.O. Box 158, Vallecito, California 95251.

quest for power was no longer the pastime of idle philosophers; it was a biological imperative. Man is either the powerless pawn in the meaningless cosmic processes, or else he is the next stage in the evolutionary process, the one who will direct the path of evolution by means of that great (and utterly unexplainable) discontinuity of nature, the human mind. Somehow, man's brain leaped the boundaries of evolution's most fundamental premise, continuous, uniformitarian change, and now it must take over from random variation and natural selection as the new lord of the universe.

The doctrine of evolution, as with all anti-biblical religious systems, requires the self-transcendence of man. Impersonal random natural selection miraculously provided man, the evolutionary product, with a brain vastly more powerful than his stone-age body needed. That a randomly evolved organ such as the incomparably complex human brain could have experienced such a gigantic evolutionary "leap of being," or leap beyond man's environment, is not consistent with original Darwinism, with its doctrine of nature's evolving by tiny steps. This inconsistency was later admitted by the co-discoverer of "evolution through natural selection," Alfred Russel Wallace, who then began investigating the occult, but Darwin refused to admit it.[18] Man has therefore transcended the evolutionary laws that created him. He must now transcend evolution's impersonal determinism by chance selection; he must now find the techniques — the *power* — to become the new god of the universe. Nothing must be left to chance in this battle against chance. Out of chance evolved everything, including the opposite of chance, human purpose. Human purpose must not be allowed to be swallowed back into chance's great belly. Man must become the great magician, pulling purpose and order out of chance's universe.[19]

The popularity of Castaneda's books should not be too surprising. Don Juan, the primitive sorcerer, communicates well with the skeptics of modern culture, for he shares the central vision of modern thought: the quest for magical power. He offers men a new evolution. The ancient and primitive occult origins of the New Age movement's key doctrine — the coming evolutionary leap of being for man (or at least an elite group of men) — should be apparent.

---

18. Loren Eiseley, *Darwin's Century: Evolution and the Men Who Discovered It* (New York: Anchor, [1958] 1961), ch. XI: "Wallace and the Brain."

19. North, *Dominion Covenant*, Appendix A, "From Cosmic Purposelessness to Humanistic Sovereignty."

A World of Death

Again and again during his initiation, don Juan warned Castaneda of the nameless threats that inhabit the desert and valleys that
surround them. Ritual is as important for the initiate as technique
for the bomb-defuser. It is a life-and-death affair. Water is a threat to
Castaneda; demons live there. The desert is a threat; demons live
there. A local woman is a threat; she is a scheming sorceress (he later
admitted that this story was untrue); it was a means of scaring
Castaneda into further initiatory activities. A whole host of oppressive beings inhabits the world of the sorcerer, and the initiate
knows too little to protect himself.

Castaneda had originally been interested in discovering facts
about psychedelic plants. Don Juan introduces him to "the little
smoke." A smoking mixture will reveal to him don Juan's "ally." The
old man warns him of the care that must be exercised in handling the
special pipe into which the mixture — itself specially prepared ritually
over the period of a year — must be placed. "The pipe will feel the
strain of being handled by someone else; and if one of us makes a
mistake there won't be any way to prevent the pipe from bursting
open by its own force, or escaping from our hands to shatter, even if
it falls on a pile of straw. If that ever happens, it would mean the end
of us both. Particularly of me. The smoke would turn against me in
unbelievable ways."[20] Whether the old man really believed this is
questionable; he lied to Castaneda constantly in the stages of initiation. But he never ceased to stress the importance of ritual, and it is
likely that he really saw death around them almost as often as he said
he saw it.

He did not fear the smoke as such. He feared the ally. The allies
never are referred to as demons, but are seen as separate beings, not
impersonal forces. They take animal shapes at times, but they also
take human shapes. As the fourth volume states, Castaneda's ally was
in the shape of a huge moth. These are the sources of special wisdom
and therefore unique power. These creatures must be placated. The
quest of the warrior is the quest for union with an ally — a lifetime
union. It is this that Castaneda claims to have attained, in the final
pages of *Tales of Power*.

Don Juan's ally, the little smoke, is a stickler for ritual. The old
man had to care for the pipe, keep it from the gaze of unenlightened

20. Castaneda, *Teachings*, pp. 68-70.

parties, and the man who uses it must lead a hard, quiet life. The gift of the smoke is a new vision of the world, or what the gnostics of pre-medieval days would have called a new gnosis. This was the quest of Renaissance mystics, alchemists, magicians, and illuminati.[21] "Everything is terrifying and confusing at the outset, but every new puff makes things more precise. And suddenly the world opens up anew! Unimaginable! When this happens the smoke has become one's ally and will resolve any question by allowing one to enter into inconceivable worlds."[22]

On the one hand, ritual observance is crucial. The general principle is as follows: ". . . we must follow certain steps, because it is in the steps where man finds strength. Without them we are nothing."[23] Again: "You must be infinitely careful. When one is dealing with power, one has to be perfect. Mistakes are deadly here."[24] On the other hand, human routines are to be shunned. An entire chapter of *Journey to Ixtlan* is titled "Disrupting the Routines of Life." The true hunter is "free, fluid, unpredictable."[25] In dealing with the personal sources of gnosis and power, rituals must be precise. In dealing with the affairs of life, there must be no routines. As he says elsewhere, there must not even be a personal history. There must be *total atomism of the personality*: one man, alone, in a hostile universe. The hunter must be unpredictable, for he is also the hunted. "All of us behave like the prey we are after. That, of course, also makes us prey for something or someone else. Now, the concern of a hunter, who knows all this, is to stop being a prey himself."[26]

This is the universe of the magical manipulator. All the world is like an enormous container of nitroglycerine. It must be handled with ritually exact care when it is being manipulated, and at all other times, the magician must be devious, fluid, totally unpredictable, in order to escape the manipulations of others. This is the animists' world, where living, malevolent beings strike out and trap the ritually negligent. Perfection is a matter of precise ritual. The magician must content himself with subduing only minute portions of his world on a piecemeal basis; the world is something to be escaped

---

21. Thomas Molnar, *God and the Knowledge of Reality* (New York: Basic Books, 1973).
22. Castaneda, *Teachings*, pp. 68-70.
23. *Ibid.*, p. 158.
24. *Ixtlan*, p. 147
25. *Ibid.*, p. 75.
26. *Ibid.*

from rather than brought into total conformity on a universal basis.
In order to subdue portions of the world, the magician must link
himself to mysterious powers that threaten his very existence.

Ethics or Ritual?

This perspective is almost a mirror image of the Judeo-Christian
heritage. Ethics, not ritual, is primary in Christian theology. The
prophet Micah warned Israel against the lure of ritualism:

Wherewith shall I come before the LORD, and bow myself before the high
God? shall I come before him with burnt offerings, with calves of a year old?
Will the LORD be pleased with thousands of rams, or with ten thousands of
rivers of oil? shall I give my firstborn for my transgression, the fruit of my
body for the sin of my soul? He hath shewed thee, O man, what is good;
and what doth the LORD require of thee, but to do justly, and to love mercy,
and to walk humbly with thy God? [Micah 6:6-8]

The biblical cosmology requires ethical subordination before
God and power over the created realm. Routines are tools of man's
conquest over a recalcitrant nature: routines of occupation, education, experimentation, all involving the overarching routines of
time. By this vision, Western civilization spread throughout Europe
and conquered the animistic cultures of the magicians. The animist
elevates ritual before multiple gods over against the daily routines of
life, and the result is cultural impotence and stagnation. The Christian elevates routine over ritual, and the stronger that impulse is (in
Protestant cultures as opposed to Roman Catholic ones, in Roman
Catholic cultures as opposed to primitive ones), the more thorough
the transformation of culture and the advent of ideas of progress and
external development.

The Christian vision of progress is at bottom ethical. Nevertheless, ethical decisions are supposed to influence the external world
and transform it (Deuteronomy 28:1-14). The Protestant ethic is an
ethic of self-discipline, thrift, and future-orientation. It is an ethic of
dominion. The sorcerer's world is a world of immediate amoral power
based on ritual exactitude. It is a timeless world, and therefore not a
future-oriented world. Castaneda later said in an interview:
". . . don Juan is a good existentialist. When there is no way of
knowing whether I have one more minute of life I must live as if this
is my last moment. Each act is the warrior's last battle. So every-

thing must be done impeccably."[27] Not ethically impeccable, but ritually impeccable.

It is also extremely interesting to note the nature of Castaneda's personal initiatory technique for "stopping the world" in a magical timeless sense. When asked by the interviewer, "Of the many techniques that don Juan taught you for stopping the world, which do you still practice?" Castaneda's reply is stunning; it is the heart of the difference between Western development and primitive backwardness, between Puritanism on the one hand and social dissipation on the other: "My major discipline now is to disrupt my routines. I was always a very routinary person. I ate and slept on schedule. In 1965 I began to change my habits. I wrote in the quiet hours of the night and slept and ate when I felt the need. Now I have dismantled so many of my habitual ways of acting that before long I may become unpredictable and surprising to myself."[28] This is the discipline of randomness. The interviewer was correct in linking this remark to an old Zen Buddhist story. And once again, the year 1965 appears. It was his year of transition, despite five years of prior initiation. In this sense, he was a product of his era.

Escape from the Ordinary

Don Juan emphasizes the necessity of ritual because the world that he inhabits is potentially infused with personal power, and death lurks everywhere. Page after page of Castaneda's books is filled with the old man's observations that death is very near, at times even actively stalking them. The awareness of death is an avenue to power. The knowledge of their own helplessness before animistic forces is the way men build up their own magical potency. Not humility before a personal God, but constant wakefulness and wariness amidst animistic forces. A world of imminent destruction must replace the world of daily routines if the initiate is to be successful in his quest for power. This was the message of don Juan's own teacher, and the old man passed it along to Castaneda:

My benefactor said that when a man embarks on the paths of sorcery he becomes aware, in a gradual manner, that ordinary life has been forever left behind; that knowledge is indeed a frightening affair; that the means of the

27. Interview by Sam Keen, "Sorcerer's Apprentice," *Psychology Today* (December 1972); reprinted in *Seeing Castaneda*, p. 88.
28. *Ibid.*, p. 90.

ordinary world are no longer a buffer for him; and that he must adopt a new way of life if he is going to survive. The first thing he ought to do, at that point, is to want to become a warrior, a very important step and decision. The frightening nature of knowledge leaves one no alternative but to become a warrior.

By the time knowledge becomes a frightening affair the man also realizes that death is the irreplaceable partner that sits next to him on the mat. Every bit of knowledge that becomes power has death as its central force. Death lends the ultimate touch, and whatever is touched by death indeed becomes power.

A man who follows the paths of sorcery is confronted with imminent annihilation every turn of the way, and unavoidably he becomes keenly aware of his death. Without the awareness of death he would be only an ordinary man involved in ordinary acts. He would lack the necessary potency, the necessary concentration that transforms one's ordinary time on earth into magical power.[29]

It is obvious that no man can live in constant fear of death, and don Juan did not advise Castaneda to enter a life of worry. But some other emotion had to be substituted for fear. The next step in the path toward magical power is *total detachment*. "The idea of imminent death, instead of becoming an obsession, becomes an indifference. . . . Detach yourself from everything."[30] Understandably, a man detached in this manner is not bound by earthly conventions.

It is at this point that don Juan displays another of the important intellectual and philosophical premises he shares with modern man. *Don Juan is an existentialist.*[31] I think it is likely that a student could pass off the following quote as if it were part of a formerly unpublished letter from Martin Heidegger, the German existentialist philosopher:

Only the idea of death makes a man sufficiently detached so he is incapable of abandoning himself to anything. Only the idea of death makes a man sufficiently detached so he can't deny himself anything. A man of that sort, however, does not crave, for he has acquired a silent lust for life and for all things of life. He knows his death is stalking him and won't give him time to cling to anything, so he tries, without craving, all of everything.

A detached man, who knows he has no possibility of fencing off his death, has only one thing to back himself with: the power of his decisions.

---

29. Castaneda, *A Separate Reality: Further Conversations with Don Juan* (New York: Pocket Books, [1971] 1974), pp. 149-50.

30. *Ibid.*, p. 150.

31. *Ibid.*

He has to be, so to speak, the master of his choices. He must fully understand that his choice is his responsibility and once he makes it there is no
longer time for regrets or recriminations. His decisions are final, simply because his death does not permit him time to cling to anything.[32]

Castaneda may be inserting bits and pieces of Western philosophy into the old man's mouth, but the basic themes are repeated over
and over in various contexts. The themes of death and detachment,
coupled with total affection for earthly life, pervade his teaching. At
the end of the fourth volume, Castaneda quotes the old man: "This
earth, this world. For a warrior there can be no greater love."[33] This
same perspective undergirds the widely publicized Church of Satan
in San Francisco, run by Anton LaVey: "Life is the great indulgence
— death, the great abstinence. Therefore, make the most of life —
HERE AND NOW!"[34] Don Juan's philosophy is simple enough,
and it is exceedingly modern: "Life in itself is sufficient, self-explana-
tory and complete."[35]

Escape from Meaning

Total detachment is supposed to give a man a lust for life. A universe in which death lurks — death that literally stalks a man — is supposed to promote the philosophy of life. Life is everything, yet it is
nothing. This is the vital attitude that don Juan calls "controlled folly."
"But we must know first that our acts are useless and yet we must
proceed as if we didn't know it. That's a sorcerer's controlled folly."[36]
This perspective must be used with everyone else at all times. The
sorcerer is an actor; he does not let those around him know that he
thinks that they are irrelevant. "Once a man learns to *see* he finds
himself alone in the world with nothing but folly."[37] In short, "everything I do in regard to myself and my fellow man is folly, because
nothing matters."[38] The *modernism* of don Juan's outlook is striking.
A meaningless universe must be dealt with in terms of a philosophy
of ultimate meaninglessness and the concomitant quest for power.

---

32. *Ibid.*, p. 151.
33. *Tales of Power*, pp. 284-85.
34. Anton Szandor LaVey, *The Satanic Bible* (New York: Avon, 1969), p. 33. By
late 1972, this book was in its eighth printing.
35. *Tales of Power*, p. 59.
36. *Separate Reality*, p. 77.
37. *Ibid.*, p. 81.
38. *Ibid.*, p. 80.

For in a meaningless world, nothing counts except personal power. "But you want to find the meaning of life," he taunts his pupil. "A warrior doesn't care about meanings."[39] In such a world there can be neither true nor false: "An average man cares that things are either true or false, but a warrior doesn't."[40] The warrior acts the same in either case.

This is a philosophy of death parading as a philosophy of life. It professes indifference and clings to life tenaciously. It denies that anything matters, yet concludes that power matters greatly. By asserting the total autonomy of detached man, it turns into a philosophy of *action* — a kind of pseudo-fascism. Then again, it is equally a defense of passivity or *inaction*: "For me nothing matters, but perhaps for you everything will. You should know by now that a man of knowledge lives by acting, not by thinking about acting, nor by thinking about what he will think when he has finished acting. . . . Nothing being more important than anything else, a man of knowledge chooses any act, and acts it out as if it matters to him. His controlled folly makes him say that what he does matters and makes him act as if it did, and yet he knows that it doesn't; so when he fulfills his acts he retreats in peace, and whether his acts were good or bad, or worked or didn't, is in no way part of his concern."[41] As he puts it toward the end of Castaneda's training, controlled folly embraces "the possibility of acting without believing, without expecting rewards — acting just for the hell of it."[42] This is the goal of the man of knowledge — the man who has achieved gnosis.

Yet the old man cannot really believe his own philosophy. It leads him to equate man and animals. We and the snakes are on a par, he says.[43] But when he describes the death of his mother at the hands of Mexican soldiers, he says: "They killed her for no reason at all. It doesn't make any difference that she died that way, not really, and yet for me it does. I cannot tell myself why, though; it just does."[44] There are still traces of human sympathy left in the man. Some of his actor's makeup has rubbed off, and there is still a human being underneath. Yet he is unable to make sense of his feelings of the injustice of the murder. To make sense of any act implies — demands

39. *Ibid.*, p. 181.
40. *Ixtlan*, p. 191.
41. *Separate Reality*, p. 85.
42. *Tales of Power*, pp. 232-33.
43. *Separate Reality*, p. 63; *Ixtlan*, pp. 25, 249.
44. *Separate Reality*, p. 137.

—that there is sense in this world, and that is the premise that his philosophy of life explicitly rejects.

Though all things are meaningless, there is one standard by which all events are measured, by which all things are tested, *death*: "Death is the only wise adviser that we have."[45] Nevertheless, adopting the language of a Zen monk, don Juan announces: "Death is a whorl. . . . Death is the face of the ally; death is a shiny cloud over the horizon; death is the whisper of Mescalito [the Peyote god] in your ears; . . . death is me talking; death is you and your writing pad; death is nothing. Nothing! It is here yet it isn't here at all."[46] This kind of philosophical mishmash is supposed to be rare wisdom. The old Indian is correct: "To be a sorcerer is a terrible burden."[47] Especially philosophically.

Prisoners of Power

The apostle Paul, writing to the church at Rome, warned them of the inescapability of service in the world. The question is never to serve or not to serve; it is always *whom* to serve. "Know ye not," Paul asks, "that to whom ye yield yourselves servants to obey, his servants ye are to whom ye obey; whether of sin unto death, or of obedience unto righteousness?" (Romans 6:16). Don Juan's discussion of power demonstrates how clearly he understands this principle. On the one hand, union with a demonic ally gives the sorcerer power: "From then on you can summon your ally at will and make him do anything you want."[48] These allies are supposedly neutral forces, "neither good nor evil, but are put to use by the sorcerers for whatever purpose they see fit."[49] Yet on the other hand, he warns Castaneda against becoming a "slave to the devil's weed" (jimsonweed), for "it will never let you go." The weed is the means of obtaining revelations from the female spirit that is associated with it. "She will cut you off from everything else. You will have to spend your life grooming her as an ally. She is possessive. Once she dominates you, there is only one way to go—her way."[50]

Don Juan's references to the "protectors" of some friends and rel-

---

45. *Ixtlan*, p. 34.
46. *Separate Reality*, p. 195.
47. *Ibid.*, p. 199.
48. *Ibid.*, p. 40.
49. *Ibid.*
50. *Teachings*, p. 120.

atives—Jesus Christ, the Virgin Mary, Our Lady of Guadalupe—
indicate his contempt for their lack of visible power. But they also indicate how frivolous was his relatives' worship of these occasional
church visitors. He contrasts their worship of the traditional Mexican deities with the worship demanded by Mescalito, the god of
peyote. "If they were real protectors they would force you to listen,"
he argues. "If Mescalito becomes your protector you will have to
listen whether you like it or not, because you can see him and you
must take heed of what he says. He will make you approach him
with respect. Not the way you fellows are accustomed to approach
your protectors."[51] Power demands respect.

The problem with power is always the same: the user is simultaneously subjected to it. The man who wields the scientific power of
the modern world must have a theory of the transmission of power.
If causes have effects, then by becoming an intermediary cause a
man must admit that his decisions are also effects of prior causes. If
he denies that he is necessarily determined, then he must also deny
his own power to determine certain effects. Similarly, if a magician
uses the power of an ally or demon to produce certain effects, he inevitably places himself under the power of the ally. At the very least,
he is subjected to a rigorous series of rituals that must be used when
calling forth occult power. To command power—any power—is to
acknowledge the sovereignty of the source of that power, whether
God, demons, natural law, random variation, or whatever. Men will
serve that which they believe to be sovereign.

At the very end of his training, Castaneda is warned of his new responsibilities by his teacher: "The fate of all of us here has been to
know that we are the prisoners of power. No one knows why us in particular, but what a great fortune."[52] Simply and less enthusiastically
put, "We are dregs in the hands of those forces."[53] Ghosts, spirits,
mysterious forces: these are the gods of the world of the sorcerer.[54]

Since the attainment of the gnosis was basic to the attainment of
power, and power involved Castaneda in a new and fearful world,
what kinds of power did he actually see or experience that would
seem to have made the bargain worthwhile? As a result of the various drugs, he did achieve several nonrational experiences, a few of

51. *Separate Reality*, p. 64.
52. *Tales of Power*, p. 280.
53. *Ixtlan*, p. 88.
54. *Separate Reality*, pp. 232-34.

them terrifying. Learning how to enter into these states of "higher consciousness" apart from the use of drugs, and apparently without hypnosis, also went with his training. But these visions and nonordinary perceptions were more the price paid for power than a benefit. If power was crucial, what signs of power were revealed? The books list a very few examples:

1. The ability to see in the dark on certain occasions.[55]
2. Limited powers of divination — "second sight" — through the combined use of jimsonweed and lizard familiars.[56]
3. Possibly astral projection; it may have been a dream.[57]
4. Mind reading; don Juan seemed to possess this ability, though Castaneda may have related certain events during one of his hallucinatory dreams.[58]
5. Teleportation; two actual cases are related. It is attributed to a local sorceress, and Castaneda says that he saw her do it. He and don Juan also experienced it.[59]
6. Floating, flying, defying gravity.[60]
7. Feats of strength — a claim of don Juan concerning his earlier days of sorcery.[61]
8. Some prestidigitation tricks that may truly have been feats of mind over matter.[62]

When one considers that Castaneda's readers hacked through four volumes of material to glean these few items of occult power, it would seem that the appeal of these books in 1975 lay not in their tales of power, but in their presentation of a world of nonrational perceptions. Castaneda is a spinner of first-rate ghost stories. If he has in fact become a practicing *brujo*, then he may prefer to tell us very little but it seems more likely that his intention is to convey a vision of another conceptual world. He is telling us about occult "knowledge" — magical gnosis — which is essentially anti-rational.

---

55. *Teachings*, pp. 97-98.
56. *Ibid.*, pp. 116-17, 155-57.
57. *Ibid.*, pp. 126-29.
58. *Ibid.*, pp. 140-41; *Separate Reality*, pp. 29-31.
59. *Separate Reality*, p. 240; *Tales of Power*, pp. 147-62.
60. *Tales of Power*, pp. 166, 182, 253, 261.
61. *Teachings*, p. 66.
62. *Tales of Power*, p. 51.

Christ posed the question concerning the price a man would pay for his soul. If he were to gain the whole world, he could not redeem it (Mark 8:36-37). Castaneda was tricked, according to don Juan, into leaving the common world of the West in order to enter the sorcerer's world of imminent destruction. The old man is quite correct: no sober-minded man would want to become a "man of knowledge" without having been tricked into it. But those who pursue power for its own sake are not sensible.

Shattered Reality

The gnosis of the primitive sorcerer is an intensely and consistently antirational cosmology. *Time* summarized his perspective: "At the core of his books and Don Juan's method is, of course, the assumption that reality is not an absolute. It comes to each of us culturally determined, packaged in advance."[63] Castaneda's own summary of the sorcerer's perspective, in contrast to the familiar and popularized version of Western rationalism, is very much to the point: "In fact, the reality of the world we know is so taken for granted that the basic premise of sorcery, that our reality is merely one of many descriptions, could hardly be taken as a serious proposition."[64]

Several comments are in order. Van Til's point must never be forgotten: Western rationalism has always had a kind of alliance with Western irrationalism. Western materialism has always had an alliance with Western mysticism. Post-Newtonian science has been at bottom dualistic, simultaneously absolutist and relativistic. Einstein protested loudly against any interpretation of his theory of relativity which concluded that everything is relative, but to little avail. He asserted in 1931 that "Belief in an external world independent of the perceiving subject is the basis of all natural science."[65] He was correct, and as that faith has waned, so has the coherence of modern natural science.

Despite Einstein's protests, the relativist genie that he let loose from the Newtonian bottle is now loose in the world. The growth of relativism in every academic discipline, including physics, has stead-

---

63. *Seeing Castaneda*, p. 106
64. *Ixtlan*, p. ix.
65. Albert Einstein, *The World As I See It* (New York: Covici-Fried, 1934), p. 60. Cited in Stanley Jaki, "The Absolute Beneath the Relative: Reflections on Einstein's Theories," *Intercollegiate Review*, XX (Spring/Summer 1985), p. 29.

ily undercut Einstein's old-fashioned defense of an independently coherent reality. First, Kant triumphed over Newton, as men were told
that the innate categories of their minds provide order to the random
noumenal world "out there." Then, after 1964, a world view close to
don Juan's began to triumph over Kant, at least within a growing
segment of the student population, as well as inside the American
book-buying public. People began to take Castaneda's anti-rational
proposition quite seriously: there *is* a separate reality. In fact, there
are many realities. Each autonomous man makes his own, in terms
of his own categories. The linguistic confusion of the tower of Babel
is now paralleled by the confusion of the "universal language" of
Kant's categories. (This is the essence, I suspect, of the prevailing
epistemology of all those in hell: total autonomy and isolation.)
Kant's faith that universal categories of the human mind necessarily
exist and give order to the world is being abandoned; it is "every
man for himself." The acids of philosophical relativism had finally
eroded the confidence that intelligent Western people once had in the
distinctly absolutist world view of nineteenth-century philosophical
mechanism.

Don Juan's vision rested on a philosophical premise: all is not
what it appears to our reason. The Western process of intellectual rationalization of the perceived world is explicitly rejected. "But to be a
sorcerer in your case means that you have to overcome stubbornness
and the need for rational explanations, which stand in your way."[66]
Again: "We men and all the other luminous beings on earth are per-
ceivers. That is our bubble, the bubble of perception. Our mistake is
to believe that the only perception worthy of acknowledgment is
what goes through our *reason*. Sorcerers believe that *reason* is only one
center and that it shouldn't take so much for granted."[67]

What the old man is attacking is the assumed sufficiency of phenomenal knowledge. He forces Castaneda to look at the noumenal
side of perception; and unlike Kant, who simply used the noumenal
realm as a silent backdrop or limiting concept to deal with the problem of philosophical contradictions in human thought, don Juan
really believes that the noumenal realm is accessible. Not accessible
to reason, however, but accessible to the *nagual*: the actually existing
magical half of man's dualistic existence. The *nagual* is the occult

---

66. *Tales of Power*, p. 193.
67. *Ibid.*, p. 249.

double. It is also known in Western occultism as the *Doppelgänger*. But he did not reveal this secret to Castaneda until the end of his initiation.

The three earlier volumes present don Juan's thought in the tradition of Western philosophical dualism. Castaneda quotes the old man as saying: "The world is a mystery. This, what you're looking at, is not all there is to it. There is much more to the world, so much more, in fact, that it is endless. So when you're trying to figure it out, all you're really doing is trying to make the world familiar. You and I are right here, in the world that you call real, simply because we both know it. You don't know the world of power, therefore you cannot make it into a familiar scene."[68] In short, "the world is incomprehensible," don Juan asserts. "We won't ever understand it; we won't ever unravel its secret. Thus we must treat it as it is, a sheer mystery."[69] This is the heart of the sorcerer's conception of the world. The world is fundamentally mysterious.

Escape from Reason

Western reason in the Newtonian sense is anathema. Man's ability to understand reality is futile. By emphasizing the impotence of rationalism, and by pointing to the mysterious conception of the world as the fundamental one — the most sophisticated, the wisest — the old man steadily breaks down Castaneda's world view. This is the goal of the initiation. "The warrior lowers his head to no one, but at the same time, he doesn't permit anyone to lower his head to him. The beggar, on the other hand, falls to his knees at the drop of a hat and scrapes the floor for anyone he deems to be higher; but at the same time, he demands that someone lower than him scrape the floor for him."[70] Then the old man drives home his point: "You like the humbleness of a beggar. . . . You bow your head to reason." What the reader watches for four volumes is the destruction of Castaneda's reason. He admits it in the final volume: "My rational structure was falling apart."[71] This had been the old man's goal. "You're chained!" don Juan had shouted at him very early in his training. "You're chained to your reason."[72]

---

68. *Ixtlan*, pp. 135-36.
69. *Separate Reality*, pp. 219-20; cf. 126, 258.
70. *Tales of Power*, p. 27.
71. *Ibid.*, p. 47.
72. *Separate Reality*, p. 260.

In the earlier stages of his training, Castaneda had been given an explanation of the relationship between the human will and reason in distinctly western terminology. Reason has its limits. The *will* is the link between men and the world.[73] We perceive the world in the combined activity of reason and will. The human will shapes our perception of the world; it is an active perceiving. This is the sorcerer's secret ability. "When we perceive the world with our will we know that it is not as 'out there' or as 'real' as we think."[74] In language similar to that of Professor Eisenbud, don Juan argues for a conception of man as the sustainer of the world: "We talk about our world. In fact we maintain our world with our internal talk. . . . We renew it, we kindle it with life, we uphold it with our internal talk."[75] Don Juan is not using figures of speech; he accepts the potency of men as sustainers of the world. "For instance, our rings of power, yours and mine, are hooked right now on the *doing* in this room. We are making this room. Our rings of power are spinning this room into being at this very moment."[76]

Castaneda, in his more simplistic rationalism, rejected this hypothesis initially, but had he been more familiar with Kant's *Critique of Pure Reason*, he might have recognized don Juan's line of reasoning. Though he did not speak of "rings of power," Kant certainly would have seen the sophistication of the old sorcerer's argument, although he preferred to focus his attention on the human understanding rather than the noumenal side of man. It was Kant, after all, who had asserted that "the understanding is something more than a power of formulating rules through comparison of appearances; it is itself the lawgiver of nature. Save through it, nature, that is, synthetic unity of the manifold of appearances according to the rules, would not exist at all. . . ."[77] The old sorcerer saw what Castaneda's simplistic nineteenth-century rationalism did not prepare him to see, but what humanistic philosophers have maintained for two hundred years: "The world is such-and-such or so-and-so only because we tell ourselves that that is the way it is. If we would stop telling ourselves that the world is so-and-so, the world would stop being so-and-so."[78]

73. *Ibid.*, p. 147.
74. *Ibid.*, p. 148.
75. *Ibid.*, p. 218.
76. *Ixtlan*, p. 211.
77. Kant, *Critique of Pure Reason*, Section A 126-27.
78. Castaneda, *Separate Reality*, p. 219.

The goal, then, is to "stop the world," to alter our perception of the world. "To change our idea of the world is the crux of sorcery," he tells Castaneda. "And stopping the internal dialogue is the only way to accomplish it. The rest is just padding."[79] The rest — drugs, bodily exercises, secrecy, special foods — is mere padding. *The goal is a higher consciousness.* At last, he reveals the sorcerer's secret:

> We, the luminous beings, are born with two rings of power, but we use only one to create the world. That ring, which is hooked very soon after we are born, is *reason*, and its companion is *talking*. Between the two they concoct and maintain the world.
>
> So, in essence, the world that your *reason* wants to sustain is the world created by a description and its dogmatic and inviolable rules, which the *reason* learns to accept and defend.
>
> The secret of the luminous beings [living beings] is that they have another ring of power which is never used, the *will*. The trick of the sorcerer is the same trick of the average man. Both have a description; one, the average man, upholds it with his *reason*; the other, the sorcerer, upholds it with his *will*. Both descriptions have their rules and the rules are perceivable, but the advantage of the sorcerer is that *will* is more engulfing than *reason*.
>
> The suggestion that I want to make at this point is that from now on you should let yourself perceive whether the description is upheld by your *reason* or your *will*. I feel that is the only way for you to use your daily world as a challenge and a vehicle to accumulate enough personal power to get to the totality of yourself.[80]

The true prestidigitation of the sorcerer is intellectual and philosophical. It is the same trick employed by the humanist. From a position which insists that man is no better than an animal, that it is a crime to think of oneself as superior to the animals, we come to man as the sustainer of the universe, man as the total being. What matters to a warrior "is arriving at the totality of oneself."[81] Man is the focus. Man is central once again. It is the same sleight-of-brain trick that modern evolutionists indulge in: man, the product of chance, the product of slime, somehow becomes man the mind-endowed discontinuous leap in the continuous evolutionary chain. Man-the-director-of-evolutionary-processes somehow emerges from man-the-

---

79. *Tales of Power*, p. 22.
80. *Ibid.*, p. 101.
81. *Ibid.*, p. 13.

developed-amoeba.[82] It is the lure of Satan: to be as God.

Man is dualistic, don Juan teaches. He is composed of reason (the *tonal*) and will (the *nagual*). It is man who rules, not God. "God is an item of our personal *tonal* and of the *tonal* of the times. The *tonal* is, as I've already said, everything we think the world is composed of, including God, of course. God has no more importance other than being a part of the *tonal* of our time."[83] Spoken like a true professor of freshman courses in logic. God is simply a part of the climate of opinion.

So far, this old sorcerer has proven himself to be a very hip old man. He could sail through a sophomore class in ethics without cracking a book. A bit of relativism, a strong dose of philosophical dualism, a few swipes with the "climate of opinion" paint brush, and the quest for the totality of man. Not to mention a large chunk of existentialism. The don Juan of Castaneda's books in many ways is a modern figure. If anything, it is Castaneda, the old-fashioned nineteenth-century mechanist, who sounds like an epistemological fuddy-duddy.

Nevertheless, the modernism of don Juan is deceptive, for beneath the slogans so dear to the modern climate of opinion lies an ancient faith. Don Juan does not simply see man as epistemologically dualistic; man is *actually* a dualistic construct. There are two sides to man, literally. The *tonal* and the *nagual*—reason and will—occupy man's body in a special way. Yaqui dualism is complete. *There are two creatures that exist in man.* It is the training of the sorcerer that enables the *nagual*—pure will—to capture the body of a man when the *tonal* is asleep. Astral projection somehow involves the use of a single personality and two bodies. Or else one body is an imitation: it is not clear from the explanations of the old man. But he believes that sometimes we are watching one "don Juan" and sometimes the other. This is the occult doctrine of the *Doppelgänger*, or double. The *nagual* can soar to unseen realms, defy gravity, or see the sleeping *tonal*.[84] If the *tonal* should touch the *nagual*—if a man should touch his double

---

82. This is one of the recurring themes in my writing. Cf. North, *Dominion Covenant*, Appendix A: "From Cosmic Purposelessness to Humanistic Sovereignty." At the time that I wrote this chapter of *None Dare Call It Witchcraft*, I was also working on a book on evolution. That book never was finished, but one chapter appeared as Appendix C of *Dominion Covenant*: "Cosmologies in Conflict: Creation vs. Evolution."

83. *Tales of Power*, p. 127.

84. *Ibid.*, pp. 182, 252.

—it means death.[85] The *tonal* maintains order. The *nagual* provides the sorcerer with his power. "Let's say that a warrior learns to tune his *will*, to direct it to a pinpoint, to focus it wherever he wants. It is as if his *will*, which comes from the midsection of his body, is one single luminous fiber, a fiber that he can direct at any conceivable place. That fiber is the road to the *nagual*. Or I could also say that the warrior sinks into the *nagual* through that single fiber."[86]

Christ informed his followers that rivers of living water can flow out of men's bellies—a distinctly ethical analogy (John 7:38). Don Juan understands the belly as the source of the fibers of power and the entrance place of death—a kind of Achilles' chink in man's armor. Spirits and demons can penetrate the belly. It is also the source of rays of light so strong that they can supposedly support the body, propelling it aloft.[87]

From Universe to Multiverse

What does it all mean? The sorcerer sees the world as a multiple reality held together by the rational side of man. In this, he agrees essentially with all post-Kantian logic. But man is also multiple. When don Genaro and don Juan threw Castaneda from a cliff, he did not die in the fall. Instead, he experienced wholly new sensations. He felt his clothes fall off, then his body seemed to fall off, leaving only his head. Then he was nothing but a pebble-like residue —awareness itself. All of a sudden, he found himself back on the ledge of the cliff. They told him they had pulled him back. They tossed him again. "I again had the sensations of being tossed, spinning, and falling down at a tremendous speed. Then I exploded. I disintegrated. Something in me gave out; it released something I had kept locked up all my life. I was thoroughly aware then that my secret reservoir had been tapped and that it poured out unrestrainedly. There was no longer the sweet unity I call 'me.' There was nothing and yet that nothing was filled. . . . I was a myriad of selves which were all 'me,' a colony of separate units that had a special allegiance to one another and would join unavoidably to form one single awareness, my human awareness."[88]

---

85. *Ibid.*, pp. 185, 189.

86. *Ibid.*, p. 178.

87. *Separate Reality*, pp. 23, 148, 197-98, 216-17, 242; *Ixtlan*, p. 161; *Tales of Power*, p. 166.

88. *Tales of Power*, p. 262.

When he came back to normal, he felt a loss. "I longed for the 'unknown' where my awareness was not unified."[89] He had experienced a form of pseudo-transcendence. He had attained a higher consciousness. His own multiple reality had entered into new realities of perception. He longed to attain other perceptions like this one. As the book ends, he apparently recaptures the state of altered consciousness.

What is man in this perspective? He is simply a cluster of perceptions held together by we know not what. "At death, however, they sink deeply and move independently as if they had never been a unit."[90] Man is dispersed to "the vastness."[91] There is no threat of judgment, for there is no guilt, "because to isolate one's acts as being mean, or ugly, or evil was to place an unwarranted importance on the self," as Castaneda summarizes don Juan's teaching.[92] There is no second death. These words are no doubt as comforting to the minds of modern men as they were to Indian mystics a thousand years ago. When it comes to questions concerning final judgment, man—the creator and sustainer of the rational universe—is not to worry, for to worry about such questions is to place "unwarranted importance" on his insignificant self. Strategically professed humility is the escape hatch of ancient as well as modern man.

"One," says don Juan, "can arrive at the totality of oneself only when one fully understands that the world is merely a view, regardless of whether that view belongs to an ordinary man or to a sorcerer."[93] Such a world is indeterminate, and an indeterminate universe does not hand out final judgments. The appeal of such a cosmology to modern man should be obvious. Man the perceiver-creator is safe. The perceived unity of the world is an illusion—a convenient illusion, as well as an inexplicable one—so there are no ultimate questions worth asking. Since man constructs his universe, he is not answerable to anyone else.

Don Juan, an "uneducated" Indian of the Southwest, has the same view of the world and man's role in it that Immanuel Kant struggled to attain by means of rigorous logic. Man makes up the rules and serves as the game's only umpire. "The *tonal* makes the

---

89. *Ibid.*, p. 263.
90. *Ibid.*, p. 266.
91. *Ixtlan*, p. 155.
92. *Ibid.*, p. 183.
93. *Tales of Power*, p. 240.

world only in a manner of speaking. It cannot create or change anything, and yet it makes the world because its function is to judge and
assess, and witness. I say that the *tonal* makes the world because it
witnesses and assesses it according to *tonal* rules. In a very strange
manner the *tonal* is a creator that doesn't create a thing. In other
words, the *tonal* makes up the rules by which it apprehends the
world. So, in a manner of speaking, it creates the world."[94]

Kant never said it any better; in fact, he never said it as well.
There is no world-in-itself but only a description of the world that
men learn to visualize and take for granted.[95] The only judgment
that matters to man is man's own judgment. This sounds very reas-
suring, except for one minor point. What are all those shadows in
the night, and why do they seek to kill unwary men?

Timeless Dreaming

For the sorcerer, dreams are a source of power.[96] For the
sorcerer's apprentice, they are a means of internal discipline in the
initiation process. "Think of it as something entertaining. Imagine
all the inconceivable things you could accomplish. A man's hunting
power has almost no limits in his *dreaming*."[97] Don Genaro, the sorcerer who served as Castaneda's "benefactor" (don Juan was only his
instructor), later told Castaneda that "the double begins in *dreaming*."[98] This is the means by which the self manifests itself as the
nagual. As the discipline continues, this second personality can take
over, the Indians believe, thereby dreaming the self. It becomes impossible to know for sure at any given time whether one is perceiving
the world as the *nagual* or the *tonal*. Sometimes a man dreams his
double, and sometimes the double dreams the man.[99] "No one
knows how it happens," reveals don Juan. Truer words were never
spoken. Nevertheless, the escape of the *nagual* as a second being is
made possible by these special dreams.

This is the doctrine of "magical time."[100] It is the *nagual's* time:
beyond time, independent of time. When in the *tonal's* time, men are
not to be irrational; when in the *nagual's* time, men are not to be ra-

---

94. *Ibid.*, p. 125.
95. *Ibid.*, p. 123.
96. *Ixtlan*, p. 91.
97. *Ibid.*, p. 98.
98. *Tales of Power*, p. 67.
99. *Ibid.*, pp. 81-82.
100. *Ixtlan*, p. 143.

tional.[101] When an untrained man faces the *nagual*, his *tonal* may die; *he* may die. The sorcerer must discipline his rational side not to collapse in the face of control by the irrational. Don Juan offers this crucial bit of instruction: "The goal of a warrior's training then is not to teach him to hex or to charm, but to prepare his *tonal* not to crap out. A most difficult accomplishment."[102] But apart from a man's entrance to this magical time, he cannot become a sorcerer. Sorcerers are beyond the limits of time.

Castaneda's description of his training is significant: "In my experience with don Juan I had noticed that in such states [of altered consciousness] one is incapable of keeping a consistent mental record of the passage of time. There had never been an enduring order, in matters of passage of time, in all the states of nonordinary reality I had experienced, and my conclusion was that if I kept myself alert a moment would come when I would lose my order of sequential time. As if, for example, I were looking at a mountain at a given moment, and then in my next moment of awareness I found myself looking at a valley in the opposite direction, but without remembering having turned around."[103] He very properly suspected hypnosis as the cause of his altered perceptions. But hypnosis really cannot explain anything. It is the deus ex machina used by scholars to avoid explanations.

Access to such magical timelessness inescapably involves *self-transcendence*. "Do you know that you can extend yourself forever in any of the directions I have pointed to?" asked don Juan. "Do you know that one moment can be eternity? This is not a riddle; it's a fact, but only if you mount that moment and use it to take the totality of yourself forever in any direction."[104] This, of course, is the *nagual's* time. It is, in the words of the title of Castaneda's second book, a separate reality. "For the *nagual* there is no land, or air, or water. . . . So the nagual glides, or flies, or does whatever it may do, in *nagual's* time, and that has nothing to do with *tonal's* time. The two things don't jibe."[105] The goal is the *abolition of time*. " 'There's no future!' he exclaimed cuttingly. 'The future is only a way of talking. For a sorcerer there is only the here and now.' "[106] Everything that

101. *Tales of Power*, p. 159.
102. *Ibid.*, p. 174.
103. *Ixtlan*, p. 239.
104. *Tales of Power*, p. 17.
105. *Ibid.*, p. 192.
106. *Ibid.*, p. 206.

points to time or history, including personal history, is to be ruthlessly abolished: "Don Juan explained that by the time a warrior had conquered 'dreaming' and 'seeing' and had developed a doubt, he must have also succeeded in erasing personal history, self-importance, and routines."[107]

Don Juan had told him early in his training that personal history must be dropped. Explaining his own past — a contradictory use of that which must be abolished — the old man had revealed: "One day I found out that personal history was no longer necessary for me and, like drinking, I dropped it."[108] Castaneda was told that it would be the same with him: "But there is no way to go back to Los Angeles. What you left there is lost forever. By then, of course, you will be a sorcerer, but that's no help; at a time like that what's important to all of us is the fact that everything we love or hate or wish for has been left behind. Yet the feelings in a man do not die or change, and the sorcerer starts on his way back home knowing that he will never reach it, knowing that no power on earth, not even his death, will deliver him to the place, the things, the people he loved."[109]

The sociological premise of sorcery is *radical atomism*. The sorcerer is cut off from all social institutions, all sense of history, all sense that one thing is any more important than another — except for the quest for power. With respect to the world and the flesh, it is possible to say: "Everything is equal and therefore unimportant."[110] But one had better not say this about the devil; the philosophy of pure relativism, or "controlled folly," does not apply to the agents of his satanic majesty: "My ally and Mescalito are not on a par with us human beings. My controlled folly applies only to myself and to the acts I perform while in the company of my fellow men."[111]

Primitivism and Timelessness

Over and over in primitive cultures, and now in contemporary occult groups, the abolition of time and the attainment of altered states of consciousness are seen as central operations. They are the fundamental goals of human action. Mircea Eliade, the comparative anthropologist, has placed this theme of timelessness at the center of

---

107. *Ibid.*, pp. 52-53.
108. *Ixtlan*, p. 11.
109. *Ibid.*, p. 265.
110. *Separate Reality*, p. 82.
111. *Ibid.*, p. 91.

his numerous brilliant studies of primitive religion. The shaman's quest for the "time before time"—the time of precreation and the creation of the world—is part of his training. Culturally and ritually, the abolition of time is symbolized in chaos festivals like Carnival, Mardi Gras, Macumba, and the ancient Saturnalia. The transcendence of time is to be achieved ritually by the temporary abolition of all standards of right and wrong. Ritual evil enables man to breathe new life into a dying world. Law is deadening; ritual violations of law are the source of new life.[112] It is *power from below*, as Rousas Rushdoony has called it.[113]

Primitive cultures have no concern with earthly time. The dream time is central. The future is now. Because of their lack of concern for the future, they are lower-class cultures. They do not place a high value on saving, economic growth, or progress. They are intensely present-oriented. This is true of the aborigines of Australia, some of whose magical beliefs are similar to don Juan's.[114] It is true of various African tribes. It is true of the culture that produced don Juan. The focus on timelessness requires the abolition of daily routines, normal perceptions, and law. It is the death of culture.

The West's Fading Shield of Rationalism

In this regard, perhaps the most important teaching of don Juan concerns Castaneda's rationalism. The culture of the West is still essentially rationalistic, both intellectually and as to routine. Industrial civilization could not function efficiently apart from the existence of clocks. This world of conventional routines is the barrier against the sorcerer's world of shadows and death. After experimenting with psychedelic plants, seeing visions of monsters, wrestling with the peyote god, and generally immersing himself in the world of the occult, Castaneda is warned by the old man that he is now totally vulnerable to the dark forces of the wilderness. "You have lost your shields," don Juan tells him. "What shields? What are you talking about?" replies Castaneda. The answer is straightforward:

---

112. Mircea Eliade, *Cosmos and History: The Myth of the Eternal Return* (1959); *The Sacred and the Profane: The Nature of Religion* (1961); *Myths, Dreams, and Mysteries* (1967); *Myth and Reality* (1963); *Rites and Symbols of Initiation: The Mysteries of Birth and Rebirth* (1958): all published by Harper Torchbooks. This is only a small sample of Eliade's voluminous output.

113. R. J. Rushdoony, "Power from Below," *Journal of Christian Reconstruction*, I (Winter, 1974).

114. Ronald Rose, *Primitive Psychic Power* (New York: Signet, [1956] 1965), p. 192.

Well, look around. People are busy doing that which people do. Those are their shields. Whenever a sorcerer has an encounter with any of those inexplicable and unbending forces we have talked about, his gap opens, making him more susceptible to his death than he ordinarily is; I've told you that we die through that gap, therefore if it is open one should have his will ready to fill it; that is, if one is a warrior. If one is not a warrior, like yourself, then one has no other recourse but to use the activities of daily life to take one's mind away from the fright of the encounter and thus to allow one's gap to close. . . . At this time in your life, however, you can no longer use those shields as effectively as an average man. You know too much about those forces and now you are finally at the brink of feeling and acting as a warrior. Your old shields are no longer safe.[115]

When danger approaches, Castaneda is told to write. Take notes, write, concentrate: here is his old rationalistic activity, and it is a very Western activity. His notebook will act as his shield. It is the only one he has left. His mind has been shattered by what he has seen, whether in visions or in the phenomenal world. He has left the world of Western rationalism, and he is in danger of destruction by real beings that wield tremendous power.

Western man is progressively losing his shields. Since 1965, loss of faith in traditional nineteenth-century philosophical mechanism has been obvious. People are steadily learning about the paranormal universe around them, even as Elisha's servant learned to see the angelic host around him (II Kings 6:16-18). An Associated Press story released in May 1974 is symptomatic; and the reaction of establishment scientists, clinging desperately to the world of simplistic nineteenth-century thinkers, is typical—and futile:

NEW YORK—The scientific elite were somewhat taken aback on being informed that amid all the modern technological advances, a new, national study shows people are believing more and more in the active reality of the devil.

When told of it, participants in a recent meeting in San Francisco of the American Assn. for the Advancement of Science "were absolutely shocked," says Clyde Nunn, a social researcher who reported the findings to them.

"It didn't fit their presuppositions," he adds. "It was mind-blowing for them."

He said the fact that Americans are increasingly convinced of the devil's existence runs counter to the scientific community's general assumption of

---

115. Castaneda, *Separate Reality*, pp. 216-17.

"progressively increasing rationalism as an automatic evolutionary process."

Most scientists "want to believe that society has become so rationalized that it has moved out of the nonrational world," he said. But he added that the newly gathered data reveal an opposite trend at work.

The new study, made by the Center for Policy Research here, found that in nine years the number of people believing in the certainty of the devil has risen from 37 to 48 per cent of the population, with another 20 per cent considering his existence probable.

ALTOGETHER 68 PER CENT is either sure about it or thinks it likely.

Nunn, the center's senior research associate, linked the upsurge in such belief to "times of great stress, when things seem to be falling apart, when there is great uncertainty in society and limited resources to cope with it.

"It's apparently an attempt to make sense of a world of ambiguities and to explain the evil in it," he said in an interview. He said it also made for an atmosphere vulnerable to demagogic promises to hunt out the devil's instruments.

It has the potentiality of "some new round of witch hunting," said Nunn, a University of Nebraska sociology professor before joining the center, which aims to search out trends so social policy can be shaped to deal with them.

The new study, involving a scientifically selected cross section of 3,546 people, was made last spring. Consequently, the results don't reflect the recent movie-stirred interest in demonology but derive from other conditions.

Nunn said the study, by using identically phrased questions as a parallel survey in 1964, provides the first comparative measurement of shifts in intensity of beliefs about the supernatural.

While the major change was the sharp 11 percent[116] upturn in those considering the devil's existence "completely true," the 68 per cent total either certain or partly so also rose by 3 per cent.

IN REGARD TO GOD, HOWEVER, absolute certainty about His existence dropped 8 per cent, from 77 to 69 per cent, although another 25 per cent believed in God with some reservations.

Only 6 per cent registered no belief, but the disbelief was 3 per cent higher than before.

"Whatever advantage God has had over the devil in the polls of the past, the devil now appears to be getting his due," said Nunn, a Kentuckian who has a master's degree in religion from the Southern Baptist Theological Seminary in Louisville and a doctorate in sociology from the University of North Carolina.

---

116. This is incorrect. The increase was 11 *percentage points*, from 37% to 48%. This is a remarkable 30% increase: 11 divided by 37 equals .30, or 30%.

He said the rising certainty of the devil's activity — along with the slight drop in certainty about God — suggests people have difficulty seeing any good purpose or reason in events and consider the balance of "good versus evil to be tipped in the direction of evil."

The study also brought out that those convinced of the devil's reality are much more likely than others to feel that threatening forces are at work in modern life, and that things are likely to get worse.

Faith in God is slipping, but faith in demons is increasing. We are back to Screwtape's letter to Wormwood: the materialists are beginning to believe in demons but not in God. This is the very heart of the demonic cause. The culture that indulges itself in demonic experimentation faces the loss of its shields.

Power Religion and Dominion Religion

Again and again in my writings, I return to this theme. The essence of biblical religion is ethics. The ethical self-government of the redeemed man is the foundation of society. God's law, not the autonomous laws of the universe, or the mind of man, or the dreams of men, is the basis of all order, including social order.[117] It is from ethics that we proceed to dominion.

This world view is future-oriented and confident. It sees man's primary struggles as ethical, not metaphysical. We struggle against powerful forces, but we use biblical law as our guide, and call upon God's Holy Spirit to enable us to apply that law successfully in our lives and institutions. Progress is ethical, intellectual, and also cultural and external. Progress is real, but it is necessarily progress in terms of a permanent standard: biblical law.[118] Self-discipline is of greater importance than precise ritual.

The world of the sorcerer is the mirror image of the dominion religion's conception of God's world. It is a world inhabited by powers. These powers battle against man in terms of ritual; any ritual error on man's part, or any flinching, leads to disaster. Men try to harness these powers: by ritual, by subservience, or by calling even stronger powers against them. Ethics is irrelevant.

If all is power, then the most powerful gets to impose his concept

---

117. R. J. Rushdoony, *The Foundations Of Social Order: Studies in the Creeds and Councils of the Early Church* (Fairfax, Virginia: Thoburn Press, [1969] 1978).

118. Greg L. Bahnsen, *By This Standard: The Authority of God's Law Today* (Tyler, Texas: Institute for Christian Economics, 1985).

of the world over the weaker. Temporarily, one view may prevail. But this view can be defeated by yet more powerful forces. Nothing is stable; nothing is perpetual. This is why each man is ultimately autonomous if he is a "warrior." He makes his own reality.

This view destroys the division of labor. Men cannot cooperate successfully. It is no accident that don Juan was a kind of hermit, that he had no contact with Yaqui institutions. He was a witch, and a witch takes this view of power very seriously. He cannot cooperate, except as an initiator initiates a successor. He must remain almost invisible. As Castaneda told the interviewer, "To weasel in and out of different worlds you have to remain inconspicuous."[119] (This is especially true if you are a 50-year-old man who is selling millions of books to people under 30 who think you are one of them.)

The essence of his initiation was deception. Don Juan lied to him, misinformed him, frightened him, blew his mind with dope, and generally manipulated him. The world of a sorcerer is a world of continual flux, especially flux with respect to everything one says. In short, it is a world of shadows and lies, yet always close to a very real world of intensely powerful beings who hate man, and who serve him only to trap him later on. Man is promised to be able to transcend the limits of ordinary mortals with their ordinary reality. The result is backwardness, hermit-like existence, meaninglessness, and impotence. The true power which is made available to man through social cooperation is renounced in favor of the warrior's autonomous existence. Let us not be deceived: don Juan was a poverty-stricken drifter—without community, without nation, without friends, and without a fortune in book royalties. Castaneda got those, for he was still a Western man.

Conclusion

What are we to make of Castaneda's books? Are they works of fiction? One reviewer concluded that whether or not these events took place is irrelevant: "What difference does it make whether one *believes* in astrology or I Ching or sorcery? As though a vote in some cosmic ballot is going to establish its truth or utility. The real issue is what it says, whether the disturbance it causes in the normal ways of knowing will lead to more imaginative ways."[120] No doubt about it: our shields are down. If don Juan is correct, it makes all the differ-

---

119. *Seeing Castaneda*, p. 86.
120. *Los Angeles Times* (June 8, 1975).

ence in the world whether people believe in astrology or sorcery. It made all the difference to Castaneda's training and his safety during that training. The question concerning the actual historicity of don Juan may not be crucial; what is crucial is whether the universe conveyed in the writings of Castaneda is true or not.

If these are works of pure fiction, totally unrelated to any concrete historical individuals named don Juan and don Genaro, then Castaneda is one of the great writers of fiction in our era. But if he is a writer of fiction, he is also a master of folklore — the greatest that UCLA has ever produced. His reconstruction of the sorcerer's image of this world is striking in its power and its correlation with what we know of other primitive beliefs. As we might paraphrase that old slogan, if don Juan did not exist, it has certainly been useful to invent him. The teachings of don Juan ring true. The reader has entered the mental universe of a primitive sorcerer. What we have found is a remarkably modern thinker.

Did Castaneda really experience these events? I think he did. Were these events historical events, that is, events that could have been photographed or recorded on tape (neither medium was permitted Castaneda in his research)? Some, but not all. He suspected hypnosis.[121] Furthermore, after having experienced a particular nonordinary experience, the disappearance and reappearance of his car, he was told by don Juan that don Genaro had not really moved his car from "the world of ordinary men," but that he had "simply forced you to look at the world as sorcerers do, and your car was not in that world. Genaro wanted to soften your certainty."[122] The *nagual's* time is not the *tonal's* time.

This is not to say that such events were absolutely impossible. If Satan could transport himself and Christ to the top of the temple, then the Christian who takes the Bible seriously cannot safely say that teleportation by occult means is categorically impossible. But the ability of men to distinguish fact from fiction is limited. The apostle Peter, upon his miraculous release from prison, was convinced that what was happening to him was in fact some sort of vision. Only when he was outside the city's gate was he sure that an historical event had taken place (Acts 12:9-11). The apostle Paul's description of one man's heavenly vision (no doubt his own) is open to this same confusion: he did not know whether he was in the body or

---

121. Castaneda, *Ixtlan*, p. 239.
122. *Ibid.*, p. 155.

out of it (II Corinthians 12:2). Don Juan admitted that Castaneda's body was in the bushes during his first experiments with astral projection.[123] Nevertheless, the reality of the vision may have been historically important. Did he have the ability in his trance to witness, that is, divine, real historical events at a distance? The old man thought so, Castaneda thinks so, and accounts of other people's out-of-body experiences indicate that on occasion such visions do correspond to actual events at a distance.

Primitive fire-walkers really do walk across coals that are measurably hot. They can be photographed performing this feat. It cannot be explained alone by hypnotism. It cannot be explained at all by the accepted canons of modern science. Sometimes these events are real. Yet sometimes they are not. Ronald Rose, an anthropologist interested in the kinds of psychic abilities studied by J. B. Rhine, spent many months with several tribes of aborigines. One of the stories told to him concerned the belief that magicians had the ability to produce "clever ropes"—long, slimy cords—out of their mouths. Natives insisted that they had seen these sorcerers climb up these ropes into the air. Rose was given a demonstration. The native lay down on his back, reached into his mouth, and then pulled his hand out as if he were pulling something. "Did you see the cord?" he asked. One of the other natives insisted that he had. But Rose saw nothing. When he told the magician that he had not seen it, he was assured that he would see it the next time. The motions were repeated, but this time he drew out a thin line of saliva. The other native saw it as a cord; Rose saw nothing. He believes that the other native was reporting honestly what he thought he saw. Explanation: hypnosis.[124] Of course, there is always the problem of who was being hypnotized. Presumably, Rose's observations were correct. Presumably. Western men presume a great deal, given their epistemological relativism.

Don Juan offers us a philosophy conforming to many of the most cherished tenets of the modern world: power, relativism, anti-rationalism, existentialism, higher consciousness, self-transcendence, autonomy. As an interpreter, Castaneda has struck a responsive chord in the hearts of hundreds of thousands of readers. Most everyone likes a good ghost story, and Castaneda throws in enough philosophical justification to convince his readers and reviewers that these

123. *Teachings*, p. 129.
124. Rose, *Primitive Psychic Power*, pp. 101-2.

tales of power have redeeming social value. He offers the world of
the sorcerer as a legitimate alternative to the doubt-filled culture of
the modern world.

The world of the sorcerer and the world of the self-proclaimed
autonomous scientist are not that far apart. Miss Yates, concluding
her fine study of Renaissance magic, remarks on the nature of the
differences between these two universes: "The basic difference between the attitude of the magician to the world and the attitude of
the scientist to the world is that the former wants to draw the world
into himself, whilst the scientist does just the opposite, he external-
ises and impersonalises the world by a movement of will in an entirely opposite direction. . . ."[125]

Don Juan, like his Renaissance cousins, provides Castaneda
with the training necessary to internalize the world so thoroughly
that Castaneda is no longer able to distinguish between his perceptions of the external world and the distortions of his pseudo-trans-
cended mind. But, then again, the self-professed autonomous scientist
can be no more confident of his own observations, given the relativism
of his own epistemological presuppositions. Castaneda, followng don
Juan, is simply more willing to follow the call of the voices and visions of the *nagual*.

The book on Castaneda, *Seeing Castaneda*, reprints many reviews
and opinions concerning Castaneda. He is interpreted as a Buddhist, a mystic, a guru, a gifted novelist, a serious anthropologist, a
poet, a fraud, a psychologist, a scholar of remarkable vision, and,
most eloquently, a pimp (don Juan's evaluation of him in his pre-
initiated phase — a gatherer of ideas and stories for others to enjoy).
One possibility eluded the reviewers, namely, that Carlos Castaneda
is exactly what he says he is in seven volumes: a witch, or a *brujo*,
who received initiation from an older sorcerer who possessed power
through his connection to the devil or demons. Castaneda himself
told an interviewer: "If you read the history of the Spanish conquest
of Mexico, you will find that the Catholic inquisitors tried to stamp
out sorcery because they considered it the work of the devil."[126] What
no reviewer even so much as mentions is the possibility that the
Catholic inquisitors were quite correct in their analysis. What is not
understood is that Castaneda, the victim of psychotropic drugs,

---

125. Frances Yates, *Giordano Bruno and the Hermetic Tradition* (New York: Vintage,
[1964] 1969), p. 454.

126. *Seeing Castaneda*, p. 78.

brainwashing, hypnosis, primitive occult initiation, and an old man's unique charm, has become exactly what he says he is. The commentators do not recognize that he opened a once-forbidden and hostile world to hundreds of thousands of avid readers. The reviewers believe in neither God nor the devil. Castaneda and don Juan have abandoned half the skepticism of the moderns, and in doing so, they have helped to widen the crack in Western rationalism's shield.

5

PSYCHICS

If there arise among you a prophet, or a dreamer of dreams, and giveth thee a sign or a wonder, And the sign or the wonder come to pass, whereof he spake unto thee, saying, Let us go after other gods, which thou hast not known, and let us serve them; Thou shalt not hearken unto the words of that prophet, or that dreamer of dreams: for the LORD your God proveth you, to know whether ye love the LORD your God with all your heart and with all your soul.

Deuteronomy 13:1-3

I have argued elsewhere that the crucial doctrines that undergird any culture are the doctrines of God, man, and law.[1] Almost equally important is the doctrine of time. The two rival views of time are cyclical time and linear time. Western Civilization since the days of the Christianization of the Roman Empire has been based on linear time.

In its biblical version, linear time allowed for the possibility that God-blessed prophets and demon-influenced false prophets would possess the ability to foresee the future. Foretelling the future was understood as a supernatural gift, that is, a gift not normally given to most people. It was seen as a unique ability, but it was not seen as impossible. Tests of the bearers of this gift were established in the Old Testament. The tests were practical (does the prophecy come true?) and theological (in the name of which god does the prophet come?).

The secularization of Western culture during and after the seventeenth century modified the acceptable view of linear time. (So had medieval scholasticism, for that matter.) Time was seen as inflexibly bounded by the present. There is no way for anyone to predict future events, except as extensions of present events and forces, in-

---

1. Gary North, *Unconditional Surrender: God's Program for Victory* (2nd ed.; Tyler, Texas: Geneva Divinity School Press, 1983), Pt. I.

164

cluding social and historical laws. Especially after Darwin, the scientific mind has become religiously anti-teleological. The future in no way can influence the present, except as a vision which motivates men to action. The entire body of modern science rests on this presupposition. Any break in this universal law — that the future cannot be known except as an extension of present forces — threatens the foundation of modern science, and therefore threatens atheistic secular humanism.

It is understandable that the claim of anyone to be able to forecast specific future events that are not the product of measurable social forces — "random" events — must be rejected by modern science. Any aspect of the realm of "paranormal science" will be believed by large numbers of conventional scientists before psychic forecasting will be believed. This supernatural skill, above all others, will be ridiculed and denied. The Heisenberg principle of indeterminacy may somehow offer modern science an epistemological escape hatch from odd events and odder human abilities, but it offers no rational hope for explaining the ability of some people to see the future.

Thus, the psychic is the last hurdle in the traditional humanist's race. If he trips on this one, he loses the race. When humanists begin to believe in the ability of psychics to forecast specific future events, the hole in the dike will have grown to dam-busting proportions.

In the mid-1960's, some humanists began to believe in psychic forecasts.

David Hoy

David Hoy is a psychic. Given his publicly demonstrated abilities, he is *the* psychic — the most baffling mind-reader, prognosticator, and diviner practicing his talents anywhere in the world today. He performs without any mysterious atmosphere, esoteric wisdom, Eastern philosophy, vibrations, or anything else. His special gift, if one could call it a gift, is instant revelation. Not revelation about God or the universe, but revelation concerning the more mundane affairs of life, such as where someone has lost her false teeth. As *Newsweek* reported: "It was phone-in time on radio station KCMO in Kansas City. 'Mr. Hoy,' lisped a woman caller, 'my false teeth are missing. Can you figure out where they are?' David Hoy, KCMO's guest expert in extrasensory perception, needed only a few seconds to decipher what he calls his 'ESP flash.' 'Your dog got them and put them under the stove,' he confidently informed her. 'Would you go check and see?' She did and found her bridge where Hoy said it was."[2]

Incredible? Routine for Hoy and for several other practitioners of radio ESP. Hoy is the one who first developed the call-in ESP format, and it is Hoy who best typifies the fully modern, no-nonsense entertainer on the ESP circuit. Several nights a week, he goes on live radio and takes phone calls from listeners. There are no restrictions on the kinds of questions asked: lost objects, missing persons, job opportunities, future events, identifying thieves, solving family squabbles, and almost anything else that curious callers can devise to thwart and/or tap his proclaimed powers. He claims that his answers are correct about 80% of the time, which is the top limit ever claimed by serious psychics. Over thirty stations carried his broadcasts in 1974. An example of his skills is provided by John Godwin, author of a book on Hoy:

In some instances David himself isn't sure of the meaning of his perceptions, though the other party catches them instantly. In November, 1972, a Cincinnati man called KMOX and wanted to know who had broken into his tool shed and made off with his new lawnmower.

"Hm," David mused, "all I see is a battered Volkswagen, painted with psychedelic designs and flowers. Does that make any sense to you?"

"It sure does," said the man grimly. "Thank you."

David learned the full story from a letter he received two weeks later. The psychedelic VW belonged to the man's teen-age nephew, a full-fledged juvenile delinquent. He had gone over to the boy's home and although he didn't find his lawnmower there, he discovered several other items from his tool shed. The young man finally confessed that he had sold the mower the same day he stole it.[3]

Reporters who have investigated Hoy's powers have been aided by the existence of tapes of the radio shows, as well as a large collection of letters to Hoy from those who have been given information through the radio broadcasts or through written contact with Hoy. (In 1974, he received about 10,000 letters each month.) Thousands of replies, each date-stamped and marked with the address of the sender, are in his files. There are no doubt many people who are skeptical about Hoy's claims, but thousands of people have acknowl-

---

2. *Newsweek* (April 8, 1974), p. 61.

3. John Godwin, *Super-Psychic: The Incredible Dr. Hoy* (New York: Pocket Books, 1974), p. 109.

edged that his ESP revelations on highly specific subjects have been remarkably accurate.

As for the telephone calls, there is almost no way that they could be faked. For one thing, radio stations are not eager to be involved in any broadcasting fraud analogous to those which rocked the television networks in the mid-1950's. Professional broadcasters do not want to find themselves stuck with another Charles Van Doren with inside information to specially prepared questions. The stations have to take precautions with men like Hoy. Technologically, there is little possibility that Hoy could be using plants in his telephone audience. (By plants, I mean people, not plants.) The telephone lines jam up whenever he goes on the air. The law of large numbers — so dear to the hearts of scientific investigators — takes over, keeping any given phone call purely random. A letter in his files from Northwest Bell Telephone informed him that on August 10, 1973, some 100,000 phone calls came into the station in a half-hour period. The telephone company contacted the station and asked that Hoy limit calls each night to phones whose numbers ended in a specific digit, and he complied with the request. The letter ends: "Although the increasing popularity of the show may necessitate stronger measures in the future, it appears that the control procedures were instituted just in time." (Letter dated August 17, 1973.)[4]

Hoy's ability to predict the future is uncanny. He avoids the typically vague prophecies of the fortune cookie variety. His most famous documented example was given on radio station KDKA of Pittsburgh (the nation's oldest commercial station) on Halloween night of 1967. "Within sixty days a bridge spanning the Ohio River will collapse with tremendous loss of life. It will be brought out, after the collapse, that eighteen months before, a heavily laden barge going upriver had hit a major pylon of the bridge, backed up, and gone on without reporting the accident." On December 15, thirty-seven days later, the Silver Bridge — linking West Virginia and Ohio south of Pittsburgh — collapsed during the peak hours of the Christmas shopping rush. A dozen people died. A subsequent investigation revealed that the cause of the disaster had been an unreported ramming of the bridge supports by a barge proceeding upriver.[5]

(A note of caution is in order at this point. With respect to this particular prophecy, there was nothing exceptional about Hoy's pre-

---

4. *Ibid.*, p. 106.
5. *Ibid.*, p. 21.

diction—exceptional in the realm of occultism. For months before the collapse of the Silver Bridge, the occult world, including the "flying saucer contactee" world, had been filled with the prophecy of this event. This was especially true in occult groups nearby the bridge. There were also a great number of "flying saucer" sightings in the area.)[6]

David Hoy was born into a Southern Baptist household, attended Bob Jones University, the independent fundamentalist school in South Carolina. (One of Hoy's former classmates informs me that Hoy always requested housing in "Graves" dormitory hall—an odd request, even sinister, given the nature of his subsequent career.) He later graduated from Southern Seminary in Louisville. He then became a missionary to Brazil. From his days at Bob Jones, he had occasionally received flashes of precognition. He had predicted his father's death on the morning that he died, hundreds of miles away (March 10, 1952). Later, when he was working at Calvary Baptist Church in New York, he met a young pianist who was then studying at Juliard School of Music, Van Cliburn. Cliburn was deeply into the occult: astrology, numerology, and the tarot. He tried to interest Hoy in such matters, but Hoy responded negatively. Hoy was convinced that spiritualist phenomena were just that: phenomena. It was all gadgetry and dexterity, mixed in with a lot of mumbo-jumbo and showmanship, he believed. He himself was quite skilled at "magic"—prestidigitation—which he had learned from his Baptist minister father.

Yet he was curious about psychic and similar phenomena, and his interest continued through seminary. He continued to receive precognitions—so often, in fact, that the seminary's authorities had to forbid any further prophecies, since the local newspaper was reporting that a local seminarian had been predicting local events. He agreed to cease.

During his time on the mission field in Brazil, he attended a Voodoo ceremony out of curiosity. He kept returning to the all-night sessions of dancing, rhythms, and ecstatic outpourings. He was fascinated by the fact that glowing coals could be placed on the bodies of ecstatic worshippers, leaving no scars and producing no pain. He saw the priestess pick up a scorpion with her mouth without being stung; he watched her tell the color of a cloth placed in her hand

---

6. John Keel, *UFOs: Operation Trojan Horse* (New York: Putnam's, 1970), pp. 276-78.

while she was bandaged around the eyes. Once, she even hexed him mildly. She asked him to hold out his hand, fingers stiff and spread apart, and when she opened her own hand and touched his, palm to palm, he was subsequently unable to close his fist. His fingers were frozen. Finally, she touched his hand again, and his muscles relaxed. On one occasion, he explained to her that he was a Christian missionary, and she replied: "You no belong to them. You belong to us."[7] She turned out to be a prophet; not long thereafter, Hoy left the ministry. He returned to the stage as a "magician." The flashes of information continued. He would devise elaborate acts of "mind-reading," only to find that on occasion he did not actually need the signals of the accomplice in the audience. Pick a word, he would tell a companion. He could tell him the word. He wrote a book, published by Doubleday in 1965, *Psychic and Other ESP Party Games*, in which he encouraged his readers to develop their latent psychic skills. Yet this was prior to his own remarkable development as a psychic. The flashes of information kept coming. In 1967, he predicted that President Johnson would not run again the following year, and this prophecy was confirmed by a Louisville *Courier-Journal* reporter. He predicted in 1966 that Jackie Kennedy would marry a Greek shipping magnate. Time and again, his prophecies came true.

Hoy began to tour college campuses with a serious ESP act in 1966. This was the period of the beginning of the great epistemological earthquake which opened the door to every kind of new idea in university and college atmospheres. Naturally, college administrations and self-conscious department chairmen fought against Hoy's appearances, but students welcomed him. The accepted truths of the Establishment, as certified by Harvard, Princeton, Yale, and Berkeley faculty members (tenured), were being thrown out in every department by the students, as the hostility to the war in Vietnam—itself a product of messianic Liberalism—overflowed into every area of Liberal domination on the campus, which meant, basically, everything outside of the department of engineering. The students of 1965-70 were like the Athenians of St. Paul's day, spending their time "in nothing else, but either to tell, or to hear some new thing" (Acts 17:21b). Hoy marched into the campuses of America, predicting the outcome of forthcoming athletic events, finding lost books, pointing out the dormitory thieves (not by name, but by the location of the

---

7. *Super-Psychic*, p. 35.

stolen goods, which would sometimes be in a particular student's locker), reading minds, and generally disrupting every established theory of what the human mind is capable of accomplishing. The students loved it.

Knowledge is power. People generally seek knowledge, especially technical knowledge, in order to gain control. Hoy acknowledges that his type of mental power works two ways. He claims that he can control the thoughts and actions of others. He worries about this, he says, which is understandable, since it is his contention (as it is with most professional psychics) that everyone has latent psychic abilities, and that it just takes time and practice to bring these powers into action. Author Godwin wanted a demonstration. Hoy gave him a good one. Hoy asked him to go into the next room and bring him a vase of flowers.

We were sitting in the downstairs living room of the Hoy home in Paducah. The adjoining room was the dining room, which lay in darkness. I opened the door and walked in. The room was almost pitch black. I groped my way to the table, banging my shin against a chair en route. I felt over the table top until I touched the vase, nearly knocking it over. Then I picked it up and brought it back.

I handed David the vase and rubbed my sore shin. "Now what?" I asked.

In answer he handed me a slip of paper. On it was written: "You will not switch on the light in the dining room."

I spent the next hour or so trying to figure out why I hadn't switched on the light. I knew where the switch was, and by all the rules of logic and common sense my first action should have been to turn it on. Yet I didn't. The thought never occurred to me.[8]

It is possible, of course, that Hoy had noticed that he did not switch on the light and hastily scribbled down the note before Godwin returned. But why would he have selected this particular experiment? How many possible combinations of activities by Godwin would have allowed Hoy to single out one of them — clearly peculiar — to scribble down? Godwin was convinced.

Mind over mind: we come to one of the central impulses in all systems of magic, witchcraft, and occultism. The desire to take control over another's will is a dominant theme of all forms of messianic humanism. In other words, "scientific" humanists and liberals share

8. *Ibid.*, p. 115.

with occultists a similar presupposition regarding the legitimacy of techniques of manipulation. The psychologist's use of brain implants on animals, or drugs to control their actions, is not very far removed from the occultist's use of drugs for purposes of mind control — or the hippie's. The same is true of biofeedback machines: same technology, different "laboratories." This "brave new world of the mind" was enthusiastically popularized in the early 1970's by Maya Pines' book, *The Brain Changers: Scientists and the New Mind Control*.[9] Equally messianic are: the hypnotist's use of a totally unknown force to bring out secrets or control the personality; the brainwashing techniques of the Communists; the psychodrama techniques of Jacob L. Moreno; and sensitivity training techniques of therapists and social revolutionaries. All are part of the same basic motivation, namely, *to be as God*. Men wish to invade the personality centers of their fellows, taking away the power and responsibility of someone else's actions.

There is a lot of hypocrisy in modern liberalism. The same reformers who castigate the use of Madison Avenue advertising techniques to sell laundry products are delighted to hire these same firms for political campaigns or for moving a recalcitrant and "reactionary" public along "progressive" paths. Religious revivals are terrible, they believe, because people are manipulated by exploiting preachers; Esalen is wonderful, because it breaks down stultifying personality barriers to total intimacy. Criticism or praise from secular humanists too often depends on whose ox is getting gored.

Hoy admits that his techniques of mind over mind can be used commercially. In fact, he made a lot of money by applying his techniques to a specific product line of men's hairdressing, Roffler products. He designed a kind of "power of positive thinking" training course for salesmen — in this case, barbers — in which they would direct their thoughts to the customer. "This product will make you look terrific. This product will increase your self-confidence." The barber was to visualize the product in relation to the customer. The company used Hoy's 21-page typewritten course for six months with its 4500 barbers. By the end of the period, sales were up seventy percent.[10]

Those familiar with the so-called science of mind movement will recognize the origins of Hoy's techniques. It is fundamentally a religious response to the world. Bryan R. Wilson, an Oxford sociologist specializing in comparative religion, has argued that there are eight

---

9. New York: Harcourt Brace Jovanovich, 1973.
10. *Super-Psychic*, p. 101.

basic types of supernaturalist responses to the world: one type accepts things as they are (orthodoxy, in his terminology), and the
other seven are concerned with changing the world. His catalogue:
conversionist, revolutionist, introversionist, manipulationist, thaumaturgical, reformist, and reconstructionist.[11] (As reasonably
close-fitting examples of each, we could list: fundamentalist, Marxist, Mennonite, science of mind, primitive magic, social gospel, and
Puritan.) Hoy is obviously a manipulationist.

Hoy's approach is very much like the approach of "Rev. Ike," the
former fundamentalist black preacher who by 1975 had become a
science of mind, "God-is-within-you" proponent. He worked the manipulationist psychology (or metapsychology) into the language of
the ghetto. He drove a $90,000 pink Rolls-Royce in 1975, and en-
couraged his followers to do the same. His philosophy is straightforward: "We are not interested in Pie in the Sky bye and bye. We want
our pie now, with ice cream on it, and a cherry on top."[12] Anyone
who has ever seen Rev. Ike on television will instantly recognize
Hoy's technique, outlined in Lesson Four of Hoy's Roffler products
training manual: the hair stylist (read: expensive barber) is supposed
to *feel* the prediction of increased sales . . . the touch of crisp new
dollar bills in his hands . . . the motion of the new car he will be
driving . . . his sense of personal greatness. Napoleon Hill's *Think
and Grow Rich* is a similar handbook; so are the writings of the multimillionaire insurance entrepreneur, W. Clement Stone.

The difference between David Hoy and the other manipulation-
ists is that he frankly acknowledges that the name of this game is
mind over mind. He does not appeal to gods within us; he does not
use the jargon of the psychologist; he does not propose this system of
salesmanship as a program of self-transcendence. He simply says
that with sufficient concentration, the person who has developed
these powers can get other people to do what he wants them to do.
Hoy realizes the danger of sinister men who would make use of these
techniques, but he is convinced that these powers are in everyone
anyway, and sooner or later the word will get out.

Remember that bit of historical paradox that was repeated everywhere in 1964: Lincoln was elected in 1860; Kennedy was elected in

---

11. Bryan R. Wilson, *Magic and the Millennium* (London: Hineman, 1971), pp.
21-26.

12. William C. Martin, "This Man Says He's the Divine Sweetheart of the
Universe," *Esquire* (June 1974).

1960 — both had seven letters in their last names — both were slain on Friday, in the presence of their wives, etc? That, according to Hoy, was Hoy's gift to the American Historical Association. The world is filled with paradoxes, coincidences, and mysterious, unexplainable forces. There is free will, Hoy says, but there is also *destiny*. Or, as Godwin titles the chapter, there is "The Finger of Fate."

For those who do not recognize this philosophy, it is the same interpretation of the world which dominated the Roman Empire and which led to its collapse. Prof. Charles Cochrane, in his crucially important book, *Christianity and Classical Culture* (1940), writes: "The acceptance of such beliefs involved a picture of nature in terms either of sheer fortuity or (alternatively) of inexorable fate. By so doing, it helped to provoke an increasingly frantic passion for some means of escape. This passion was to find expression in various types of supernaturalism, in which East and West joined hands to produce the most grotesque cosmologies as a basis for ethical systems not less grotesque."[13] Gnosticism was the most characteristic form of this philosophical crisis — the crisis of total impersonal chance vs. total impersonal fate (destiny). The breakdown of classical philosophy undermined classical culture, leaving the field to Christianity, which proposed a wholly new cosmology, namely *cosmic personalism*, in which all things come to pass because a creator God has a universal plan of history. It was the philosophy of Augustine, argues Cochrane, which provided a concept of personalistic history that could undergird a new civilization.

David Hoy is very mod, both in terms of his dress and his language. He does not attempt to build an overarching theoretical structure to explain or justify his abilities. He can cover the field with the letters "ESP," and everyone is happy. But the fact of the matter is that Hoy does have a philosophy, however vague it may appear. It is that same philosophy which brought forth the flourishing of magic and occultism at the end of the Roman Empire. A world of blind destiny must be mastered, thereby making it conform to man's goals, man's dreams, and man's nightmares. It is man who rules this universe of cosmic impersonalism. It is man's mind that is the capstone — not the narrow definition of mind given to us by eighteenth-century or nineteenth-century rationalists, but man's mind, the

---

13. Charles N. Cochrane, *Christianity and Classical Culture: A Study in Thought and Action from Augustus to Augustine* (2nd ed.; New York: Oxford University Press, [1944] 1957), p. 159.

master of the cosmos. The mysterious *synchronicities* (to use Carl Jung's term) of the universe serve as avenues for man's mysterious sovereignty over the universe (including over other men). The powers of occultism need not be accompanied by tappings, philosophies of reincarnation, or creeping ectoplasm. Twentieth-century humanism serves occultism quite well.

Gerard Croiset

On January 6, 1957, a Dutch psychic, Gerard Croiset, met with W. H. C. Tenhaeff, a professor of parapsychology at the University of Utrecht, along with biologist L. H. Bretschneider and physicist J. A. Smit. Croiset was handed a seating plan for a meeting to be held 25 days later. The room to be used for the meeting would contain 36 chairs. The guest list had already been made up. Croiset was asked to select a chair. He chose chair #9. He was then asked to describe the person who would sit there. He spoke into a tape recorder and gave a dozen specific facts about the person, plus some additional material relating to four of the twelve general features. Some of the facts included were as follows:

1. She would be a middle-aged woman. She is interested in child care.
2. Between 1928-30, she was around a circus in the town of Schevenigen.
3. As a child, she lived in a cheese-making district.
4. There was a fire on a farm in her childhood.
5. Three boys came to mind. One is working in British territory.
6. She has been looking at a picture of a maharajah.

After the recording was finished, this session ended. On Feb. 1, two packs of cards, numbered 1-30, were selected by the experimenters (but not Croiset). As the meeting was about to begin, both sealed packs were opened independently. One set was used to place a card on each chair; the other was distributed on a random basis to the guests who were in another room. The guests went in and sat down in chairs bearing the number corresponding to their cards. They were instructed not to touch any other chair. Once seated, they awaited Croiset, who entered a few minutes later. The tape was played back to the audience. The lady seated in chair #9 admitted that several of Croiset's observations did apply to her.

1. She was 42 and interested in child care.
2. Her father used to take her to the circus in Schevenigen.
3. She had visited farms; butter was the main product (not a solid hit).
4. She had been looking at a photo of an Indian yogi a few days earlier.

Another direct hit concerned her interest in opera, specifically the opera *Falstaff*. Croiset had felt strongly that this particular opera was the first one she had ever seen. She admitted that it had been the first one. She had fallen in love with the tenor. Furthermore, Croiset had predicted that on Feb. 1, the lady would take her daughter to the dentist. The lady admitted that she had taken her daughter to the dentist that afternoon.[14]

Once again Croiset had performed his now-famous chair test, an experiment that has been repeated in many countries under many different conditions. Again and again, his predictions have come true with startling accuracy. Like many psychics (or paragnosts, as Prof. Tenhaeff prefers to call them), Croiset hates the ESP card experiments. But the chair test contains many of the same elements of randomness that the Zener card experiments contain, and the results are far more impressive to anyone who is not a total captive of the methodology of authoritative randomness. Sometimes the chair is selected by that ultimate of randomness, a geiger counter. Other times, the biblically traditional method of choice by lot is used. Sometimes Croiset receives no impressions whatsoever; on those occasions, the chair winds up empty. He can see the individual's past and sometimes the future. Prior to a test before a group of intellectuals in Hilversum in October of 1953, Croiset informed Prof. Tenhaeff: "The person who will sit in that chair was away for a few weeks in another country. I see him walking in a large city. His shoelaces are loose. He leans forward to tie them. As he does so, I see a gentleman walking behind him who bumps into him." A direct hit. The person seated in the chair said that he had been visiting London, and this very incident had occurred.[15]

---

14. Jackson Harrison Pollack, *Croiset the Clairvoyant* (London: Quality Book Club, 1965), pp. 47-52.

15. *Ibid.*, p. 165.

Croiset is perhaps the most famous psychic in Western Europe. Television specials have been made about him. One was shown in the United States in the mid-1960's. (I remember watching it.) Most Hollanders seem to have heard about him. He performs services for detectives in solving crimes, especially crimes involving missing children. Less well known is the fact that he performs psychic healings for a fee.[16] He is a gifted *psychometrist*, i.e., he works with objects that belong or did belong to an individual about whom he is giving the reading. (That other famous Dutch psychic, Peter Hurkos, is also a psychometrist.) He says that he "sees" pictures associated with the owner of the object — sometimes incredibly detailed pictures.

In April of 1963, a young boy, Wimpji Slee, disappeared. The boy's uncle contacted Croiset. Croiset told him that the boy had drowned in a particular canal. Dragging the canal for the body proved useless, however. Four days later, the body was found floating in the canal at precisely the spot designated by Croiset.[17]

A similar case had taken place in May of 1960. Another young boy, Toontje Thooner, had been missing for several days when a local resident contacted Croiset. Prof. Tenhaeff happened to be with Croiset at the time, and he switched on the tape recorder (which he begs Croiset to use in every case, but which Croiset uses only sporadically), recording the conversation on Croiset's end of the phone. Croiset's biographer reports on the contents of that tape:

Is the playground where the child was last seen in a new suburb? [*Yes.*] When you leave it at the left, is there some open ground? [*Yes.*] When you follow the border of this open ground, do you reach a canal? [*Yes.*] Is this canal 200 to 500 metres from the playground? [*Yes.*] Croiset paused, and then inquired, "Are you a member of the child's family?"

"No. I'm a neighbour," was the reply.

"Well," sighed the sensitive, "I can then tell you that the outlook isn't good. In about three days, the child's body will be found in the canal I mentioned, close to a bridge and near a bucket of zinc."

Three days later I checked up. Unhappily enough, the police of Eindhoven had just found the child's body next to one of the piers of the bridge over the canal near a bucket of zinc. . . .[18]

---

16. Norma Lee Browning, *The Psychic World of Peter Hurkos* (Garden City, New York: Doubleday, 1970), pp. 190-91.

17. Pollack, *Croiset*, p. 99.

18. *Ibid.*, p. 36.

These are documented cases. Dutch police departments have used Croiset and other psychics working with Prof. Tenhaeff on many difficult cases. Police officials are seldom willing to resort to such aid unless they regard it as absolutely indispensable, since psychic methods of detection are hardly what fellow law enforcement agents would call professional. This may not be the kind of evidence which impresses scientific investigators of the paranormal, but generally scientists are so hostile to such phenomena that they are willing only to accept negative findings. Police departments do not continue to use potentially embarrassing assistants in order to produce negative findings.

What is the source of Croiset's abilities? He claims that they are gifts from God. But there is a curious side to these abilities. They come upon him while he is in a state of altered consciousness — "lowered consciousness," as his biographer puts it. He obtains visual images of the person or event. With other psychics, this state of altered consciousness may resemble a trance; with Croiset, it is barely noticeable by an outsider.[19] Sometimes these visions are intensely religious, and he places great importance on them. One of them is crucial for an understanding of the source of his powers, for it indicates the link between psychic visions and magic.

In one of these visionary states, at the age of thirty, there appeared to him a host of angels in a blaze of golden light. He also 'saw' two guardians holding trumpets. The next day these guardians again appeared to him, standing by a curtain which was slightly pulled aside. Through the opening a stage was visible and a man clad in oriental dress, wearing a turban with a splendid diadem, stepped forward. Suddenly, Croiset saw that the Oriental's face began *to show his own features!* "To Croiset, the Oriental symbolized a paranormally gifted superman," explains Dr. Tenhaeff. "Croiset's vision meant to him the promise that, in the future, he would accomplish great things as a Magus — the more so because the Oriental's face started to show his own features. Croiset felt that he was receiving the call from a Higher Power."[20]

It is not uncommon for people who exhibit psychic powers to have developed them at a very early age. Sometimes an adult trains the child in occult practices. (The grandmother of the little boy in Thomas Tryon's novel, *The Other*, has had real-life counterparts for

---

19. *Ibid.*, p. 20.
20. *Ibid.*, p. 27.

thousands of years; Tryon based his novel on universal themes in folklore and actual historical practice.) In other instances, moody children, especially teenage children, seem to come upon their powers suddenly. Gerard Croiset fits neither of these categories. In his book on Croiset, Pollack fails to mention anything about the man's childhood, but in a 1964 article in *True Magazine*, he does provide some basic information. Croiset's parents were Jewish theater people, always on the road. He had no home life. At the age of eight, he was placed in a foster home. He was to go through six sets of foster parents over the next five years, until he finally ran away at the age of thirteen.

Croiset had been an introverted child who lived in a world of his own fantasies. He was a prodigious daydreamer. He was sickly, and he suffered from rickets. When he spoke of imaginary playmates and imaginary places, people no doubt thought him to be a trifle immature. When he began to describe people and places he had never seen, but describe them accurately, adults grew concerned for his sanity. He began to predict events on the basis of his fantasies, and they would occasionally turn out to be true. "These daydreams which Gerard didn't understand, together with his telepathic relations with people, were the first signs of his paranormal abilities," wrote Pollack.[21]

Unlike David Hoy, Croiset had little education. He had failed at several occupations by the time he was out of his teens. In 1935, he suffered a nervous breakdown at the age of 26. He joined a spiritualist group at one point, but quit shortly thereafter. He says that he does not believe in spiritualist explanations for odd phenomena. It was only as his reputation grew as a psychometrist (object-handling psychic), from 1937-40, that he began to believe that he had something unique to offer the world.

Croiset's abilities may be questioned by professional skeptics, but police departments throughout Europe are not so skeptical, and families who have been helped in locating lost children or lost property are not skeptical. The chair tests have also added to his reputation. He has become a prophet in his own time. To know in advance when and where a body will float to the surface of a canal is a startling sort of knowledge. There is little doubt that the man's talents are unique.

Modern scientists, not being able to deal with such phenomena in terms of the categories of pure rationalism, have preferred to ig-

---

21. *True* (April 1964), p. 125.

nore him completely. That is the safe approach; it is also the dishonest approach. But at least it had one healthy byproduct: up until the shattering of faith in orthodox science which began after 1964, professional skepticism kept the Croiset-type phenomena from spreading into the mass media. Skepticism served as a barrier to truth, but it also served as a barrier to the highly personal and deeply hostile demonic threat to man and culture. As a result, for many years Croiset had few imitators with access to popular culture, at least in the United States. The problem today, however, is that skepticism is no longer an effective barrier, and once the public has concluded that mere denial of such powers is not a valid critique, that same public is left without a guide as to what, in fact, the sources of such power really are. Modern science had but one defense, skepticism, and that defense no longer convinces millions of readers.

Peter Hurkos

If Croiset's abilities came as a result of an overactive imagination, or if his overactive imagination came as a result of his discovery of his powers, these powers were nevertheless developed gradually. Not so with Pieter Cornelius van der Hurk. His paranormal psychic abilities came almost in an instant. As a young man, he had assisted his father as a house painter. In July of 1941, he was painting the outside of a building four stories up. He slipped and fell to the earth, breaking his shoulder and suffering a concussion. When he awoke, he found that he had "another mind." He could not remember many facts about his past, but he could remember facts about other people's lives. Furthermore, he had other arcane abilities: psychometry, astral projection, visions, and most significantly, *voices*. More accurately, a single voice which spoke to him about secret things. As he was to say years later, "I felt I had no mind of my own."[22]

Multimillionaire C. V. Wood, Jr., president of McCulloch Oil Corporation and the developer of Arizona's Lake Havasu, was cofounder of an organization called Mind Science Foundation. He has been associated with numerous research projects into psychic abilities. He writes: "Within the Mind Science Foundation we have studied many persons who have had certain psychic abilities, and in almost all cases the ability developed after either experiencing a fall or being hit on the head, or after having an extremely high fever."[23]

---

22. Browning, *Hurkos*, p. 48.
23. *Ibid.*, p. viii.

Why this should be the case, no one knows for certain, and orthodox scientists are hardly likely to explore the topic. (At best, they might say that people who think they are psychic are suffering from physically induced mental disorders.) Hurkos' mind(s) may be disordered, but it (they) cannot be said to be powerless.

During his stay in the hospital, Hurkos demonstrated his new abilities on several occasions. At first he inspired fear. It was wartime, Holland was under Nazi domination, and Hurkos seemed to know things that only a spy should be aware of. This suspicion almost cost him his life. Then, when he convinced the physicians that he was no spy, they thought he was mad. Finally, by revealing some very personal and embarrassing facts to one of them concerning the latter's extra-marital affair, he received a confused sort of respect.[24]

He was as confused as the professionals about his powers. Walking the streets of The Hague, one night he stopped in a cemetery to rest. He claims that he began to hear voices — voices of the dead, he says. He ran home, but he could still hear them. His "gift," which he quite correctly regards as a curse, was to bring him under bondage to these voices for the next three decades, at least. As his biographer writes: "Whatever it was he had about cemeteries didn't go away. Peter gets some of his strongest vibrations at gravesites and from clothing or objects that have belonged to dead people, especially when he works on murder cases. If the body is buried in the ground, he is usually taken to the gravesite. 'But I don't like to go in cemeteries,' he says. 'Not that I'm afraid, but if I walk in a cemetery for half an hour I'm completely exhausted, as tired as if I worked fourteen days. Even when it is cold, I am sweating like hell when I go in a cemetery. Because I get the vibrations, and then comes the mental picture and then the voices.' "[25]

One of the more familiar words of the "youth culture" of the 1960's was "vibrations." Good vibrations, bad vibrations, no vibrations: these terms were supposed to convey information about the setting or person involved. The Beach Boys had their biggest hit record, "Good Vibrations," during this period. (Shortly thereafter, Dennis Wilson, a member of the group, befriended a bearded hippie guru named Charles Manson and his many followers, who proceeded to eat his food, steal his wardrobe, borrow and then smash up his uninsured $21,000 car. These events finally were interpreted by Mr.

---

24. *Ibid.*, p. 51.
25. *Ibid.*, p. 54.

Wilson as being of the bad vibration variety, having cost him an estimated $100,000, and after weeks of such nonsense, he finally asked
the group to leave — but not before recording one of Manson's songs
as the flip side of a Beach Boys' hit single, however. The song, prophetically, was titled, "Cease to Exist," which Wilson prudently
changed to "Cease to Resist."[26])

Peter Hurkos (who himself later worked on the Manson case —
successfully, says his biographer; disastrously, says Manson prosecu-
tor Vincent Bugliosi[27]) is a man who lives in a world of vibrations. So
do countless others inside the world of the occult: vibrations are everywhere and everything. He gets vibrations from the objects he investi-
gates. Sometimes, they are "bad vibrations." But they are vibrations.[28]

Hurkos does not regard himself as a healer, psychic or otherwise.
This is to his advantage, given the attitude of physicians and state
medical boards toward uncertified competition. But on one occasion, witnessed by several people, he performed an act of miraculous
healing on himself. (Fortunately, he forgot to charge himself a fee,
thus staying inside the law.) He is unable to explain the following; he
simply thought to himself, "I don't want to be in a hospital." (You
don't have to be a psychic to figure *that* out.)

If Peter Hurkos could heal nobody else, at least apparently he could
heal himself. Even Henry Belk, though no longer friend or believer, still
swears by this incident. It happened on the evening of May 17, 1958, in
Belk's New York apartment. A group of Belk's friends and business associates had gathered there for a sociable evening. Peter was there, too. At
some point during the evening, Peter tripped over something and fell,
twisting his leg so badly that, according to Belk, "One of the bones broke
clear out of his skin. There was blood all over the place."

While Peter cried out in pain, some of the men lifted him onto a bed. As
Belk tells the story, Peter bowed his head as though in prayer, "And before
our very eyes, the bone went back into place and the torn skin healed and
became smooth. I was there. I actually saw the bone stick out and go in,"
Belk himself told me. Those are his words verbatim from my notes. He also
told essentially the same story to Jess Stearn (*The Door to the Future*) and
played him a taped recording of that memorable night, with testimonials
from the other eyewitnesses.[29]

---

26. Vincent Bugliosi, *Helter Skelter* (New York: Norton, 1974), p. 250; Ed Sanders, *The Family* (New York: Dutton, 1971), p. 97.

27. Bugliosi, *Helter Skelter*, pp. 55-56; Browning, *Hurkos*, pp. 253-55.

28. Browning, *Hurkos*, pp. 65, 95, 201, 206.

29. *Ibid.*, pp. 84-85.

Hurkos became famous, like Croiset, for his investigations of criminal cases. He worked on many of them, with varying degrees of success. One police officer who believes in Hurkos was police chief Robert White of the Palm Springs police department. Hurkos had helped his department locate the body of a missing youth, Stephen Gallagher. He had told them where to search for the body (December, 1968); the following September, they located it very close to the location described by Hurkos. Even more eerie, however, was the way in which Hurkos presented the information. Chief White reconstructs that original meeting:

"I had heard a lot about Peter Hurkos," said Chief White. "I knew of his reputation on the Boston Strangler case, and I was interested in meeting him. While he was in my office he asked whether we had any complicated cases we were trying to solve. I told him yes, as a matter of fact we had several. I asked Captain Richard Harries to bring in some of the folders of unsolved cases. He brought in several.

"Peter Hurkos laid his hand on the top folder, which happened to be the Gallagher case, and began verbally telling us almost verbatim what was in the report. Both my captain and I were amazed. We had never seen Peter Hurkos before. He had no way of knowing what was in that folder. The case was a year old, and it hadn't been in the news recently. Yet Peter began telling us about it exactly as though he were seeing through that folder.

"He said it was the case of a missing boy. He named the correct number of persons involved—three. He identified the vehicle they were driving. He told us there had been a little 'party' and there were lots of narcotics involved. This also was correct. The three boys had been off on a little 'trip' on LSD."[30]

Hurkos is able to perform before large groups. He is a professional psychic. His gifts are not limited to dark halls and seances filled with credulous people. He can do his work on television as well as on a Las Vegas stage. In August of 1969, he appeared on *The David Frost Show*. Columnist Leonard Lyons handed him a sealed box and asked him to identify its contents. Not even Frost knew what was inside. His biographer writes:

Peter began rubbing his hands over the box. His reading, as many will remember, went something like this:
"I see wires, yes . . . wires and hooks . . . steel hooks shaped like this

---

30. *Ibid.*, pp. 110-11.

[moving his arm in an arc]. . . . Oh, my God, terrible. What this man did to this world, it is too terrible. He's a genius but a bad man for what he did to the world. Yes, wires and hooks. . . . Wait, I see now. It's a telephone. I see a telephone. We must pray for this man's soul."

When the box was opened, there it was—a telephone. Not the kind of telephone familiar to most of us, to be sure, but nonetheless a telephone and a very special one.

It was Hitler's telephone, the one he had had in his mountain villa at Berchtesgaden.[31]

How does Hurkos do it? He answers: "I tell only what I see and hear, what the voice tells me." What voice? "The voice that came back with my other mind."[32] His "other mind" came with the blow on his head. It has never left. At other times, he sees pictures along with, or in place of, the mysterious voice. The voice and psychic pictures: *these are the same phenomena described by Carlos Castaneda that he encountered during his experiments with divination by means of lizards.*[33] The Yaqui sorcerer uses "familiars"—animals associated with demonic power, at least under ritual conditions—in the same way that Western witches have traditionally been linked to special animals. But in Hurkos' case, there are no animals involved—only the voice and the visions. Nevertheless, the basic goal in both psychic phenomena and occult divination is the same: *access to secret knowledge.* In other words, the basic urge is *gnostic*: salvation through knowledge, especially secret knowledge.

The voice gives Hurkos advice. "I never painted before my fall. Only house painting. Then a few years ago I start painting. Somebody said, 'Paint. Paint what you saw.' And I am painting." His biographer asked, "Who was the somebody who told you to start painting?" Hurkos gave a two-word answer: "The voice."[34] The voice not only gives information about the external world—past, present, and future—but it also gives instruction in the arts. It sounds very much like the techniques used by the Soviet hypnotist, Vladimir Raikov, who is able to "reincarnate" great masters of painting in the minds of his subjects, thus producing competent artists in a few sessions.[35]

---

31. *Ibid.*, pp. 235-36.
32. *Ibid.*, p. 241.
33. Castaneda, *The Teachings of Don Juan: A Yaqui Way of Knowledge* (New York: Bantam, [1968] 1974, pp. 110-17.
34. Browning, *Hurkos*, p. 272.
35. Sheila Ostrander and Lynn Schroeder, *Psychic Discoveries Behind the Iron Curtain* (New York: Bantam, [1970] 1973), ch. 12.

There is power here. Power to give information and power to direct and control personal development. That power is *personal*: being to being.

The doors of perception swing both ways.

There are problems associated with voices. Take the case of one Robert F. Roy, a self-professed "student and disciple of demonology," accused burglar, arsonist, and murderer. He admitted to the murder of a mother of nine children. Police in Camden County, New Jersey, said that he informed them that an inner spirit seemed to be telling him "to kill an elderly female." He led them to a hidden recess in a wall of the Berlin Hotel, where he was living, and produced a 12-gauge shotgun which he said was the murder weapon. The woman had indeed been cut down by a shotgun blast.[36] There is no guarantee that the voices, whatever they are, are reliable, factually or ethically. Yet psychic after psychic relies upon some form of spirit voice to guide him in his mystical revelations.

Jeane Dixon

"As I touched her hand I saw the death symbol over her. It was high above the ground. I saw life on the ground around her, and thus knew that if she would keep her feet on the ground she could elude danger. It was a sort of inner voice that said, 'Six weeks.' This voice comes to me frequently, and I always listen to it."[37] Jeane Dixon, like Peter Hurkos, gets messages from a voice. These voices get around.

Mrs. Dixon is undoubtedly the most prominent American psychic of our time. Ruth Montgomery's bestselling introduction to her powers, *A Gift of Prophecy* (1965), was almost prophetically timed to coincide with the initial detonation of the occult explosion. It appealed directly to the literary tastes of those who take seriously the in-depth articles of the *Ladies Home Journal*. Unlike Peter Hurkos, who feels burdened by his talent, Jeane Dixon (as interpreted by Ruth Montgomery) seems to revel in her gift. Being a prophet may not be easy, the book informs us, but it certainly is spiritually rewarding, and it certainly can make a person the envy of her neighbors. The underlying message of the book is that while everyone is not equally gifted — contrary to David Hoy — it certainly is nice for those who are, especially those who Do a Lot of Good with their gift.

---

36. *Philadelphia Bulletin* (May 30, 1974).
37. Ruth Montgomery, *A Gift of Prophecy* (New York: William Morrow, 1965), p. 19.

Undoubtedly, Mrs. Dixon has performed some important services for people. She calls ambulances for people who have not yet had a heart attack but who will in a few minutes. She tells people to see a doctor quickly because they have a serious and previously undiagnosed disease. She keeps people from flying on airplanes that are about to crash. She warns people about business deals that are not going to work out. The book is filled with first-hand testimonials of the beneficiaries of such prophecies. All in all, it makes psychic powers look like a true gift from God, just as Croiset and Mrs. Dixon maintain. Why object to prophecies of this nature?

The biblical quote which introduces this chapter provides one answer. It is not simply the accuracy of the prophecies concerning the events which is crucial; it is the philosophy and theology that undergirds the prophecies. Furthermore, the apparent benefits conferred on both the prophet and the recipients of the advance information (providing that the recipient does *exactly* what the prophet has instructed) almost guarantees that some readers will imitate the techniques of the prophet, and that others will somehow feel cheated that no such gift has been bestowed on them. The market for materials about or by Mrs. Dixon indicates just how curious the public is. The sale, for example, of the Dell Purse Book titles that deal with the development of prophetic skills indicates how widespread the imitation factor is. *The Book of Omens: Your Guide to Good Luck; Numerology; Palmistry; Develop Your ESP*: the titles, as they say, "tell all."

Mrs. Dixon was first informed of her powers by a gypsy. It sounds like a plot in some Hollywood B-grade film of the 1940's, but she insists that it is the truth. When she was eight years old, her mother took her to see a gypsy woman in northern California, close to their home, and the woman said that the young girl had a unique palm. (Eastern mystic types apparently have said the same thing, for what it is worth.) The woman told them that when the girl grew up, she would have special powers. Then she went into her covered wagon home and produced a crystal ball, which she gave to young Jeane Pinckert. (Her brother is Ernie Pinckert, who became an All-American football player.) Almost immediately, she received visual messages in it, including the fact that the old gypsy would scald her hand in a cooking accident. Sure enough, it happened. (Crystal balls in the hands of psychics seem to be good for a long life of "I told you so's," not generally regarded as a sure way to win friends and influence people, as Cassandra's biographer, a Greek by the name of Homer, informed us a few years back.)

The use of quartz crystals by Yaqui sorcerers and aborigine magicians is a curious parallel. Special properties are supposed to be associated with crystals. They permit the focusing of power as well as inducing visions. But crystal gazing has a separate history. It has been practiced by psychics and magicians for thousands of years, East and West. Lewis Spence, in his *Encyclopedia of Occultism* (1920), reports that in ancient times, an elaborate ritual preparation was used by diviners, but that in modern times, scryers (gazers) have dropped much of the ceremonial periphera. He argues that the object of the crystal ball has always been to induce hypnosis. The problem with this theory, as Nandor Fodor points out in his *Encyclopedia of Psychic Science* (1934), is that hypnotic symptoms are rarely found in crystal gazers. He writes: "The most arresting question, of course, is whether the pictures are ever objective. In many experiences this appears to be the case. There are instances in which the pictures grow larger under a magnifying glass, may be reflected in a mirror and may be seen by several persons. Sometimes they have even been photographed. It is very likely that in these cases the vision is due to spirit-operators. The pictures are built up as a means of communication just as messages may be given in the crystal in writing. The fact that in some cases the messages are spelt out backward points to a conscious effort on the operator's part to furnish proof of the exclusion of the medium's subconscious mind."

This is not to say that in all cases the pictures inside the crystal are objective; in the majority of cases, such as with Mrs. Dixon's visions, they are not. But there are sufficient documented cases of several people seeing the same vision, including actual photographs, that would indicate the validity of Fodor's central thesis: *the source of the vision is an outside being or beings.* In Mrs. Dixon's case, the most likely candidate is the mysterious voice.

She claims that she can peer into her crystal and see future events as clearly "as if she were watching a T.V. screen."[38] Sometimes the channels come in a bit fuzzy, however, such as the time she forecasted that the Soviets would beat us to the moon.[39] (Perhaps this particular revelation was from the voice or in a general, run-of-the-mill vision, in which she places less trust.) But at other times, she is uncannily accurate. Jeane Dixon's world, like Hurkos', is filled

---

38. Montgomery, *ibid.*, p. 16.
39. *Ibid.* p. 111.

with vibrations. It is not just a catchy phrase with psychics. In fact, it became a catch phrase in the late 1960's only when the language of the occult was transmitted by the counter-culture to the general population. The literature of occultism reveals a continuing theme: the whole universe is composed of vibrations. Donald Hatch Andrews, a professor of chemistry, has attempted to fuse this religious perspective with modern, post-Heisenberg physics, and he has concluded that the universe is not so much a huge machine as an enormous melody. He thinks that "the universe is composed not of matter but of music."[40] It is not surprising that his book was not published by a scientific publishing house but by Unity Books, an organ of a prominent science of mind type of organization.[41]

Mrs. Dixon finds that vibrations can reveal many things about a person's life. She once diagnosed the health of a friend of Ruth Montgomery's. "Ruth, I have picked up your friend's vibrations. She was suffering some pain in the intestinal region a few minutes ago, which I believe is a chronic condition caused from nervous strain."[42] Her diagnosis proved completely accurate. But not only do vibrations come from people, they come from objects, especially her old pack of playing cards, also a gift of the mysterious gypsy: "The sweet old gypsy gave me those cards when I was eight years old, and because she blessed them they carry good vibrations. I don't know a single thing about telling fortunes with cards. I simply have a person hold them so that I can pick up his vibrations. It sometimes helps me to pull out his channels."[43]

Houses also give off vibrations. These can sometimes be significant. "The moment that I walked into that Nineteenth Street house I seemed to feel God putting his arms around me. I knew it was for me. All the vibrations were right."[44] Even the future gives off vibrations, which is why they can be used for prophetic purposes. Mrs. Dixon said throughout 1948 that Truman would beat Dewey, and a week before the election, she announced once again that Truman would be the victor. She went down to campaign headquarters to give a donation the Saturday before the election, and she said to a friend who was working there, "Madeline, everyone thinks I'm

40. Donald Hatch Andrews, *The Symphony of Life* (Lee Summit, Mo.: Unity Books, 1966), p. 9.

41. Richard Rhodes, "Heaven on Earth," *Harper's* (May 1970).

42. Montgomery, *Gift*, p. 25.

43. *Ibid.*, p. 26.

44. *Ibid.*, p. 74.

crazy. [Not because she likes to peer into crystal balls, you understand, which for Washington is not all that weird, but because she
was predicting a Truman victory, which involved the essence of
craziness as defined by Washington, namely, arguing against the
polls.] Let's try it again with the cards, to see if I still get the same vibrations."[45] She did, and Truman won.

My favorite Jeane Dixon prophecy about politics was announced in the *Los Angeles Times* (May 11, 1973, Part IV): "Dixon:
Watergate Will Help Nixon." Speaking before the Mary and Joseph
League, she prophesied that Watergate "may not help the President's
image now, but it will later." Watergate "will put Nixon in a position
to right a great wrong for the United States. . . . This will come to
pass." What else will come to pass? National unity. "I feel that President Nixon will unite us as we have not been united for a long time
and, strange as it seems, Watergate will be the catalyst." It was, too:
the whole country was *united against Nixon*, and fifteen months later,
he resigned in disgrace. Her crystal ball must have been a little
cloudy that day.

Crystal balls, cards, vibrations, voices, visions: What is left? *Astrology*. She claims that she never uses astrology. Not that she thinks it
is nonsense. Quite the contrary; she was taught the art, she says, in
her teens by a Jesuit priest (a statement which will be readily believed by all Dominicans). The problem with astrology, according to
her, is that it takes too much time.[46] There are more efficient ways of
divining the future. Instead of constructing complex astrological
charts, Mrs. Dixon has found a short cut, vibrationally speaking: in
reading for Miss Nichols and other strangers, Jeane almost invariably asks their birthday. "I do that for the rising and setting signs,"
she explains, "because it helps in my meditation to see which direction they're going. I don't ask for the minute of their birth, because I
don't want to be influenced by what their horoscope charts would
say. I just like to know their rising and setting signs, so that I can
pick up their correct vibrations."[47]

Jeane Dixon is, if nothing else, a vibrant woman. How is it that
a crystal-gazing, card-consulting, vision-receiving reincarnation-
believing wife of a divorced man could be regarded by everyone, including the Roman Catholic Church, as an orthodox and upright

---

45. *Ibid.*, p. 83.
46. *Ibid.*, p. 26.
47. *Ibid.*, p. 94.

member of that ancient institution? Simple: at the heart of her theology is the humanistic god of *ecumenicism*. This is also the god of modern Protestantism and modern Catholicism. It is part and parcel of the humanist culture of our day. No one in the Church was about to excommunicate her for her book, *Reincarnation and Prayers to Live By* (1970), in which she includes a Jewish prayer, a Hindu prayer, a Hindu prayer to Buddha, a Japanese prayer, an American Indian prayer, and a Mexican Indian prayer, the "Hymn to the All-Mother."[48] The dedication tells all:

> Dedicated to
> Man
> Believing and Unbelieving

Ecumenicism is a basic theme of all theosophist, occult, and science of mind cults. Most of these cults believe that a single universal religion is the solution to man's problems and the foundation of a messianic one-world political order, or as it has also been called, the *New World Order*. Whether by means of the dry rationalism of university training or the irrationalism of mystical visions, modern humanists have again and again come to the conclusion that *man*—the best representative of divinity, or else the highest being in a universe devoid of divinity—*must be united politically and spiritually*. This perspective is the very essence of humanism, and it has been dominant since the time of the Enlightenment. As Rushdoony writes, "humanity is the true god of the Enlightenment and of French Revolutionary thought. In all religious faiths one of the inevitable requirements of logical thought asserts itself in a demand for *the unity of the Godhead*. Hence, since humanity is the god, there can be no division in this godhead, humanity. Since Enlightenment philosophy was monistic, this means an intolerance of differences as being unessential."[49] In short, he concludes: "The goal is not communion but uniformity."

Bearing this fact in mind, consider Mrs. Dixon's vision of Feb. 5, 1962. She "saw" Queen Nefertiti and her husband, the Pharaoh, just outside her window. She saw a pyramid, too. They were carrying an infant from whom were emitted rays of light. The queen walked

---

48. Jeane Dixon, *Reincarnation and Prayers to Live By* (New York: William Morrow, 1970).

49. R. J. Rushdoony, *This Independent Republic: Studies in the Nature and Meaning of American History* (Fairfax, Virginia: Thoburn Press, [1964] 1978), p. 142.

away and was stabbed in the back. The child became an adult. A cross above his head expanded until it was worshipped by everyone. The task of unravelling this vision would have baffled the diviners of Babylon. (A Ph.D. candidate in psychology — Freudian, of course — might have produced his dissertation from it.) But Mrs. Dixon has laid the mystery to rest: "A child, born somewhere in the Middle East shortly after 7 A.M. (EST) on February 5, 1962, will revolutionize the world. Before the close of the century he will bring together all mankind in one all-embracing faith. This will be the foundation of a new Christianity, with every sect and creed united through this man who will walk among the people to spread the wisdom of the Almighty Power."[50]

If this sounds a trifle messianic to you, you are not alone. The book ends on a hopeful note: "Mankind, Jeane Dixon has said, will begin to feel the great force of this man about 1980, and his power 'will grow mightily' until 1999, when there will be 'peace on earth to all men of good will.' "[51] For those who are not of good will, as defined by the creedless creed of ecumenical humanism, times will undoubtedly be tough.

Another favorite doctrine of occult humanism is the idea of the "spark of divinity" in each man. It is most highly developed as a system of belief in Hinduism, with the doctrine of karma (reincarnation) of each soul in a progressive evolution back into the formless, monistic divinity from which all diversity (illusion) originally came. But Mrs. Dixon has succeeded in fusing this humanistic creed with pre-1965 Democratic Party politics, no mean feat: "This is the true meaning of President Kennedy's life and death: that through his martyrdom he would light an eternal flame to remind peoples of the world of God's eternal flame in each of us. During John Kennedy's brief period in the public spotlight, he was able to kindle in the hearts of men an awareness that there is more to life than the narrow pursuit of personal gain. Because his life on this earth was cut short in its prime, it was possible for him to become an eternal symbol of youth, vitality, culture, and intellect. This was not of his doing but of God's. Like the courteous Washington policeman on the street corner, who radiates good vibrations to all passers-by, and like each of us who tries to develop the talents that were entrusted to us, President Kennedy was simply an instrument of God's will. Through him

---

50. Montgomery, *Gift*, p. 171.
51. *Ibid.*, p. 182.

God has demonstrated that within each of us burns this eternal flame; that our greatness lies not in the size of our bank accounts but in our faith and our development of divinely granted talents."[52] Any relationship between John Fitzgerald Kennedy, the consummate political pragmatist-millionaire, whose family has undeviatingly sought political power for its members for over five decades, and the man of Mrs. Dixon's eulogy, is purely coincidental. Any relationship between the God of the Bible and the ecumenical god of Mrs. Dixon is less than coincidental; it is nonexistent.

Conclusion

The facts of psychic power are available for serious students of the question. Too many cases that are documented by too many eyewitnesses now exist for the professional skeptics to continue to discount, ignore, disparage, or explain away by means of scientific rationalism. The positivist's universe never existed; the faith in that universe is now coming apart at the seams. Somehow, ESP must be accounted for, but not just mind-reading, but psychokinesis, precognition, and memories of past existence (*someone else's* past existence, not the psychic's). Croiset says a body will float to the surface of a canal in a particular place on a certain day in the future, and it does. Jeane Dixon predicts a specific event, and it happens. These are not "fortune cookie prophets," with vague generalities, but rather producers of concrete statements. You will find your false teeth under the kitchen sink, says David Hoy, and the caller does. You will not turn on the light, thinks Hoy, and the author doesn't.

Yet with few exceptions, there is more to the psychic's universe than just the ability to see the future or direct thoughts in externally verifiable ways. There are voices. There are odd bits of theology and cosmology that reappear, generation after generation: reincarnation, one-world religion, the divine spark in every person, the "secret doctrines" of the great teachers. Add to these the prophecy of a coming millennium, the New World Order—an era in which mankind will transcend today's limitations.

The psychics' abilities are not in accord with the Newtonian science of the past three centuries, yet they are invariably in accord with the *philosophic* humanism which supposedly created modern science. Should the faith in Newtonian science be eroded, what is to

---

52. *Ibid.*, p. 181.

prevent a new fusion: messianic humanism and the occult powers of the psychic? Is it so surprising to find that the Soviet Union should be experimenting with psychics in order to find the "laws" that undergird these most disturbing, yet most promising, impossible phenomena? The messianic state seeks power, and psychics possess power—the power of occult knowledge. The opposition of the modern humanistic culture to occult power has been methodological, not moral. When the methodology shifts, as it has clearly begun to shift, what moral restraint will be present to call a halt to mind readers, mind controllers, and humanistic prophets of the coming one-world order?

6

EDGAR CAYCE: FROM DIAGNOSIS TO GNOSIS

*And as it is appointed unto men once to die, but after this the judgment:
so Christ was once offered to bear the sins of many; and unto them that
look for him shall he appear the second time without sin unto salvation.*

Hebrews 9:27-28

I first heard of Edgar Cayce [KAYsee] in the spring of 1964. His
son, Hugh Lynn Cayce, was promoting his newly published book
about his father's work, *Venture Inward*. He was appearing on Long
John Nebel's midnight-to-dawn radio show which originated on
New York's WOR. Beamed all over the East Coast, Long John's
program drew literally millions of listeners. A former carnival
barker, Nebel opened the microphones to every sort of occultist, fundamentalist, libertarian, renegade medical practitioner, and fringe
group member imaginable. There was only one requirement: they
had to tell interesting stories — five hours' worth. A lot of them did.
None was more intriguing than the story of Edgar Cayce.

From 1901 until his death in 1945, Edgar Cayce won a following
of faithful believers and less faithful financial contributors as a result
of a unique occult facility. By putting himself into a trance, and by
assigning a "control" agent to ask him questions, he could diagnose
people's physical illnesses. Not only diagnose them, but prescribe
remedies, many of them completely unorthodox and seemingly unrelated to the illness, that would be found to be helpful and very
often completely successful. He would simply loosen his tie, take off
his shoes, lie down on a couch, and go into his trance state. The control agent would then give him the name and address of the person
to be diagnosed. Then would come the familiar words: "Yes, we have
the body." The diagnosis would then begin. A secretary would record
the diagnosis and recommendations, and these notes would then be
put into Cayce's permanent files. By the time of his death, the Cayce

foundation, the Association for Research and Enlightenment (A.R.E.) had almost 9,000 of these medical "readings," as they were called. The files also contained letters from patients that had been sent in unsolicited, plus others that had come in as a result of follow-ups made by the A.R.E. Cayce's followers claim, with considerable justification, that this is the largest body of paranormal documentation relating to methods of healing that has ever been assembled. The A.R.E. has opened these files to qualified researchers, which again is unique within most occult circles. They do not regard Cayce's talents as occult, however; they see him as a man who possessed certain visionary skills that we all supposedly possess.

An amazing story, if true. An amazing story even if false, since Cayce gave his "readings" for over four decades, received considerable (one time only) attention by the press, was investigated by medical and university officials, and was never convicted of fraud. He made almost no money at his trade, built no impressive institution, received criticism from skeptics, wrote no books, made no speeches on the lecture circuit, conducted no seances, and in general devoted his entire life to a seemingly lost cause. He was arrested once, in 1931, on the charge of fortune-telling, but it was dismissed. He was never sued by one of his patients (clients?) and he returned the small fees charged for the readings in later years upon request. What, in short, was in it for him? He said that his work had to go on. If it was a fraud, why could he not impart his "skill" to his son? If it was not a fraud, how can we explain what he did? Psychic healing is an ancient tradition, especially in so-called primitive cultures. Psychic diagnosis and prescriptions are not common. They are unheard of. Yet the press took only sporadic interest in his work, although millions of people knew of it. In the early 1900's, the story was picked up by newspapers in the South. In 1910, Cayce received national coverage, including the *New York Times*. Yet for the remainder of his life, newsmen simply stayed away or forgot about him. There were books by his followers: *There is a River* (1942), by Thomas Sugrue, sold well if not spectacularly, and Gina Cerminara's *Many Mansions* (1950) received some attention. For the most part, however, the Cayce story was buried. Hugh Lynn's book was superbly timed; it hit the market about the time that the Beatles hit New York and shortly before riots hit Berkeley. The occult revival created a market, and in 1967, Jess Stearn filled it, or at least gave every impression of having filled it. *Edgar Cayce—The Sleeping Prophet* was hardly a sleeper. Released in January, it went through eight hardback printings by July. The next year Bantam published a paperback version, and by 1975 it was into its fifteenth printing. That, by any standard, is a best-seller. Yet it was only the beginning. The A.R.E. began issuing books based on Cayce's life and readings, and there are at least twenty titles in print, plus another book by Cayce and a reissue of a second book by Sugrue. Millions upon millions of copies of these books have been sold. There are even Edgar Cayce study groups — the final test of a true movement-cult — operating around the country. There was a brief advertisement for an Edgar Cayce study group which appeared in the Long Beach *Pennysaver* (a local throwaway advertiser) as I was writing this chapter — three decades after his death. The occult revival, fittingly, created the whole Cayce movement. Without it, he would be remembered only by a handful of relatives, both of Cayce and his patients, plus a few occult researchers. Cayce's supporters may try vainly to argue that Cayce's talents had nothing to do with the occult, but the movement has everything to do with it.

History

Edgar Cayce was born in Hopkinsville, Kentucky, in 1877. He had his first vision at the age of six, according to one biographer.[1] His grandfather had been a dowser, or more properly, water-witcher, and his grandmother told young Cayce that the old gentleman had also been able to make tables and chairs move without touching them, although he had only performed these feats in front of her.[2] His dowsing abilities had been well known, however. His father's only seemingly occult ability was his highly undesirable attraction to snakes. They followed him out of the fields, wrapped themselves around his hat when he would set it down, and generally made life unpleasant for him. He never liked snakes. He finally had to move away from the farm into the town to avoid them.[3] Other than that, his son later explained to Harvard psychologist Hugo Münsterberg, he was completely normal. (Münsterberg had come to expose Cayce as a fraud in 1910; he left convinced that Cayce had

---

1. Doris Agee, *Edgar Cayce on ESP* (New York: Paperback Library, 1969), p. 14.
2. Thomas Sugrue, *There Is a River* (rev. ed.; New York: Holt & Co., [1943] 1948), pp. 60-61.
3. *Ibid.*, p. 7.

some sort of legitimate, though unheard-of, abilities.) *Normal*: that was one term that had never fit young Edgar.

As a child, he claimed to be able to see "little people" — companions in the fields. Unlike most children, Cayce never doubted that he had. At the age of thirteen — the age most frequently associated with poltergeist activity — he was reading his Bible through for the twelfth time. Not a good student, he was at least faithful in this activity. He experienced a vision of a lady with wings. She asked him what he wanted, and he said he wanted to be of service to people. (Part of the appeal of the Cayce story to a lot of people is that he was a perpetual do-gooder. He always seemed so sincere.) She granted him his wish, he later said.[4] This incident cannot be dismissed lightly; the next day Cayce demonstrated a most remarkable ability. He was a poor student. His teacher, who happened to be his uncle, had told his father that the boy was hopeless, and his father, like so many fathers before him, was determined to beat a little knowledge into his son. He began to drill him on his spelling lesson. Blank, as always. He grew furious, striking the boy. Edgar later claimed that at this point, he heard the lady's voice: "if you can sleep a little, we can help you." He asked his father's permission to doze for five minutes. Granted. He put his spelling book behind his head, dozed off for five minutes, and when his father returned, he knew every word in the book, including the page number and the line on which the word appeared.

He brought home his geography book, slept on it, and the next day had it completely memorized. He did this with every school book he had. His teacher could hardly believe it. His father was disturbed; this was too spooky. Yet he was proud of his son. (Some of Cayce's classmates, when interviewed several decades later, still recalled how they had resented his effortless learning technique.[5]) Just before his son's graduation from school (from the seventh grade, according to Hugh Lynn Cayce; from the sixth, according to legend[6]), his father had bragged to former Congressman Jim MacKenzie that his son could memorize anything by sleeping on it. MacKenzie was understandably skeptical. A test was proposed by MacKenzie. Years before, he had delivered a speech favoring the repeal of the tax on

---

4. *Ibid.*, pp. 23, 45-46.

5. Harmon H. Bro, *Edgar Cayce on Religion and Psychic Experience* (New York: Paperback Library, 1970), p. 24.

6. Hugh Lynn Cayce, "Introduction," H. L. Cayce (ed.), *The Edgar Cayce Reader* (New York: Warner Paperback Library, [1969] 1974), p. 8.

quinine. He had become known as "Quinine Jim" in the House. He was on his way to Peru as American ambassador, and Peru was the major source of quinine. Therefore, said the Congressman, have Edgar sleep on a copy of this famous speech. His father went one better, or so he thought: he would read it to his son while he was asleep. He did, twice, and two evenings later, Edgar delivered the hour and a half oration to the students and parents of the graduating class, to the delight of Quinine Jim and, presumably, the utter boredom of the audience.[7] The story is marred by the fact that his graduation came in 1892, when he was fifteen years old. If he had developed this ability at age thirteen, why had he not progressed more rapidly? Hugh Lynn repeats on several occasions that his father's ability in this regard later faded, forcing him out of school early.[8] But years later, Edgar memorized the entire catalogue of a book and stationery store, astounding the owner and customers.[9] The less obvious reason for his apparent failure to go on was the level of achievement common to sixth grade drop-outs. Take a look at the sixth McGuffey reader. Poetry by Shakespeare, Dryden, Whittier, Poe, Tennyson, and others; essays by Edmund Burke, Macaulay, Samuel Johnson, Oliver Goldsmith, Patrick Henry, Daniel Webster. Can you imagine assigning Blackstone's essay on the origin of property to the typical product of today's government high school, let alone a sixth grader?[10] How about William Pitt's answer to Robert Walpole? College freshmen in most of the "better" state universities would have trouble with the sixth McGuffey reader. Furthermore, after the grammar school education of the 1880's and 1890's, sheer memorization would not have been sufficient to get a young man through. The curriculum involved higher mathematics, rhetoric, foreign languages, and the liberal arts. Not what the average farm boy needed. Edgar quit. But he was not soon forgotten by his classmates.

---

7. Sugrue, *River*, pp. 55-56.

8. Bro, *Religion*, p. 9; *Reader*, p. 8.

9. Sugrue, *River*, p. 106.

10. An added note: 1986. Years after I wrote this passage, I was told by Prof. Bertel Sparks of Duke University's prestigious School of Law (from which Richard Nixon graduated) of the following test. Sparks mimeographs Blackstone's essay on property and hands it out early in the first semester to his first-year law students. When they come back at the next class to discuss it, they have extreme difficulty with its concepts. Only after they have struggled with it does Sparks reveal that he took it from the sixth McGuffey reader. It humbles them early, he says.

In the spring of 1900, he developed a hoarse throat. It steadily became a whisper. Out of desperation, he became a silent apprentice to a photographer; he could no longer sell books and stationery supplies. A travelling hypnotist visited town and heard about the young man's plight. He guaranteed to restore his voice for $200. When hypnotized, his voice returned; as soon as he came out of the trance, his whisper reappeared. After several attempts, the hypnotist gave up. But another local amateur hypnotist and amateur osteopath, Al Layne, remembered an incident from Cayce's youth. He had been hit on the head by a baseball. Dazed, the boy became feverish and then delirious. Yet out of his delirium, he had told his parents to apply a poultice to his neck. They did, and he recovered quickly. He had no memory of his diagnosis afterward. Layne put Cayce into a trance and then asked him to diagnose his problem. Immediately, the fateful words came forth: "Yes, we can see the body."[11] The voice diagnosed the problem as insufficient circulation. Layne gave a suggestion that the body cure itself. Cayce's neck grew pink, then bright red. Twenty minutes later, it became normal again. Layne told Cayce to wake up, and when he did, his voice had returned.

This was the beginning, not only of Cayce's diagnostic ministry, but of a lifetime of trouble with his voice. His biographers seldom refer to the fact that throughout the remainder of his life — 45 years — Cayce had recurring voice failures. He was completely dependent upon his trance state and its circulation stimulation to return his waking voice to normal.[12] No one could give a physiological reason for the loss of his voice. Those familiar with demon possession would immediately recognize the cause: occult bondage. Cayce could not abandon the physical "readings" once they had begun. He was trapped.

Layne, the hypnotist, immediately saw possibilities for himself and Cayce. He could put Cayce under, question him concerning the ailments of others, get a prescription, and then mail the prescription to the "patient." Cayce was initially suspicious, both of his talent and of Layne's proposition. Layne asked him to diagnose his own illness, and when he followed Cayce's advice, he said that he felt much better. Cayce gave in, but he refused to accept any payment for his services. Layne, however, had no qualms about fees.

---

11. *Ibid.*, p. 121.

12. Hugh Lynn Cayce, *Venture Inward* (New York: Harrow Books, [1964] 1972), p. 51.

In 1902, Cayce moved to Bowling Green. His voice plagued him. Layne had to come up every few weeks to treat him. Then Layne came more often, bringing cases. Then, in the summer of 1902, Cayce received the crucial telephone call of the healing stage of his career. C. H. Dietrich, the former superintendent of schools in Hopkinsville was desperate. His five-year-old daughter had been ill for several years; now she was suffering as many as 20 convulsions a day. She could no longer speak. The physicians, several from out-of-state clinics, had given up on her. Could Cayce help? Cayce got on the train and returned to Hopkinsville. Eight years later, Dietrich had the following statement notarized:

March 1st, 1902, she was taken to Dr. Hoppe, of Cincinnati, Ohio, who made a most thorough examination. He pronounced her a perfect specimen physically, except for the brain affection, concerning which he stated that only nine cases of this particular type were reported in medical records, and every one of these had proved fatal. He told us nothing could be done, except to give her good care, as her case was hopeless and she would die soon in one of these attacks.

At this period our attention was called to Mr. Edgar Cayce, who was asked to diagnose her case. By auto-suggestion he went into a sleep and diagnosed her case as one of congestion at the base of the brain, stating also minor details. He outlined to Dr. A. C. Layne, now of Griffen, Ga., how to proceed to cure her. Dr. Layne treated her occasionally to follow up the treatment, as results developed. Her mind began to clear up about the eighth day and within three months she was in perfect health, and is so to this day.[13]

The trance voices informed them that the girl had suffered a fall from a carriage three years earlier. Sure enough, her mother remembered the incident. Layne was told how to adjust her spine. Once her mind had cleared, she advanced rapidly intellectually until she was a normal child of her age. By having achieved a major success with a prominent, educated citizen, Cayce established a precedent which led to other cases and other successes.

The readings continued. A man in New York heard of the work, wrote to Layne, and he asked him to have his "associate" diagnose his case. Cayce did, from hundreds of miles away, and without any statement in advance of the man's symptoms. He had prescribed

13. Jeffrey Furst, *Edgar Cayce's Story of Jesus* (New York: Coward-McCann, 1969), pp. 340-41.

something called clarawater to the man, only there was no such product listed. Cayce was put under again and the voice came up with the formula. Yet at no time could Cayce remember any of this.[14] His voice would give remarkably detailed anatomical descriptions, and they were sometimes confirmed by physicians, yet Cayce read nothing other than the Bible and simple Sunday school literature. He had not received training in anatomy by sleeping on his grammar school textbooks, however advanced they would seem in today's educational context. In 1902, Cayce also developed a game for adults which he called "Pit." People liked it, so he sent a sample to Parker Bros. He received their thanks, several free sets, and a letter stating that it had been copyrighted by them and it would henceforth be illegal for him to produce them. So much for Edgar Cayce, businessman.[15]

Word finally got out to the press about Cayce's diagnoses. This was in 1903.[16] The medical authorities immediately moved in on Al Layne, who agreed to quit practicing until he graduated from a school of osteopathy. Cayce's voice again departed. Now, however, he had learned that he could put himself into a trance, and with a "control" agent, he could still have himself temporarily cured. A local physician agreed to act as an assistant, but was surprised when Cayce's chest turned red, then returned to normal, and upon awakening, his voice was normal.[17]

Cayce worked with some young physicians in Bowling Green, then returned to Hopkinsville, where he teamed up with a doctor of homeopathy, Wesley Ketchum, who quietly used Cayce to diagnose a hundred cases over the years. It was Dietrich's testimonial on behalf of Cayce that helped to reduce his initial skepticism. But the occult nature of Cayce's power became increasingly blatant. On one occasion, he had prescribed something called "balsam of sulphur." Years later, Ketchum described the scene: "One day, there were a couple of doctors and druggists in Cayce's [photographic] studio on a complicated case, for which Cayce had prescribed balsam of sulphur. They began scratching their heads. Nobody had ever heard of it. One of the druggists, an elderly man named Gaither, was convinced there was no such thing. They pored over a copy of the dis-

14. Sugrue, *River*, pp. 137, 145-46.
15. *Ibid.*, p. 126.
16. H. L. Cayce, *Venture Inward*, pp. 33-35.
17. Sugrue, *River*, p. 146.

pensatory, listing all available therapeutic drugs. There was no balsam of sulphur. Then, in the attic, they stumbled across an old defunct catalogue, put out fifty years before. They dusted it off, opened it, and there found balsam of sulphur."[18]

Even more eerie was his prescription, "oil of smoke." Again, no catalogue listed it. No one had heard of it. They took another reading. The name of a Louisville drugstore was given. Ketchum wired the store for a bottle. The reply: never heard of it. "We took a third reading. This time a shelf in the back of the Louisville drugstore was named. There, behind another preparation — which was named — would be found a bottle of 'Oil of Smoke,' so the reading said. I wired the information to the manager of the Louisville store. He wired back, 'Found it.' The bottle arrived in a few days. It was old. The label was faded. The company which put it up had gone out of business. But it was just what he said it was, 'Oil of Smoke.' " This story was related to Professor Münsterberg, or so Sugrue reports.[19] It is unlikely that Ketchum would make himself appear to be a fool in front of a Harvard professor. Cayce did possess astounding powers. Or, to put it more accurately, astounding powers possessed Cayce.

Ketchum related some of the Cayce stories to a convention of homeopathic physicians at a 1910 convention. He was asked to put his thoughts down on paper by Dr. Krauss, who then read it before a Boston meeting of the American Association for Clinical Research. The *New York Times* picked up the story and ran it on October 9, 1910. These were before the days of the "new journalism" or "interpretive journalism"; hence, it was run as a straight news story. Other papers picked up the story from the *Times* (some things never change), and an army of reporters descended on Hopkinsville.[20] Local physicians began crying for Ketchum's scalp, but he backed them down successfully. It was the first and last time that Cayce was to receive national attention from the media. Only with the publication of Sugrue's book in 1942 did the nation have the opportunity to hear the story of Edgar Cayce during his lifetime. Cayce finally broke with Ketchum over the question of his using his readings to do a bit of gambling with fees paid into a supposed hospital fund. He moved to Selma, Alabama for a time. He tried to find oil by means

18. Jess Stearn, *Edgar Cayce — The Sleeping Prophet* (New York: Bantam, [1967] 1971), p. 105.

19. Sugrue, *River*, p. 21.

20. H. L. Cayce, *Venture Inward*, pp. 36-39.

of his trance; again, to raise money for a hospital. None was found. He worked as a photographer. He taught Sunday school in the Christian Church. He became a prominent leader in Alabama's Christian Endeavor organization. And all the while, he continued to give his readings on people's ailments. Finally, in 1923, came a distinct break in his thirteen-year-old pattern. In that year, Cayce became a philosophical occultist. The second stage of his career, by far the more enduring, began.

The Occult Readings

In 1923, a supposedly wealthy Dayton printer, Arthur Lammers, visited the Cayces in Selma. He had heard of Cayce's paranormal powers, and he had decided that Cayce could answer many questions concerning the philosophy of life — occult philosophy. He asked Cayce for a reading, but not a physical reading. He wanted an astrological reading. Furthermore, he wanted it in Dayton. He asked Cayce to drop everything and come to Dayton. Cayce did precisely that. The Sunday school teacher travelled to Dayton, Ohio, in order to provide an astrological reading — name, date of birth, location of birth — for a devotee of mystery religions. It was so very easy. At the end of the horoscope reading, the trance voice announced: "He was once a monk." These five words sealed Cayce's fate, and may have sealed the fate of millions of his modern followers. A new world, totally hypothetical, and historically compelling, opened up behind his closed eyes: the world of reincarnation.[21]

Lammers wanted to pursue this new avenue. When was he a monk? Had he lived many lives? His was the first of what came to be known as the "life readings." Lammers' money ran out before he could get his questions answered to his satisfaction — a problem which seemed to plague all of Cayce's well-heeled and temporary devotees — but the pattern was established. Of the 14,249 readings still on file with the A.R.E., 2,500 of them are life readings. Bridey Murphy stuff.[22] Taylor Caldwell stuff.[23] Not just a stream of old ladies of

---

21. Sugrue, *River,* p. 237.

22. *The Search for Bridey Murphy* was a best-selling book of the mid-1950's, an account of a woman who had been hypnotized, and under hypnosis she had discussed in great detail her former life in Ireland as a girl named Bridey Murphy. No evidence that such a person had ever existed was discovered.

23. Jess Stearn, *The Search for a Soul: Taylor Caldwell's Psychic Lives* (New York: Fawcett Crest, 1973). Yes, this one-time heroine of the conservative movement and best-selling novelist wound up a reincarnationist in her old age. She had said that

both sexes asking "Who am I?", but "Who *was* I?"

At first, Cayce rejected the whole idea of reincarnation. He was convinced that the Bible rejected the concept. He was absolutely correct. But slowly and steadily, he changed his beliefs. He began to apply twisted interpretations to biblical passages (but never to Hebrews 9:27-28) in order to discover reincarnation. As one of his longtime followers puts it: "The active membership of the A.R.E., as it is usually called, is made up of people of all religious faiths and many nationalities, including foreign countries. Strangely, they all seem to be able to reconcile their faiths with the philosophy emerging from the Cayce readings."[24] Cayce set the pattern. The fact is that these people *do* have one religion, the Cayce religion. They ignore the teachings of their secondary, official religious memberships.

The importance of his self-conversion, if that is really the accurate way to describe the relationship between his conscious mind and the messages that proceeded from his trance-induced voice, cannot be overstressed. One follower hit the nail on the head when she wrote: "Had his physical readings not been proven accurate and useful in all the years he had been giving them, he probably would have turned from this new development in his psychic work and never given another reading of any kind."[25]

Cayce knew his Bible. He had asked himself and his wife for many years whether his work was of God or the devil. Since his philosophy after 1923 denied the existence of the biblical devil, his followers ignore the crucial question. Yet they should know that he once asked it. He concluded, using the argument of pragmatic humanism, that if good is accomplished, a work must be from God.[26] Healing people's sick bodies is obviously good. For thirteen years he had been doing just that. The voice had never lied before. Always before, he explained to Lammers, the voice had confined itself to healing. Nothing was ever said about reincarnation. He had always believed in the Christian view of life: ". . . souls born into the earth,

---

she had not agreed with *The Search for Bridey Murphy*: p. 10. She had herself hypnotized in the early 1970's in order to explore the possibility of past lives. She had often wondered where the vivid material for her historical novels had come from: pp. 18-19. She had long been visited by a "nameless Presence." She could only sense it, she said. "It was often her guide late at night when she was writing; and when she was traveling in some distant corner of the globe, it would often appear at her elbow and remind her that this was the ground she had traveled before" (p. 20).

24. Bro, *Religion*, p. 264.
25. Agee, *ESP*, p. 31.
26. Sugrue, *River*, p. 147.

to live a while, die, and be judged." He had *always* believed this. Yet he had watched the force he had been given for many years. "It hasn't ever done evil, and it won't let me do it. . . . But what you've been telling me today, and what the readings have been saying, is foreign to all I've believed and been taught, and all I have taught others, all my life. If ever the Devil was going to play a trick on me, this would be it."[27] This is Sugrue's reconstruction of that initial discussion, as Cayce and his wife must have related it. They saw this encounter as the watershed in their lives, and so do the historians of the movement. Cayce laid it on the line, and then abandoned his previous religious commitment. The voice he could never remember took precedence over the Bible he had read through so many times. He was never to return to orthodoxy.

Reincarnation was only the beginning. About 30% of the life readings dealt with the lost continent of Atlantis — that secular and occult version of Noah's flood.[28] The recently published paperback, *Edgar Cayce on Atlantis*, contains the choicest of these visionary historical tidbits. Stearn devotes chapter thirteen of his best-seller to Atlantis. We even have a chronology of Atlantis and its West Coast precursor, Lemuria (the West Coast always gets there first!):

1,000,000-800,000 B.C. — Early Lemurian development.

500,000 B.C. — Lemuria inundated by water, peoples scattered.

400,000-300,000 B.C. — Lemuria inhabited and civilization advanced.

250,000 B.C. — Second Lemurian catastrophe, possibly by fire.

200,000 B.C. — Early Atlantean culture emerged.

80,000 B.C. — First Atlantean disturbance. Final Lemurian submergence.

28,000 B.C. — Second Atlantean disturbance. Recorded biblically as the Great Flood.

10,700 B.C. — Final destruction and sinking of Atlantis.

10,390 B.C. — Completion of the Great Pyramid in Egypt by the priests Ra-Ta and Hermes.[29]

---

27. *Ibid.*, p. 247.
28. Agee, *ESP*, p. 203.
29. Furst, *Jesus*, p. 41.

Where is Atlantis? Cayce's followers find hints in the record that would point to Bimini. Cayce prophesied a great series of cataclysmic geological upheavals for the period 1958-98. *Edgar Cayce on Prophecy* is filled with specific prophecies, so far completely erroneous, relating to these upheavals. Jess Stearn, as late as 1967, somehow took Cayce's rambling prophecies quite seriously. Part of Atlantis will reappear soon, he said in 1940. Atlantis had broken into five islands. One of them was called Poseidia. (Why anyone bothered to name a handful of islands as they were breaking up is a mystery.) In any case, a June, 1940 reading was quite specific: "And Poseidia will be among the first portions of Atlantis to rise again. Expect it in sixty-eight and sixty-nine. Not so far away."[30] Not so far away in 1940, but just far enough away so that nobody was likely to be able to challenge the prophet in his lifetime. His geological predictions were equally as specific and equally as accurate. Yet Stearn saw fit to devote chapters 3-5 to earthquake predictions, plus chapter 13 to Atlantis. Even more pathetically, there is some poor Cayce convert who apparently has professional credentials as a geologist, who is devoting his career to a search for Atlantis. He serves as the official apologist for the geological portion of the Cayce readings. His name is not given by Stearn (a sign of Stearn's charity), but Stearn reverently refers to him as "the Geologist." The Geologist fully expects to see the fulfillment of Cayce's prophecies that, among other earth-shaking events, parts of the West Coast will break up and slide into the sea, probably in the latter portion of the 1958-98 period.[31] Japan will also slide into the sea.[32] The earth's axis will tilt.[33] The Great Lakes will empty into the Gulf of Mexico.[34] In 1932, he predicted a great catastrophe for 1936, which would involve a shaking of world powers, both politically and geologically.[35] In retrospect, it is not clear whether this prophecy referred to the annexation by Italy of Ethiopia, the abdication of Edward VIII of England, the coronation of King Farouk of Egypt, the exile of Trotsky from the Soviet Union, the Presidential candidacy of Republican Alf Landon, or the Spanish Civil War. Take your pick.

Two of the criteria of demon possession used by the Roman

---

30. Stearn, *Prophet*, p. 229.
31. *Ibid.*, p. 40.
32. *Ibid.*, p. 27.
33. *Ibid.*, p. 39.
34. *Ibid.*, p. 34.
35. *Ibid.*, p. 35.

Catholic Church are: 1) the ability of man to gain access to information not otherwise attainable by normal means, and 2) the ability to speak in foreign languages without prior instruction. Cayce's career exhibited both traits. The medical diagnoses certainly can be categorized as information unnaturally obtained. Stearn reports that he spoke in French, Italian, Spanish, German, teutonic German, and several unknown tongues.[36] Doris Agee claims that he spoke an even two dozen languages at various times.[37] It seems clear enough that his trance states were abnormal. (The third trait used by the Catholics is the demonstration of superhuman strength, which Cayce never exhibited.) His philosophical and cosmological speculations indicate that his trance states were demonic.

Cosmology

"What do witches believe in? First of all, we believe that each person has the ability to develop magical powers within himself. We seek ancient wisdom through psychic forces, and know that each individual has a personal link with the Godhead. Secondly, we believe in reincarnation, the survival of the spirit after death; it is essential to our faith."[38] So writes Sybil Leek, America's most famous self-proclaimed witch. The divinity of man, his access to supernatural power, ancient wisdom, psychic revelation, and reincarnation: here, in a nutshell, is the creedal position of the Cayce movement. Our thanks to Miss Leek for pinpointing the origin of this statement of faith, or if not the ultimate origin, then at least the competing organizational claims to its use.

The divine-human link is asserted in Cayce's theory of *pantheism-monism*. The doctrine of evolution is basic to Cayce's theory of *reincarnation-karma*. The source of manipulative power over nature, he taught, is man's control over specific *vibrations*. The theoretical foundation of his system is *humanism* — the deification of man. It is significant that these beliefs are shared by most, if not all, of the more prominent occult-theosophist-mental healing cults. Where such ideas are prominent, witchcraft casts its dark shadow over the organization or movement in question. Witchcraft, as Miss Leek correctly argues, is not simply magical spells or specific rituals, however important ceremonial magic is to witchcraft. Witchcraft is, above all, a

---

36. *Ibid.*, p. 257.
37. Agee, *ESP,* p. 65.
38. *Argosy* (Feb. 1975), p. 75.

way of life undergirded by a specific philosophy. This is why the overwhelming number of books dealing with witchcraft and occultism only skim the surface; they do not deal with the heart of witchcraft, namely, its world-and-life view. The rituals of occultism vary far more than the presuppositions that provide the philosophical and emotional support for the various rituals. The heart of witchcraft is not "bell, book, and candle"; the heart of witchcraft is its *humanism.*

Monism

"Wherever the Law of One has been taught, there truth has lived."[39] All is ultimately One. This doctrine is fundamental to mysticism, both eastern and western. God, man, and the universe are fundamentally one. The Creator-creature distinction, so crucial to orthodox Judaism and Christianity, is specifically denied. The so-called "spark of divinity" in each man supposedly leads all men back into oneness with God. One "life reading" announced: "The body, the mind, the soul are one within the physical forces; for the body is indeed the temple of the living God. In each entity there is that portion which is a part of the Universal Force, and that which lives on. All must co-ordinate and cooperate."[40] God is *impersonal*; only man is truly personal. This is another central theme of monist systems. Man is the personal agent of the impersonal God. "For in the measures ye mete to others — in worshipfulness or in hate, in consideration or in disregard — ye actually mete the material activities in relationship to Creative Forces, God."[41]

There are many passages in these readings that would appear to be orthodox; their content is not. The essence of Cayce's cosmology is simple: "While individuals differ, let the first principle be the starting point. ALL is One!"[42] It is the same cosmology that underpins Hesse's *Siddhartha*, Charles Manson's favorite novel. Man, in this scheme, becomes the co-creator with God, a co-sovereign of the universe, for man partakes of the very being of God. This is the humanism of the ancient pagan kingdoms, and it blends well with the godless humanism of the twentieth century which, by denying God, raises man's position to that of co-creator with the impersonal laws of evolution — the humanist's substitute for providence. Cayce's voice stated:

---

39. Sugrue, *River*, p. 351.
40. Mary Ann Woodward, *Edgar Cayce's Story of Karma* (New York: Berkeley Medallion, 1971), p. 46.
41. *Ibid.*, p. 84.
42. H. L. Cayce, *Venture Inward*, p. 112.

As has been indicated by some, ye are part and parcel of a Universal Consciousness, or God. And thus (part) of all that is within, the Universal Consciousness, or Universal Awareness: as the stars, the planets, the Sun and the Moon.

Do ye rule them or do they rule thee? They were made for thine own use, as an individual. Yea, that is the part (they play), the thought which thy Maker, thy Father-God, thinks of thee. For ye are as a corpuscle in the body of God; thus a co-creator with Him, in what ye think and in what ye do.[43]

A few "ye's" and "thee's" and "thy's" do not orthodoxy make. Those people who associate the sixteenth-century grammar of the King James Bible with the content of the Bible are apt to be misled by such revelations. No doubt, that is why the Cayce readings often (though not always) used such stilted phrases.

Cayce incorporated the philosophy of the readings into his own Sunday school lessons, but he was careful to update the language. *The Edgar Cayce Reader* presents his own interpretations of the voice messages that he could not remember, but which were taken down by his secretary. He became a *pantheist*: "Life isn't a bit different today from what it was a million years ago. Life is One. God is Life— whether in the oyster, the tree, or in us. Life is God and a manifestation of Him."[44] Yet men, in this karma-directed life, are not yet one with God, despite the fact that all life is a manifestation of God's being. A reading revealed that "there has been given to each soul that privilege, that choice, of being one with the Creative Forces."[45] Man was once a part of God, was separated from God, still is a manifestation of God, and is slowly—ever so slowly—returning to be in God once again. The process of evolutionary karma gives all souls not only second chances, but an infinite number of chances, to work off the effects of transgression. Given enough time and reincarnations, men can pay off their debts—debts owed not to an omnipotent, personal God, but to the very karmic laws.

In Cayce's theology, God is identified with Universal Forces, also called Universal Awareness. Ultimately, however, God is identified with man's own "higher consciousness"—a concept which is common to virtually all occult and New Age groups. In Cayce's readings, as in some of the other cults, this is referred to as the "I Am" consciousness. "Let yourself enter into deep meditation so that the I AM con-

---

43. Furst, *Jesus*, p. 52.
44. *Reader*, p. 23.
45. *Ibid.*, p. 111.

sciousness may make you more aware of how the purpose of this experience may be applicable in your life now. This is highly to be desired."[46] This is the search for the *deity within.* "It is not, then, to be a calling upon, a depending upon, a seeking for, that which is without, outside of self; but rather the attuning of self to the divine within, which is a universal, or the universal, consciousness. . . ."[47]

Because man can venture inward, he can tap the infinite powers of the universe. The goal, ultimately, is *power.* "What is the power of the soul, then? All that is within the infinite itself! All of that! It is ours!"[48] Hugh Lynn Cayce, summarizing the essence of his father's religion, points to the internalization of the universe—a mystical quest which leads, in Van Til's superb phrase, to the *integration into the void.* "It seems reasonable that the path of the spiritual quest, the returning to a state of spiritual awareness, must surely at times lead inward, past the dark areas of accumulated guilt and prejudice, fears and frustrations resulting from many false starts, to the lighted areas of the creative or God-mind. Unless we can believe that such areas of the self exist—where we can meet God face to face—we are doomed to a self-created world of confusion and perhaps self-annihilation. . . . This is a venture inward."[49]

Jesus, Karma, and Evolution

Karma, the doctrine of reincarnation, is *the central dogma* of the Cayce movement, just as it is in Sybil Leek's version of witchcraft. Karma is the ancient Eastern belief that all souls—to the extent that they are personal at all—must live numerous lives, sometimes rising toward God, sometimes falling away from God, but always getting another chance. The good or evil that a man does in each life has an effect on all subsequent lives.

A phrase which appeared in many of the readings, and which appears in all of the Cayce books, is the biblical phrase, "You must reap what you sow." Not in a final judgment, as the Bible affirms, but in endless incarnations. It does not take a genius to understand that this view of man must affirm that *man is fundamentally good*; no evil act, no matter how perverse, can alienate man from God forever. His good deeds can, given a sufficient number of reincarnations,

---

46. Furst, *Jesus*, p. 232.
47. Agee, *ESP*, p. 77.
48. Furst, *Jesus*, p. 19.
49. H. L. Cayce, *Venture Inward*, pp. 206-07.

overcompensate for the evils of all previous lives — denying the biblical view of law affirmed by the Apostle James: "For whosoever shall keep the whole law, and yet offend in one point, he is guilty of all" (James 2:10). The Apostle Paul wrote: "Therefore by the deeds of the law there shall no flesh be justified in his sight . . ." (Romans 3:20). Only because of the perfect fulfilling of the law by Jesus Christ, which he came to fulfill (Matt. 5:17), can men be viewed by God as righteous; Christ died for the sins of many (Romans 5:6-11). To use a crude analogy, one transgression of the law is like a zero. In all schemes of reincarnation, zeroes are added up, and positive deeds can register. They can offset the zeroes. In the biblical view, zeroes are multiplied into the string of deeds: one zero negates the entire product. The two systems are antithetical.

Out of One came many. This is the religion of the East. It is Cayce's faith: "In the beginning was the Word, the Word was God, the Word was with God. 'HE MOVED.' Hence, as He moved, Souls, portions of Himself, came into being."[50] This rewriting of the first chapter of the Gospel of John is a mirror image of that gospel. Souls did not come out of a God who moved; they came from a God who *spoke*. His fiat creation was by the power of His word. Not so in Eastern systems of thought, and the Creator-creature distinction is blurred. Therefore, the process of souls over time is back into the One. Cayce's trance readings are the revelations of the East.

The revelations are peculiar, even by Eastern standards. They affirmed a very strange story of the origin of men. There were two separate waves of souls. The first were "thought forms" that tried to imitate God's creation. These were the "Sons of Man." (They were not, of course; they turn out to be the fathers of animals and stones.) These thought forms immersed themselves in the earth — in rocks, trees, and animals. They could not escape their own creations, however, so a second wave of souls, the "Sons of God," intervened. They came to rescue their brethren. This wave was led by The Master, who is known to us, among other incarnations, as Jesus. They fashioned or evolved human bodies by means of thought forms. Meanwhile, the first wave went on creating, producing monsters: winged, feathered, hoofed, and clawed "men," plus dragons and other weird beasts. But the master's souls continued to create, and thus the five races of man were formed at one time. This took place about one

---

50. Furst, *Jesus*, p. 32.

million, B.C.[51]

Later on, Atlantis was formed (300,000 B.C.). The Master took on a human form at this point — 700,000 years after the creation of the five races. He was called Amilius, or Adam. Here is the heart of Cayce's *soteriology* — his doctrine of salvation. The Master, as Amilius-Adam, fell ethically.

Question: When did Jesus become aware that he would be the Saviour of the world?
Answer: When he fell in Eden.[52]

Eden, as later readings seem to imply, was Atlantis. Then the Master began his series of incarnations. He subsequently became, among others: Enoch, Melchizedek, Joseph (son of Jacob and Rachel), Joshua, Zend (father of Zoroaster), Asapha or Alfa (an Egyptian), and finally Jesus.[53] He was incarnated for a total of 30 times, which the voice affirmed as a very low number to achieve perfection.[54] The Master's real name was Jeshua. He was also Hermes, the builder of the Great Pyramid of Egypt. Amazingly enough, his partner in this important task was the priest RaTa, who was an early incarnation of . . . Edgar Cayce![55] The identification of Jesus with Hermes is extremely significant in occult circles. The Egyptian god Thoth was identified as Hermes by the Greeks, also referred to as Hermes Trismegistus (thrice great). The importance ascribed to Hermes Trismegistus by early medieval magicians, astrologers, and occultists cannot be overstressed. The development of Renaissance magic around the legends of Hermes has been studied in an exhaustive fashion by Frances Yates. Hermes was understood as the real founder of the magical arts. Miss Yates makes a shrewd observation concerning the "cult of Egypt" in the second century, when the legend of Hermes originated. It fits the Cayce cult quite well:

The men of the second century were thoroughly imbued with the idea (which the Renaissance imbibed from them) that what is old is pure and holy, that the earliest thinkers walked more closely with the gods than the busy rationalists, their successors. Hence the strong revival of Pythagoreanism

---

51. *Ibid.*, pp. 32-35, 40-41.
52. *Ibid.*, p. 23.
53. *Idem.*
54. *Ibid.*, p. 71.
55. *Ibid.*, pp. 78-79.

in this age. They also had the impression that what is remote and far distant is more holy; hence their cult of the "barbarians," of Indian gymnosophists, Persian magi, Chaldean astrologers, whose approach to knowledge was felt to be more religious than that of the Greeks. In the melting-pot of the Empire, in which all religions were tolerated, there was ample opportunity for making acquaintance with oriental cults. Above all, it was the Egyptians who were revered in this age. . . . The belief that Egypt was the original home of all knowledge, that the great Greek philosophers had visited it and conversed with Egyptian priests, had long been current, and, in the mood of the second century, the ancient and mysterious religion of Egypt, the supposed profound knowledge of its priests, their ascetic way of life, the religious magic which they were thought to perform in the subterranean chambers of their temples, offered immense attractions.[56]

That Hermes-Jesus and RaTa-Cayce had once worked together on that greatest of all magical and occult projects, the Great Pyramid, no doubt sent a wave of anticipation down the spines of Cayce's followers. Here was Cayce, RaTa reincarnate, launching yet another work of mysterious power and mysterious knowledge.[57] They would be a part of it. Hugh Lynn Cayce may not have accepted the mumbo-jumbo of reincarnation, preferring instead to see the venture inward as a psychological operation, but his followers do not seem to have been equally sophisticated. The stories of the reincarnations, especially concerning Jeshua-Jesus, are referred to in numerous Cayce-related volumes.

The Master, Jesus, was a man. Until the very end of his reincarnation cycles, Jesus was a fallen man. When he went into the wilderness, he went "to meet that which had been His undoing in the beginning."[58] What we have in the life of Jesus of Nazareth, therefore, is a fine ethical *example*: "In that the man, Jesus, manifested in the world the Oneness of His will with the Father, He becomes—from man's viewpoint—the only, the first begotten of the Father. Thus he is the example to the world, whether Jew, Gentile or any other religious force."[59] Jesus is the humanistic example of the good life, even the final good life which overcomes all our former and imperfect lives.

---

56. Frances Yates, *Giordano Bruno and the Hermetic Tradition* (New York: Vintage, [1964] 1969), p. 5.

57. I can't stand it any more! I have to say it! "RaTa, RaTa . . . RaTa, RaTa, ring, ring, ring." There. I feel a lot better. Now let's get back to our story.

58. Furst, *Jesus*, p. 172.

59. *Ibid.*, p. 173.

Q. What is the significance and meaning of the words "Jesus" and "Christ" as they should be understood and applied?

A. Jesus is the man — the activity, the mind, the relationships that He bore to others. Yea, he was mindful of friends, He was sociable, He was loving, He was kind, He was gentle. He grew faint. He grew weak, and yet gained that strength which He has promised in becoming the Christ, by fulfilling and overcoming the world. Ye are made strong in body, in mind, in soul and purpose, by that power in Christ. The pattern is Jesus.[60]

There is nothing in these words that could offend the nonorthodoxy of three generations of Social Gospel preachers, seminary professors, and run-of-the-mill humanists. What is fundamental in Cayce's doctrine of Jesus, which he shares with practically every other occult group now popular with the young, is not Jesus the God-man whose death satisfied the justice of a personal, holy God, but rather the *Christ-Consciousness* which is available to every man. The Protestant idea that every man, regenerated by Christ, serves as prophet, priest, and king, because Christ was the ultimate prophet, priest and king, becomes in the philosophies of the occult groups the idea that every man is his own Jesus, his own savior.

Q. 16 The problem which concerns the proper symbols, or similes, for the Master, the Christ. Should Jesus be described as the Soul who first went through the cycle of earthly lives to attain perfection including perfection in the planetary lives also?

A. 16 He should be. This is as the man (he was), see?

Q. 17 Should this be described as a voluntary mission (on the part of) One who was already perfected and returned to God, having accomplished His oneness in other planes and systems?

A. 17 Correct.

Q. 18 Should the Christ Consciousness be described as the awareness within each soul, imprinted in pattern on the mind and waiting to be awakened by the will, of the soul's oneness with God?

A. 18 Correct. That's the idea exactly.[61]

When asked the meaning of *resurrection* from the dead, the voice replied that it meant reincarnation, "which is what the word meant

---

60. *Ibid.*, pp. 173-74.
61. *Ibid.*, p. 68.

in those days."[62] Since all men are reincarnated, all men are continually resurrected. There is a doctrine of atonement in the Cayce readings, and it involved the shedding of blood for the unjust.[63] But he who died was only a man — a perfect man, of course, but a man. It was a man who fully restored himself to God. The example of Jesus is clearly the example of self-atonement and personal self-sacrifice. Jesus "is an example for Man and only as a man, for He lived only as a man. He died only as a man."[64] If Jesus was a savior, then each man must also be a savior. "Each and every soul must be the Savior of some other soul, to even comprehend the purpose of the entrance of the Son into the earth."[65] This is the salvation of humanism — the soteriology of Satan.

Cayce gave 2,500 of these "life readings" throughout his career. People were fascinated with the information regarding their supposed past lives. An amazing number of the ones recorded in the Cayce books were lives of people who had some connection to the ministry of Jesus. One which fills up many pages in *Edgar Cayce's Story of Jesus* concerns a woman, Judy, who in a former life was Josie, the teacher of Jesus. It seems that Jesus was an Essene, the sect about which very little is known, conveniently for the life readings. The life readings of "Judy" and others reveal that the Essenes were deeply involved in the "secret wisdom of the East": astrology, numerology, kabbala, reincarnation — all the things so dear to middle-aged ladies from Pasadena, former LSD trippers, and drop-outs from Berkeley. It was Josie who helped Mary and Joseph flee from Palestine and go to Egypt. Predictably, the readings revealed that Jesus was initiated into the secrets of Egypt. (The way the stories have been getting out for 2,500 years, it is amazing that there are any secrets of Egypt left.) She was also there when Jesus studied in Persia and India.[66] (Over and over, the story of Jesus' training in Eastern mysteries comes up in the literature of the higher-consciousness cults.) Jesus may have been a Jew, but his connection to Egypt was crucial: "For as indicated oft by this channel (Cayce) the unification of the teachings of many lands were [sic] brought together in Egypt; for that was the center from which there was to be the radial activity of influence in the earth. . . ."[67]

---

62. *Ibid.*, p. 26.
63. *Ibid.*, p. 220.
64. *Ibid.*, p. 247.
65. *Ibid.*, p. 284; cf. 270.
66. *Ibid.*, pp. 164-66.
67. *Ibid.*, p. 171.

There is not a single shred of evidence that Jesus ever stepped foot in an Egyptian temple, for his family returned after the death of Herod (Matt. 2:15), who died in 4 B.C. Since Herod had executed the children around the Bethlehem region two years after the birth of Jesus (Matt. 2:16), this indicates that Jesus was two or three years old when his family returned. Only if it is assumed that there was a large gap of time between the slaying of the children and Herod's death, for which there is no evidence, could Jesus have been initiated into the mysteries. At age twelve, he was in Jerusalem, arguing with the priests (Luke 2:42). How young were boys initiated into super secret Egyptian mysteries? As for his travels to Persia and India, there is not a word. This legend is the product of the desire of generations of occultists and neo-gnostics to insert their anti-Christian ideas into religious circles that are at least officially Christian. Yet it is not simply a strategy of men; the voices of the trances affirm this secret tradition over and over. There is a source of this historical tradition, and it is not earthly, any more than Cayce's ability to report on druggists' shelves from a trance condition was earthly.

There is no final judgment. Judas Iscariot is still working out his salvation on earth, the readings informed the Cayce circle. In fact, one of Cayce's clients was the reincarnated Judas, file number 5770, "a fine man today," the voice affirmed.[68] If Judas gets a second chance, anyone seems safe! "For the Father has not willed that any souls should perish and is thus mindful that each soul has again — and again — the opportunity for making its paths straight."[69] There need be no final judgment, for there is no ultimate ethical debt:

Q. What debt do I owe J. M.?

A. Only that ye build in thine own consciousness. For every soul, as every tub, must stand upon its own self. And the soul that holds resentment owes the soul to whom it is held — much. Hast thou forgiven him the wrong done to thee? Then thou owest naught![70]

What we have, then, is "not a karmic debt *between* but a karmic debt of *self* that may be worked out *between* the associations that exist in the present."[71] This revelation may not be too clear, but it does

---

68. *Ibid.*, p. 314.
69. Woodward, *Karma*, p. 23.
70. *Ibid.*, p. 22.
71. *Ibid.*, p. 21.

relieve men of worrying about a final judgment—or would if it were true. Furthermore, the voice affirmed that this karmic debt of self "is true for every soul."[72] Man saves himself, for he can cancel debts owed to other souls by forgiveness, while he cancels his only other debt— the self-owed karmic debt—by working out his salvation through his own labor.

Salvation is therefore an evolutionary process. "Then, karmic forces—if the life application in the experience of an individual entity GROWS to a haven of peace and harmony and understanding; or ye GROW to heaven, rather than going to heaven; ye grow in grace, in understanding."[73]

Q. Are souls perfect, as created by God in the first? If so, why is there any need of development?

A. The answer to this may only be found in the evolution of life, in such a way as to be understood by the finite mind. In the first cause or principle all is perfect. That portion of the whole (manifested in the creation of souls) may become a living soul and equal with the Creator. To reach that position, when separated, it must pass through all stages of development, in order that it may be one with the Creator.[74]

This is the theology of ancient gnosticism. It involves a steady evolution of spirit back into God. Hugh Lynn Cayce, summarizing his father's faith, writes: "Through the guidance of the Christ-Soul the earth has been made a ladder up which souls may return to a consciousness of atonement with the Creator. Through a series of incarnations in matter in human form the soul can learn to cleanse itself of selfish desires blocking its more perfect understanding and to apply spiritual law in relation to matter. Urges created in the material plane must be met and overcome, or used, in the material plane."[75] This concern with matter, in contrast to ethical rebellion, is characteristic of all gnostic sects.

Orthodox Christianity teaches that men will have their bodies restored to perfection—material bodies. We shall be like Jesus, the incarnate son of God, in His perfect humanity (I Cor. 15). Men were made in the image of God; they do not partake of God's divinity. For

---

72. *Idem.*
73. *Ibid.*, p. 17.
74. *Ibid.*, p. 255.
75. H. L. Cayce, *Venture Inward*, p. 75.

gnostics and mystics, perfect humanity, being material, is imperfect. Nothing less than divinity, than reigning co-equal with God and in God, will suffice. Man is, in the final analysis, God. At the end of evolution, he enters the Godhead. Man, by his own labors, creates his own divinity. "In the day ye eat thereof, then your eyes shall be opened, and ye shall be as gods . . ." (Gen. 3:5). Some ideas never lose their glitter in the eyes of those who are not satisfied with the limitations of their creaturehood.

The process of salvation, in Cayce's scheme, is one of increasing one's own merit. Each man receives such information as he merits, the voice informed Cayce's stenographer.[76] Thus, it is a system based on the affirmation of autonomous man, the self-savior of his soul. Gina Cerminara, the most straightforwardly anti-Christian, pro-reincarnation of the Cayce writers, summarizes the essence of Cayce's doctrine of salvation. What she writes is applicable to any system of karmic cosmology. Where the doctrine of reincarnation is preached, this perspective, in one form or another, will invariably be present:

For almost twenty centuries the moral sense of the Western world has been blunted by a theology which teaches the vicarious atonement of sin through Christ, the Son of God. Even skeptics, in the face of the strange events and the tremendous influence that emanated from this man, may concede that Christ was in a sense a Son of God and that—noble and compassionate—he lived and died so that men might be free. But more and more, in the light of the advances of modern physics, people are coming to feel that all life in the universe, down to the minutest power-charged atom, is in essence related to each other life in the universe by virtue of a common sustaining source in one central energy, or God. By this view it seems necessary to conclude that all living things, and all men and women, are the sons of God—like rays from some vast central sun. It can be felt then that perhaps the personality called Jesus was different from us only in that he was closer to the central light than we are.

Moreover, Christ's giving of his life that men might be free is no unique event in history; the study of comparative religions reveals other saviours, among other peoples, who suffered martyrdom and death. In our own Western culture, many idealists have given their lives willingly for humanity's sake, Mazzini, Bolivar, Lincoln, St. Francis, Toussaint L'Ouverture, Semmelweiss, St. Teresa—a hundred names and more can be cited of men and women who lived and died that other human beings might be free. But

---

76. Furst, *Jesus,* p. 308.

no one feels that their effort redeems us from effort, or that their sacrifice absolves us of our own personal guilt.

To build these two statements, therefore—that Christ was the Son of God and that he died for man's salvation—into a dogma, has been the great psychological crime not of Christianity but of some of its theologians. It is a psychological crime because it places responsibility for redemption on something external to the self; it makes salvation dependent on belief in the divinity of another person rather than on self-transformation through belief in one's own intrinsic divinity. It violates the sense of justice and psychological verisimilitude because it declares that belief in vicarious atonement is necessary, the penalty for non-belief being everlasting damnation. Twentieth-century minds, trained rigorously in physical and psychological sciences, find it difficult to take such a doctrine seriously.[77]

I have quoted this statement at length, since it is one of the finest statements of what Christianity does hold and why a person with a Ph.D. in psychology, such as Dr. Cerminara, is willing to swallow the Cayce cosmology hook, line, and sinker. *It conforms far better with the humanist thought of the twentieth century!* Parapsychologists are unlikely to believe in either Cayce's karma theories or orthodox Christianity, but if it were a question of one or the other, Cayce would win every time. The humanist's dream of a man-centered universe is shared by the trance message-giver of Edgar Cayce. Karma is another form of humanism, or better yet, humanism is a modern version of the traditional view of man held by reincarnationists. It is a rival religion. Furthermore, Dr. Cerminara makes clear, it must be believed in, just as Christians claim that Christ must be believed in. He who refuses to believe in the reality of karmic laws must suffer karmic justice: "But whether karma is regarded as a debt or a deficit or a sort of spiritual deficiency, the fact remains that its redemption must be approached in a spirit of willingness rather than of rebellion. To 'deny' its existence partakes more of the nature of rebellion than of acquiescence; for such a 'denial' is expressive of the self-will and desire for convenience of the present personality, rather than the long-term wisdom of the eternal identity."[78] And also like Christianity, for those who believe, there is perfect peace: "In the universe of order and justice and beneficence which the reincarnation principle reveals, there is no need for fear."[79] Hebrews 9:27-28 says there is a

77. Gina Cerminara, *Many Mansions* (New York: Signet, [1950] 1967), p. 63.
78. *Ibid.*, pp. 72-73.
79. *Ibid.*, p. 75.

whole eternity to fear. One cannot hold both positions. Each side knows it. Or at least the consistent representatives do.

If we are to believe Dr. Cerminara, the doctrine of reincarnation has an important social and political corollary: *the irrelevance of institutional forms.* "Marriage as an institution is, by the reincarnationist view, less sacrosanct than many people think. If society wishes to make marriage indissoluble, well and good; if not, again well and good. Cosmic law will not be thwarted by either system — if man fails to meet an obligation in one existence, he will irrevocably be called to task in another. The outer forms which man sets up are almost as arbitrary and almost as unimportant as the rules he devises for gin rummy. In the last analysis it matters very little what rules are set up for any game, because through the forms and conventions of all of them it is skill and honesty in playing which are their intrinsic value."[80]

On the one hand, this is radically antinomian. It denies that there is any form of social order that is dictated by the limits and needs of mankind. But this is consistent with the humanism of karma: man is ultimately limitless. Therefore, by becoming radically antinomian, the reincarnationist opens up the possibility of radical authoritarianism. There is no ethical principle, no higher law, to which men can appeal other than social convention. Men must conform, in a Dewey-like fashion, to the rules of society. The Moloch state, as Rushdoony has called it, is set free from the restraining features of godly law. Men are left defenseless to play the institutional games of the totalitarian regime. The worst, as Hayek has said, will tend to get on top of such a coercive state system.[81]

Cayce's movement has proven to be quietistic and retreatist, waiting for Atlantis and California earthquakes. They wait for China to become the new cradle of Christianity, as predicted.[82] (Unfortunately, China did not become democratic in 1968, as predicted.[83]) They wait for the Soviet Union to change its present leadership, for a prophecy told them, "out of Russian comes again the hope of the world."[84] Not from Bolshevism, but from a reawakening of freedom: Russia's future will be crucial. So they wait, and hope,

---

80. *Ibid.*, p. 154.
81. F. A. Hayek, *The Road to Serfdom* (Chicago: University of Chicago Press, 1944), ch. 10.
82. Furst, *Jesus*, p. 333.
83. Stearn, *Prophet*, p. 90.
84. Furst, *Jesus*, p. 332.

and study the great prophecies. And the A.R.E. collects its royalties and continues its training in ESP techniques, one of the gateways to "higher consciousness" or "Christ Consciousness."

Vibrations

An occult corollary to the doctrine of karma is the theory that life is essentially a series of universal vibrations. As mentioned in a previous chapter, the use of the term "vibrations" by the counter-culture was no accident. The sources of the phrase are the many groups that are in, or on the fringes of, the occult underground. Everything is a vibration. One Cayce reading revealed: "The human body is made up of electronic vibrations, with each atom and element of the body, each organ and organism, having its electronic unit of vibration necessary for the sustenance of, and equilibrium in, that particular organism."[85] There is no fundamental difference between the realm of spirit and the realm of matter. "For things spiritual and things material are but the same conditions of the same element, raised to different vibrations. For all force is one force."[86] The emphasis on the healing ministry of Edgar Cayce is obvious in the literature, although it is subordinate to the emphasis on his philosophy-cosmology. Healing is an activity of vibrations. "Life in its expression in a human body is of an electrical nature. The vibrations from low electrical forces, rather than high vibrations, produce life-glowing effects."[87] Even more specifically, the color *green* "is the healing vibration."[88]

Vibrations relate to the human aura. The idea that each man possesses an aura is common to the occult tradition. The attempt by occultists to link the aura to the radiations revealed by Kirlian photography is an example of the relationship between paranormal scientific research and occultism. Cayce claimed that he could see auras around people — not in his trances, but during the normal daily activities. (The same claim is made by Castaneda and by don Juan.) This ability which Cayce claimed to have is mentioned by several of his followers.[89] He was supposedly able to diagnose people's moods by the color of their auras, indicating that the supposed phenomenon is not constant, but reflective of the human personality. These

---

85. Sugrue, *River*, p. 288; cf. 363-64.
86. Agee, *ESP*, p. 41.
87. Stearn, *Prophet*, p. 163.
88. *Ibid.*, p. 84.
89. Agee, *ESP*, ch. 7; Bro, *Religion*, ch. 5; H. L. Cayce, *Venture Inward*, p. 73.

auras are visualized vibrations.[90]

Nevertheless, the most important teaching connected to the vibration theory is that *God is a vibration*. Understanding this fact, the trance voice informed its listeners, is the key to one's personal salvation. This is the soteriology (doctrine of salvation) of vibrations. "For without passing through each and every stage of development, there is not the correct vibrations to become one with the Father. . . . Then in the many stages of development throughout the Universe or in the great system of the Universal Forces, each stage of development is made manifest through the flesh—which is the testing portion of the Universal Vibration. In this manner, then, and for this reason, all are made manifest in flesh and there is the development through aeons of time and space, called Eternity."[91] Vibrations, in short, are the key to evolution. They are also related to astrological influences: "Each planetary influence vibrates at a different rate of vibration. An entity entering that influence enters that vibration: (it is) not necessary that he change, but it is the grace of God that he may! It is part of the Universal Consciousness, the Universal Law."[92] Nevertheless, it is not the planets that determine life; it is *the will of man*. The voice was very specific on that point: "But let it be understood here, no action of any planet or any of the phases of the sun, moon, or any of the heavenly bodies surpass the rule of man's individual will power. . . ."[93] God, the Great Vibration, is secondary at best, probably tertiary, and possibly not half so powerful as the color green.

Garbled Messages

One problem faced by all occult mediums is that the messages from "the other side" are often incoherent. It is as if the wisdom of the spirit world gets short-circuited from time to time, leaving the recipients of this wisdom with the vague feeling that the spirits have been drinking steadily for several hours. Yet the language is always very profound, totally self-assured. For example:

First, the continuity of life. There is no time; it is one time; there is no space; it is one space; there is no force; it is one force; other than all force in its various phases and applications of force are the emanations of men's

---

90. Agee, *ESP*, p. 69.
91. Furst, *Jesus*, p. 57.
92. *Idem.*
93. Agee, *ESP*, p. 54; cf. Appendix B on astrology in Furst, *Jesus*.

endeavors in a material world to exemplify an ideal of a concept of the creative energy, or God, of which the individual is such a part that the thoughts even of the individual may become crimes or miracles, for thoughts are deeds and applied in the sense that these are in accord with those principles as given. That [which] one applies will be applied again and again until that oneness, time, space, force, or the own individual is one with the whole, not the whole with such a portion of the whole as to be equal with the whole.[94]

Got that? If so, then perhaps you are ready for the voice's answer to a question concerning the Sons of the Highest in Atlantis and the second coming of souls to earth:

There was, with the will of that as came into being through the correct channels, of that as created by the Creator, that of the continuing of the souls in its projection and projection—see? While in that as was of the offspring, of that as pushed itself into form to satisfy, gratify, that of the desire of that known as carnal forces of the sense, of those created, there continued to be the war one with another and there were then—from the other sources (worlds) the continuing entering of those that would make for the keeping of the balance, as of the first purpose of the Creative Forces, as it magnifies itself in that given sphere of activity, of that that had been given the ability to create with its own activity—see?[95]

Frankly, I am perfectly willing to admit that I simply do *not* see. It is way, way beyond my powers of comprehension. When one worker asked the sleeping Cayce in 1932, "How can the language used in the readings be made clearer, more concise and more direct?" the voice was concise and direct: "Be able to understand it better."[96] Doris Agee nevertheless gives us hope: "Just as you found when you first encountered Shakespeare or Chaucer, familiarity with the particular 'shape' of the language will make you more comfortable with it."[97]

I never did get used to Chaucer's 600-year-old English, but at least there are translators and commentators for Chaucer. So far, at least, Cayce's 1932 English is without a translator for a considerable portion of his revelations. But it is not really a translation problem. Those who made up the messages did not wish to communicate anything of substance. Why should they? They themselves have no substance.

94. *Reader*, p. 159.
95. Furst, *Jesus*, p. 36.
96. Agee, *ESP*, p. 28.
97. *Idem.*

Conclusion

Edgar Cayce was a man who saw auras, he said; read people's minds, he said; received visions and revelations throughout his life, he said; and was not an occultist, he said. He did go into something like 25,000 trances over the years, and the records of over 15,000 of them are still available for inspection by researchers. He has been the subject of dozens of books. There seems to be no serious evidence available that he faked the trances; if he did, the motive is obscure. Some of his prophecies and diagnoses — of a minutely detailed kind — did turn out as he had said. These served as the bedrock for the construction of a humanistic, occult cosmology: reincarnation, vibrations, evolution, monism, pantheism, etheric planes of existence, and so forth. What is central to the Cayce movement is his cosmology, not the "signs and wonders" that served as the magical validation of the later philosophy.

Max Weber, the great German sociologist, defined charismatic authority as that possessed by some unique personality because of certain magical qualities or demonstrations — the Bible's signs and wonders — "by virtue of which he is treated as endowed with supernatural, superhuman, or at least specifically exceptional powers. . . ."[98] Because of these powers or qualities, he is considered a leader. His rule is characterized by hostility to all other forms of authority, whether bureaucratic (rational) or traditional. He comes with the words, "You have heard it said. . . . but I say unto you. . . ." To a very great extent, this classification applies to Cayce. He possessed the unique abilities, and once he had established a small following, primarily confined to his family and close friends, he was then able to take the traditional language of Christian orthodoxy — "you have heard it said" — and transform the meaning into the commonplace, but seemingly revolutionary, interpretations of gnostic mysticism — "but I say unto you." Given the enormous popularity of Cayce-related materials, it would seem that as a charismatic prophet, he was quite successful.

The reasons why the movement has spread are varied. First, it is basic to the post-1964 times: anti-establishment, inquisitive, curious about the unexplained, interested in new avenues of power, desperate to establish new forms of community. Yet at the same time,

---

98. Max Weber, *Economy and Society* (New York: Bedminster Press, [1924] 1968), p. 241.

Cayce's philosophy is so thoroughly at one with the underlying presuppositions of modern thought: relativistic, man-centered, hostile
to Christian dogma, universalistic, messianic. His is a system of
process philosophy, so deeply ingrained in Western thought since Darwin. "Now is Truth such a thing that those who have been followers
of Mohammed have *all the truth*? Have those who have been the followers of Moses, the law-giver, all of the truth? Or hasn't it been,
rather, a growth in our individual lives; and what may be truth for
one individual may not, in the experience of another individual, answer at all? Does that make the other any less true for the other individual. . . . Then if this be true, it is possible that truth is a
changeable thing — is a growth."[99]

Truth is totally man-centered, "the essence with which an individual builds faith, hope and trust." It is, in "theologian" Paul
Tillich's popular phrase, an "ultimate concern." Man constructs his
own truth, his own God: "[W]hat you hold before yourself, to create
that image you worship — that is what will develop you always upward, and will continue to enable you to know truth."[100] Cayce then
came to a doctrine of truth and God which is essentially Hegelian-
fascist-Marxist: "Truth, then, being a growing thing; truth, being a
thing that will develop you; is a something that is *entirely in action*!
That's what God is! For in every *movement* that has ever been, there
has been a continual upward development — upward toward that
which is Truth. . . . What is prayer but simply attuning yourself to
that which you are seeking assistance through? That's all prayer is
— the attunement to that very same thing; and *that becomes Truth when
it becomes an action*. When it goes into action, to you it becomes
Truth. . . . You go on whichever way your standard is set."[101]

Hegel writing of the movement of the dialectic, Marx writing of
the unity of theory and practice, or Mussolini writing of the necessity of a life of pure action: the evolutionary thrust leads to *total, un-
compromising relativism*. No wonder Cayce's cosmology — on the surface so archaic — could have attracted so many modern followers. It
holds out that most ancient of modern heresies: the desire to worship
oneself as God. Man, made in the image of God, wishes to worship
an image rather than the Creator. The second commandment prohibits this practice, but Cayce asks: "Why not? Because if you make

99. *Reader*, pp. 31-32.
100. *Ibid.*, p. 33.
101. *Ibid.*, p. 34.

an image, it becomes your God. But if you have for your God that which is within your own individual self—you yourself being a portion of the Creator—you will continue to build upward, to it!"[102]

Or downward, downward, downward—into the fiery void.

Edgar Cayce's writings, and the writings about him, reflect a striking continuity of thought, from gnostic speculations in the century following Christ to the present. He was not a profound man. He did not build a large organization. But he left a huge body of written materials—so vital in this day of footnotes and verification. As a representative of occultist philosophy, he is far more personal and believable than a Madame Blavatsky, more readable than Alice Bailey and the publications of her Lucis Trust. He shares most of the central ideas of the rival gnostic groups, but his work seems so human, and his modesty was so remarkable, that the average middle-class humanist can hardly resist "the sleeping prophet." They do not recognize the source of his revelations. It all seems so curious; at worst it seems innocuous.

The Cayce movement is indeed a curiosity. It is not innocuous. Ideas do have consequences.

---

102. *Idem.*

7

DEMONIC HEALING

Thou shalt not bow down to their gods, nor serve them, nor do after their works: but thou shalt utterly overthrow them, and quite break down their images. And ye shall serve the LORD your god, and he shall bless thy bread, and thy water; and I will take sickness away from the midst of thee.

Exodus 23:24-25

There is probably no educational guild more outspoken in its claim to a technical monopoly than modern medicine, and none more confident in its claims than American medicine. The idea that alternative forms of healing exist is immediately treated as the promotion of quacks — quack being defined as anyone who claims to be able to accomplish healing apart from the techniques and presuppositions of modern medicine. While the overwhelming number of sicknesses are treated outside the office of a physician — home remedies, self-diagnosis and cure, chiropractic, and the old favorite, two aspirins and plenty of rest — there is little doubt that most modern Americans believe that healing is accomplished by means that are scientifically explainable in principle, if not in fact at the present. (No one knows exactly how an aspirin relieves a headache.) This is the very essence of modern intellectualism. Max Weber, the great German scholar, set forth the basic principles of the modern world view in 1918:

Scientific progress is a fraction, the most important fraction, of the process of intellectualization which we have been undergoing for thousands of years and which nowadays is usually judged in such an extremely negative way. [The anti-rationalistic themes of the post-1965 counter-culture were in vogue half a century earlier — G.N.] Let us first clarify what this intellectualist rationalization, created by science and by scientifically oriented technology, means practically. Does it mean that we, today, for instance, everyone sitting in this hall, have a greater knowledge of the conditions of life under which we exist than has an American Indian or a Hottentot? Hardly. Unless he is a physicist, one who rides on the streetcar has no idea how the car happened to get into motion. And he does not need to know. He is satisfied that he may 'count' on the behavior of the streetcar, and he orients his conduct according to this expectation; but he knows nothing about what it takes to produce such a car so that it can move. The savage knows incomparably more about his tools. . . . The increasing intellectualization and rationalization do *not*, therefore, indicate an increased and general knowledge of the conditions under which one lives.

It means something else, namely, the knowledge or belief that if one but wished one *could* learn it at any time. Hence, it means that principally there are no mysterious incalculable forces that come into play, but rather that one can, in principle, master all things by calculation. This means that the world is disenchanted. One need no longer have recourse to magical means in order to master or implore the spirits, as did the savage, for whom such mysterious powers existed. Technical means and calculations perform the service. This above all is what intellectualization means.[1]

The disenchantment of the world: here is one of Weber's most powerful and influential themes. Unquestionably, the development of modern, Western thought, especially since 1660, has promoted this process of disenchantment. The average man believes in God, but he also believes in technology and science, and he looks to these for answers to problems of physical pain and biological affliction. The escape from pain is perhaps the most revered development of the modern world. Ask anyone which scientific advance over the last century that he would least be willing to abandon forever, and if the list includes anesthetics, it will be checked off more readily than any other. Yet the use of anesthetics is primarily surgical; modern man believes in cutting. Four centuries ago, only elitist scientists and occultists believed such a thing (and both were served by the illegal services of grave robbers). But the cutting must be guided by rational, scientific knowledge.

It should not be surprising that Edgar Cayce's feats of trance-induced medical diagnosis and prescription are dismissed out of hand by professional medical men. Such practices must be invalid, by definition. Not only are they unsubstantiated claims made by un-

---

1. Max Weber, "Science as a Vocation" (1918); in H. H. Gerth and C. Wright Mills (eds.), *From Max Weber: Essays in Sociology* (New York: Oxford University Press, 1946), pp. 138-39.

professional occultists and mystics, the claims are, by their very nature, unverifiable by the *only* valid criteria of validation: the investigative techniques of rationalization. Such claims must be the products of fraud, self-delusion, madness, or ignorance of valid testing procedures. Interestingly enough, this same set of explanations was used by Reginald Scot to deny the occult power of the social phenomenon of witchcraft. He wrote his *Discoverie of Witchcraft* back in 1584, and the same old rationalistic arguments are still in current use by his intellectual heirs.

Nevertheless, in the field of non-rationalistic healing, or paranormal healing, or most accurately, demonic healing, Cayce was remarkable only within the confines of urbanized America. He left more records than anyone else — a peculiarly Western concern. But in terms of volume of healings, rapidity of diagnosis, and the rationalistically impossible nature of the cures, no one in man's recorded history has ever approached Brazil's José Arigó. (I avoid the accent, since his biographer did.)

Arigo

The story of Arigo is now known by millions of people outside of Brazil. The *Reader's Digest*, which has the largest circulation worldwide of any magazine, included a condensed version of John G. Fuller's *Arigo: Surgeon of the Rusty Knife* (1974) in its March 1975 issue. Fuller's study of flying saucers, *Incident at Exeter*, was one of the important books of the mid-1960's which helped to revive public interest in this aspect of the paranormal. *Arigo* is even more startling. It chronicles the life of Jose Pedro de Freitas, who was known from his youth as Arigo (jovial country bumpkin), a Brazilian peasant who possessed incomparable powers of healing. During the two-decade period, 1950-70, Arigo treated as many as *two million* patients; it may have been less, but only due to the fact that some may have returned more than once. He saw over 300 patients per day, five days a week, for almost 20 years. He ran them through his "clinic" for about six hours a day. He spent only about one minute on each patient: diagnosis, treatment, and/or written prescription. If St. Paul could claim historical justification for the resurrection of Christ because Christ was seen by 500 people (I Cor. 15:6) and also defend himself and his account of the resurrection in a court of law by arguing that "this thing was not done in a corner" (Acts 26:26b), then the fact that two million people saw Arigo at work should be very solid evidence.

When the Brazilian authorities began an investigation of his healing ministry in order to convict him of that crime of crimes—practicing medicine without a license—they could find no one to testify that he had injured anyone or defrauded them of their money. They finally could convict him only by using the testimony of supporters that he had healed them, since this admission proved that he was indeed practicing medicine, and he did not have a license. When no complaints out of two million possible clients can be ferreted out by the authorities, it seems safe to say that Arigo had a most remarkable practice. If he were in the United States today, he might well be the only medical practitioner who might be profitably insurable by the insurance companies against malpractice suits at rates that anyone could reasonably afford.

The volume of patients is only the tip of the implausible iceberg. His method of operation was to take a simple pocket knife, jab it into the body of the patient (usually his eye), twist it around violently, reach in and pull out the growth or whatever, seal up the flesh in a matter of seconds without stitches, and send the patient on his way. And most implausible by the standards of modern medicine, he accepted no pay. ("The story *has* to be false, then," the skeptic will say.) There was no pain on the part of the patients, no fear, little bleeding (if there was, he could command it to stop), and no scarring. This process was recorded on movie film on numerous occasions, witnessed by physicians at close range, run and rerun in slow motion. No one ever detected a single sign of fraud, manipulation, or sleight-of-hand. On occasion, he would leave the knife stuck in a person's eye while he turned around to pick up tweezers or another implement, returning to his jabbing and twisting a few moments later. This was hardly a repeatable stunt, yet physicians witnessed it on many occasions. (We are still waiting for The Amazing Randi to offer to duplicate it on the Johnny Carson Show in front of a team of M.D.'s. No doubt he will claim that he could do it, but he is busy doing stage work in Cincinnati.)

Like so many of the faith healers and miracle workers, he had not been a good student. Several of his brothers had gone on to higher education, but after dropping out of third grade, Arigo returned to the family farm. From his earliest years, he had experienced flashes of eerie light and hallucinations, but they were relatively infrequent and he refused to discuss them. Also like so many occultists who display paranormal powers, he would hear a voice which spoke in a strange language.[2] He grew up where he finally died, in a small town about 250 miles north of Rio, Congonhas do Campo. He married in 1943 at the age of 25.

In his early working days as an adult, he worked as a miner, walking to the mine seven miles each way. He became a union organizer and then its president. The union struck, was compelled by the authorities to return to work, and that ended Arigo's years in the mines. When he resigned his presidency, he opened a restaurant, dabbled in real estate, and sold used cars. His visions increased, too, primarily in dreams. The voice continued to speak to him in these dreams, and he recognized the language as German. He kept dreaming of a hospital operating room.[3]

Finally the voice identified itself. It claimed that it was the spirit of Dr. Adolpho Fritz, a German physician who had died in 1918. He announced that he intended to use Arigo to complete his as yet unfinished work. He did not explain why a Brazilian peasant was necessary to complete the work of a German physician. Arigo awoke from this dream-hallucination and ran screaming into the streets, naked. Friends had to lead him home. Headaches began, and nothing could cure them, including an official church exorcism. Finally, he capitulated to "Dr. Fritz," consenting to participate in his work. According to Arigo, the headaches immediately ceased, beginning again only when he later temporarily agreed to discontinue the healings. Like Edgar Cayce, Arigo was possessed; without becoming a healer, he could not avoid the headaches and dreams, just as Cayce could not maintain his voice. Arigo was trapped.

The healings began on a small-scale basis. He would issue verbal commands for them to get well. They were not spectacular, although they gained enough notoriety to gain the warnings of the Roman Catholic Church to cease them. He put up a sign: "IN THIS HOUSE, WE ARE ALL CATHOLICS. SPIRITISM IS A THING OF THE DEVIL."[4] The headaches returned, along with daytime blackouts. He was in desperation.

It was at this point, in 1950, when a unique event took place. Senator Bittencourt, a pro-labor union politician, swung through Arigo's district in search of votes for the presidential candidate, Var-

2. John G. Fuller, *Arigo: Surgeon of the Rusty Knife* (New York: Pocket Books, 1975), p. 58.

3. *Ibid.*, pp. 58-60.

4. *Ibid.*, p. 64.

gas. Arigo still controlled the union's loyalty, and he promised to support Bittencourt. The senator invited Arigo and other miners to attend a rally in nearby Belo Horizonte. Both he and Arigo spent the night in a hotel in Belo Horizonte.

The senator had recently been informed that he was suffering from cancer of the lung. He was told that he required immediate surgery and that he should go to the United States for treatment. He intended to do just that as soon as the campaign was over. That night, as he lay on his bed, Arigo entered his room. He seemed to be in a trance. He was carrying a razor. Bittencourt blacked out. When he awoke the next morning, his pajama top was slashed, there was blood on both his chest and pajama top, and there was a neat incision on his rib cage. He got up, staggered to his closet to get dressed. He was in a state of shock. He went to Arigo and told him what he had seen. Then Arigo went into a state of shock. He had no memory of such a thing. He helped the senator to a taxi, got into his jeep, and drove home.[5] The senator went to his physician. When X-rayed, he learned that all traces of the cancer were gone.[6] This was a miracle. He began to tell people what had happened. He spoke of it in his political speeches. Arigo became an instant celebrity known throughout Brazil. The sick and wounded began streaming to his door. For the next two decades, they continued to come.

Brazil was the perfect place for a man of Arigo's talents. As Prof. Bryan Wilson writes, "perhaps there is no society with so rich a profusion of thaumaturgical cults as Brazil. . . ."[7] Elements of African tribal healing magic were imported with the slaves centuries ago. Catholicism, while officially hostile to magical practices, tended to absorb and modify the aboriginal healing traditions. The ancient practices continued. "Tribal deities and deities associated with fixed location," writes Wilson, "necessarily lost significance or acquired new functions among detribalized slaves. The integrative functions of religion for tribal groups were now no longer relevant, but the therapeutic and psychic functions of traditional religion, the practice of thaumaturge in putting individuals into contact with ancient and traditional sources of power and reassurance, acquired new appeal."[8]

---

5. *Ibid.*, pp. 55-56.
6. *Ibid.*, pp. 66-67.
7. Bryan R. Wilson, *Magic and the Millennium* (London: Hineman, 1971), p. 106.
8. *Idem.*

The primary forms of occult healing in Brazil are associated with one of three groups: umbanda, quimbanda, and Kardecism. Umbanda is an outgrowth of macumba, an African-originated religion of spirit possession. A rudimentary form of spiritualism, Western in origin, fused with macumba to produce umbanda. The umbanda priests seek communication with long-dead saints. Animal sacrifices are rejected. The priests practice occult healing, although they deny that they are involved in black magic. They distinguish their practices from the outright witchcraft of quimbanda. During spirit possession, umbanda priests and participants frequently speak in tongues, the same phenomenon known in Christian Pentecostal circles as glossalalia.[9] Quite frequently, members of the umbanda cult register as Roman Catholics. Umbanda developed as an independent movement in the early 1930's, but it has gained a mass audience only since World War II.

Far more curious than either umbanda or quimbanda is Kardecism. Named after Alan Kardec, a pseudonym of Leon Hyppolyte Denizart Revaill, a French spiritist (1804-69), Kardecists believe in a healing system based on guidance from deceased spirits who guide physicians in both consultations and actual operations. Instead of operating on the physical body, however, Kardecists operate on the "etheric body," which is suspended a few inches above the physical body. These healer-mediums actually use surgical instruments in these spirit operations. Supposedly, this operation can heal the physical body, too. The same occult technique is used by the British medium, George Chapman, although he does not use instruments, only his hands.[10] Well-trained Brazilian physicians who are licensed to practice medicine by the equivalent of the A.M.A., use Kardec techniques. They refer to these techniques as "supplements" to normal medical practice. By 1951, about the time that Arigo began his ministry, there were 21 Kardec associations in Brazil.[11] It is extremely interesting to compare the doctrines of Kardecism with those of the Cayce "readings."

According to Prof. Bryan Wilson, "The principal doctrines of Kardecism are: (1) the possibility and ease of communication with spirits; (2) reincarnation; (3) no cause exists without an effect, so that no one can escape the consequences of his acts; (4) the plurality

---

9. *Ibid.*, p. 113.
10. Hans Holzer, *Beyond Medicine* (New York: Ballantine, 1974), pp. 65-66.
11. Wilson, *Magic*, p. 118.

of inhabited worlds, each of which represents a stage of spiritual progress; (5) no distinction of natural and supernatural, or of science and religion: there is no grace, and individual progress depends exclusively on personal merit accumulated in earlier incarnations; (6) the principal virtue is charity as exercised toward the dead, the disembodied, and the living; (7) God is an immense distance from men; (8) there are important spirit-guides who help men; (9) Jesus Christ was the greatest incarnated being."[12]

With the exception of the idea that God is at an immense distance from men (Cayce's system was monistic, identifying God and the creation), and with the exception of showing charity to the dead, the doctrines are practically identical. Occult healings in Western settings generally are accompanied by a comprehensive and almost universally accepted cosmology, and Wilson's summary of Kardecism is a very useful summary for all of the other groups.

The setting was perfect for Arigo. Almost immediately, spiritists throughout Brazil began to claim Arigo for their own. This was especially true of Kardecist leaders. Although Arigo initially dismissed the theory, since he wanted to remain in good standing with the church, by 1968 he openly stated: "All my family are Catholic. I am a spiritist. But I believe that all religions take people to God."[13] By that time, the church and the civil authorities had ceased their efforts to stamp out his ministry.

His earliest spectacular cure which was witnessed by a number of people was of a woman with cancer of the uterus. She was dying, and the priest had administered the last rites. Arigo was a friend of the family, and he had come to pay his respects. Suddenly, the tingling sensation which accompanied a visit by Dr. Fritz—a sensation common to table-raising, ouija boards, and seance activity—rushed through his system. In a trance, he rushed to the kitchen, grabbed a knife, and ran back into the room. In front off the dazed family, he pulled down the sheet which covered the woman, thrust the knife into her body, and began to twist and jab, widening the opening. Finally, he reached into the wound, yanking out an enormous tumor, which was the size of a small grapefruit. Apart from the blood on the tumor, there was almost no bleeding at all. He returned to the kitchen, dropped the knife and tumor into the sink, and collapsed into a chair. When the family came into the kitchen, he was sobbing.

---

12. *Ibid.*, p. 118n.
13. Fuller, *Arigo*, p. 200.

The physician who had diagnosed the cancer was immediately called to the scene. He found no hemorrhaging. The "patient" claimed that she felt completely relieved. He took the tumor for examination, and the woman subsequently recovered.[14] There was no possible medical explanation for the tumor's removal, her survival, and the disappearance of all traces of cancer. Arigo had performed a miracle, according to the family.

The lines lengthened in front of his door. He would treat people for hours, yet after he was finished, he claimed that he remembered nothing. He wrote long, complicated medical prescriptions in a matter of half a minute, while staring blankly into space. He operated with a pair of scissors, a knife, and perhaps some tweezers. The prescriptions were sometimes for long-forgotten drugs, yet on other occasions they were so new that they were not yet imported into Brazil. The best pharmaceutical firms were used.[15] This later was an important point raised by his defense lawyer in opposition to the charge brought against Arigo of witchcraft. As his biographer writes: "In order to prove witchcraft, it was necessary to prove that a defendant had personally distributed concoctions of roots and herbs. This was clearly a thing Arigo never did."[16] Yet these weird prescriptions, often of abnormally high dosages, did not work when any other physician imitated them. They worked for Arigo and his immediate patients, but not for anyone else. His ministry was non-repeatable.

Carlos Paranhos da Costa Cruz was a dentist in Belo Horizonte, and had his office in the same building as the British consul, H. V. Walter. He reported the story of one of Arigo's operations to Walter, who was to become a frequent observer at Arigo's "clinic." Sonja, Cruz's sister-in-law, had cancer of the liver. This, at least, was the diagnosis of several physicians, including her own father. She was considered inoperable. In desperation, she, Cruz, and her father journeyed to Congonhas do Campo. She got in line, and when she came to Arigo, he asked no questions. He told them she had a tumor on her liver. He insisted on performing an operation. The description of what followed is nothing short of fantastic:

Within minutes, Sonja was placed on newspapers on the floor of Arigo's small room. Arigo brought some cotton and several instruments, including

---

14. *Ibid.*, pp. 20-21.
15. *Ibid.*, p. 75.
16. *Ibid.*, p. 125.

scissors and knives. He selected a penknife and made an incision. Both Cruz and his father-in-law knew that it was impossible to cut into the liver without massive hemorrhaging, and neither could explain why they permitted this to be done, or why they stood by passively as Arigo cut into the patient with an unsterilized knife and no anesthesia. Perhaps, they thought later, it was because this was the last chance: all else had been given up.

They watched for the blood to spurt out, but only a thin tickle slid from the sides of the wound. Then, Cruz claimed, an even stranger thing happened. Arigo inserted the scissors deep into the wound, removed his hand, and the scissors seemed to move by themselves. Cruz turned to look at his father-in-law, who nodded and exchanged glances. Later, they were to compare notes and confirm, at least to themselves, what they had seen. In moments, Arigo removed the scissors, reached into the wound, and pulled out a tumorous growth. With a showmanlike flourish, he slapped the tumor into Cruz's hand. Then he took the cotton and wiped it along the incision. When he was finished, the edges of the wound adhered together without stitches and Arigo momentarily placed a crucifix on it. Then he told Sonja to rise, which she was able to do. She was weak and shaky, but felt no pain.[17]

The biopsy of the tumor confirmed that the growth was cancer. The liver regenerated itself—it is the one major organ that can do this—and the woman lived. Neither Cruz nor his physician father-in-law had any rational explanation for what they had seen. Obviously not; there is no rational explanation, i.e., an explanation in terms of laws known to men or conceivably knowable to men. What they had seen was a denial of what Weber described as Western rationalization. It could not happen, rationally speaking. Only it did happen.

Prominent patients now joined the long lines of hopeful visitors. They waited for hours in line; it was first come, first served. (I wonder if "patient" refers to what people have to be in order get in to a physician's inner offices. No other profession has patients rather than clients—only those in the healing profession.) President Kubitschek, the builder of that majestic political pyramid, Brasilia, sent both his daughter and his pilot to visit Arigo, and both were cured. The head of his security police also was treated, and if Arigo was a fraud, this would have been a predictably harsh culmination of his career. Investigating physicians, who were willing to put their reputations on the line, publicly announced that the operations, while unexplainable, were successful: few scars, tissues removed skillfully,

17. *Ibid.*, p. 82.

valid diagnoses.[18]

Operating on Mrs. Maria Silveiro, in the presence of a visiting physician, Dr. Ladeira Margues of Rio, Arigo removed a piece of tissue 31 inches long and 15 inches wide from her ovaries. Dr. Margues later described the incision: "Arigo was taking hold of one half of the scissors. Then we [he and a safely anonymous physician friend] began to see the other side of the scissors start to move alone. It was as if another hand had taken hold of the free handle and was beginning to make clear motions, causing the scissors to snip and cut. The sound of metals and tissues being cut was obvious. In moments, 'Dr. Fritz' removed the scissors. When he saw bleeding begin, he ceased what he was doing, and said: 'Lord, let there be no more blood.' There was no further hemorrhage, as the operation went on."[19]

The possession of Arigo by a demon should be clear to anyone who takes seriously the biblical doctrine that it is appointed once for man to die and after this, the judgment. It was not a floating soul of a dead physician. Physicians do not have the power to perform the kind of surgery Arigo performed, not even dead Prussian physicians. The ability of Arigo to halt the flow of blood — an ability demonstrated on numerous occasions — is not medical; it is supernatural. The claims of the wife of Czar Nicholas II of Russia concerning the similar abilities of Rasputin with respect to the young Czarevitch, Alexie, become much more plausible in light of Arigo's skills. The charges of Rasputin's opponents, that he was sinister and even satanic, also seem more believable.

Arigo never signed any of the prescriptions that he was seen to write with lightening speed. Yet the local druggist did a land office business in filling the complicated prescriptions. The author does not explain the intricacies of Brazilian law respecting medical prescriptions, but since the druggist was never shut down, it appears that the practice was legal. Then again, maybe there were other ways of skinning the bureaucratic cat.

In 1963, Arigo was visited by a pair of investigators into the paranormal, Henry Belk and Henry (Andrija) Puharich, M.D. Both are well known within occult and paranormal circles. Puharich's other books, *The Sacred Mushroom* and *Uri*, have created considerable controversy, especially the latter. The word had filtered back to the

---

18. *Ibid.*, p. 91.
19. *Ibid.*, p. 99.

United States that a Brazilian peasant was performing impossible feats. They had come to test these abilities. Jorge Rizzini, who had previously photographed color moving pictures of Arigo's operations, joined them. His own wife had been cured of arthritis, and his daughter had been cured of leukemia. (Fuller's book reports on several astonishing cures of leukemia by Arigo's prescriptions.)

Arigo welcomed them. Almost immediately, he performed an operation. It was to leave Belk and Puharich totally dumbfounded. He picked up a four-inch paring knife, plunged it into an elderly man's eye socket, and began to scrape. The patient made no sign of being in pain. He also was not afraid. Arigo had Puharich place his finger on the eyelid in order to feel the blade beneath. Puharich confirmed that it was under the flesh. This, Arigo explained, was one of his methods of diagnosis. When he removed the knife, it had pus on it. There had been no bleeding and no scar remained. Total time elapsed: one minute.[20]

At eleven A.M., he left his "clinic" to go to his job as a receptionist in the local social security office. This was his sole source of income, other than his wife's sewing. The job took four hours a day. The Brazilian government obviously had its employees on the dole.[21]

Puharich had developed a non-malignant growth just under the skin of his right elbow. It was called a lipoma. He knew that it normally took twenty minutes to remove one, under ideal conditions. He decided to test Arigo. Arigo agreed. With Rizzini manning the movie camera, Puharich stepped up for his operation. A feeling of calm came over him. Arigo had him look away. He rubbed the knife over the elbow for a few seconds — Puharich estimated about half a minute — and then slapped the moist growth in Puharich's hand. The films revealed later that the whole operation had taken *five seconds*. It was medically impossible. Then, in his traditional medical care, he wiped the knife on his shirt and went on to the next patient. Yet no infection appeared in Puharich's arm. He took his lipoma back to New York.[22]

Anyone might have been baffled by what they saw, day after day, in Arigo's "clinic." A peasant healer who could write complicated prescriptions and spoke with a German accent. Knives in peoples eyes. Instant diagnoses. Hundreds of patients streaming through the

---

20. *Ibid.*, p. 19.
21. *Ibid.*, pp. 23-25.
22. *Ibid.*, pp. 35-36, 43.

lines each day. Yet Belk and Puharich took all these events in stride, or at least in staggering progression. What they could not grasp was Arigo's straightforward explanation of his talents:

The very fact that Arigo claimed to be "incorporated" by the spirit of a deceased German physician was enough to turn off most of the scientists who might be otherwise interested. This bothered Puharich and Belk too, and strained their own credulity. It was incredible enough to accept the documented empirical evidence, without having to consider a concept so foreign to the practical mind that it might shut off intelligent inquiry before it started. And yet this strange claim of spirit "possession" could not be ignored or buried, since Arigo insisted it was not only an integral part of his work, but was the entire essence of his skills and powers. Far from enhancing an explanation of what Arigo did and how he was able to do it, this was a stumbling block. A scientist who stood up before a meeting of a professional organization and began with a statement about Arigo and "Dr. Fritz" would be likely to be laughed off the podium.[23]

This is an extremely revealing fact. Modern science cannot handle the facts of paranormal science. Each of the major researchers will go so far into these studies of the scientifically impossible, convincing himself, step by step, that he is only investigating the statistically improbable. Dr. Thelma Moss calls her book, *The Probability of the Impossible*, which she then tries to make acceptable by dealing with these scientifically impossible facts by appealing to the "as yet unknown." What they will not face is the fact that there is a demonic realm of life — not just a metaphor of evil, but demonic activity in the realm of Kantian phenomena, i.e., the denial of Kant's neat cleavage between the unknown and the scientifically known. Puharich's account of Uri Geller is so totally improbable that one wonders why, apart from the expectation of enormous profit, any respectability-seeking publisher would have touched it. Messages from intergallactic robot ships, self-destructing cassette tapes, and on and on: Puharich could put his name on *Uri*, yet he feared, back in 1963 anyway, to consider the possibility that spirit possession is a fact of life. Anything might be true, except that. Let spirits of dead men into your universe, and the idea of a God who acts in history gets much too close for comfort. Let demons in, and you cannot protect yourself any longer without allowing God in, too — and that, above all, is what secular man dares not contemplate.

---

23. *Ibid.*, p. 45.

In the spring of 1957, Arigo had been convicted of practicing medicine without a license. Both the Roman Catholic Church and the medical association were behind the prosecution. He was put on probation, and in May of 1958, President Kubitschek pardoned him.[24] Throughout 1961, 1962, and 1963, the authorities once again began to build a case against him, now that Kubitschek was out of office and barred by the Brazilian constitution from holding the top office again. This time, however, the authorities also were planning to try him for witchcraft, a far more serious crime. Arigo had to be very careful. He knew that his visitors were collecting data that could be used against him, if only by subpoena. Nevertheless, he consented to have the photographs and movies taken. He hoped to have a full-scale investigation by scientists of his powers.

Belk and Puharich, as paranormal researchers, wanted more data. They were still operating under the delusion that if you can just gather enough examples of impossible events, orthodox scientists will accept their reality and reformulate their concepts of what is and is not possible. But all you should expect is that numerous impossible events are only marginally more difficult to dismiss than a single impossible event. It becomes a matter of rejecting a large sample of events as being either statistically insignificant (which is almost always the case, given the non-repeatability of most occult phenomena) or else insignificant because of a statistical fluke. The scientists will send the researcher back to tighten his controls and/or increase his sample until signs of the paranormal disappear. Only then will the orthodox scientist accept the verdict of the experiments. *The conflict is at bottom religious.* The orthodox scientist stands at the edge of a bottomless pit, daring the paranormal scientist to present another fact that cannot be explained by means of orthodox categories. Then he tosses it over his back and calls for more facts.

Puharich, like almost all paranormal researchers, has not understood the game establishment scientists play. After all, "para-scientists" have found the evidence compelling — up to a point. Not "over the line" into the occult, but compelling to an extent great enough to get them laughed off any orthodox podium. Once they have the facts, they try to explain them. They simply cannot do this, given their commitment to the standards of scientific investigation and correlation. But they try. They reach for explanations, like Dr. Eisen-

24. *Ibid.*, p. 134.

bud's psychoanalytic explanation of Ted Serios' mental photography. They press on, undaunted by skepticism, although not unaffected by it. They cease asking questions that are too embarrassing — the absolutely crucial questions, in other words. As Fuller writes: "Puharich himself had already challenged Arigo with his own lipoma operation. On the surface, this would be reasonably good evidence, if not proof, of the worthiness of further study of Arigo. So were the films. But these still would not be enough for the exacting requirements of scientific-journal publication, which demands, in addition to prolific footnote references of past practices and observations, some pragmatic frame of reference on which a theory could be built and accepted. It had taken centuries for acupuncture to be even considered worthy of scientific study. Arigo's practices went so far beyond acupuncture that they almost soared out of sight."[25]

Fuller's reference to acupuncture is quite appropriate, though totally misleading. It had not taken centuries for acupuncture to be taken seriously by the American medical profession. It is still not taken seriously by most members, and those few who have begun to consider the possibility that acupuncture might have anesthetic effects were converted in a few months, not centuries. For centuries, the whole idea was rejected out of hand. Then came President Nixon's repudiation of a quarter century of foreign policy toward Communist China. Ping-pong diplomacy was born in 1971-72, Nixon visited Red China, and he took along the usual contingent of reporters, all of whom seemed hypnotized by the clean streets of Peking. The atrocious, hysterical, preposterous "art form" of anti-imperialist "ballet," invented by Mao's wife, was hailed as being deeply significant, though of course alien to Western taste. All things Chinese — Red Chinese — were up for reconsideration. After all, if this progressive, rationalistic, Marxist democracy still used acupuncture, then acupuncture must be progressive, rationalistic, and democratic. Then *New York Times* columnist James Reston suffered from an attack of appendicitis, and the Chinese physicians used acupuncture as the anesthetic. Reston felt no pain, survived, and began to sing the praises of this ancient medical practice. That, and that alone, converted a small minority of American physicians, not a careful investigation of centuries of accumulated data on acupuncture. *We are dealing with religious conversion when we deal with the acceptance by former*

25. *Ibid.*, p. 143.

orthodox rationalists of some facet of paranormal science. The impetus in the case of acupuncture was the religion of democracy, as interpreted by the *New York Times*.

Unfortunately for Arigo, he was not a physician in Red China. His story did not fit the editorial policies of the *New York Times*. When Arigo was sent to jail in 1964, James Reston failed to drop in for an instant diagnosis and lightning-fast operation. It would have been better for the free world if Arigo, rather than the Red Chinese, had received the credit for curing Reston. Arigo's demons did not possess ballistic missiles and a messianic ideology of Communist domination. Arigo's demons had not slaughtered thirty million people. Arigo's demons did not play ping-pong.

When Puharich returned to the United States after his first visit to see Arigo in action, he had begun a series of experiments that are only too typical of the pathetic attempted fusion of demonic possession and orthodox scientific inquiry — as if the two were not totally antithetical in both theory and practice. He felt compelled to continue true research. Not acknowledging the demonic nature of Arigo's healing abilities, Puharich and Dr. Luis Cortes of the New York University School of Medicine attempted to imitate Arigo's techniques. First, they took rats as their victims. "Using painstaking care, Cortes held a rat firmly while Puharich tried to insert a small knife under the lid and up toward the sinus cavities. They found that it was literally impossible to do this on a conscious, unanesthetized rat unless its head was held in a vicelike grip."[26] Surprise, surprise! Rats simply do not like to have knives stuck into their eyes. But rats are not people, as even a fairly large percentage of experimental psychologists know. What would people think of having a physician stick knives into their eyes? Fortunately, a subject was eagerly awaiting just such an experiment. A young laboratory assistant, fascinated with the stories she had heard about Arigo, insisted that they try Arigo's trick on her. Neither of them wanted to try this, the author writes, but "she kept on insisting. . . ."[27] Cortes took a small knife and began to insert it into her eye. It went in only a fraction of an inch under her eyelid, when the girl signalled that she could not stand the pain. "The experience convinced all three that they were dealing with an extraordinary case in Arigo that would be a mam-

---

26. *Ibid.*, p. 115.
27. *Idem.*

moth challenge to science."[28] Puharich and Cortes caught on really fast; yes, siree, Bob: they were really scientific fellows. After rigorous experimentation like this, they proved, at least to themselves — and, yes, even to me — that normally it hurts someone when you poke a knife into his eye, at least in a statistically significant number of cases, if the sample is large enough. *Paranormal science marches on!*

The scientific investigating techniques that are affirmed as exclusively valid by the cosmologists of human autonomy and neutral observation are impotent to handle the manifestations of the demonic. The questions that must be asked regarding the origins of such occult phenomena are denied from the start as being legitimate questions. Thomas Kuhn's enormously influential book, *The Structure of Scientific Revolutions*, explains why it is that apparently rational men such as Puharich would perform such meaningless and irrational experiments as probing the eyes of rats and a laboratory assistant in order to demonstrate the obvious. "Effective research scarcely begins before a scientific community thinks it has acquired firm answers to questions like the following: What are the fundamental entities of which the universe is composed? How do these interact with each other and with the senses? What questions may legitimately be asked about such entities and what techniques employed in seeking solutions? At least in the mature sciences, answers (or full substitutes for answers) to questions like these are firmly embodied in the educational initiation that prepares and licenses the student for professional practice. Because that education is both rigorous and rigid, these answers come to exert a deep hold on the scientific mind."[29]

A strong element of *arbitrariness* is inevitably involved in scientific research, Kuhn concludes. Conventional science thinks it knows what the universe is really like, at least insofar as it can be known at all. Conventional science, therefore, "often suppresses fundamental novelties because they are necessarily subversive of its basic commitments." Kuhn is convinced, however, that this suppression of the novel cannot go on very long. Men like Puharich who are involved in paranormal science are doing their best to undermine orthodoxy as it now stands, thereby creating a scientific revolution. But in order to accomplish this goal, *they dare not depart from formally established procedures.* They are attempting to use the investigative tools of ortho-

---

28. *Ibid.*, p. 146.

29. Thomas Kuhn, *The Structure of Scientific Revolutions* (University of Chicago Press, 1962), pp. 4-5.

dox science as wedges (or crowbars) to break open the hard shell of
establishment orthodoxy.

The overwhelming problem with this approach is in the very nature of the tools they are using, including the assumptions about the
universe that are accepted by all supposedly reasonable participants
in scientific research. If the subject studied does not, by its very nature, fall within the post-Kantian laws of science, what good are the
operating assumptions of post-Kantian science in determining what
factors are involved in the observed phenomena? Orthodox scientists
conclude that there must be some flaw in the observational capacities
of paranormal researchers. They are being tricked by sleight-of-
hand artists. They have not studied enough cases. The cases are not
repeatable. The anomalies are a product of the inherent randomness
of the universe. The researchers are liars and involved in a massive
conspiracy against their colleagues. The researchers are mad. The
paranormal researchers reply that the orthodox leaders are blinded
by prejudice, unwilling to examine the facts, suppress evidence, lie
about paranormal researchers, and are too stodgy and wrapped up
in pre-1965 concepts of what constitutes the possible to be accurate
judges. Yet both groups claim allegiance to the increasingly shaky
canons of post-Kantian rationalism. Yet it is precisely this — the
operating presuppositional foundation of all modern science — that is
being undermined by the realization that men like Arigo do exist,
and that neither orthodox medicine nor paranormal science can
make any sense out of the facts. The hard reality of the facts are, like
a knife, jabbing their way into the eyes of the scientists. The orthodox scientists act like Arigo's patients: they seem oblivious to what is
taking place. The paranormal scientists understand that what is
happening is impossible, but they also claim that there is no discomfort involved. They are self-deluded. Arigo's knife is cutting away
the public's faith in the world of the scientists. The public is coming
to believe that scientific rationalism cannot account for the miraculous events that are being reported in book after paperback book,
and even in that Establishment organ of conventional wisdom, the
Reader's Digest. The public, feeling no pressure to publish in respectable scientific journals, and not having gone through the mind-
directing program of scientific initiation, sees that Arigo's knife is
cutting out the heart of science's most cherished presupposition: that
the rational, categorizing mind of man can give an account, at least
in principle, assuming sufficient facts are available, of any known

phenomenon. The key word, of course, is "known." *If science is unable to explain it, it is not known.* The public, slowly but surely, is becoming aware that orthodox science is involved in a sleight-of-hand trick far more comprehensive than anything dreamed of by peasant healers. Peasant healers sometimes fake miracles; orthodox scientists who face the facts of the demonic are constantly faking non-miracles. "Give us time; we can explain this," they say, paraphrasing the "Amazing Randi's" challenge: "Give me time, and I can duplicate this." Then orthodox scientists scurry away, hoping that both the unexplained phenomena and the public's memory of their challenge will somehow fade away.

Arigo was again convicted of practicing medicine without a license in 1964. This time he was sent to jail. Predictably, he began healing prisoners. The public kept coming to him, and the jailers looked the other way. He even was given a key to allow him to come and go when he wished. The world-wide effects of the occult revival were making themselves felt in Brazil in 1964-65. The Roman Catholic Church, like a growing minority of formerly orthodox scientists, was involved in a holding operation called "redefinition." If an occult practice could not be stamped out, or at least suppressed enough to keep the public from making it into a fad, it was redefined as "parapsychological" in nature. Parapsychology was seen more and more as a legitimate subdivision of scientific investigation, thereby sanctioning the observation of occult abilities. Somehow, by calling demonic possession "parapsychological behavior," the church's leadership hoped to justify their retreat from the fray. This was neutralizing the old hostility to witchcraft.[30] In Arigo's case, the authorities were growing tired of trying to suppress him. He had become one of Brazil's half a dozen most widely recognized citizens. He was front-page news, year after year. He had treated people from every station in life. He was paroled in June of 1965, after having spent seven months in jail.

The following summer, Puharich led a well-equipped team back to Congonhas do Campo. They watched, charted, and recorded events for three days, involving about 1,000 patients. With a tape recorder, they took down each of Arigo's 965 diagnoses. They checked to see if the patient had brought along his own physician's written diagnosis. In 545 cases, they had. Out of these 545, Arigo had made diagnoses in accord with the physicians in 518 cases, or a total of

---

30. *Ibid.*, p. 62.

96%. The researchers, being men of good faith, assumed that in the 27 discrepancies, the physician was correct and Arigo was wrong. These diagnoses, remember, took about 30 seconds each. Movies were made of the operations. More photographs were taken.[31] Still, they needed more data. Always more data were required. Paranormal scientists are forever fearful of the standard charge: insufficient observations to permit statistically significant correlations. If one instance of a knife being poked in someone's eye does not convince the orthodox scientists, then perhaps 500 instances will. If he thinks you have faked one set of films, possibly 500 sets will convince him.

Another expedition would be needed. This time, the questions to be asked would be restricted even more — so restricted, in fact, as to be virtually irrelevant in making any sense out of the observed data: "Paramount in the plans was the study of those aspects of Arigo's work which could be explained and related to accepted modern medical theory and practice. . . . The 'voice' that told Arigo his amazingly correct diagnoses would be considered, but the statistics on the actual diagnoses and treatment would come first."[32] As for the Kardecist explanation of Arigo's non-miracles, that he was a vessel for a God-given energy, or higher form of energy, it could be ignored completely. "These concepts were interesting, but utterly useless for the medical researchers, who needed more statistical information on the hard, observable facts. It is one thing to be convinced by direct observation. It is another to articulate the facts in a form acceptable to the editors of a scientific journal, who must have precedents and previously documented material to fall back on."[33]

This hope in getting published was naive. Here we find the old "egg before the chicken, chicken before the egg" routine: no precedents can be set without access to the journals, but the journals require precedents. The thousands upon thousands of cases of impossible events compiled by Charles Fort and his followers never crept into respectable journals. The idea of these journals is to *keep out overly disturbing precedents*. One can never be sure just where a precedent may lead, so editors handle them very carefully. Anyone who doubts that outright suppression goes on should read Alfred de Grazia's *The Velikovsky Affair*, which demonstrates how members of major universities, including Harvard, pressured Velikovsky's publisher, Mac-

---

31. *Ibid.*, p. 168.
32. *Ibid.*, p. 174.
33. *Ibid.*, p. 195.

millan, into dropping his books. These books did not get back into print until 1965 — in the midst of the occult revival. Unlike Arigo's knives in the eye, the knives of the scientific guild, delivered very often from behind, can maim and kill a man's reputation, sometimes affecting his ability to get an academic job, especially if he is not yet tenured.

It was Arigo's dream to establish a hospital. This had been Edgar Cayce's dream, too. This was why he had hope in the investigations of these North American scientists. He did not understand that they were basically pariahs in their profession for even daring to promote his story back home. When the team returned in 1968 to make more films, gather more statistics, and play the data game once again, it was driven out by the press, which had received reports on the clandestine visit of the North Americans. Nothing fills a paranormal scientists' heart with greater fear than the attention of journalists prior to the full and final report, written in the discipline's jargon, addressed to one's skeptical colleagues. In an academic world where the mere writing of a *textbook* may tarnish a man's reputation, as Kuhn reveals, a summary by a journalist of a "major breakthrough" is nothing short of suicidal.[34] The team left when the reporters appeared. Arigo was not going to get his hospital.

Why did he want a hospital? This is the anomaly. What would a hospital have provided for him? He could treat 300 patients a day. No one else in the world had his talents, so there was no possibility of the division of labor, which is one of the primary functions of a hospital's medical staff. He could perform feats of surgery that no medical team could imitate. His powers were vastly beyond those ever dreamed of by a medical technician. Indeed, the very nature of his ministry was a denial of the need for medical technicians. What need was there for a hospital? What need did a demon-possessed peasant who cured men with a rusty knife in a filthy room have for a hospital — the product of centuries of slowly improving medical techniques? What need did he have for sanitary conditions, teams of researchers, diagnostic equipment, anesthetics, or any other product of Western technology and theoretical science?

This is the central *social* implication of the conflict between Western science and primitive healing. It is not that Western techniques, being rational, are therefore the only successful avenues of medical treatment. That may be what the orthodox scientists think, but what

---

34. Kuhn, *Scientific Revolutions*, p. 21.

they think and what happens in the world are very often two entirely different processes. It is not that peasants are too stupid, generation after generation, to recognize the difference between staying sick and getting well. It is not that the monopoly of Western rationalism really is what it claims to be: solely efficacious. What is at stake is the idea of *progress*.

It is a fact that only by means of Western science has a centuries-long period of constant improvement of skills, equipment, and treatment been maintained. Scientific progress, which was originally grounded on the Christian ideas of providence, progress, and the subduing of the earth to the glory of a pre-eminently rational and personal God, was exponentially increased by the social and intellectual aftermath of the Reformation.[35] The idea that men can increase their control over nature by an ever-increasing division of labor, including intellectual labor, is at the heart of Western progress. Simple men, with only average or slightly above-average intelligence, can perform almost miraculous feats through the use of painstakingly devised techniques and equipment. The "uncharismatic" plodders who are the troops of any scientific organization steadily advance certain aspects of the discipline. Scientific progress is not the product of centuries of such plodding—a continuous addition of minute improvements—but it certainly is aided by such narrow but progressive additions of human knowledge. Teams of researchers are able to participate in a systematic, cost-effective program of investigation. It is only through such incremental additions to knowledge, when coupled with occasional breakthroughs by "scientific revolutionaries" like Newton and Pasteur, that the West has achieved universal dominance through science and technology. And science and technology would not have been possible without the capital produced by thrift, intelligent investing, and continual economic progress.

Systematic testing, trial-and-error investigations, double-blind experiments, widespread publication of results (however controlled) in over 100,000 scientific periodicals in the world, and all the other features of incremental and progressive and scientific advancement are not possible in a culture dominated by an occasional charismatic magician leader and his association of enchanted priests, shamans, and visionaries. The whole society becomes dependent on a tiny

---

35. Robert K. Merton, *Science, Technology and Society in Seventeenth Century England* (New York: Harper Torchbooks, 1970); Merton, *Social Theory and Social Structure* (New York: The Free Press, 1969), ch. 18.

handful of religious healers, whose powers stem from unpredictable and hostile occult forces. The rule of terror is prominent. There is no hope of progress culturally; there is only the *ad hoc* healing of physical ailments. Short-term healing of specific ailments is as much as anyone can hope for. If the charismatic healer dies, or loses his gift, the society cannot escape from its illnesses. By *personalizing* the techniques of healing, primitive societies have in principle abandoned the idea of medical, economic, or any other kind of progress through more impersonal organizations of human talent.

Arigo worked in unsanitary conditions. Why not? His magic worked. No ideal of Western cleanliness was present in his peasant surroundings, nor was he expected to conform to Western standards of sanitation. He did not use his prestige to promote voluntary local programs of personal and community sanitation. His teaching did not include cause-and-effect doctrines of the nature of good health. "Dr. Fritz" was the source of health, not public sanitation.

Arigo was incomparable, but he died in January of 1971. What did he leave behind? What healing is accomplished today by his legend? Who relieves human suffering now? He established the tradition of spirit possession much more firmly in the minds of both Brazilian peasants and upper-class products of Western education in Brazil. He gave the Kardec movement new impetus. Today, some 30 million or more spiritists live in Brazil.[36] The knife is gone; the spiritism remains.

Demonic healing is the denial of progress, the denial of widespread public health, the denial of cause and effect, not because it is invariably and necessarily fraudulent, but because it is externally, visibly, miraculously successful in a "statistically significant number of cases." The curse of demonic healing is not that it never really works, except in cases of psychosomatic illness — and all healings that do take place, say orthodox scientists, by definition were psychosomatic in origin — but that it so often relieves the visible symptoms of sickness. The primitive peasants who go to these healers, not being trained in modern universities, have no *a priori* incentive to shut their eyes to the obvious manifestations of healing. They permit themselves to accept what their eyes can see, unlike Western scientists. They are therefore willing to place their bodies under the control of the agents of demons and demons themselves. The epistemological protection of autonomous Western science is not present.

---

36. "The Land Where Spirits Thrive," *Christianity Today*, (Dec. 13, 1985), p. 48.

Christians must understand the nature of a society like Brazil. It may be able to telescope its progression from primitive religion to Western science and religious skepticism to post-1965 paranormal science and parapsychological fascination. It may be able to skip the rationalist phase. Skeptical rationalism may never get a strong enough foothold, even among the intellectual elite, to secularize the culture. This fact is extremely important, for it has made it very difficult for Christian evangelism by denominations that have a puritan-like commitment to education and rational techniques. Long-term economic growth is made far less likely; mass inflation will be the substitute. The foundations of progress are simply not present, for the primary foundations are matters of faith and attitude.[37] The only Western churches that have access to these people are those that hold very similar conceptions of the universe. Writes Wilson: "In Brazil and elsewhere in Latin America the appeal of Pentecostalism, which in America and Europe we should regard as a conversionist movement, may have much less to do with the specific elements which have been significant in its spread in Protestant societies, and more to do with those thaumaturgical aspects which are a part of its inheritance. Thus we find that in missionary activity . . . the ostensible configuration of doctrine, organization, and practice that is offered, is not accepted as a whole: certain elements are more readily embraced than others. In cultures with strong indigenous religious traditions it is entirely expectable that the appeal of any missionary denomination which includes thaumaturgical elements should be precisely these, rather than other features of its teachings, activities, or organization."[38]

In short, it is very difficult to deliver societies in occult bondage by means of evangelism that is based on similar manifestations of occult healing. The Protestant ethic, which was firmly grounded in a de-emphasis on charismatic signs and wonders, and placed great emphasis on self-discipline, education, thrift, and material uplift, cannot be implanted readily in the hearts and minds of the newly "converted" population. Those in bondage may stay in bondage, or at best, may not experience the fruits of total redemption from occult power.

---

37. P. T. Bauer, *Dissent on Development* (Cambridge, Mass.: Harvard University Press, 1972).
38. Wilson, *Magic*, p. 121.

The Philippine Healers

Arigo was unrivaled as a demonic healer. His powers were the least disputed, most consistent, utterly baffling, and most widely witnessed of any healer on record. Yet what Arigo did for two decades in Brazil differs only in degree from what other demonic healers in primitive cultures have performed for centuries. When we examine the healing arts of another widely publicized group of peasant spiritists, the Philippine wonder healers, we find the same basic patterns, both theologically and methodologically. Their abilities have been challenged more successfully, since some instances of fakery have been detected, and far fewer people have been treated by any one of these men. Nevertheless, in the aggregate, a large number of films, photographs, and first-hand accounts have been assembled that demonstrate that successful operations are being performed which are impossible to explain in terms of known biological and physical principles.

One of the earliest "psychic" healers in the Philippines whose work was observed and reported by American visitors is Brother Eleuterio Terte. Gert Chesi's New Age book, *Faith Healers in the Philippines*, says that Terte performed the first Philippine "bloody operation" in 1945.[39] *Fate*, a popular magazine of occult and "Fortean" anomalies, ran an April 1960 article which dealt with Terte's powers. Two moving picture producers recorded several of his bare-hand operations. His techniques were analogous to Arigo's, although they were far more explicitly religious in nature. He uses a female medium in a trance state to add to his power; she, rather than Terte, is visibly entranced. J. Bernard Ricks, a clairvoyant and self-professed medium, journeyed to Terte's tiny village in 1963 to see him in action, and his report appeared in *Fate* in the same year. The editors of the magazine decided to include this essay in a compilation published in 1965, *The Strange and the Unknown*, an anthology gleaned from the pages of *Fate*. Again, notice the date of publication: 1965.

According to Ricks, villagers in the little town of 400 gather together in order to form a choir. They sing hymns before each operation, supposedly in order "to stir up the vibrations." After the hymns, Terte recited the Lord's prayer and went to work. A middle-

39. Gert Chesi, *Faith Healers in the Philippines* (Wörgl, Austria: Perlinger Verlag, 1981), p. 10.

aged man who claimed to be suffering from a blood clot was seated on the operating table. Terte's hand began to massage the man's chest area. Within ten seconds, according to Ricks, a small, black object began to appear on the chest—actually coming out through the chest! Yet there was no opening visible to Ricks, who was standing on the other side of the operating table. The clot fell into Terte's hands. Ricks said it was the size of his thumb. The man claimed that he felt nothing.

The next patient had an acute case of appendicitis. The choir sang for a while, then stopped, Terte said his prayer, and commenced. He washed his hands and the patient's body with rubbing alcohol—the only condescension to Western standards of cleanliness—and began to massage the man's abdomen. A one-inch hole appeared. A few seconds later, the appendix rose up through the small opening. Terte lifted the organ and placed it in Ricks' hand. There was almost no sign of blood. By pressing on the opening with his hand, Terte closed the wound. A few seconds later, Ricks reported, there was no sign that there had ever been an opening.

Ricks watched the third operation from a distance of a few inches. Terte made an incision on the back of a patient and drew out long strands of foul-smelling flesh. As always, the patient felt no pain.

This phenomena of internal organs or objects located inside the body passing through the flesh, even apart from openings larger than the pores, is relatively common with primitive forms of demonic healing. Ronald Rose, in his study of Australian aborigines, records a conversation he had with one native concerning an alleged healing. Rose is convinced that such operations involve trickery:

When the old Birri full-blood from Bowen (Queensland), Harry Monsell, told me about seeing a doctor suck a stone about the size of a hen's egg from the body of a woman who was suffering from abdominal pains, I put it to him that the doctor had deceived them.

"Oh, no," he said firmly. "That same old doctor I saw once fix up a man who had a chest pain. He said the man had got a porcupine [echidna or spiny anteater] spike in him. The doctor sang a song, and I saw with my own eyes the quill come out of the body of the man."

"Do you mean that it seemed to come directly out of his flesh?"

"Yes."

"Did the doctor perhaps pull it out?"

"No. He just sang and it came up. When it came right out, it fell down onto the ground."

"Was there any blood or any mark where the quill had come out?"
"No, there was no mark. The man got better."[40]

The native could have been telling a tall tale, or he could have
been hypnotized, but in the light of the scenes photographed and at-
tested to by numerous Western visitors to Philippine healers, it is
more likely that the "old doctor" did remove the quill by a song. What
he claims to have seen is not different in principle (or at least different
in its nonconformity to Western science) than what Mrs. Bobbie
Gironda, of North Hollywood, California, saw in the Philippines.

Her son had a crippled leg. He had been operated on, but still he
could not walk without crutches. He was nine years old. She took
him to Juan Blanche, one of the more prominent healers. Blanche
placed a copper coin on the back of his leg, close to the tumor which
was causing the trouble. Then he put a piece of oil-soaked cotton on
top of the coin. Then he lit the cotton with a match. By placing a
glass on top of the coin, Blanche put out the flame. He tapped the
top (i.e., bottom) of the glass, and a circle of blood appeared beneath
the rim of the glass. He grabbed the hand of the boy's grandmother,
closed it into a fist, and left her forefinger extended. He made a
slashing motion above the circle of blood, and a pink slash appeared
in the skin, eight inches beneath her forefinger. He then reached in
and withdrew a piece of hard tissue. Actually, he removed it part
way, allowing them to snap a photograph. Then he pulled it out.[41]
After a few more chiropractic-like treatments, the boy's leg was healed,
and there are signed statements by American physicians to that effect.[42]

Mrs. Gironda was so impressed that she convinced the Philippino
housegirl, Fanny, that she too should visit Blanche to have her red
rash cured. Mrs. Gironda's description of what took place follows:

Fanny shyly approached the table. Blanche, after a cursory examination, began picking little seed-like objects from her arms, face and neck. I
have been busying myself getting the camera loaded but the sound of the
things plinking into a bowl partly filled with water caught my attention. At
my hard look at the bowl, the helper held it out to me for closer inspection.

"He's got to be a magician!" I thought to myself. "It's the hand quicker
than the eye. Where else could these things be coming from?"

40. Ronald Rose, *Primitive Psychic Power* (New York: Signet, [1965] 1968), p. 87.
41. Harold Sherman, *"Wonder" Healers of the Philippines* (Santa Monica, Calif.: De
Vorss, [1967] 1974), p. 275.
42. *Ibid.*, pp. 279-80.

The instant my thought was completed, I felt Blanche's eyes on me. He was grinning broadly, as if he had heard my thoughts aloud. Then he spread his hands wide, slowly turning them over, back and front. I was so embarrassed, I wished the floor would open up and let me drop out of sight. Since my skepticism was already in plain sight, I was going to satisfy it. Blanche's helper snickered aloud and the psychic surgeon kept grinning pleasantly as he watched my face stop blushing and determination take its place. I looked Blanche up and down, all sides too, carefully checking for any hidden gimmicks which might contain a reservoir of these magical seeds. His hands and arms were bare and the short-sleeved cotton shirt he wore was too damp to offer any concealment.

I put my nose within four inches of Fanny's arm. Blanche obligingly, and in slow motion, pressed two fingers on either side of a skin pore. The tip of another seed began emerging. His hands were visible at all times and since we were standing hip to hip in that cubbyhole, I felt satisfied no tricks were underway.

Blanche paused for my benefit as the seed was half out, and again, at the three-quarter mark. These things, well over fifty removed, resembled what I would imagine long grain rice with husks would look like. The amazing thing was that they were much larger than the pore from which they were taken. Blanche then simply grasped the seed, with the tips of his fingers, and picked it out of the skin.[43]

Many of the prominent healers are members of the Union Espiritista Cristiana de Filipinas, a self-confessed "Christian" spiritist association. It is explicitly religious in outlook, and members view their powers as stemming from God. They admit quite readily that similar powers can be given to men by evil spirits.[44] Very significantly, the Union has officially adopted Allan Kardec's *The Spirits' Book* as one of its official documents. The members believe in reincarnation, karmic law, and the universal salvation of all mankind. "The basic belief of a spiritual healer," writes Chesi, "is the belief in reincarnation. This contradicts the basic teachings of Christianity, according to which death terminates life on earth."[45]

Prof. Guillermo Tolentino, a famous sculptor and leader of the organization, puts forth the standard humanist-spiritist doctrine that all religions lead to God, but his, being eclectic and universalistic, is undogmatic and therefore superior. "All religions set up barriers when they say there is no salvation outside their own belief. Without

43. *Ibid.*, p. 277.
44. *Ibid.*, p. 89.
45. *Faith Healers in the Philippines*, p. 43.

exception, they are all commercialized. Christian Spiritism, on the other hand, sets up no barrier because it embraces mankind as a whole — since all are One in worshipping God in Truth and in Spirit. . . . All, without exception, will be saved through *multiple reincarnations!*"[46] This is Kardecism, pure and simple. Remove the doctrine of reincarnation, and it is just another run-of-the-mill brand of humanism. Man saves himself by merit; God does not discriminate on a permanent basis between good and evil; everyone gets a second, third, or infinite number of opportunities in life to reform himself. Man is therefore divine.

Terte's background is revealing. At 20, he married a spiritist. He took little interest in her religion. But he got sick and began to experience hallucinations. In a dream, two angels appeared to him. They promised that he would recover if he became a healer. He then visited the spiritist church that his wife belonged to, and they welcomed him. He was baptized by a medium. She announced that he had been given the power to heal. He continued to heal people, until World War II.[47] Before 1945, however, he had used a knife rather than his bare hands.[48]

Tolentino revealed some of the background of Terte. He discovered his "knife-less" talents in 1948 (Chesi says that it was in 1945), the same year in which the stream of outsiders began to seek out psychic healers.[49] There were many healers to choose from. They all had one factor in common beside their healing abilities: none had advanced beyond the fourth grade.[50] By these standards, Edgar Cayce was a post-doctoral candidate. Like Arigo, they had dropped out very early. This is indicative of the inverse relationship between Western rationalism and primitive demonism. Where rationalistic education flourishes, and where it still retains the confidence of the students and faculty members, psychic healing techniques are infrequently manifested. Chesi writes: "Education and training as we understand it can inhibit the faith healer in the same way as it hampers any spiritually gifted person. Only an 'ignorant' healer is able to work with his gift without being hampered by rational deductions of his own. He acts as the instrument of a superior being who demands of him no

---

46. Sherman, *"Wonder" Healers*, p. 125.
47. Chesi, p. 191.
48. *Ibid.*, p. 192.
49. Sherman, p. 16.
50. *Ibid.*, p. 88.

more than that he execute a given task. The medium's spirit guide does not want to be interpreted or corrected by him. The healers with the least education apparently command the greatest power. . . ."[51] The inverse relationship between education (knowledge) and power is characteristic of primitive societies; in the West, knowledge and power are believed to go together. One major reason why primitive societies stay primitive is that they have not adopted the Western view.

In an age of *confident* rationalism, demonic phenomena are minimized; people refuse to accept the validity of non-rationalistic phenomena. Such phenomena are regarded as mythical. But when the confidence in the monopoly of rationalism weakens, primitive cultures, especially the demonic aspects of primitive cultures, receive new attention from a growing minority of disaffected rationalists. This disaffection with rationalism has quite clearly influenced the clients of the faith healers. Chesi states that about 90 percent of the patients of the Philippine faith healers come from abroad, meaning from the industrial West.[52]

In 1948, the Philippines experienced a spiritist revival. Similarly, the Kardec movement and umbanda became major religious forces only after World War II in Brazil, with Arigo appearing in 1950. By the early 1960's, word about healings in both nations began to filter back to the United States, and after 1964 there was a growing flood of interest. *The rise of occult humanism is presently offering an alternative to a growing body of formerly materialistic humanists who are losing their faith in materialism, but not in the tenets of humanistic religion.*

Of all the Philippine healers, Tony Agpaoa is by far the most famous — or infamous. He was trained (initiated?) by Terte.[53] Two books written on the subject of psychic healing in the Philippines, one by Harold Sherman and the other by Tom Valentine, deal most heavily with Agpaoa's ministry. He does not belong to the spiritists' organization, and is therefore regarded as a renegade by the members of that group. He also accepts donations to his "research foundation," a practice hotly criticized by the spiritists. Apart from a simple prayer before each operation, his healing techniques show no traces of being religious in nature. But in one crucial respect, Agpaoa's ministry does maintain a basic continuity with the work of

---

51. Chesi, *Faith Healers in the Philippines*, p. 11.
52. *Ibid.*, p. 43.
53. *Ibid.*, p. 194.

Arigo, Terte, and all the rest: the lack of sanitation. These healers have an almost philosophical commitment to unsterile operations.[54] This is not to say that people are actually infected. Indeed, from the reported cases of infection — virtually none — there is far less infection in one of these primitive clinics than in a typical North American hospital, with its staph infections and other horrors. The bodies of those treated are not infected, but what is infected is the attitude of the public toward standards of cleanliness. The lack of sanitation is a visible testimony against the law of cause and effect in the medical realm. The relationship between cleanliness and health is symbolically rejected by these healers. Those peasants who are treated by them remain in a kind of microbiological bondage to their primitive culture. They remain dependent upon the charismatic healers who alone seem to be able to provide efficacious treatment within the framework of the traditional culture to which these people are clinging. These static cultures are kept static, in part, by the very success of these healers. As one Western physician remarked during a television documentary on a group of doctors who use light aircraft to bring Western medicine to African tribes: "I'm always the second doctor called in for consultation."

Agpaoa normally treats 30 to 50 people per day, seven days a week.[55] His absolute maximum was Arigo's average day: 300.[56] His operations generally take as "long" as five minutes, five times as long as Arigo's. His trance state, like Terte's, affects only his arms and hands.[57] When the power comes upon him, he says, there is a tingling sensation — a phenomenon which is reported as preceding numerous forms of demonic activity. Then he goes to work.

Occasionally, one of these healers will use a razor blade, but normally they use only their bare hands to enter the body. Juan Blanche, as reported earlier, uses the index finger of an onlooker to make the slit in the flesh — eight inches away from the body. Then they enter the cavity of the body with their hands.[58] Typically, the healer begins by massaging the flesh for a few moments. When it opens, he inserts his hands and makes the necessary "repairs." Sometimes they may use a pair of old scissors to cut the internal organs; other times, most

---

54. Sherman, pp. 24, 58, 61, 192.
55. *Ibid.*, p. 59.
56. *Ibid.*, p. 163.
57. *Ibid.*, p. 68.
58. *Ibid,.* pp. 54, 288.

horrifyingly, they simply pull out the organs — supposedly diseased — by the handful.

Moving pictures and photographs of these operations are now relatively common. Valentine reports that by the early 1970's, there were at least 200 different home movies of various healers in action that circulated in the Chicago area alone.[59] Other more professional films have been made over the last fifteen years. Harold Sherman showed one to the late Louis Lomax, who had one of those curiously popular and short-lived "harassment of weirdos" television programs that were made popular by Joe Pyne (who was a debunker of Agpaoa.) (The earliest of the shows using this format, at least in the Los Angeles area, was run by a cocky Irishman named Tom Duggan, who was as responsible as anyone for introducing Malcolm X to white television viewers in the early 1960's. Five years later, Lomax, a Negro, had his own show, and Duggan had sunk into obscurity.) Lomax indicated to Sherman before the show that he would not be easy to convince, but a showing before they went on camera of one of Sherman's films of Agpaoa in action shocked Lomax into confused neutrality. The film was shown to the studio audience as it went over the airwaves. People were stunned. Lomax did not adopt the typical attitude of the knowing rationalist while he was on camera, yet he could not wholly escape the intellectual's usual assumption that if a phenomenon is not reported by the *New York Times*, it probably is not true and/or relevant to the public. He displayed this bias when he responded to a UCLA student from Upper Volta in Africa, who stepped up to the microphone and thanked Sherman for having shown the film. He claimed that he had witnessed numerous bare-handed operations conducted by tribal healers in his own country. Lomax seemed shocked.

"My dear man!" said Lomax. "If this is true — how come the newspapers of the world have not headlined this great event? That's the same question I might ask Mr. Sherman? If these bare hand operations are true — why hasn't the world heard about them before now?"

Mr. Guirma's reply was self-contained but potent.

"Your foreign missionaries and medical doctors with your foreign missions have known about these kinds of operations for years — *but apparently they do not consider what our native doctors have been doing of any value to their culture.*"[60]

---

59. Tom Valentine, *Psychic Surgery* (New York: Pocket Books, 1975), p. 17.
60. Sherman, *"Wonder" Healers*, p. 252.

This answer touches on one aspect of the stone wall of silence encountered by all who would point out that such phenomena exist. The typical Western rationalist, being a materialist, cannot accept the possibility that there are forces that can affect the visible, measurable world that do not conform to the laws of that world—laws that are at bottom the laws of the self-proclaimed autonomous reason of man. This is especially true of American physicians, but it is even true of missionaries, including fundamentalist missionaries. Occasionally, missionaries will report home about the existence of demonic activity, but for many years, the people back home, especially the ordained pastors, preferred not to believe in such reports. The missionaries stopped sending back such reports, for their financial support was dependent upon the cooperation of the churches back home.

Yet it goes even deeper than this. Western rationalism is today overwhelmingly *Darwinian*. All progress is evolutionary. Progress in nature is blind, random, and totally unplanned. It is dependent upon the response of random genetic mutation in existing species to the randomly changing environment. Out of competing randomness comes the order of progress. In human affairs, this same evolutionary perspective persists; indeed, it was assumed even before Darwin published his investigations. Therefore, the *primitive* is said to be primitive because it is *temporarily prior*. Not because primitive cultures are perverse, present-oriented, demonic, envious, or whatever, but because they are temporally prior. This is the great sin of primitivism, not the particular characteristics displayed by any given culture. Therefore, that which has come after is, by definition, better —better being defined as rationalistic and materialistic.

The argument is rigorously circular, as Nisbet has demonstrated so forcefully in his important book, *Social Change and History* (1969). It assumes that what has come later *in the West* is that which is truly progressive. *Later* is therefore defined as whatever the West has done, and *West* means those peculiar aspects of culture which are distinctly rationalistic and materialistic. If progress has not come to one or another culture, it must be because there have been *institutional impedances* to progress, and obviously the belief in the power of tribal medicine men is one such impedance. Therefore, to assist a culture in becoming progressive—to speed up the blocked processes of cultural evolution—it is necessary to convince primitive people that their medicine men do not have occult powers, for to be progressive is to rely totally on human reason and natural laws as defined by human reason. It is not simply that what native doctors can do has no value to Western rational culture; it is that what they claim to do, if accepted even as a possibility, denies the very premises of Western rational culture.

Sherman describes one of Agpaoa's operations that he witnessed personally. He was accompanied by Dr. Hiroshi Motoyama, a professor in religious studies at the University of Tokyo.

Tony patted the abdomen with the flat of his hand, then held both hands up, fingers extended, to show he had nothing in them.

"I am going to open the body here," he said, and placed the fingers of his right hand against the body, pushing downward. As he did so, it appeared as though the flesh separated and rolled back. Using both hands, he now quickly pulled the body open, widening the "incision." His hands went quickly inside and what appeared to be blood oozed out. Tony looked across at me and smiled.

"You think I am not *in* the body?" he said. "Here, put your hand in here beside mine!"

I hesitated.

"Go on — it is all right," he reassured, as he held the wound open.

Dr. Motoyama's face was a study. I had heard that no infections ever resulted but the possible chance of infection crossed my mind. A decision had to be made.

I extended my hand toward the body opening. I felt my fingers go down beside Tony's. I felt blood and tissue of some sort. When I extracted my hand it had turned red in color. Louie [Agpaoa's assistant] handed me a piece of cotton to swab it off.[61]

When Sherman delivered a lecture on what he had seen before the Los Angeles Breakfast Club on April 13, 1966, the large crowd was fascinated. But two weeks later, a physician who had been in attendance demanded that the club's manager repudiate the speech. The facts claimed by Sherman, in the eyes of this critic, were nothing short of preposterous — an outrage. In short, demonic healing did not conform to the standards laid down in the nation's medical schools.

In response, Sherman invited the club's manager, the critic, other important members of the club, and any surgeons who wanted to come to see his films of Agpaoa's operations. Then he intelligently

---

61. *Ibid.*, pp. 139-40.

covered his flanks. He invited numerous former patients of Philippine healers who lived in Southern California, and Southern California being what it is, a roomful showed up. But he did not announce who they were until after the showing of the movie.

Three surgeons, friends of one of the important members, asked
to come and received invitations. Sherman showed the film. Then he
announced his little surprise: several carloads of cured patients who
had brought before-and-after certificates from licensed physicians
concerning the post-Philippine absence of the previously diagnosed
medical problems. He offered to let any of the physicians examine any
of the patients. The result, as Sherman wisely had guessed, was instant victory — the opposition folded. "There was an instant stir among
the three surgeons up front. Without giving the patients a chance to
open their mouths, they got up and walked out, giving no expression
of appreciation for the courtesies extended them. It was plainly obvious that they did not wish to face this kind of evidence and testimony. It might be one thing to criticize the picture, to brand it fraudulent, to say that the operations on film were faked — but to have to admit to having met actual patients who had gone to the Philippines
with medical records of operations and other ailments, and had returned greatly benefited by psychic surgery, was just too much. They
did not even want it known that they had been there, I learned later,
and one of them had said he would sue if whoever was taking flash-
light pictures ever published one with his likeness in it. Brave men."[62]

This is orthodox science in action — or inaction. Stand your
ground where you know you can win; otherwise, remain anonymous and clear out quickly.

Nevertheless, orthodox skepticism is not entirely wasted. Sherman and Valentine report that they had seen several cases of apparent sleight-of-hand manipulations by psychic healers. It is also true
that on several occasions, psychic healers refused to appear before
Western investigators, or failed to operate when the investigators
sought them out. It is almost as if Western rationalists possess some
sort of negative aura about them which in some way hampers the activities of the demonic control agents. This, in fact, is precisely what
old don Juan told Castaneda: the everyday activities of Westerners
serve as shields against the powers of the spirit world.[63] The barrier

---

62. *Ibid.* p. 301.
63. Carlos Castaneda, *A Separate Reality* (New York: Pocket Books, [1971] 1974),
pp. 217, 219.

can seemingly work in an offensive fashion as well as defensively.

All things are fair in love and war, the slogan says. In epistemological confrontations, the rules of war prevail. While the psychic healers would sometimes do a bit of fakery when the flesh was willing but the spirit was weak, their rationalistic opponents were also not above a little sleight-of-hand. Valentine reports on an experiment he conducted. "With the help of a Filipino-American medical doctor who was in Baguio when we were, I carried out an informal placebo test on a clinic. Two genuine gallstones removed from a living patient were sent to a laboratory, but the clinic was informed that the stones had been removed by psychic surgery. The report came back without detailed analysis, but it carried a flat statement that the stones were not organic."[64] This, as might be suspected, was the invariable answer whenever researchers sent in products of admittedly psychic operations. The specimen might be animal, vegetable, or mineral, but it was never human.

Physicians predictably claim that the only possible healings resulting from psychic surgery are psychosomatic illnesses. ("Take that knife out of his eye, and I'll prove it!") Again, there are indications of just this kind of mental healing, but consider the case of Joseph Ruffner. Ruffner had suffered an industrial accident in 1956. He had been put on crutches permanently. In 1966 he visited Agpaoa. Here is his description of what took place in 1966: "I was scared, but I didn't feel any pain. I saw him cut into me with his bare hands and dig something out. I saw it open, I saw it close, and I saw blood. A guy who said he was a doctor asked me if he could put his hand into my wound. I said it was okay by me if it was clean. He put his hand in [what — no washing with soap and water for 20 minutes?], and I could feel it. When he drew it out, it was covered with blood. Then Tony took his hands out, and the wound was instantly healed. He said to me, 'Get up and walk.' I didn't think I could — you know, after surgery and all — but I did."[65]

He never used crutches after that. Yet upon being X-rayed when he returned to the United States, he learned that his bones were still broken. He should not have been able to walk. He could walk, though, and without any pain.[66] If this is psychosomatic healing, it is a very peculiar kind.

---

64. Valentine, *Psychic Surgery*, p. 160.
65. *Ibid.*, p. 51.
66. *Ibid.*, p. 52.

Others who had journeyed to the Philippines to be healed by Agpaoa were not equally happy. In fact, several later said that they had not been helped. Some had gone as skeptics and had returned skeptics. Others went in hope, and came back disappointed. Still others had felt better after the treatments. But the later patients tended to give mixed reviews.[67] Tony Agpaoa is no Arigo.

Tony and many of the other healers are expert tooth-pullers. They simply reach in with their bare hands and yank out the tooth, and the patient feels nothing. P. L. Katigbak, the Philippines' general manager of the Detroit-based Parke-Davis Co., and an M.D., visited a tooth specialist, Batangas. (Who says these healers are not following modern medical practice? Now, if Batangas can just persuade the Philippine government to prohibit other psychic healers from pulling teeth without a license. . . .) Katigbak says that "in a split second my tooth was out with no pain. Unbelievable."[68] Yet when confronted with a similar display of psychic healing in the tooth extraction field, in this case a series of extractions made by Agpaoa, Dr. Seymour Wanderman, a friend of Sherman's and one of the great professional skeptics in medical history, simply remarked: "Means nothing. Anyone can do that."[69] He had seen this at close range, peering directly into the patient's mouth. No pain, no resistance from the tooth, just instant removal. Fraud, said Wanderman. No fourth-grade drop-out was going to fool Seymour Wanderman, M.D. Agpaoa had even opened up a woman's stomach in front of him, using his bare hands, in front of a movie camera clicking off eighteen frames per second. He offered to let Wanderman stick his hands into the wound. Wanderman refused. Agpaoa then offered him samples of the woman's blood. "No, that's not necessary," said Wanderman.[70] How about the bottle containing the growth that he had just removed? Again, unnecessary.

When questioned about his opinion later by Sherman, Wanderman said the whole thing was sleight-of-hand. How about the blood? "It wasn't real blood." What about the tissue in the bottle? Animal tissue, he said, two or three days old. But what about running clinical tests? "I haven't been trained for years to observe tissue and handle it as I have, not to be able to tell. That growth was not taken from that woman's body." Why did he refuse to put his hand into the wound? "I didn't need to, to know what was going on. I am a trained observer. I was seeing what you did not see."[71] Anyway, that is the reconstruction of the exchange between them offered by Sherman. But Wanderman was in the moving picture film. He was there. He did not believe.

Why should he have believed? Why should he trust his eyes? Men make mistakes in viewing facts. What should he do, throw out a life's career based on one set of absolute presuppositions, in favor of a 27-year-old medicine man? What is reality, anyway? Isn't it what our minds say it must be? When Sherman had warned him that he was going to have to put aside all his medical training and view these events as a separate type of phenomenon, he stoutly refused. "I can't put aside a medical background of over fifty years in viewing any operations of whatever kind on the human body. If it is not right, in my judgment, based upon proved and established standards, it is not right, no matter who does it or how it's done."[72] Wanderman was testifying to a faith in Western medical techniques. It was his deeply felt religion. It was filled with oughts and ought-nots, like any respectable religion. Western medicine is the product of Western religion, a religion which denied the use of spirits in healing, although it did permit prayer and ritual anointing (James 5:14-15). That religion had produced religious techniques and standards unparalleled in the recorded history of man. Was he to throw out the standards of Western medicine just because of a sight which, by definition, *had* to be produced by trickery? Was it not preferable to assert what *had* to be true—fraud—rather than to admit that he was not quite sure how it had been accomplished. Isn't it far better to admit that a peasant can fool you rather than to admit that a peasant can have access to powers that dwarf anything a trained physician can do? Why should he abandon his faith in exchange for nagging doubt all the rest of his life—not to mention ridicule by his peers if he should lend support to such *a priori* nonsense? Why, in short, should any Western physician who is not an amateur ghost-chaser abandon his faith in rational medical techniques?

There is only one answer: because what they are confronting is a real phenomenon. It can be tested. It is, to use an overworked term, the real thing. What is *not* real is the Kantian phenomenal realm—a

---

71. *Ibid.*, p. 199.
72. *Ibid.*, p. 193.

hypothetically autonomous world which man's mind can comprehend, thereby giving man power over phenomena. But unlike the
religion of Christianity, rationalistic materialism cannot successfully
deal with such phenomena. Materialists can try to bottle up occult
facts, as they did for two centuries, but the genie is out of the bottle.
The only defense is an epistemological system which accounts for the
phenomena of occult powers, while simultaneously denying their
long-run efficacy in comparison to an even more powerful system of
thought and practice that employs both spiritual power *and* the
power inherent in rational thought. In short, the proper defense is
Christianity, which gave birth to the bastard system we call Western
materialism. For if Christianity does not win the battle, then either
we continue to bury the truth, or else we return to the primitive, or
worst of all, we witness the fusion of technocratic power and occult
immoralism. The Wandermans of the world have been unable to
bottle up the genie of occult power. Who, then, is prepared to step in
where the Wandermans have failed?

What this chapter has described has been referred to as primitive
healing. But primitivism is not the monopoly of the underdeveloped
nations of the world. *Primitivism is a philosophy of life.* There are now
signs that demonic healing has become popular in urban America.
The point of entry, it seems, is California.

California Dreaming

At a "festival" put on by the greater Los Angeles chapter of the
International Cooperation Council (your instinctive reaction to the
name is no doubt correct), called the "New Consciousness Celebra-
tion," which was held on July 28, 1974, several hundred weirdos and
I listened to a day of speeches by yogis, swamis, experimental educators, sufi dancers, and goofy singers, who informed us about the possibilities of higher living and greater power. The highlight of the day
came when Rev. Roslyn Winsky appeared—late, it turned out,
because her car had broken down. (Bad vibes? Bad plugs?) She is a
truly charismatic person, in the Bishop Sheen sense, as well as the
Tony Agpaoa sense. Vibrant, confident, Winsky convinces an audience that her story is the truth. She is a psychic healer. Operating
from a trance, Rev. Winsky (who appeared to be in her early thir-
ties) and her spirit mediums perform such feats, she claims, as re-
building spinal discs by mental power. She operates on a regular
basis, and she trains people in these techniques. She assured us, as

they usually do, that "anyone can do these things." When we broke off into discussion groups—some things never change—her group session was absolutely jammed with enthusiastic people. Next door were the Chaneys, of Astara fame, more traditional Los Angeles instructors in metaphysics.[73] About a dozen people came by, mostly middle-aged ladies. Healing was clearly where the action was understood to be.

Rev. Harold G. Plume is regarded by some as being the most powerful medium in central California. This may not mean very much, since California's more sane people—farmers, oil rig workers, country music singers—live and work in central California. One does not even capitalize the "c" in central California, it is so normal. But Rev. Plume is not normal. He uses the same operating techniques that the Philippine healers use. He sticks his fingers into the body. He is pastor of St. John's First Chapel of Healing, which has lots of prayers, hymns, passing of collection plates, and other spiritual activities. If he did not have spiritual activities, he might be in jail for practicing medicine without a license.

Like Tony Agpaoa, who had visions as a youth, Plume had visions. But he had them at age three, which may be a record of some kind. People would appear to him in his room. He saw the disembodied spirits of the departed. He is now controlled by a Chinese physician who lived 2,500 years ago. His name is Hoo-Fang. Honest. And he does something even Dr. Fritz and Agpaoa's "protector" never tried: he operates right through clothing. Complete modesty prevails in his church; he is British, not some simple barbarian. Things are done properly. Furthermore, he inserts only his fingers whenever possible, not his hands, plus a piece of Kleenex. There is no muss, no fuss, and no blood. Ladies in knit dresses bought in California shops do not appreciate bloody performances.[74] (Agpaoa is different in this respect; he loves a bloody show.)

The Reality of Hexes

If the power of healing by demonic possession exists, as the external evidence indicates, then a secondary problem appears: the ability to produce illness by these same occult forces. The belief in primitive cultures that certain "holy men," meaning unholy men, have the

---

73. On Astara, see David St. Clair, *The Psychic World of California* (New York: Bantam, 1973), pp. 253-56.

74. *Ibid.*, pp. 160-61.

power to inflict illness and even death, is widespread. Western observers almost always regard such beliefs as being totally superstitious, yet the evidence is overwhelmingly on the side of the primitive accounts. The problem with the Western explanation of death from sorcery, namely, that the "victim" commits suicide, against his will, by means of his psychosomatic power, raises the question of the kinds of mental power possessed by primitive people. How does the human mind self-destruct the human body within a few hours or at most a few days? How does it come about that this power of self-destruction is triggered, time after time, by the fear of a particular man's threat to kill the victims?

One absolutely incomprehensible example of primitive witchcraft is reported by Valentine. One of the Philippine healers, Mercado, who had been trained by Agpaoa, healed a young woman whom he had diagnosed as a witchcraft victim. She had not been aware of her plight and was horrified. She had only thought that she was ill for some physical reason. Without doubt, her case is the strangest that appears in this book. Valentine describes what he saw:

Again Mercado worked rapidly on the patient's lower abdomen. The girl was not in pain, but she was evidently upset at the thought of being a witchcraft victim. She covered her face with her arms and sobbed convulsively during the operation. I leaned in for a closer look; my nose was about eighteen inches from the action. Suddenly several large, flat leaves from some tropical plant popped up from the surgical opening like a jack-in-the-box. I stared in blank disbelief as the crowd behind me gasped in unison. Mercado plucked the leaves out of the girl and waved them to onlookers.

"Witchcraft," he explained with a toothy grin.

Kurt Osolsobie's eyebrows were raised—he too was seeing but not understanding. Jack Netchin, standing at the head of the table taking pictures, just shrugged and kept on filming. I picked up a leaf that had missed the wastebasket and examined it closely. It looked and felt like the leaf of a plant. It was spattered with blood and about ten inches long and three inches wide at its widest point. If Mercado had palmed the leaves, they would have been crumpled; that leaf was perfectly smooth. I'd already made routine checks of the sheet and the cotton. Before the girl got off the table, I examined her, with Lolet's help; the waistband of her skirt was tight. Those leaves had been inside the girl.

In Don Wild's film, Marcello Jainar removes about two feet of "plastic wrap" from a patient's abdomen as Tony looks on. The slowest of slow motion cannot detect any sleight of hand. Certainly it's illogical, but the whole phenomenon is illogical.[75]

---

75. Valentine, *Psychic Surgery*, pp. 142-43.

How can we explain this? Fakery? At eighteen inches, in front of cameras and many witnesses? Yet how could leaves get into a woman's intestinal area? Aborigines in Australia believe that when a hex using a "death bone" is made, a second bone literally enters the victim and kills him, either directly or by the sorcerer burying the death bone, burning it, or in some way destroying it.[76] Can this be correct? Is this analogous to the Filipino housemaid's rash, which was treated by pulling rice-sized pellets through microscopically small pores? What does a leaf have in common with pellets? There is no logical answer, simply because such phenomena are not governed by rational categories. What is more likely than the idea that such items do reside inside men's systems is to assume some form of demonic transformation. The pellets and the leaves are literally materialized, either by the healer's control agent, or else by some other occult source of power. In other words, the victim of witchcraft is under spiritual bondage, and this bondage has physical aspects, such as a feeling of illness or discomfort. But these feelings are not those that would be caused if real leaves were inside the body. No Western physician could operate on the victim and discover leaves inside the body, or pellets instead of a rash. The visible signs that are produced when the spirit control agent of the healer works on the bodies of the victims are a means of confirmation to primitive people that the occult is directly involved. The leaves become *tangible symbols of demonic power*—confusing to the Western observer, but understood in principle by the local population. The local tribesman nods in agreement with the healer's diagnosis: yes, it must have been witchcraft. The sight of the abnormal affirms the existence of occult power, thereby increasing men's fear of the local medicine man or village sorcerer who must have produced the hex. Seeing, after all, is believing—unless you are a *Western* observer. For the Westerner, seeing is also believing, but the belief is in sleight-of-hand by men, not a kind of sleight-of-hand by demons. But the effect on the tribe is the same, whoever is playing games: continued occult bondage and perpetual fear in a world of unfamiliar laws and hostile forces—intensely personal forces.

Kurt Koch, the Protestant exorcist whose books are filled with case histories of occult bondage, relates a remarkable story of a native pastor in Nigeria, a member of the Izi tribe. He had been suffering from a serious disease of the lungs, and his physicians believed

76. Ronald Rose, *Primitive Psychic Power*, pp. 28-35.

that he was close to death. His X-rays indicated that both lungs were filled with blood. He was literally drowning in his own blood. The pastor had asked the local missionary to come and visit him.

"I sensed I am not going to die," he told the missionary. "It seems to me as if this is only an attack of the powers of darkness. Please, will you command these powers to leave me." The missionary, however, hesitated, for he was more inclined to believe what the doctors had told him than to believe what his native brother said. But the pastor urged him again. Finally he agreed and he prayed roughly with the words, "Lord Jesus, if my brother here is right, and this is only an attack of the enemy, then deliver him. But forgive me if what I am saying is silly." The missionary then commanded the evil powers to go, although in his heart he doubted if he was doing the right thing. What happened? Suddenly the pastor vomited and brought up a vast amount of blood. The doctor was called immediately, but he said that this was the end. Yet instead of dying, the man began to recover. A few days later he was X-rayed again. A miracle had taken place. The massive caverns in his lungs had closed up, and instead of certain death, the native Christian was wonderfully healed by the hand of the Lord.[77]

The missionary's reaction was typically Western. It is hardly surprising. Orthodox Protestant theological seminaries never offer courses in demonic possession. Demons are covered during one week, or even less, in one semester of systematic theology. ("Angels, fallen.") That men are possessed today, or that missionaries might face problems relating to actual occult power, is (or was in the mid-1960's and earlier) never even considered.

Koch then goes on to say: "Events of this nature are nothing we can copy. God cannot be forced to do the same for all who are suffering in this way. He alone is sovereign. It is he, and not us, who decides who is to be healed and who is not." Understandably, Koch is totally hostile to the full-time faith healers in Christian churches, or even more often, the independent healers with their tents or their regularly scheduled miracles at the Shrine Auditorium or Sports Arena. God is not a kind of injection that is at the beck and call of flamboyant faith healers. He is not a package of instant healing mix (just add holy water, stir under a spotlight, and pour). The Christian ministry of healing is to be done quietly by prayerful elders in the home or in a hospital (James 5:14-15). And God's healing is not to be

---

77. Kurt Koch, *Occult Bondage and Deliverance* (Grand Rapids, Michigan: Kregel, 1972), pp. 78-79.

accompanied by three to five collection offerings. (Rev. Gerald Latal, an Orthodox Presbyterian Church minister, was asked in the 1940's to co-sponsor the appearance of a subsequently well-known but now-deceased healing lady. It was at the beginning of her career. He was skeptical, but he and his elders met with her. She wanted her organization to handle all the mechanics, including the promotion. He insisted that if she appeared, any sponsoring churches had to be given credit as co-sponsors. "All *right!*" she replied to him. "But I'll take the *collections*." Rev. Latal wisely decided not to have anything to do with the project. The lady kept taking those collections for 25 years.)

Koch makes some telling comments on the ministry of Oral Roberts, who established himself as a faith healer. Today, Roberts' television programs are modeled along the lines of the more conventional evangelists: a weekly "intimate" get together, with a small studio audience, plus clean-cut "up-beat" singers. He has abandoned the mass healings; he just bows his head and prays that God will heal people in the audience. This is valid enough. But in the early 1950's, before he had joined the Methodist Church, before he had built a college and a heavily recruited basketball team of NCAA tournament caliber, he was on the sawdust trail. He did not have one-hour travelog specials on Alaska in full color; he had live broadcasts from his tent. The walking wounded hobbled up to be healed, and he laid hands on them all—or at least those who were screened to come up onto the stage. Koch comments on Roberts' appearance at the World Congress of Evangelism held in Berlin in 1966. Roberts was the leader of a subcommittee.

There were about 300 delegates present including the Rev. Pagel, the evangelist Leo Janz and myself. Roberts had been speaking on the subject of healing when one of the Americans present asked him, "Mr. Roberts, isn't it true that during your television programs you have sometimes asked the viewers to place a glass of water on the television during the actual broadcast?" After receiving an affirmative answer, his questioner went on, "And isn't it also true that at the end of the programs you have told the viewers to drink the water if they are seeking healing?" Again, in the presence of the 300 or so delegates, Oral Roberts replied, "Yes." That was honest of him. But what type of healing is this? Occasionally during similar programs one of the viewers has been asked to place his hand on the television set and with his free hand to either touch or to form a chain with other viewers present. But this is the sort of practice one finds in connection with spiritistic table-lifting, when chains are formed in order to encourage the flow of mediumistic forces.[78]

Roberts admitted publicly that when he was younger, an old Indian once healed him. Koch speculates that this may have been the origin of his healing powers.[79] Transfers of such powers are reported again and again by healing mediums. (Rev. Plume is one example.)

Conclusion

Western rationalism is as one-sided and narrow as any other world-and-life view. Those who hold to its premises have exercised great power over the last two centuries. Much of this power is well deserved. By refining the techniques of science, Western thinkers have made possible a flowering of human culture which is the envy of the primitive, magical world. The whole underdeveloped world wants a piece of our action, but they do not usually want to give up the other aspects of their culture that guarantee continued poverty. By turning their leaders into socialists, materialists, bureaucrats, and rationalists by giving them scholarships to our better universities, we have cut off the leaders from their popular support. Democracy cannot flourish in these nations for many reasons, not the least of which is the undemocratic nature of all bureaucratic rule, and it is bureaucracy, far more than democracy, which has been the West's major organizational export — bureaucracy financed by government-to-government foreign aid and heavy taxation inside the recipients' nations. But democracy also cannot flourish where demonism is present. The essence of demonism is an elitist manipulation of the common tribesmen. The means of power are personal asceticism, demon possession, trances, visions, dreams, and total immersion into the occult. *Ritual*, not a study of the regularities of nature, is the law of primitive cultures. The ideology of bureaucracy may be in conformity with some of the aspects of demonism, but democracy is in total opposition. No one but a Western intellectual could have believed that India was democratic, or that its traditions and institutions might permit the limited democracy of the liberal West. Indira Gandhi did not cut down Indian democracy at the roots; there never were any roots, except in the dreams and visions of Western commentators and in Indian newspaper editorials. And what is true of India is true of the whole so-called Third World. Where demonism is a

---

78. *Ibid.*, p. 55.
79. *Ibid.*, p. 54.

part of the culture, democracy cannot take root. Neither can the rationalistic production methods of free-market capitalism.

What is so disturbing today is the growing popularity of the Eastern cosmologies within Western circles, especially among the formally educated young. It is not possible to import Western versions of Eastern philosophy — all nicely sterilized by the professors of Eastern religion on the campuses — without simultaneously opening up one's mind and soul to all the rest of Eastern culture: monism, mysticism, asceticism, irrationalism, and finally magic. The East is coming West. It represents the importation of intellectual and cultural stagnation at best; at worst, it will destroy the very foundations of Western productivity. It is integration into the void.

Everyone wants to "do good." Healing seems to do good. Occult healing seems to do good a lot cheaper. So argues Henry Belk, the rich psychic investigator who helped to popularize both Arigo and the Philippine healers, and who is rich because his staunchly Presbyterian father established a cost-effective, economically rational chain of stores. He described the "benefits" of healing by spirits: "They don't eat, they don't pay taxes, and they supply the labor."[80]

At the heart of all magic is the quest for power, but at low cost. Asceticism is personal, not cultural. Economically, it is the philosophy of something for nothing. Westerners who think they can make use of Eastern and primitive healing techniques without the personal asceticism required of the healing adepts will find that the price of their power is far, far higher than they think.

Westerners who do accept the validity of the stories concerning psychic healing may say to themselves: "What a shame that we in the West have closed off ourselves to such wonderful powers." Wonderful indeed: *filled with wonder.* But the same person who is saddened by the absence of occult healing techniques in the West lives in a clean environment and has at his disposal skilled medical diagnosticians operating in terms of the division of labor (meaning physicians can check out each other's progress and learn). Western citizens may want the blessings of both cultures, not realizing that what primitive man has is a *curse.* Now we find men who are out to fuse Western technology and Eastern irrationalism. They are out to build an electric Tibet. They fail to comprehend that in an electric Tibet, not

---

80. Valentine, *Psychic Surgery,* p. 214.

even the machines would be healthy. A Tibetan culture does not accept a Western view of the world in which men can gain access to electrical power, thereby increasing the productivity of all people, not just the demonic elite. We cannot fuse the two cultures; the two cultures are at war.

If your head hurts, take two aspirin and go to bed. Let the Arigos of the world remain where they belong: struggling in the jungles.

8

MAGIC, ENVY, AND FOREIGN AID

But it shall come to pass, if thou wilt not hearken unto the voice of the LORD thy God, to observe to do all his commandments and statutes which I command thee this day: that all these curses shall come upon thee, and overtake thee.

Deuteronomy 28:15

One of the characteristic features of the Christian West is its commitment to the concept of linear history. Westerners seldom give the concept much thought. They assume, almost automatically, that no other idea of history could be held by anyone. But the concept of linear history — a unique past, present, and future — is very much the product of religious faith. It was the Hebrew concept of the creation as an unrepeatable event that gave the West its belief in historical time. By affirming the doctrine of creation, Christianity transformed the West — indeed, created the West. It is quite proper, therefore, for Charles N. Cochrane to end his book *Christianity and Classical Culture* (1940) with a chapter on Augustine. It was Augustine's formulation of linear history in *The City of God* that served to transform the thinking of Western scholars. The concept of cyclical history, held by classical culture and the ancient pagan kingdoms, was overturned by Augustine.[1] His words served as a kind of intellectual touchstone: "The education of the human race, represented by the people of God, has advanced, like that of an individual, through certain epochs, or, as it were, ages, so that it might gradually rise from earthly to heavenly things, and from the visible to the invisible."[2]

The source of the idea of progress is Christianity. The pagan concept of historical development, with its inevitable cycles of growth and decay, did not leave room for long-term progress. But Christian-

---

1. Augustine, *The City of God*, XII:17.
2. *Ibid.*, X:14.

ity offered hope to men: by conforming themselves to the image of Christ, men might see progress spiritually. This, in turn, was understood by Protestants, and especially Calvinists, as undergirding the possibility of external, cultural, and economic progress—a literal fulfillment of the promises of Deuteronomy 8 and 28. Thus, during the sixteenth and seventeenth centuries came a new concept of applied Christianity: economic growth.

This is not to say that medieval Catholicism entirely ignored economic growth. In fact, one of the continual problems of the church in the Middle Ages was its constant tendency to grow rich. The legendary productivity of the Benedictine monasteries became a recurring source of embarrassment. Benedictine monks, though they owned no property personally, were energetic, thrifty, and innovative farmers. Over and over, their monastic communities prospered, occasioning cries for reform. The external economic blessings were simultaneously a sign of efficient management and a source of embarrassment. In one sense, the Protestants made every man an industrious monk, and by affirming the legitimacy of private property, the Protestants opened the door to the expansion of riches. Nevertheless, they cautioned against the dangers of wealth, even as Moses had cautioned his listeners in the oft-quoted Deuteronomic passages. The idea of compound growth over time was the product of an explicitly theological interpretation of time.

Primitive Culture

Because Western thinkers operate by some version of the idea of progress, they inevitably think of primitive cultures as those which are *historically prior.* Somehow, they have not been able to "progress" along the linear time model. They have been held back, and the supposedly innate tendencies toward progress that can be found whenever men form communities have not been able to flourish. But this approach to the question of economic or cultural development is fundamentally in error. The existence of what *we* might call expansionary pressures is in no way automatic. What is normal, that is, historically most common, is for a few members of a culture to be innovative, with the vast majority content with things as they are. There is no confidence in progress; in fact, the whole idea is absolutely foreign. Traditional approaches are assumed to be satisfactory for most problems; social change is therefore not expected, nor even appreciated. Two distinctly Western beliefs are absent: first, the belief in linear history, and second, the belief that reason is capable of unlocking the secrets of nature. Without a future-orientation, primitive cultures do not possess an inner dynamic favorable to social advancement. Without a concept of practical reason — the link between the laws of the mind and the laws of nature — these cultures lack the engine of progress.

It is not enough to argue that primitive cultures are historically prior. The reason why they are primitive is that the concept of "historically prior" has no meaning for them, for the concept of "historically future" is meaningless. The remarkable scholarly writings of the cultural anthropologist, Mircea Eliade, have dwelt on this subject at length. Cyclical history (or, as he calls it, the myth of the eternal return) has placed a premium on the escape from the burdens of history. Only through ecstatic release, or ritual chaos, do primitive cultures expect to retain the lost paradise of the age of gold. Magic is central to this quest. Through magic, the holy men of the tribe or community can recreate the conditions of the original creation — an evolutionary creation — thus permitting the community to participate ritually in that original creative act or series of acts. The festivals of Mardi Gras and Carnival are the product of the pagan faith in cleansing chaos and the annual abolition of conventional behavior.

The bondage of law, which is itself the product of the degeneration of the ages, is one of the primary targets of ritualistic chaos. The ages of gold, silver, bronze, and now iron (to use Hesiod's traditional outline in his *Works and Days*) have brought with them the increasing bondage of men to law. Lawlessness is therefore a ritual affirmation of a better way of life, a kind of regeneration socially. It is the philosophy of "power from below," in Rushdoony's words.[3]

Pagan cultures deny the doctrine of Darwinian evolution. They affirm the doctrine of *devolution*. The hope of these men is in some magical discontinuous event — a messianic magical savior, a successful revolution, the discovery of a magical formula — that will restore the lost paradise. They see life's problems as metaphysical — the lack of some attribute of being — rather than moral and ethical. The problem of man is therefore not covenantal disobedience to a holy and sovereign God, but a flaw in the creation. Men will restore the

---

3. R. J. Rushdoony, "Power from Below," *Journal of Christian Reconstruction*, I (Winter, 1974).

lost paradise, not by repentance and godly labor in every area of life, but by the magical exercise of power.

The heart of cultural primitivism is the desire to transcend time, to abolish time's burdens. The Christian idea of slow economic progress that is the product of continual spiritual discipline and conformity to God's ethical laws, is absolutely foreign to the pagan culture. In magical society, there is a distinctly revolutionary impulse, as Eliade notes: "The wish to abolish time can be seen even more clearly in the 'orgy' which takes place, with varying degrees of violence, during the New Year ceremonies. An orgy is also a regression into the 'dark,' a restoration of the primeval chaos, and as such precedes all creation, every manifestation of ordered form. The fusion of all forms into one single, vast, undifferentiated unity is an exact reproduction of the 'total' mode of reality. I pointed out earlier the function and meaning of the orgy, at once sexual and agricultural; at the cosmological level, the 'orgy' represents chaos or the ultimate disappearance of limits and, as time goes, the inauguration of the Great Time, of the 'eternal moment,' or nonduration. The presence of the orgy among the ceremonials shows the *will to abolish the past totally by abolishing all creation*."[4]

The concern is not with ethics but with the limitations of all created being. *The attempt to abolish the limits of creaturehood is the very heart of all demonic religion.* It is this impulse that militates against human progress. The existence of both law and the limits imposed by law is denied. But without law, the tool of progress is denied, for it is by the systematic application of the laws of nature that men subdue the creation, causing it to become fruitful (Genesis 1:28). Magic substitutes meaningless ritual for law, and rituals do not change. Discovery is left to the random event; illumination is understood as ecstatic rather than intellectual. Progress dies.

Subsidizing the Primitive

Western commentators generally and correctly associate magic and primitivism. The explanation, unfortunately, tends to be environmentalistic: these societies still practice magic because they are primitive. The assumption seems to be that the West, by massive doses of foreign aid, the Peace Corps, scholarships for their bright

---

4. Mircea Eliade, *Patterns in Comparative Religion* (New York: Sheed & Ward, 1958), p. 399.

young men to Cambridge, Oxford, or Harvard, plus free public, secular education, can bring these primitive cultures "into the twentieth century." At that point, magical practices will slowly fade away. Yet the analysis is fatally flawed. The reason why these cultures are primitive is that magic, which involves a definite world-and-life view, dominates all of them. The cultures are the product of the religion of magic, not the other way around.

It is not what man possesses externally that counts in the long run. What is crucial is the *attitude* toward God and the world that permeates the culture. By failing to recognize this fact, modern foreign-aid administrators have produced one folly after another, and this is as true of the Soviets as the West.[5] *Primitivism is a state of mind, a set of attitudes.* All attempts to overcome cultural backwardness, apart from a prior change of mind by the members of the culture in question, are doomed to failure. P. T. Bauer, a professor of economics at the London School of Economics, has written several important books on economic development, but in his 1972 study, *Dissent on Development*, he lays it on the line. The key to the economic development of a society is the character of the people. What they believe is vastly more significant than what they presently own:

Examples of significant attitudes, beliefs and modes of conduct unfavourable to material progress include lack of interest in material advance, combined with resignation in the face of poverty; lack of initiative, self-reliance and of a sense of personal responsibility for the economic future of oneself and one's family; high leisure preference, together with a lassitude often found in tropical climates; relatively high prestige of passive or contemplative life compared to active life; the prestige of mysticism and of renunciation of the world compared to acquisition and achievement; acceptance of the idea of a preordained, unchanging and unchangeable universe; emphasis on performance of duties and acceptance of obligations, rather than on achievement of results, or assertion or even a recognition of personal rights; lack of sustained curiosity, experimentation and interest in change; belief in the efficacy of supernatural and occult forces and of their influence over one's destiny; insistence on the unity of the organic universe, and on the need to live with nature rather than conquer it or harness it to man's needs, an attitude of which reluctance to take animal life is a corollary; belief in perpetual reincarnation, which reduces the significance of effort in the course of the present life; recognized status of beggary, together with a lack of stigma in the acceptance of charity; opposition to women's

---

5. Victor Lasky, *The Ugly Russian* (New York: Trident, 1965).

work outside the household.[6]

Bauer's list, coming after a lifetime of research into the question of economic underdevelopment, must be taken seriously. Obviously, no society is ever totally categorized by such a list, just as each Western, industrial nation will possess certain features found in the list. It is an ideal type, a kind of master model, and not a summary of any given culture. But where a significant number of these features are found in a culture, all the Western foreign aid available will not, in and of itself, succeed in transforming the culture. To believe that money or technical training can bring permanent economic growth is simply to believe in environmentalism.

Bauer's list is extremely informative, given the information found in previous chapters of this book. A close look at the so-called counter-culture reveals that most of the elements of the backward economic society are part of the world-and-life view of the counter-culture. The hippie movement of the 1960's did not begin with magic, seances, occultism, blood sacrifice, and ritual murders. It began with pessimism concerning rational methodology. It began with pessimism concerning the future, at least the Establishment's future. Vegetarianism, Eastern religion, philosophical monism, mysticism, and chemical escape from the rational world were standard tenets of the counter-culture. Only toward the end of the decade did the faith in reincarnation, occultism, spirits, and other elements of witchcraft become commonplace. "Tune in, turn on, drop out" was Timothy Leary's antirational slogan, and it rested on a view of life that fundamentally corresponds with Bauer's outline of the underdeveloped society. As to the stigma associated with charity, a generation of the welfare state had eroded the older concepts of full personal responsibility and personal labor. The affluence of the society led young people to believe that wealth is automatic. Begging and outright scrounging became a way of life because of the easy availability of vast wealth in urban trash cans. As God warned the people of Israel, covenantal obedience produces wealth, but wealth brings temptation, the temptation to forget the God whose covenantal law-order made possible the wealth (Deuteronomy 8:6-20).

The occult epidemic threatens the very foundations of Western culture. Middle-class morality is the distant heir of the Puritan work

6. P. T. Bauer, *Dissent on Development* (Cambridge, Mass: Harvard University Press, 1972), pp. 78-79.

ethic. As such, it has produced abundance. But this historically un-precedented economic prosperity is not a self-sustaining process. It is the product of certain attitudes and presuppositions about the nature of reality. It rests, ultimately, on a religious perception of the world. By introducing a new (and very ancient) set of religious prin-ciples — the religion of magic — the counter-culture serves as a kind of Pied Piper. Religious transformation will inevitably produce cultural transformation. Western capitalism cannot possibly survive in a so-ciety that is committed to the tenets of magic.

Envy and Backwardness

Bauer mentions magic as one factor that retards economic devel-opment, but the German sociologist Helmut Schoeck has developed this theme in relation to another retarding factor: envy. Schoeck's book, a masterpiece, traces the impact envy has had on thinkers, cultures, and economies. Its thesis is straightforward: envy toward the wealth or achievements of others reduces the ability of individ-uals to advance themselves economically. Envy is not mere jealousy, as Schoeck defines it. It is not simply one man's desire for another man's possessions. It is a strong resentment against the very exist-ence of another man's wealth or status. It involves the desire to reduce another man's wealth even when this reduction in his wealth in no way improves the position of the envious person. Nowhere is envy more devastating than in so-called primitive cultures.

If a person or a family should get ahead of the accepted tribal minimum per capita wealth, two very dangerous things may easily occur. First, the offending party may be suspected of being a wizard or witch. Second, he may become fearful of being the object of the envious evil magic of others. As Schoeck writes: "The whole litera-ture on the subject of African sorcery shows the envious man (sor-cerer) would like to harm the victim he envies, but only seldom with any expectation of thereby obtaining for himself the asset that he envies — whether this be a possession or a physical quality belonging to the other."[7] Understandably, this envy is present only where there is *close social proximity* between the envious and the envied. It is always regarded as very difficult to bewitch a stranger with any suc-cess.[8]

---

7. Helmut Schoeck, *Envy: A Theory of Social Behavior* (New York: Harcourt Brace Jovanovich [1966] 1969), p. 37.
8. *Ibid.*, p. 40.

The efficacy of demonic magic is strong in these non-Christian cultures. The fear of magic is pervasive. Thus, the threat of its use against the truly successful man causes men with talents to conceal them from their fellows. Men become secretive about what they own. They prefer to attribute any personal successes to luck or fate, both impersonal. *"Institutionalized envy* . . . or the ubiquitous fear of it, means that there is little possibility of individual economic achievement and no contact with the outside world through which the community might hope to progress. No one dares to show anything that might lead people to think that he was better off. Innovations are unlikely. Agricultural methods remain traditional and primitive, to the detriment of the whole village, because every deviation from previous practice comes up against the limitations of envy."[9]

Furthermore, Schoeck writes: "It is impossible for several families to pool resources or tools of any kind in a common undertaking. It is almost equally impossible for any one man to adopt a leading role in the interests of the village."[10] While Schoeck does not discuss it, the problem of institutionalized envy and magic for the establishment of republican institutions in primitive cultures is almost overwhelming. Once a chief's link to traditional authority is officially denied by secular educators in a culture, who is to lead? If a man cannot point to a long tradition of authority or his semidivine status as a leader, who is to say who is to lead? Whoever dares to proclaim himself as leader had better be prepared to defend his title not merely at the polling booth, but from envious magic. In a culture in which the authority of traditional rulers has been eroded by Western secularism and Western theories of individualism and democracy, the obvious alternative to traditional authority is military power.

In April 1975, the tiny, poverty-stricken African "nation" of Chad had a military coup. Months later, the news media briefly picked up the story of the deposed leader, Ngarta Tombalbaye, who had been executed by the military. He had imported Haitian witch doctors — one of Haiti's few products that can compete successfully in the international division of labor — and had used Radio Chad to broadcast what were purported to be spirit messages. Men in every station of life were told to return to their tribal villages and participate in initiation rites from Chad's Stone Age past. (Chad's Stone Age, chronologically speaking, ended a couple of centuries ago.) From 1962,

---

9. *Ibid.*, p. 47.
10. *Ibid.*, p. 48.

when Tombalbaye took control of the government, until his death, Christians who refused to participate in these rites were tortured, murdered, or forced to flee the country. One pastor, Moussa Bopen, opposed the rites for a year, and when he was threatened with execution, asked if he could preach one last sermon. His request was granted. His topic: "The Evils of Idolatry." He was fatally clubbed from behind before he could finish. One European-educated college professor returned home to his village, underwent initiation, and later claimed to have been born free. He wears a suit now (he had worn a loin cloth during his initiation), but sleeps with magical knives under his bed.

What finished the man's rule was his attempted purge of the army. He arrested two high officers and promised to reorganize the army. He was seized and executed shortly thereafter. It was not Western democracy that replaced the rule of the magicians, but military despotism.[11] Similar reports have come from other Third World areas for a decade. The centuries-long, or millennia-long, paralysis produced by demonic power cannot be overcome by Western checks and Western educations. The winners are those who have mastered one aspect of Western technology: weaponry. Military despotism has been the secularized West's major export to the Third World. "General" Amin of Uganda was only the loudest, most flamboyant of the corporals who came to power when the Western colonial administrators gave up and went home. He was the symbol of transported Western administrative techniques — the strange hybrid of tribalism, occultism, and secular technology.

Envy has crucially important implications for a culture's concept of time. Schoeck concludes: "In a culture incapable of any form of competition, time means nothing."[12] Men do not discuss their private plans with each other. Shared goals, except of a traditional nature, are almost absent in magic-dominated societies. "Ubiquitous envy, fear of it and those who harbour it, cuts off such people from any kind of communal action directed toward the future. Every man is for himself, every man is thrown back upon his own resources. All striving, preparation and planning for the future can be undertaken only by socially fragmented, secretive beings."[13] Is it any wonder, then, that primitive cultures stay primitive, despite massive doses of

---

11. *Los Angeles Times* (Oct. 9, 1975).
12. Schoeck, *Envy*, p. 41.
13. *Ibid.*, p. 50.

foreign aid, that is, government-to-government aid. Schoeck does not exaggerate when he writes, "As a system of social control, Black Magic is of tremendous importance, because it governs all interpersonal relationships."

Power, Cause, and Effect

"The fundamental aim of all magic is to impose the human will on nature, on man or on the supersensual world in order to master them." With these words, E. M. Butler introduces her book, *Ritual Magic* (1949). The goals, however, are rigorously materialistic: fame, power, fortune, success. Anton Szandor LaVey, the self-ordained (1966) minister of the Church of Satan in San Francisco, is quite open about the goals of Satanism: "Anyone who pretends to be interested in magic or the occult for reasons other than gaining personal power is the worst kind of hypocrite."[14] Further, says LaVey:

White magic is supposedly utilized only for good or unselfish purposes, and black magic, we are told, is used only for selfish or "evil" reasons. Satanism draws no such dividing line. Magic is magic, be it used to help or hinder. The Satanist, being the modern magician, should have the ability to decide what is just, and then apply the powers of magic to attain his goals.

During white magic ceremonies, the practitioners stand within a pentagram to protect themselves from the "evil" forces which they call upon for help. To the Satanist, it seems a bit two-faced to call on these forces for help, while at the same time protecting yourself from the very powers you have asked for assistance. The Satanist realizes that only by putting himself in league with these forces can he fully and unhypocritically utilize the Powers of Darkness to his best advantage.[15]

In short, concludes LaVey, "Satanism is not a white light religion; it is a religion of the flesh, the mundane, the carnal — all of which are ruled by Satan, the personification of the Left Hand Path."[16]

The Left Hand Path: here is one of the familiar slogans of the occult underground. The Right Hand Path is the path of mystical illumination, higher consciousness, white magic, and philosophical monism. Members of these seemingly innocuous groups constantly

---

14. Anton Szandor LaVey, *The Satanic Bible* (New York: Avon, 1972), p. 51.
15. *Ibid.*, pp. 51-52.
16. *Ibid.*, p. 52.

warn newcomers against the Left Hand Path, that is the quest for occult power for selfish ends. LaVey regards all this as hypocrisy; occult power is occult power, so why mix in remnants of Christian morality? It is ultimately the power of man, says LaVey, that Satan symbolizes. "Man, the animal, is the godhead to the Satanist."[17] What's more, "The Satanist realizes that man, and the action and reaction of the universe, is responsible for everything, and doesn't mislead himself into thinking that someone cares."[18] Therefore, he says, men should live consistently with this faith.

There are no standards except those forged by each individual Satanist. "Death to the weakling, wealth to the strong! . . . I break away from all conventions that do not lead to my earthly success and happiness."[19] The great enemy is a conservatism that is grounded in Christian principles. "Behold the crucifix; what does it symbolize? Pallid incompetence hanging on a tree. I question all things. As I stand before the festering and varnished facades of your haughtiest moral dogmas, I write thereon in letters of blazing scorn: Lo and behold; all this is fraud. . . . The chief duty of every new age is to upraise new men to determine its liberties, to lead it towards material success — to rend the rusty padlocks and chains of dead customs that always prevent healthy expansion. Theories and ideas that may have meant life and hope and freedom for our ancestors may now mean destruction, slavery, and dishonor to us! As environments change, no human ideal standeth sure!"[20] This is relativism.

The hope of LaVey is that his recommended system of power will produce "healthy expansion." Yet the religion of magic is calculated to destroy the very foundations of social progress. By creating a social system based on fear of other men, magic destroys the possibility of a systematic division of labor. It destroys the concept of linear time, for in a world of flux, especially moral flux, it becomes impossible for men to calculate the difference between good and bad results over time. Moral flux reduces time to chaos; indeed, the very chaos cults of the ancient world and today's primitive cultures acknowledge this fact: moral flux, ritually applied, recreates the eternal moment where time's bounds are broken. Without the ability to distinguish good from evil, men cannot distinguish cause from effect

---

17. *Ibid.*, p. 89.
18. *Ibid.*, p. 41.
19. *Ibid.*, p. 30.
20. *Ibid.*, p. 31.

over time. If whirl is king, who can comprehend the kingdom? Science becomes impossible, for the regularities of nature are forever being transcended by the power of the magicians. As don Juan told Castaneda, without faith in his everyday world and its everyday activities, the occult world of power threatened him day and night. The radical autonomy of the philosophy of Satanism, like the radical autonomy of existentialism and modern philosophy, cannot help but result in cultural impotence and stagnation. It is the death of culture.

Lawlessness and Impotence

The fruits of magic, economically speaking, are not productivity and unlimited wealth, but just the opposite: the erosion of capital, the stagnation or even decline of per-capita wealth, and the end of economic growth. The society of Satan lives off the stolen capital of two thousand years of Christian culture.

The Christian premise is that the fear of God is the beginning of wisdom (Proverbs 1:7), but that those who live in the fear of the Lord need not fear other men (Psalm 27:1). The Satanic premise is that the Lord of heaven need not be feared, but that both Satan and other men are to be feared. This creates a sense of bondage; the creation, rather than the Creator, is feared. The source of *Christian activism* is the knowledge that under God's providence, the faithful servant triumphs, if not during his stay on earth, then at least on the final day of judgment. Thus, the command that the earth be subdued to the glory of God (Genesis 1:28) can be taken seriously. Passivity toward the affairs of life is clearly prohibited. Christian men, as God's delegated superiors over the creation, are required to take positions of leadership. The source of their strength is their faith; the source of their power over earthly affairs is their commitment to the tool of social reconstruction: the revealed law of God.

On the other hand, the Satanist lives in a universe devoid of predictable laws. Ritual rules supreme, but there is always the fear that some minute aspect of ritual will be neglected or transgressed, or that some other magician can master the terms of the prescribed ritual even more efficiently. The source of man's power is therefore in the hands of a created being who is fundamentally hostile to man's desires, basically the liar of liars whose solemn word cannot be trusted, whose tongue is a snare to the unwary. There is a marvelous science-fantasy short story about a young man who was failing his class in mathematics. He then discovered an old book of magic, and decided to master the ritual and summon up a demon. After going through nights of preparation, he drew the protecting pentagram on the floor of his room and called forth the hideous demon whose power he would command. The awful creature appeared, sending terror through him, but he knew that he was protected by the chalk marks on the floor. "I need help with my geometry," he announced. "You certainly do," the demon replied, as he stepped easily across the hexagram.

The spirit of the law has no place in demonic rituals. It is the form that counts, above all. Men are in bondage to the outward forms, in contrast to the biblical perspective that states that God has no need of our sacrifices, but desires justice, mercy, and a humble walk before Him (Micah 6:6-8). Christian men can be confident in the face of the creation precisely because it is the trustworthiness of God that reassures them, not confidence in the ritualistic works of their own hands. This element of trust is what is totally absent from the world of Satanic intervention. The idea of the compact with the devil is that the ultimate goal is to break it. Mutual distrust is its very foundation. In contrast the idea of the covenant with God is based on the hope that God will honor it even in the face of our weaknesses (Romans 8:28-31). A society can be constructed on the basis of mutual trust and the fulfilling of contractual (covenantal) obligations precisely because each man sees every obligation as one made under God's ultimate sovereignty and authority. A man's word can be regarded as his bond, not because he is autonomous, but because no man is autonomous.

Man as God

The implicit humanism of all Satanism—that men shall be as God, knowing [determining] good and evil (Genesis 3:5)—has been made explicit in the writings of LaVey and the man on whose model LaVey is obviously acting, Aleister Crowley. Crowley's important book, *Magick in Theory and Practice*, which was originally written in 1911, has spelled out the Satanic premise: man is God. "For the Gods are the enemies of Man; it is Nature that Man must overcome ere he enter the kingdom. *The true God is man. In man are all things hidden.* Of these the Gods, Nature, Time, all the powers of the universe are rebellious slaves."[21] He then informs his readers that it is in Crowley's

---

21. Aleister Crowley, *Magick in Theory and Practice* (New York: Castle, n.d.), pp. 152-53.

name that all others should conquer nature. He was no shrinking violet. Yet the result of his faith was a kind of impotence. All money, he admitted, slipped through his fingers. "Every human affection that He had in His heart — and that heart aches for Love as few hearts can ever conceive — was torn and trampled with such infernal ingenuity in His intensifying torture that His endurance is beyond belief." As he says, his children died, his wives drank themselves to death or went mad.[22] In short, his life was a disaster. But he invariably capitalized his name and spoke of himself in the third person, as if he were a god.

Crowley was at least consistent. He knew the origin of his faith, for he spoke of "Chaos, the All-Father."[23] There is no law in the world, no truth, except for his own writings.[24] He had to believe in "Gods," for these are nothing more than the laws of nature, "and thus their 'Wills' are immutable and absolute."[25] Yet there is no law, except for his famous dictum: "Do what thou wilt shall be the whole of the law."[26] There is no devil. There are demonic hosts who can serve men.[27] These demons are fallible, and they can be manipulated emotionally. Every fact is autonomous; there is no law-order that stands in relation to man.[28] Yet the magician is nonetheless sovereign: "For there is no power either of the firmament or of the ether, or of the earth or under the earth, on dry land or in the water, of whirling air or of rushing fire, or any spell or scourge of God which is not obedient to the necessity of the Magician!"[29] And to achieve this absolute sovereignty over nature, the magician must submit entirely to the invisible forces of secret intelligence — demonic spirits who are not infallible, as he informs us: "It is equally necessary that the muscles with which he manipulates the apparatus of divination must be entirely independent of any volition of his. He must lend them for the moment to the intelligence whom he is consulting. . . ."[30] Chaos, in Crowley's world, is indeed king, the All-Father. His is the world of terror and destruction: "There is a Magical Operation of

22. *Ibid.*, p. 127.
23. *Ibid.*, p. 42.
24. *Ibid.*, pp. 36, 62, 144, 256-57.
25. *Ibid.*, p. 24n.
26. *Ibid.*, p. 193.
27. *Ibid.*, pp. 167-69.
28. *Ibid.*, p. 164.
29. *Ibid.*, p. 65.
30. *Ibid.*, p. 164.

maximum importance: the Initiation of a New Aeon. When it becomes necessary to utter a Word, the whole Planet must be bathed in blood."[31]

Conclusion

Should it be surprising that such a moral and spiritual universe is impotent? Should it startle us to find that where the philosophy of magic reigns supreme in men's hearts, they are unable to construct permanent institutional conditions favorable to the full exercise of human creativity? Should men wonder why it is that the Christian West has provided the emotional and legal incentives for men to transform the external realm of nature in order to conform it to the needs and goals of men? Embarked on a quest for autonomous power over nature, the Satanist finds chaos and ultimate impotence. Desiring to create conditions favorable to his own personal goals, the Satanist consumes the spiritual and legal capital of Christian civilization. The world of the devil is a masochistic universe that is destined to total failure. Yet secularism has eroded the commitment of Western men to such an extent that they believe that foreign aid by government decree will bring demonic societies the blessings of Christian liberty apart from the spiritual foundations, which indicates how demonic the foundations of secular humanism really are.

That Western capital should wind up in the treasuries of the Chads of the world is preposterous. To subsidize the demonic systems that have kept most of the world in spiritual darkness and economic poverty is to erode Christian capital that much faster. It is masochism — multi-billion-dollar masochism — yet the practice has gone on for a generation. We think that Western money and Western secular educations can convert savages into modernism. What we see before our eyes is one set of savages, bearing Ph.D.'s from Harvard and D. Phil.'s from Oxford, subsidizing the savages in the Third World (who sometimes have degrees from the same universities) with the earnings of less sophisticated men who have been made to feel guilty for their hard-earned prosperity. The politics of guilt and pity, as Rushdoony has called it, is the devil's tool. It is money down the devil's fiscal rathole.[32]

---

31. *Ibid.*, p. 96.
32. R. J. Rushdoony, *Politics of Guilt and Pity* (Fairfax, Virginia: Thoburn Press, [1970] 1978.

9

INVADERS FROM . . . ?

*If I become President, I'll make every piece of information this country
has about UFO sightings available to the public, and the scientists.
I am convinced that UFOs exist because I have seen one.*

Candidate Jimmy Carter

This was Jimmy Carter, the honest man from Plains, Georgia,
the man who promised American voters, "I'll never lie to you."
Would he have told this story in the middle of the race for the Presidency unless he was telling what he believed to be the truth? In 1973,
he and 20 other people saw a large, bright light in the sky which kept
changing colors. They watched it for ten minutes. Once honest Jimmy
was elected, of course, he reneged on this promise, among many,
many others.[1] He never mentioned the topic again, as far as I ever
saw — and I watched. But the reporter for the supermarket tabloid
National Enquirer who investigated the story found out that others
were with Carter when he saw the UFO, and they too had seen it.
Several others said that Carter had told them the story.[2] By the
mid-1970's, a flying saucer was still relatively odd news, but it certainly did not cost Carter many votes. Flying saucers were no longer
exclusively "cracked" saucers.

In the December 17, 1966 issue of *The Saturday Evening Post*,
Northwestern University astronomy professor J. Allen Hynek began
his feature article with this report: "On August 25, 1966, an Air
Force officer in charge of a missile crew in North Dakota suddenly
found that his radio transmission was being interrupted by static. At

---

1. A classic little paperback book has now become a collector's item, and in retrospect, a barrel of laughs: Robert W. Turner's *"I'll Never Lie to You": Jimmy Carter in his
Own Words*, published by Ballantine Books in 1976, during the Presidential campaign.

2. *National Enquirer* (June 8, 1976), headline story: "Jimmy Carter: The Night I
Saw a UFO," by Malcolm Balfour.

288

the time, he was sheltered in a concrete capsule 60 feet below the ground. While he was trying to clear up the problem, other Air Force personnel on the surface reported seeing a UFO—an unidentified flying object—high in the sky. It had a bright red light, and it appeared to be alternately climbing and descending. Simultaneously, a radar crew on the ground picked up the UFO at 100,000 feet. . . . 'When the UFO climbed, the static stopped,' stated the report made by the base's director of operations." Hynek reported that they saw it land ten to fifteen miles south of the base, but when a team was sent to investigate, their radio contact was drowned in static. Another UFO was spotted in the vicinity.[3]

When communications are disrupted at a nuclear missile base, and when the base's radar spots a vehicle close to it at 100,000 feet, we need to take such phenomena seriously. What if a whole radar screen full of such blips should appear, all headed toward SAC bases and missile sites? There is little doubt at the probable result. World War III would begin.

It came close on October 5, 1960. A formation of unidentified flying objects was picked up on U.S. radar screens at the early warning station at Thule, Greenland. These objects appeared to be headed for the U.S.A. Their origin seemed to be from the Soviet Union. The Strategic Air Command in Omaha was alerted. The B-52 crews were racing toward their planes at airfields all over the world. To confirm, SAC broadcast a signal to Thule. No answer. "Suddenly the mysterious blips on the radar screen changed course and disappeared." Later, the U.S. government issued an official explanation for the loss of communication: an iceberg had cut the submarine cable to the U.S. (Our survival communications link is dependent on a "submarine cable"?) No explanation for the blips on the radar screen was offered until three members of Parliament in Britain demanded one. The Air Force replied that radar signals had actually bounced off the moon and had been misinterpreted. The story was (predictably) buried in the *New York Times* on page 71.[4]

If our radar signals are that easily misinterpreted, we have a major high-risk problem. If they are not that easily misinterpreted, then what caused the radar to give this sort of signal? Do we have another

3. Reprinted in Jay David (ed.), *The Flying Saucer Reader* (New York: Signet, 1967), pp. 213-14.

4. John Keel, *UFOs: Operation Trojan Horse* (New York: Putnam's, 1970), pp. 13-14.

sort of high-risk problem?

The Soviets have had similar problems. In 1961, they fired a salvo of missiles at a squadron of UFO's that was hovering over a Moscow defense network. The missiles exploded before they reached their target. A second salvo was fired; the same thing happened. Then the electrical equipment of the missile base went dead.[5] Admittedly, it would be nice to believe that these failures were the result of inefficient Soviet technology, but I doubt that this explanation is adequate. Our technology suffers the same problem. The question is: Who or what is interfering with the electrical equipment? Who or what blew up those missiles?

Who Sees UFO's?

Prof. Hynek lists several myths concerning UFO sightings.[6] He spent over twenty years studying thousands of UFO reports that had been submitted to the U.S. Air Force. The four myths:

> Only UFO "buffs" report sightings.
> Scientifically trained people never report them.
> Only uneducated, unreliable people report them.
> UFO's are synonymous with "little green men."

In 1966, as the counter-culture was beginning to make itself felt, a Gallup poll was taken to determine how many Americans had seen a UFO. It was five percent. Seven years later, a second poll was taken. The figure had risen to 11 percent. Furthermore, over half of those interviewed who had heard of UFO's believed that they are real phenomena, and 94 percent had heard of them. The results of this awareness poll were among the highest in the history of the Gallup organization. Some 46 percent believed that there is intelligent life on other planets. In 1966, it had been only 36 percent. Seven out of ten who believe that there is life on other planets think that UFO's are real. Also of interest is the fact that college-educated people were as likely to have seen a UFO as persons with less formal education.[7] Yet

---

5. Ralph Blum, *Beyond Earth, Man's Contact With UFO's* (New York: Signet, 1975), p. 189; cited by Clifford Wilson and John Weldon, *Close Encounters: A Better Explanation* (San Diego, California: Master, 1978), p. 101.

6. J. Allen Hynek, *The UFO Experience: A Scientific Inquiry* (Chicago: Regnery, 1972), pp. 8-9.

7. J. Allen Hynek and Jacques Vallee, *The Edge of Reality: A Progress Report on Unidentified Flying Objects* (Chicago: Regnery, 1975), Appendix C.

all this has taken place in less than three decades, since that first great wave of publicity in June of 1947.

John Keel, a private reporter who began to collect information on UFO's in the mid-1960's, says that in 1966, he received from his newspaper clipping service over 10,000 clippings and reports of UFO sightings. This was in contrast to the Air Force's *reported* 1,060 sightings.[8] There is no doubt that UFO phenomena became widespread after 1965.

In the first edition of this book, which was published almost exactly at the time that Carter went public with his story of the UFO, I included no chapter on Unidentified Flying Objects. There were reasons for this. The literature on UFO's was very large and continues to grow. Furthermore, there are so many conflicting stories about what UFO's are or could be, and so many different opinions and interpretations regarding the reliability of the sightings, that I decided that it would be best not to open that particular can of worms. The topic deserved a whole book, perhaps, but a chapter seemed to be far too short to contain the material necessary for a full understanding of the topic. Had I been aware of John Keel's intriguing books, especially *UFO's: Operation Trojan Horse* (1970), I probably would have written this chapter earlier. I agree entirely with his conclusion: "The UFOs do not seem to exist as tangible, manufactured objects. They do not conform to the accepted natural laws of our environment. . . . The UFO manifestations seem to be, by and large, merely minor variations of the age-old demonological phenomenon."[9]

On the other hand, the thrust of this book is to demonstrate that there are certain continuing themes in occult literature. We find these same themes being repeated again and again in the literature produced by those who say they have seen Unidentified Flying Objects, and more to the point, by those who claim that they have been visited by beings from outer space. It then becomes mandatory that I devote some attention to the topic.

Familiar Occult Themes

What are some of these themes? The first and most important is the theme of the evolution of man. Man is perceived as a being who is presently limited in time and space, but who is capable of achieving a leap of being and evolving into a much more powerful being in

---

8. Keel, *Trojan Horse*, p. 18.
9. *Ibid.*, p. 299.

the future. The myth of evolution has many forms. It is perhaps the oldest sustained myth which has rivaled biblical orthodoxy from the beginning. When we find that people claim that they have been visited by creatures from outer space—creatures that have advanced technologically, psychologically, and ethically far beyond mere mankind—we are alerted to one more example of this ancient rival faith. Man the creature of the future, man the technologist of the future, man the creature who is capable of achieving vast attainments in the future if only he listens to the warnings and messages of creatures from outer space. This theme is repeated so often in the literature of flying saucers that it must be dealt with in this book.

Another continuing theme is the idea that man has failed to advance morally as rapidly as he has advanced technologically. This idea is so familiar that it has become commonplace. But the UFO version offers this variation: outer space creatures who have been able to advance morally to keep pace with their technological innovations will soon reveal to mankind (or elite representatives of mankind) the moral secrets that have enabled them to avoid nuclear destruction. Thus, the promise of a more advanced technology (which they supposedly possess) is accompanied by the promise of a more advanced morality (which they seemingly must possess, since they have not blown themselves to smithereens). Mankind is therefore about to be given, free of charge, the secrets of the ages—not just ancient mysteries, but the secrets "of a galaxy far, far away in a time long, long ago," to paraphrase the introductory scroll of "Star Wars."

A third theme is that some great catastrophe is fast approaching. Unless people on earth soon repent, and adopt the higher moral ways of the outer space invaders—who represent the forces of the cosmos—there will be a period of horrors: bad weather, wars, and so forth. But the contactee is assured that he has been selected for this task of communicating this message to his fellow man. In case after case, there is some version of the old radio warning, "please stay tuned."

Thus, the appeal of UFO phenomena is similar to the appeal of ancient mysteries. The believer joins the "cutting edge" of the next phase of evolution. He joins the ranks of the "true believers" whose wisdom, perception, and open minds have enabled them to perceive what average people will not admit is possible. The initiate (especially those who are not trained scientists, whose interest is more strictly scientific) is promised to be on the "inside track" in a new evolutionary leap of being. He will be able to command the high ground morally, for the space invaders will give to him and to other initiates a new morality. The religious aspects of this quest for new information should be obvious.

1947: The Turning Point

A question ought to be raised, however. Why is it that almost no attention was given to this topic prior to 1946 or 1947? Stories of mysterious lights in the sky have been reported for centuries. A farmer in Texas described a dark flying object as a "large saucer" in January of 1878. But this was late news. On October 27, 1180, a luminous object described as an "earthenware vessel" was seen around midnight in Japan. Similar objects were seen repeatedly in Japan in what we call the Middle Ages.[10]

On August 12, 1883, a Mexican astronomer named José Bonilla saw the sudden appearance of a long parade of circular objects in the sky. He counted 143 of them. His telescope had a camera attached to it, so he took pictures of them. "When developed, the film showed a series of cigar-and spindle-shaped objects which were obviously solid and noncelestial."[11]

In 1896 and 1897, a series of UFO sightings took place. In November of 1896, cigar-shaped airships appeared in California. The mayors of San Francisco and Oakland said they had seen such a ship.[12] Thousands of people in the United States saw airships in April of 1897.[13] Jacques Vallee and several other researchers have surveyed hundreds of newspaper accounts of these sightings in 1897.[14] And oddity of oddities, it was in April of 1897 that *Pearson's Magazine* in England began publishing as a serial H. G. Wells' classic novel, *The War of the Worlds*, which was concluded in December of 1897.[15] (I suspect Wells was simply "cashing in" on the publicity.)

Keel points out that the town of Eldora, Iowa, was the site of a sighting in 1897 and again in 1967.[16] Can you imagine creatures travelling many light years through space in order to visit Eldora, Iowa?

---

10. These events are reported by Jacques Vallee, *Passport to Magonia: From Folklore to Flying Saucers* (Chicago: Regnery, 1969), pp. 4-6.

11. Keel, *Trojan Horse*, p. 33.

12. *Ibid.*, p. 78.

13. *Ibid.*, pp. 33, 79-94.

14. *Ibid.*, p. 79.

15. *The Collector's Book of Science Fiction by H. G. Wells*, selected by Alan K. Russell (Secaucus, New Jersey: Castle Books, 1979), p. 1.

16. *Trojan Horse*, p. 92.

He says that certain regions have a high number of these sightings. One is Michigan, which had 30 percent of the sightings listed in his study of the 1897 incidents. The areas he mentions are Ann Arbor and Hillsdale. Dallas, Texas, has been another high-visitation city. Texas had 20 percent of the sightings in 1897. Sightings continued from 1897 and culminated in a major "flap" in 1909. As he mentions, this was the year after the famous explosion of the "meteor" over Siberia[17] — an event which still confuses scientists. Sightings were made in New Zealand, Finland, Sweden, and elsewhere. In New England, the "flap" took place during Christmas week.[18]

There were UFO sightings in 1914 near the Portuguese town of Fatima, three years prior to the famous "miracle of Fatima," in which an apparition (who did *not* claim to be the Virgin Mary, at least not in those words; it was called "the Lady") was initially seen in May of 1917 by three children, and which a month later was seen by a group of 50 adults, and a month after that by a crowd of 4,500; other unexplainable phenomena were seen by 18,000 in August. On that day, one man saw a "luminous globe" spinning in the sky.[19] A huge globe of light appeared before a crowd of 30,000 on September 13, and the children saw the apparition in the midst of the globe.[20] On October 13, over 70,000 people showed up. A huge silver disk which rotated rapidly appeared in the clouds and was seen by the whole crowd. For ten minutes it bobbed over the heads of the crowd. The crowd contained priests, journalists, and scientists.[21]

In 1944-45, Allied flyers over Germany saw varicolored fireballs, which they thought might be a secret weapon. These lights were harmless, although they would fly close to the bombers as if they were playing with the pilots. Sometimes they appeared in precise formations. The crews called them "foo fighters" and "kraut fireballs."[22] Mysterious projectiles were also seen in these years by Allied pilots over Sweden.[23] But interest in UFO's always faded rap-

---

17. *Ibid.*, pp. 107-11.

18. *Ibid.*, pp. 115-18.

19. Jacques Vallee, *The Invisible College* (New York: Dutton, 1975), pp. 142-45.

20. *Ibid.*, p. 146.

21. Keel, *Trojan Horse*, pp. 259-60.

22. David R. Saunders and R. Roger Harkins, *UFOs? Yes!: Where the Condon Committee Went Wrong* (New York: Signet, 1968), p. 53. For some accounts of American pilots who encountered these lights, see Vincent H. Gaddis, *Mysterious Fires and Lights* (New York: Dell, 1967), pp. 18-23. See the account by J. Chamberlain in *American Legion Magazine* (Dec. 1945).

23. Carl Jung, *Flying Saucers: A Modern Myth of Things Seen in the Skies* (New York: Harcourt, Brace, 1959), p. 3.

idly after such sightings, until 1947.

Kenneth Arnold's Flight

As far as the world's media were concerned, the advent of UFO's began on June 24, 1947. On that day, pilot Kenneth Arnold took off from Chehalis, Washington in a small private plane. Flying toward Yakima, he passed close to Mount Ranier. There was a missing Army C-46 transport plane lost in the area, so he decided to look around. He noticed a series of bright flashes off to his left. He then saw a string of bright disk-shaped objects, which he estimated to be 45 to 50 feet in length. He clocked their speed, and when his estimates were later calculated, these vehicles would have been flying in the range of 1,700 miles per hour. In 1947, there were no planes that could fly that fast.

The story got front-page attention all over the United States. Why? Initially, local editors regarded it as a hoax. But when they investigated Arnold's background, especially his skills as a mountain pilot — these men know their territories very well — they changed their minds. They switched from "hoax" to "amazing phenomena."[24]

This helps to explain the decision of local Washington state editors, but it does not explain why the story was picked up by the wire services. Nor does it explain why, from that day forth, the whole world has been besieged with thousands of similar reports. Why not in 1939? Why not in 1530? Why in 1947? As Jacques Vallee notes, it was not the first, nor was it one of the best, of the post-World War II reports on UFO's, but it was the first to gain widespread coverage by the media. Two more major waves of sightings worldwide took place in 1950 and 1954.[25]

The next wave of sightings began in early 1966. (Once again, we take note of remarkable changes that were taking place during that two-year period, from early 1964 until early 1966.) Vallee includes an appendix in *Passport to Magonia* (1969) of a century of sightings, 1868-1968. He says that his sources provide continuity for the entire period "until the recent dramatic rise in the number of reports, i.e., until the end of 1965."[26] (Vallee's *Passport* is a creative attempt to compare stories of UFO contactees with the legends of dwarves,

---

24. Edward J. Ruppelt, *The Report on Unidentified Flying Objects* (Garden City, New York: Doubleday, 1956), pp. 16-19.

25. Vallee, *The Invisible College*, chart, p. 197.

26. Vallee, *Passport to Magonia*, p. 169.

elves, sprites, "little people," and similar mythological beings in Western folklore.) John Keel says that he received over 2,000 clippings of sightings in March and April of 1966, yet the national news media ignored this huge "flap."[27] In 1973, another wave took place. This led Vallee to shift his approach, and to begin to discuss the psychology and theology of the contactees rather than the scientific basis for believing in UFO's.

I have a second question: Why should it be that if occult forces underlie the manifestation of spacecraft or creatures supposedly from outer space, they chose to reveal these "vehicles" on a continuing basis only after 1946? Why was it that prior to 1947, there were only occasional references to such creatures from outer space, and only occasional references to the spacecraft that supposedly brought them to earth? In other words, it is the question of *timing*. Why is it that now rather than before that we should be deluged with stories about creatures from the beyond? And when I say "beyond" in this case, I mean from outer space. Stories of creatures from below are as old as civilization and anti-civilization: ghosts, spirits, departed souls, etc. But why *outer* space? And why now?

The Technological Imperative

One obvious answer is that after 1945 and the advent of the atomic age, the general public became much more aware of the possibilities of destruction by unknown technology. The faster that technology has advanced, and the more specialized it has become, the less it is understood even by the elite guild of scientists, let alone by the general population. We are not really sure exactly how modern technology works, but we know some powerful new force has been given to mankind by the elite scientific planners of the world, and that this power can be used both for good and for evil. There are widespread disagreements among politicians and even voters concerning which uses are good and which uses are evil. This has created political unrest. To mention only a few areas of rabid scientific and political disagreement: national defense policy, atomic power for producing electricity, petrochemicals and the proper disposal of their waste products, and genetic engineering.

There is something else, something more important: the growing awareness that technology changes very rapidly and that technologi-

---

27. Keel, *Trojan Horse*, p. 21.

cal change is basic to our lives. We cannot escape. Jacques Ellul has called this the technological imperative: if something *can* be produced, it *must* be produced.[28] Eventually, it *will* be produced, even when from a moral frame of reference, it should not be produced. The autonomy of technology, or as Ellul calls the process, *technique*, is unstoppable in the modern world. Efficiency triumphs over morality.

This concern is legitimate. Philosophically, it is the most important contradiction in the modern world, one which C. S. Lewis has devoted many eloquent passages to, especially in *The Abolition of Man* (1947). It is the dominant intellectual antinomy of modern man, argues the Dutch philosopher Herman Dooyeweerd. As man increases power over nature through scientific knowledge, some men appear to increase their control over others. As men gain added freedom from the "random" effects of nature, they simultaneously lose their freedom to scientific planners. Thus, the nature/freedom dualism is the major inescapable contradiction of modern man.[29] There is good reason for the rise of concern about where "science" is taking us, meaning those who are the supposed masters of science and its social implementation.

This focus on technology leads men to evaluate their own lives and their own memories in terms of technological change. They are almost hypnotized by the myth of technology. They see changing technology as perhaps the essence of the modern world. They become concerned about technological changes that they don't understand. More importantly, they increasingly *define their own existence* in terms of technological advancement and technological threats.

I like John Keel's analysis: "Today we kneel before the altar of science, and our scientific ignorance receives the blame for what we do not know or cannot understand. The game's the same, only the rules have changed slightly. We no longer run to the temple when we see a strange, unearthly object in the sky. We run to the Air Force or to the learned astronomers. In ancient times the priests would tell us that we had sinned, and therefore God was showing signs in the sky. Today our learned leaders simply tell us that we are mistaken — or crazy — or both. The next time we see something in the sky, we keep

---

28. Jacques Ellul, *The Technological Society* (New York: Vintage, [1954] 1964), pp. 80-81.

29. Herman Dooyeweerd, *In The Twilight of Western Thought: Studies in the Pretended Autonomy of Philosophical Thought* (Philadelphia: Presbyterian & Reformed, 1960), pp. 46-52.

it to ourselves. But the damnable things keep coming back anyway."[30]

It is my thesis that personal occult creatures whose goal is to confuse men, delude men, and keep them in a form of bondage, can do so by manifesting themselves in a form which is acceptable to man. In other words, we are back to that being described by Screwtape in his letter to Wormwood, the "materialist magician." When men are willing to believe in supernatural forces but not in God, then mankind is very close to the end — either the final battle, or at the very least, the end of the anti-Christian world of humanism.

Not Physical Phenomena

Kenneth Arnold, the pilot whose adventure started it all, studied UFO's from 1947 until 1955. In that year, he issued a report saying that he thought that the vehicles were not airships at all, but some form of living energy.[31]

But the story is stranger than just the oddity of the physical manifestations of the "vehicles." If these invaders are from Mars, asks Keel, why is it that they seem to know exactly where state borders are in the United States? Time and again in the "UFO flaps" — mass sightings of numerous UFO's — the sightings cluster within the borders of one or two states. This was a common phenomenon in 1966-67. On August 16, 1966, for example, there were hundreds of sightings in Arkansas, in a belt running from north to south. There was not a single sighting in Oklahoma, Mississippi, Tennessee, or Louisiana, all bordering states. Minnesota and Wisconsin, far to the north, did participate in this "flap," mostly in Minnesota, with a few sightings in South Dakota, right on the border with Minnesota. Keel comments: "Certainly if the UFOs were meteors or other natural phenomena, they would also be reported in adjoining states. Cross-state sightings are not as common as skeptics would like to believe."[32] Another question Keel asks is this: Why were over 20% of the 1967 and 1968 sightings on a Wednesday, but only 7% on Tuesday?[33]

Mystery airplanes are also often sighted in UFO "flap" areas. They fly without identification markings, usually low to the ground, and at night the pilot's cabin is illuminated. They often appear in the midst of bad weather. In short, they violate all the rules of sane

---

30. Keel, *Trojan Horse*, p. 32.
31. *Ibid.*, p. 42.
32. *Ibid.*, p. 20.
33. *Ibid.*, p. 19.

flying. In 1932-34, a series of large (huge) unmarked planes began appearing over Sweden. One group of five witnesses claimed that they saw a plane with eight propellers. Yet this was the era of the tiny Ford Tri-motor, an era in which few planes ever appeared in Scandinavian skies. The Swedish Air Force could never locate the base of these ghost planes. Hitler came to power in early 1933, and the *Luftwaffe* did not yet exist. Mysterious radio transmissions sometimes accompanied these "flaps."

A mystery airplane appeared over New York City during a fierce snowstorm on December 26, 1933. It circled the city for six hours (*New York Times*, Dec. 27). But as Keel points out, in 1933 planes were not capable of operating in a blizzard for six hours straight. There was a similar incident over London in February, 1934 (*New York Times*, Feb. 4, 1934). And what is really amazing is that in numerous incidents, the planes would cut off their engines and just circle an area. Finally, just to round things out, Keel includes a section on phantom helicopters, a group of seven in New Jersey and numerous sightings in Vietnam during the war.[34]

Then there is the question of UFO design. There is none. Every report differs as to UFO shapes. Keel lists flying cubes, triangles, doughnuts, spheres, giant metal insects, and transparent flying jellyfish. Some have wheels, flat domes, pointed domes, no domes. Every color is listed by observers. There are cigar shapes. Keel thinks it is part of psychological warfare: creating confusion.[35] Can you imagine thousands of different models of spaceships all being sent out from a star system light years away?

Wilson and Weldon offer a list of major problems associated with UFO's. They play games: buzzing cars, for example. They do not crash, as far as the evidence shows. Yet they have repeatedly leaked fluids or had pieces of metal break off and fall. They stop to "make repairs," but they never crash. Keel writes: "If they are the product of a superior intelligence with an advanced technology, they seem to be suffering from faulty workmanship. Since 1896 there have been hundreds of reports in which lone witnesses have stumbled onto grounded hard objects being repaired by their pilots. In flight, they have an astounding habit of losing pieces of metal. They seem to be ill-made, always falling apart, frequently exploding in midair. There are so many of these incidents that we must wonder if they aren't

---

34. *Ibid.*, ch. 7.
35. *Ibid.*, p. 142.

really deliberate. Maybe they are meant to foster the belief that the objects are real and mechanical."[36]

Their operators have never really come out in the open, though human "contactees" have repeatedly been promised that the "space brothers" are about to reveal themselves. (Gypsy Rose Lee successfully used a similar technique to maintain interest by observers.) Furthermore, there are too many kinds of spacecraft. It is as if a stellar civilization designed hundreds of kinds of craft, and then sent them to play games with earthlings — and only in great numbers after 1945. They appear to people selectively. They appear on radar screens selectively.

What about speed? The vehicles accelerate too rapidly; they violate physical laws. They do not seem to get hot despite their speed. Sometimes they are completely silent; sometimes they are noisy — clanging, Model T noisy. They change shape, disappear, pass through clouds without moving the clouds. One spacecraft will split into two spacecraft.[37] The occupants do not splatter against the wall when ships travelling 18,000 miles per hour suddenly change course at a 90-degree angle. Hynek and Vallee put it thusly: "If UFOs are indeed somebody else's 'nuts and bolts hardware,' then we must still explain how such tangible hardware can change shape before our eyes, vanish in a Cheshire cat manner (not even leaving a grin), seemingly melt away in front of us, or apparently 'materialize' mysteriously before us without apparent detection by persons nearby or in neighboring towns. We must wonder, too, where UFOs are 'hiding' when not manifesting themselves to human eyes."[38] In short, nothing adds up in the Newtonian account book.

Problem: if they are not *physical* phenomena, how can they be phenomena at all? If they do not conform to physical laws, then what is the truth? Are the laws incorrect? (Crisis!) Are the UFO's an illusion? If so, then how can we trust our powers of observation? (Crisis!) Is our knowledge of the true physical laws incorrect? (Slightly smaller crisis, but still a crisis.) Is the universe governed by noumenal sorts of events? (Greatest crisis of all!) What are we to believe?

---

36. *Ibid.*, p. 64.

37. Clifford Wilson and John Weldon, *Close Encounters: A Better Explanation*, pp. 38-41.

38. *Edge of Reality*, pp. xii-xiii.

The Impulse to Believe

What do we find about men's ideas concerning outer space creatures? Scientists may want to believe that most people probably do not believe these space creatures exist, but scientific public opinion polls point to widespread popular belief in UFO's and "higher creatures" from outer space. A few scientists also believe, and lots more are open to the possibility. When the space probe "Voyager" was sent out of the solar system, it carried with it a drawing of a man and a woman, and it provided information concerning the location of the earth. When Voyager was sent into space there were artifacts of various kinds and messages which supposedly will be picked up by someone or something beyond the solar system. The popular 1984 movie "Starman" was based on the idea that outer space creatures do discover the Voyager and send a representative to visit earth. So the idea of the *possibility* of creatures in outer space somewhere has become at least somewhat acceptable as a theory among prestigious scientists and technologists, despite their skepticism of "spacemen here and now." They see the universe as random, and they see it as evolving; both doctrines create the possibility of almost anything.

Nevertheless, the stories of visits by space creatures, messages from space creatures, and so forth are not generally taken seriously by scientists. Such tales are regarded in much the same way that rational people regard messages received at seances. It is my contention that this interpretation of the skeptics is essentially correct, that is, the two types of messages should be equated. The theologies undergirding the two types of messages are in fact one theology. The messages to mankind from both kinds of unknown sources beyond the realm of the natural are in fact the same basic message. The message is clear: man can become something greater than he is today, and he needs a total transformation — theologically, politically, spiritually, and technologically. Mankind is about to become a higher being, a new creation, but this new creation is not the result of ethical transformation in the form of regeneration by God, but this transformation can be achieved and must be achieved by man himself. It is the doctrine of salvation by works; it is the doctrine of *self-salvation*. It is that original doctrine, "Ye shall be as gods."

Randomness and Law

What readers should understand is that all modern humanist thought, and above all scientific thought, is an amalgam of two incompatible doctrines: the doctrine of the random origins of all things, and the doctrine of fixed and unbending cause and effect. Out of randomness evolved inflexible natural law. The rigorous bondage of scientific law is therefore softened only by the occasional random event, and such events are supposed to be confined to the realm of the tiny: to electrons if possible, and nothing larger than a mutant chromosome. Thus, in principle, anything is possible if given enough time, but at this very moment, nothing is supposed to be outside the impersonal laws of scientific cause and effect.

So scientists waffle back and forth. Yes, life on other planets is mathematically possible, given sufficient evolutionary time (10 billion to 20 billion years, say the scientists), and given the existence of ten billion galaxies (some say a hundred billion) with one hundred billion stars per galaxy (the 1970's estimate).[39] Prof. Harlow Shapley, the Harvard astronomer — and Dr. Establishment in the field — speculated that there might be 100,000 life-bearing planets in our galaxy.[40] On the other hand, living beings from outer space are not actually revealing themselves to us in this century; why, the odds against that are . . . *astronomical!* (One exception to this scientific skepticism is Cornell University astronomer and popular lecturer Carl Sagan, who thinks that in the last 500 million years of life on earth, the earth may have been visited by space creatures five thousand times, or once every 100,000 years. He thinks that perhaps a million planets in our galaxy could contain civilizations.[41] But Sagan is personally skeptical that UFO's exist or are transportation devices for space visitors.)

They refuse to face "the facts" of UFO's. The facts are set forth in scientific studies by men such as Vallee, Hynek, and other serious investigators. The critics respond by trotting out every disproved sighting and representative crackpot encounters, but they studiously, scientifically avoid the hard cases where the evidence of simultaneous sightings by hundreds of people can be proven to have taken place. The skeptics perceive that if such events are true, then modern science isn't. They would then have to revise the presuppositions of modern autonomous science in order to make it into something quite foreign, something dangerously close to the cosmic per-

39. Robert Jastrow, *Red Giants and White Dwarfs: Man's Descent from the Stars* (New York: Signet, 1969), pp. 18-20.

40. Harlow Shapley, *Of Stars and Men* (Boston: Beacon, 1958), p. 85.

41. I. S. Shklovski and Carl Sagan, *Intelligent Life in the Universe* (San Francisco: Holden-Day, 1966).

sonalism of the Bible, or the cosmic personalism of primitive animist religion. They resist the temptation to investigate the facts and deal with them in terms of present-day scientific principles, but only by sacrificing their integrity as impartial observers, and by sacrificing their credibility among the growing number of people who read and believe.

The Technological Factor

There is one major difference between occult manifestations in the form of ghosts, poltergeists, healing voices, precognition, and all the rest of it. Flying saucers can be measured, technically. They can be photographed, and have been photographed by professionals and by amateurs. They affect radar screens again and again. Professional pilots, air force officers, private jet pilots, and airline crews have all reported sighting flying saucers and other kinds of Unidentified Flying Objects. There is no scientific explanation for these sightings in probably 10 to 20 percent[42] of the known cases — or at least 2 percent, if the most skeptical of scientific estimations are our standard. (This figure, 2 percent, was the agreed-upon figure at least three years before the official research was finished. In 1965 Americans were told: "Project Bluebook people in Washington, D.C., say that only two percent of the UFO cases of the past five years have not been solved. . . ."[43] This was a year before the Condon Committee was formed and three years before it issued its final report, which announced: "After investigation, there remains a small residual, of the order of 2% of all cases, that appears to represent well recorded but unidentified or unidentifiable objects that are airborne — i.e. UFO's. Yet there is insufficient evidence to assert that any one of these reports represents an unusual or extraordinary phenomenon. We find no conclusive evidence of unidentified aircraft or 'flying saucers.' "[44] In short, "we don't know what they are, but we know what they aren't!")

A discrepancy of 2 percent in scientific investigations is large, not small. Twenty percent is a huge discrepancy. Unidentified Flying Objects have been investigated by the Air Force, by private agencies

---

42. Hynek and Vallee, *Edge of Reality*, p. viii.

43. Newport News, Virginia, *Times Herald* (Jan. 25, 1965); cited in Frank Edwards, *Flying Saucers — Serious Business* (New York: Lyle Stuart, 1966), p. 281.

44. Daniel S. Gillmore (ed.), *Final Report of the Scientific Study of Unidentified Flying Objects* (New York: Dutton, published in association with Colorado Associated University Press, 1968, 1969), p. 86.

that are devoted to the topic, and by scientific panels. Again and again, the evidence for them is scientifically significant. Not so strong as the evidence for a scientifically repeatable experiment, but strong in the sense that no explanation which is given by the professionals in terms of Newtonian science makes any sense.

In this sense, Unidentified Flying Objects are a manifestation of occult ("unknown") power which can be taken somewhat seriously by scientists, reporters, and rationalists generally. People who have no particular theological beliefs, people who do not espouse the doctrines of New Age humanism, or ancient mysticism, nevertheless can be persuaded that there are such phenomena as flying saucers. They are seen as phenomena, not noumena. They can be explained as technological wonders from beings who have advanced technologically beyond mankind.

The basis of this faith in the technological reality of flying saucers is that there can be other beings outside of this world who are nevertheless limited by the natural laws and scientific laws of this world. It is assumed, in other words, that creatures beyond earth's atmosphere somehow have gained access to certain kinds of knowledge that enable them to visit the earth. This sort of knowledge, however, is knowledge which in principle can be understood by scientific man. They are better scientists than we are, but they are not occult magicians. They are better builders than we are today, but given enough money and enough formulas and enough skills, General Motors in principle will be able to produce interstellar or intergalactic or at least interplanetary spaceships. So the scientists who are interested in UFO's are willing to discuss the topic and study the topic, but only under the standard Newtonian world view. They are willing to discuss such phenomena only because they are believed to be phenomena, that is measurable, scientific, and repeatable.

This may distinguish the average investigator of UFO's from the average investigator of other kinds of paranormal phenomena. Then again, it may not. It is my guess that the average man on the street would be more willing to admit to a television audience that he believes in the existence of UFO's from outer space than he would be to admit that he believes in haunted houses. I am not arguing that serious scientific investigators of the other sorts of unexplained phenomena, or parapsychological and paranormal phenomena, are not serious scientists. Some of them are. We know of investigators who are clearly interested in such phenomena only because they believe that these phenomena really are *phenomena*. In other words, they believe these manifestations of odd powers or presently unexplainable forces, are in principle explainable by Newtonian or at least modern post-Heisenberg science. They may have to appeal to randomness more than Newton would have preferred to; they may have to appeal to the uncertainty principle more than Newton would have believed necessary, but nevertheless our scientists today, given enough time, study, and money, would in principle be able to duplicate the phenomena which are being investigated.

A New Evolution

Other investigators of UFO's are not interested in these phenomena primarily as manifestations of technological precocity, or manifestations of normal abilities of men's mind, but in fact are looking to a new evolution. They are looking for a substitute for God. Edward J. Ruppelt, formerly the head of the Air Force's Project Blue Book, and the man who coined the phrase, "UFO's,"[45] has described these people quite well: "Consciously or unconsciously, they want UFO's to be real and to come from outer space. These individuals, frightened perhaps by threats of atomic destruction, or lesser fears — who knows what — act as if nothing that men can do can save the earth. Instead, they seek salvation from outer space, on the forlorn premise that flying saucer men, by their very existence, are wiser and more advanced than we. Such people may reason that a race of men capable of interplanetary travel have lived well into, or through, an atomic age. They have survived and they can tell us their secret of survival. Maybe the threat of atomic war unified their planet and allowed them to divert their war effort to one of social and technological advancement. To such people a searchlight on a cloud or a bright star is an interplanetary spaceship."[46]

Ruppelt is a serious scientific investigator of UFO's. He is not a man who automatically dismisses all stories about such objects. He is not one, on the other hand, who wants to get involved in UFO's as a means of cosmic salvation. His point is well taken: men who live in an era of nuclear weaponry find themselves threatened by a form of annihilation which has never faced mankind in the past. They are therefore concerned and fearful that nothing they can do or even

---

45. Hynek and Vallee, *Edge of Reality*, p. x.
46. Edward J. Ruppelt, *The Report on Unidentified Flying Objects*, p. 9.

their rulers can do can release them from the thermonuclear trap. They therefore seek solace, comfort, and assistance from beyond the skies. They do not turn to God; they turn to little green men.

Old Faith, New Framework

It should not be thought that belief in outer space creatures is new. That belief goes back for hundreds of years, perhaps thousands of years. In the Renaissance, scientists so-called and philosophers so-called believed in multiple universes on multiple planets beyond the stars. The ancient Platonic idea of plenitude was combined with the discoveries of the Copernican revolution to produce a new religious faith in the *plurality of worlds*.[47] This was true of the magician-"scientist" Giordano Bruno, and it was true of many of his contemporaries. It was true of some of the crackpots of nineteenth-century rationalism, some of whom became quite influential. One example is Charles Fourier, the French socialist and certifiable nut who believed that the planets are alive and copulate with one another. Yet Frederick Engels, the co-founder with Karl Marx of Communism, praised Fourier as a man who, despite his mysticism (!!!), was an important social scientist who was characterized by his "sober, bold and systematic thinking, in a word, *social philosophy*."[48]

What distinguishes the modern concern about flying saucers from the mystical occult belief in multiple worlds that are inhabited by many forms of beings is today's confidence in technology. The faith in technology as a means of linking up creatures between the worlds was not as common in Renaissance society. One new thesis which is unique to the latter decades of the twentieth century is the thesis of popular writer Eric Von Däniken that gods from outer space, meaning space travellers, came to earth thousands of years ago, mated with our foremothers, and produced a new race of which we are the heirs. They taught them science or at least preliminary foundations of scientific thought. They showed them technological wonders and then they left. Mankind, therefore, made a major leap of being as a result of contact from outer space creatures. He argues this thesis in several books: *In Search of Ancient Gods*, *Chariots of the Gods?*, *The Gold of the Gods*, and most tauntingly, *Gods from Outer Space*.

---

47. Arthur R. Lovejoy, *The Great Chain of Being: A Study in the History of an Idea* (New York: Harper Torchbooks, [1936] 1965), ch. IV.

48. Cited by Igor Shafarevich, *The Socialist Phenomenon* (New York: Harper & Row, [1975] 1980), p. 204.

This thesis has sold millions of books. Why should it be so popular? Western civilization for over a hundred years has operated in terms of the doctrine of evolution through natural selection. The idea of evolution, however, comes in many forms, as we have already seen. There is cosmic evolution, there is evolution through natural selection, there is the inheritance of acquired characteristics, and many other explanations. People who are not skilled scientists but who have come to believe in the doctrines of evolution are therefore easy targets for the Von Dänikens of the world. Von Däniken seems to be able to answer questions that standards scientists cannot answer. How is it that mankind could have evolved so rapidly both technologically and philosophically? How is it that his intellect is so advanced compared to changes in his body? How is it that the mind of man seems to have evolved much more rapidly than changes in man's environment would have accounted for? Questions such as these baffled Alfred Russel Wallace, the co-founder of the doctrine of evolution through natural selection and led him into occultism and spiritism in the late nineteenth century.[49] Similarly, modern readers are baffled by these obvious questions or variants of these obvious questions, and when they find that modern science has no answers, they easily pick up on pseudo-scientific answers. Von Däniken's answer sold millions of copies.

Von Däniken was not alone in his quest for book sales. Consider the book by W. Raymond Drake, *Gods and Spacemen of the Ancient Past* (Signet, 1974). Here are slogans from the front cover that are intended to sell large numbers of this paperback book: "Was Jesus a great intelligence from a higher planet incarnated on earth to inspire man's spiritual evolution?" "Was the star of Bethlehem really a UFO?" "Are we children of the gods; fascinating new evidence that superbeings once ruled and mated on planet Earth!" And on the back cover these intriguing questions: "Does the blood of ancient spacemen flow in our veins?" "Were Sodom and Gomorrah destroyed by nuclear attack?" "Was the angel Gabriel, who foretold the birth of Jesus, an extraterrestrial?" "Did Martians, who had destroyed their own civilizations, actually come to Earth and teach men the game of war?" "Here are all the pieces of the jigsaw puzzle that reveals for the first time how beings from space once dominated earth, and not only ruled but actually mated with its people. Here is startling evidence about

---

49. Loren Eiseley, *Darwin's Century: Evolution and the Men Who Discovered It* (New York: Anchor, [1958] 1961), ch. XI: "Wallace and the Brain."

the seige of Troy, the ancestry of Alexander the Great and Jesus, the raising of the pyramids, the atomic wars in Indian holy scriptures, the building of Solomon's temple, and much, much more. Here is the boldest yet most convincing book you have ever read." I am sure this advertising sold its share of books, though not nearly so many as Von Däniken's. The obvious appeal is to the origins of man: Where did man come from? Where is man going.

It would be fairly easy to go through the entire book line by line, poking ridicule. Nevertheless, the book is important because of its attempt to link the stories of men from outer space with the origins of the Christian gospel. We even find that a certified scholar has produced one of these books, Prof. Roger Wescott's *The Divine Animal* (Funk & Wagnalls, 1969). Prof. Wescott was at the time chairman of the Department of Anthropology of Drew University in New Jersey. He links outer space agents to religious leaders such as Jesus, Buddha, and Mohammed.

Max Flindt and Otto Binder produced a popular paperback, *Mankind — Child of the Stars* (Fawcett, 1974), in which they argue that man is a hybrid creature whose ancestors were spacemen. It is significant that they take as their starting point the fact that man is the great anomaly of the evolution thesis: his brain is too powerful for his environmental origins. They cite A. R. Wallace's doubts in this regard.

There is no question that books such as these have been popular precisely because they have an underlying religious basis. They are substitutes for the Christian faith; they are lures to trap people to take them down paths of destruction. They have been popular in an era of supposed skepticism and science precisely because they attempt to link advanced science and ancient cosmology. They attempt to deflect men from the paths of righteousness by pointing to a new form of salvation, that is, science and technology, and then explaining science and technology in terms of ancient stories, ancient literature, ancient secret mysteries. This is nothing more than magic with the white smock coat of the scientist covering the real theology involved. The author waxes eloquent about the wonders of man: "The achievements of Science shine as a triumph of the human intellect; the mastery of Nature gives honor to Man. Daily, the crescendo of new discoveries revolutionizes life with bewilderment. This surfeit of miracles soon intoxicates men to self-destruction; even the most religious mind must mourn the intolerance of the Church, which imprisoned Man's spirit for fifteen centuries and stifled progress by the Scriptures. Today, dazzled by the wonders of Science, we watch the world drift to suicide and suspect that our materialist philosophy may be wrong, inspiring us to search again for greater, nobler Truth."[50]

Hynek's Conversion

The difficulty with dismissing such nonsense as this is that it is so popular. Another difficulty is that it is based on measurable phenomena. The philosophy, of course is based on nothing except occult speculation and the desire to sell lots of books, but the actual phenomena of Unidentified Flying Objects do exist. One of the most respectable scientific explainers of UFO phenomena was Northwestern University astronomer J. Allen Hynek. Hynek had been employed as the scientist and public relations officer to explain away UFO's for the Air Force. Originally the Air Force project which investigated UFO phenomena was called Project Sign. It was initiated in September of 1947, and on February 11, 1949, it became Project Grudge. Then in the summer of 1951 through late 1969, it was called Project Blue Book. J. Allen Hynek studied these phenomena for the Air Force for 22 years. He later claimed that he played no role during the "Project Grudge" phase, when the Pentagon treated UFO's with ridicule.[51]

Again and again, the Air Force called him forward to give explanations for essentially unexplainable phenomena. In March of 1966, he offered as a possible explanation for a particular incident burning swamp gas rather than lights from an outer space vehicle. One report had him say "marsh gas."[52] From that point on, he became known as Swamp Gas Hynek. He had not actually said that this was the explanation, but only that some people might have seen swamp gas. He had been pressured into saying something premature by an Air Force public relations officer.

Vallee's comments are important for understanding the shift in opinion that had taken place over the last few months — paralleling the wave of incidents that began in early 1966. The press jumped on Hynek, criticizing him for casting doubts on the word of a local

50. Drake, *Gods and Spacemen of the Ancient Past*, pp. 27-28.

51. J. Allen Hynek, *The UFO Experience*, p. 2.

52. "Marsh Gas in Michigan," in Jay David (ed.), *The Flying Saucer Reader* (New York: Signet Books, 1967).

farmer. "Those irate comments came from the same newspapers who for years had ridiculed witnesses just like this poor farmer, and had given no support whatsoever to Hynek himself when he begged them to report UFO cases more regularly and more accurately. Suddenly it had become fashionable to believe in flying saucers. . . ."[53] Suddenly, the older Newtonian world view was crumbling in the West in every area of life, including UFO's.

Hynek openly switched sides in 1970, the year after Project Blue Book was terminated, and he wrote a book which was basically favorable to continued serious studies of the UFO phenomena. It is called *The UFO Experience: A Scientific Inquiry* (Regnery, 1972). The title of chapter ten later became famous as a hugely successful Hollywood movie: "Close Encounters of the Third Kind." That J. Allen Hynek could be swung over to be at least a peripheral believer in UFO's seems to me to be highly significant. There are scientific facts pointing to the existence of scientifically unexplainable phenomena in the skies.

Actually, his conversion was not an overnight experience. In 1966, he wrote a Foreword to a book on UFO's written by Jacques and Janine Vallee. Like his later book, it too was published by the politically conservative publishing house, Henry Regnery Company. He insisted that there was something to the reports. It was not all nonsense. He admitted that "Perhaps I should have spoken earlier; eighteen years is a long time."[54] He blamed the difficulty of assembling the evidence. More important than raw evidence, in my view, was the date of the book's publication. His preliminary admission of at least a partial switch in opinion appeared just as the massive shift in public and intellectual opinion in every field was beginning. What was beginning to shift was men's faith in Newtonian and late-nineteenth-century explanations of cause and effect.

Six years later, Regnery published Hynek's own book on UFO's. The opening words of the Prologue are revealing; Hynek stresses the "climate of opinion" more than he does the evidence: "There is a sense in which each age is ripe for breakthroughs, for changes that were not only impossible but even frightening when imagined in an earlier age. Yet despite man's potential for discovery, there is inherent in each epoch of man's history a certain smugness that seems not

---

53. Vallee, *Invisible College*, p. 44.
54. Hynek, "Foreword," Vallee, *Challenge to Science: The UFO Enigma* (Chicago: Regnery, 1966), p. vi.

to be apparent to most participants in that age. It is a complacent unawareness of the scope of things not yet known that later epochs look back upon with a sympathetic smile of condescension, if not with polite laughter."[55] He says that UFO phenomena may be one of these breakthrough topics, "as incredible to us as television would have been to Plato." Yes, but not that startling to Plato, and especially not to his mystical followers during the Renaissance. It was pre-1965 science, not 1565 Renaissance science, that had screened out theories of life in outer space.

Hynek begins Chapter 1 of his book with this illuminating story: "During an evening reception of several hundred astronomers at Victoria, British Columbia, in the summer of 1968, word spread that just outside the hall strangely maneuvering lights — UFOs — had just been spotted. The news was met by casual banter and the giggling sound that often accompanies an embarrassing situation. Not one astronomer ventured outside in the summer night to see for himself."[56] As he says, "The almost universal attitude of scientists has been militantly negative. Indeed, it would seem that the reaction has been grossly out of proportion to the stimulus."[57] They generally take two approaches: first, ridicule of the stories or, second, that the phenomena are in fact the products of individual or group mental activity.[58] In short, a UFO sighting must be either a hoax or a delusion. This is the same sort of response that ghost stories receive. *The responses are similar because the problems that these phenomena (if they are phenomena) pose for Newtonian science are similar.*

The Condon Committee

There was an attempt in the late 1960's to wrap up and finally bury all discussions of UFO's in the scientific community. It was called the Condon Committee. Professor Edward U. Condon of the University of Colorado headed up the committee and the committee's task essentially was to kill off all further discussion of the topic within the scientific community. Its massive, unreadable report was well-designed to achieve deflection through boredom. The highly biased procedure and conclusions of that investigation are detailed in a book by Dr. David R. Saunders and R. Roger Harkins,

55. J. Allen Hynek, *The UFO Experience,* p. xi.
56. *Ibid.,* p. 6.
57. *Idem.*
58. *Ibid.,* p. 7.

UFO'S? YES! (1968). Saunders was a member of the committee until he was fired for not going along with the suppression by the committee of relevant but controversial facts, and worse, by "leaking" a memo to the press which proved that the project's coordinator, Robert Low, had deliberately adopted a two-faced strategy of dual deception. He had written in August of 1966: "The trick would be, I think, to describe the project so that, to the public, it would appear a totally objective study but, to the scientific community, would present the image of a group of nonbelievers trying their best to be objective but having an almost zero expectation of finding a saucer."[59] In short, the gentlemen clearly recognized that with respect to this issue, the public is more open-minded ("empirical") than the scientific guild is, and if the guild even suspected that a serious empirical investigation of the topic was in progress, the project would be automatically rejected by the guild.

For those interested in such examples of "normal science" (as Thomas Kuhn calls it) and scientific suppression of inconvenient evidence, you can go to the library, check out the book and read it. The book reveals that the committee itself was split, and when the group which wanted to pursue the research without negative bias published a secret memorandum that the committee had never planned to conduct such an investigation, but planned instead to spend the government's money and then issue a "nothing to this UFO business" report, Condon fired the minority faction.[60] A less inflammatory but useful critique of the Condon Committee is Chapter 12 of Hynek's book, *The UFO Experience*: "Science Is Not Always What Scientists Do." The committee's files were later deliberately destroyed — files that had cost the U.S. government half a million dollars for the committee to assemble.[61] (The bibliography produced by Miss Lynn Catoe in conjunction with the Condon Committee is excellent: *UFO's and Related Subjects: An Annotated Bibliography*, prepared by the Library of Congress Science and Technology Division for the Air Force, and published by the U.S. Government Printing Office, 1969. It contains references to 1,600 articles and materials. It is over 400 pages long. Also important is the British publication, *Flying Saucer Review*.)

What was the effect of the Condon Committee's findings? On the

---

59. David R. Saunders and R. Roger Harkins, *UFO's? Yes!*, p. 129.

60. Vallee, *Invisible College*, pp. 50-51.

61. *Ibid.*, pp. 16, 51.

public, zero effect. The public's faith in the existence of UFO's increased sharply over the next seven years. On the scientific community, it had the effect of a permanent sleeping pill. They knew that "it had all been scientifically refuted," so they would not have to think about the topic again. It had confirmed the guild's *a priori* assumptions. It had even established a record. The committee concluded, in contrast to every known government-financed study group in recorded history, that there was no further need for additional studies of the subject. While Federal agencies might keep the door open to possible future investigations "on an open-minded, unprejudiced basis," there should be no "major new agency, as someone has suggested, for the scientific study of UFOs." And then came the capper: "Therefore we strongly recommend that teachers refrain from giving students credit for school work based on their reading of the presently available UFO books and magazine articles. Teachers who find their students strongly motivated in this direction should attempt to channel their interests in the direction of serious study of astronomy and meteorology, and in the direction of critical analysis of arguments for fantastic propositions that are being supported by appeals to fallacious reasoning or false data."[62] Like some medieval committee of theologians who were worried about students deviating from Aristotelian science, the committee warned teachers of the next generation to discourage all paradigm-threatening investigations. To no avail, of course; by 1969, the epistemological dam had long since burst.

But should students be allowed to study "unprejudiced" materials? Should they study what the Condon Committee studied? In short, what became of the files of Project Blue Book? They are unclassified documents today. Unfortunately, to get into the *building* in which they are housed, you need a security clearance.[63] Ah, bureaucracy, thy ways are so utterly predictable!

The responses of the scientists are very much like the responses of Dr. Wanderman to the evidence of occult healing in the Philippines. If such evidence is what it appears to be to the untrained scientist, and therefore cannot be explained by the canons of science, then modern science is left standing naked. Its attempts to create order in terms of the presupposition of a purely autonomous world order — the realm of man-interpreted, man-measured phenomena —

62. *Scientific Study of Unidentified Flying Objects,* pp. 5-6.
63. Vallee, *Invisible College,* p. 51.

will be revealed as naive, pretentious, and false. Worse; it will leave men at the mercy of forces that they cannot control by scientific means. Scientists may worry about the Bomb, or the potential plague threat of a newly created test tube bacteria, but the idea that there are forces in this world that *in principle* cannot be explained by repeatable cause-and-effect laws scares them even more. They are men clinging to a dying paradigm — a paradigm which was never fully accepted by residents in the West, and which was never accepted at all by residents in primitive cultures. They are fighting for survival, not just as guild members who are about to be replaced, but as members of a guild which as a whole cannot survive if the evidence of an invasion from the noumenal is taken seriously.

If the saucers are in fact operated by little green men from the stars, scientists will find a way to cope with the problem. But conventional scientists smell trouble. The evidence points to something other than men from Mars. Men from Mars are in principle no different from amoebas from Mars, and scientists have been almost religious in their pursuit of evidence of life forms on the planets (as evidence of Darwinian evolution). No, what bothers them is that the stories associated with UFO phenomena indicate that we are dealing with *noumena*: invasions from a world beyond mathematical cause and effect. Such forces do not belong here. They point to even greater forces, the traditional forces of heaven and hell, of final judgment. These are far more serious than invaders from Mars.

Ironically, the very best statement from a conventional scientist concerning the question of UFO's was made by Condon. In a disparaging speech on UFO's in April of 1969, Condon revealed his contempt for the UFO topic, yet in doing so he identified the proper answer to the question, "What are UFO's?" He said: "Perhaps we need a National Magic Agency (pronounced 'enema') to make a large and expensive study of *all* these matters, including the future scientific study of UFOs, if any."[64] We do not need such an agency, but we do need this identification of the "phenomena": *magic*.

Vallee's Studies

One of the writers who has done the most to gain a hearing for the question of UFO's is the French writer Jacques Vallee. He wrote a best-selling book called *Anatomy of a Phenomenon*, published in 1965.

---

64. Cited by Keel, *Trojan Horse*, p. 46. Keel is somewhat sympathetic to Condon.

Vallee had scientific training and cannot be dismissed as a crank. This book is simply a careful summary of numerous sightings of airborne vehicles—sightings that cannot be easily dismissed. A later book, *Messengers of Deception* (Bantam, 1980), is much more important. It is subtitled, *UFO Contacts and Cults*.

Vallee claims to have had access to over 2,000 documented cases of reported contacts with UFO creatures. These files indicate that there is much that conventional science cannot explain. He understands that scientists have deliberately suppressed evidence regarding UFO sightings. He says he was present when French astronomers erased a magnetic tape on which their satellite tracking team had recorded 11 data points on an unknown flying object which was not an airplane, a balloon, or a known orbiting craft.[65] He admits that in 1967 his interests had begun to shift. In that year, the Pentagon gave $512,000 to Professor Condon to begin his studies. Vallee began to ask himself new questions: "Why is it, I wondered, that the 'occupants' of UFOs behave so much like the denizens of fairy tales and the elves of ancient folklore? Why is the picture we can form of their world so much closer to the medieval concept of *Magonia*, the magical land above the clouds, than to a description of an extraterrestrial planetary environment? And why are UFO's becoming a new religious form? I spent a year researching this angle, and emerged with a greater appreciation for the pychic aspects of the phenomenon. I could no longer regard the 'flying saucers' as simply some sort of spacecraft or machine, no matter how exotic its propulsion."[66]

Vallee continues: "In my spare time, I pursued my UFO studies, trying to find some pattern in the global distribution of sightings. What I deduced from the data was of remarkable significance: *The phenomenon behaved like a conditioning process*. The logic of conditioning uses obscurity and confusion to achieve its goal while hiding its mechanism. I could see a similar structure in the UFO stories. I am beginning to perceive a coherent picture of the 'flying saucer' phenomenon for the first time, now that I am pursuing the idea that UFOs may be a pyschological control system, and now that I am aware of their link to human consciousness. I still think there is a genuine technology at work here, causing the effects witnesses are describing. But I am not ready to jump to the conclusion that it is the

---

65. *Messengers of Deception: UFO Contacts and Cults* (New York: Bantam, [1979] 1980), p. 5.
66. *Ibid.*, p. 6.

technology of some kind of 'spacemen.' "[67]

Vallee argues that the first aspect of the UFO phenomena is physical, that the UFO does appear to be a true object operating in the atmosphere. The second aspect is psychological. People perceive some sort of space vehicle or flying object. The third aspect, he says, is social. "Belief in the reality of UFOs is spreading rapidly at all levels of society throughout the world."[68] He then asks a question. It is a lengthy question but highly significant. "The experience of a close encounter with a UFO is a shattering physical and mental ordeal. The trauma has effects that go far beyond what the witnesses recall consciously. New types of behavior are conditioned, and new types of beliefs are promoted. The social, political, and religious consequences of the experience are enormous if they are considered, not only in the days or weeks following the sighting, but over the time span of a generation. Could it be that such effects are actually intended, through some process of social conditioning? Could it be that both the believers and the skeptics are being manipulated? Is the public being deceived and led to false conclusions by someone who is using UFO witnesses to propagate revolutionary new ideas?"[69]

Vallee understands both the skeptics and the true believers. He points out that the professional skeptics, especially within the scientific guild, ridicule anyone who claims to have seen a flying saucer or who claims to have made contact with someone inside a saucer. On the other hand, the followers of many of these UFO cults are often persons who have lost faith in science and technology generally. They may believe in the scientific and technological abilities of the beings who inhabit the space vehicles, but they no longer trust the scientists and technologists who inhabit the halls of Harvard University.

Here is Vallee's conclusion, though stated early in the book: "*I believe there is a machinery of mass manipulation behind the UFO phenomenon.* It aims at social and political goals by diverting attention from some human problems and by providing a potential release for tensions caused by others. The contactees are a part of that machinery. *They are helping to create a new form of belief*: an expectation of actual contact among large parts of the public. In turn this expectation makes millions of people hope for the imminent realization of that age-old dream: salvation from above, surrender to the greater power of some

---

67. *Ibid.*, p. 7.
68. *Ibid.*, p. 8.
69. *Idem.*

wise navigators of the cosmos."[70] He goes on to say, "if you take the trouble to join me in the analysis of the modern UFO myth, you will see human beings under the control of a strange force that is bending them in absurd ways, forcing them to play a role in a bizarre game of deception."[71]

Vallee claims to have in his files records of 2,000 cases, not simply of sightings, but of actual, reported contacts. He claims that it is normal for the contacts to take place between 6:00 P.M. and 10:30 P.M., no matter where the contact supposedly has taken place. The peak number of sightings per people actually awake is 3 A.M.[72] It is his belief that these appearances are staged. The question is, of course, "staged by whom?"

Many of the contactees displayed traits that are found in other kinds of occult phenomena. One of them is by trance. Another is by some form of automatic writing. A third is peering into some kind of crystal. The contactees are told to go to some valley and take a crystal, point the crystal towards the sun, hold their minds still and wait.[73] Again, the reappearance of quartz or other kinds of crystals as a means of contacting higher consciousness or higher beings is a familiar one in other kinds of occult manipulation. Jean Dixon's crystal ball or don Juan's crystal stones are examples.

The fourth means of gathering information about UFO contacts is through hypnosis. The most famous example of this was made into a television movie and was based on the 1961 experiences of Mr. and Mrs. Barney Hill. A book about them by John G. Fuller appeared five years later, *The Interrupted Journey* (1966). The Hills had been suffering from psychological problems. When hypnotized by a psychiatrist, they gave a story about having been carried onto a spacecraft and given certain information. What is odd is that the information given to the wife concerning certain stellar formations turned out to be accurate, even though at the time scientists could not have verified the information. Three years after the book was published, Marjorie Fish identified nine of these stars, which are part of the constellation Reticulum. A triangle of background stars completed the drawing; she identified them only in 1972. Prior to 1969, the position of these three stars had been erroneously esti-

---

70. *Ibid.*, p. 20.
71. *Idem.*
72. Hynek and Vallee, *Edge of Reality*, p. 8.
73. *Messengers of Deception*, p. 33.

mated. Mrs. Fish's identification resulted from a 1969 update of the *Gliese Catalogue of Nearby Stars*. There was no possibility that anyone on earth in 1964 could have known the exact location of these stars.[74]

One question is never, ever raised by those who rely on hypnotism for background information: Is what the hypnotized person is reporting based on his memory of an actual historical event, or is another being passing along a story of his own making through the mouth of a demonically possessed person? Could the incident have been recreated mentally by outside sources — a kind of visionary memory?[75] And if it did take place as remembered, were these beings what they claimed to be? In this case, however, there was this verification: the Pease Air Force Base in New Hampshire had detected the space vehicle on radar.[76]

As part of his investigation of the philosophy and ideas lying behind the stories from the contactees, Vallee drove to Mendocino, California to hear tapes that Timothy Leary had recorded in jail. Leary, of course, was famous from the mid-1960's onward for his psychedelic philosophy of "turn on, tune in and drop out." He was of all the men of that six-year period the one who is most deserving of the Pied Piper award for leading astray that generation. Vallee listened to tapes Leary had recorded and summarizes Leary's doctrines. "He stated that every living entity had a genetic purpose, and that the problem before us now was that of the future of the human race. He implied that Man was fast approaching the end of his rope, that evolution was ready to make a new jump toward a higher form of life, and that a superior intelligence had conceived the blueprint for us on Earth. The central nervous system was its gift to us, a piece of equipment to explore and use in order to establish communication with our maker."[77] By now you are familiar with this philosophy. It is the philosophy above all other doctrines which links most of the paranormal phenomena as well as the UFO phenomena. *Men are awaiting a leap of being to higher consciousness*. This is *the* theme of both occultism and New Age humanism.

Vallee also includes a chapter on the cattle mutilations that took place in the late '60s and early '70s and are still going on. A farmer

---

74. Clifford Wilson and John Weldon, *Close Encounters*, p. 96.
75. Wilson and Weldon do recognize the occult parallels with hypnotism (p. 124), but they also have identified the occult nature of UFO phenomena.
76. Jacques Vallee, *Passport to Magonia*, p. 90.
77. *Messengers*, p. 51.

comes in his field and finds a dead cow completely drained of blood but no sign of blood on the ground with part of its body surgically opened very carefully, no footprints anywhere, no trace of anyone coming to or going from the body of the cow. Sometimes they will be found even in snow with no tracks to or from the carcass. Sometimes it will be some other form of animal, such as a rabbit or a buffalo. He says that in an 18 month period, leading up to January of 1977, there were 700 mutilations in 15 western states. Over 180 cases occurred in Colorado alone in 1975.[78] Cases go back as early as 1953.[79] "The phenomena had certain characteristics: the animals died with no evidence of struggle. There were no tracks or blood near the carcasses (although circular depressions and pod-like marks were sometimes reported). Some carcasses seemed to have been airlifted, then dropped in areas which maximized the chances of discovery. Intense blinding lights from the sky were often associated with the events."[80] He sees that one of the possible motives behind these mutilations is that it is a challenge to the law enforcement community and to the military.

One explanation of the UFO phenomenon which Vallee discusses is basically my interpretation: that the UFO phenomenon is an aspect of occultism. Vallee writes: "Many of the phenomena reported by witnesses involve the poltergeist effect, levitation, psychic control, healing, and out-of-body experiences: things quite familiar to those who know the occult literature."[81] Vallee rejects this theory and substitutes a very peculiar alternative. He argues that the UFO phenomena represent the manifestation of a reality that transcends our current understanding of physics. He says, *"It is not the phenomenon itself, but the belief it has created, which is manipulated by human groups with their own objectives."*[82] He goes on to say: "I believe there is a system around us that transcends time as it transcends space. I remain confident that human knowledge is capable of understanding this larger reality. I suspect that some humans have already understood it, and are showing their hand in several aspects of the UFO encounters."[83] He then goes on to break with modern physics, and yet in a sense does not, for modern physics itself is becoming increasingly ir-

---

78. *Ibid.*, p. 180.
79. *Ibid.*, p. 181.
80. *Ibid.*, pp. 189-90.
81. *Ibid.*, pp. 224-25.
82. *Ibid.*, p. 230.
83. *Idem.*

rational. He points to a natural phenomenon, but one that is not yet understood by conventional or even unconventional physical theory.

The most useful chapter in the book is the chapter from which I have been quoting, "The Stratagem Theories." He has a section called, "The Six Social Consequences." These are very, very important. He lists the first consequence: the belief in UFO's widens the gap between the public and scientific institutions. The second is that contactee propaganda undermines the image of human beings as masters of their own destiny. Third, increased attention given to UFO activity promotes the concept of political unification of this planet. Fourth, contactee organizations may become the basis of a new high demand religion. Fifth, irrational motivations based on faith are spreading hand-in-hand with beliefs in extraterrestrial intervention. Sixth, contactee philosophies often include belief in higher races and in totalitarian systems that would eliminate democracy.

We can see in this summary that Vallee, as a representative of the older humanism, finds that the new religion of UFO's challenges the basic world-and-life view of conventional democratic social theory. He does not like the implications of this new philosophy, but he recognizes that they exist. He is like a man who is defending a sinking ship. Worse; his own books are like torpedoes that are widening the holes in his own ship.

The Breakdown of the "Treaty"

To return once again to Van Til's analogy, there is a secret treaty between the humanist's two worlds, the phenomenal realm of science and measurement on one side, and the noumenal realm of personality, mystery, the unmeasurable, the irrational, the ethical, the theological, and the "things in themselves" on the other side. (The question to ask is: "The other side of *what*?") As Van Til writes: "Irrationalism has a secret treaty with rationalism by which the former cedes to the latter so much of its territory as the latter can at any given time find the forces to control."[84] That which is unknown must remain in the shadows of external impotence. No invasion from the beyond— the noumenal—can be tolerated by the scientific, logical mind. Every effect has a cause. Every cause must be *in principle* knowable, even though not yet known.

To repeat: Max Weber, the great German social scientist, dealt

---

84. Van Til, *The Defense of the Faith* (2nd ed.; Philadelphia: Presbyterian & Reformed, 1963), p. 125.

with the same problem. He said that we do not know as much about
the tools we use as the primitive savage knows about the operations
of his tools. We use sophisticated equipment even though we know
next to nothing about it. What modern rational science proclaims is
that "if one but wished one *could* learn it at any time. Hence, it means
that principally there are no mysterious incalculable forces that
come into play, but rather that one can, in principle, master all
things by calculation. This means that the world is disenchanted."[85]
This was one of Weber's constant themes: *the disenchantment of the
world.* It is basic to all Western rationalism.

What UFO's represent, along with psychic healing and other occult phenomena, is a threat to this world view. It represents a *re-
enchantment of the world.* It represents a break with Western rationalism and Western science. The very words "occult phenomena" are
considered illegitimate by definition — an implicit breaking of the
treaty. Phenomena by definition cannot be occult. In principle, phenomena are capable of being explained through rational calculation.
This is basic to the faith of Western rational science.

The Dilemma of Empirical Science

Scientists seem to recognize that studying anything which does
not conform to this rule borders on the heretical. Science is supposed
to be open minded, *within reason.* Science is supposed to be willing to
investigate anything, *if relevant.* Science is supposed to be empirical,
but only when *the facts are real.* Here is twentieth-century science's dilemma: the measurable manifestations of the phenomenal realm are
beginning to depart from any known set of scientific rules. The
counting devices of science cannot deal with the phenomena, for the
phenomena keep violating the rules of calculation. A few scientists —
perhaps a hundred of them in 1975, worldwide, what Vallee calls
"the Invisible College" — keep on investigating the occult, or UFO's,
in the hope that they will discover some overarching theory, some
new means of integrating knowledge. They believe that they are investigating anomalies that are comparable to other oddities in
nature, other "not yet explained" facts. They admit that these facts
do not conform to the *presently known* laws of phenomenal science.
Only a tiny handful of scientists on the very fringe of the fringe are

---

85. Max Weber, "Science as a Vocation" (1918), in H. H. Gerth and C. Wright
Mills (eds.), *From Max Weber: Essays in Sociology* (New York: Oxford University
Press, 1946), p. 139.

willing to say that Western science must be rewritten. The question is: *Rewritten in terms of what kind of paradigm?* In terms of what sorts of *regularities?* In a universe of what sorts of *limitations?*

Hynek and Vallee are not to this point yet. Their book is well-titled: *The Edge of Reality.* They are operating at the edge of the boundary, the edge of the secret treaty between rationalism and irrationalism, between the phenomenal and the noumenal. What they are unwilling to admit is that they are operating at the boundary between the natural and the supernatural, or better put, between the fixed patterns of the creation and demonic intervention.

The Edge of Reality is a delight to read. Most of it is a transcription of a three-way discussion between Hynek, Vallee, and a psychologist, Hastings. At the end, they "pull out the stops" and allow their imaginations to run wild. What can account for the phenomena? What could they be? Outside aliens? Earth-bound aliens? Secret weapons of very bright humans? Or genetic programming of some kind? Why do they never seem to contact scientists? Why are the stories of the contacts familiar—basic patterns, leading nowhere? What are the implications for mankind?

Hynek reports that at a lecture in the mid-1970's, he asked the audience how many had seen a UFO or who has a close associate who has? About 18 percent raised their hands. "How many of you reported it?" One hand. He estimates that there are a hundred sightings per day around the world.[86]

The three just cannot explain these phenomena. He ends the book with a section on "interlocking universes," meaning the edge of reality. But that other universe sounds suspiciously like the occult: mind over matter, out-of-body experiences, and so forth. But they want to think of it as a world that men can eventually understand. They want it to be phenomenal, not noumenal.

No News Is Safe News

A most important observation by the authors is this one: the UFO stories stay the same. "The reported sightings that remain unexplained after serious examination fall into a relatively small number of fairly definite patterns of appearance and behavior. These patterns have been well delineated by UFO investigators and especially by the present authors. The patterns have not changed during the

---

86. *The Edge of Reality,* p. 254.

past quarter of a century [1975]. There is little new in the contents of recent UFO reports: a 1975 report generally does not differ in basic content from a 1955 or 1965 UFO report. UFOs in a real sense do not constitute news."[87] There is nothing new about them any more.

This is extremely important for understanding why scientists have not and do not take flying saucers seriously. They have nothing to gain from further studies, and everything to lose if this assault on Kantian reason is based on noumenal events. The UFO creatures do not contact scientists and show them how to improve theory, science, or technology. They do not do what the space invader Klaatu did in "The Day the Earth Stood Still": go to the office of a great scientist and correct his blackboard errors in mathematics. *That* would gain their attention! If these invaders were to single out one or two scientists in any field and give them better knowledge, so that they could publish the new information and become famous within their profession, word would get out. Even if the new knowledge was impractical, if it was theoretically compelling to scholars in the field, the invaders would have no trouble enlisting true believers and followers in the scientific community. Non-tenured scholars would search out the invaders and beg to be taught. Science would develop, and eventually word would get out as to who was providing the new information. Scientists, especially academically employed scientists, will do whatever it takes to get published in scholarly journals, including meeting with little green men.

Scientists see that the contactees are not scientists generally, and even when they are scientists, these men do not bring forth innovative new scientific information. So there is little likelihood that contacts with the invaders will in any way bridge the gap between man's knowledge and theirs. We will not be able to transform today's "not yet known" into data that are usable in the scientific tool kit. In short, conventional scientists smell trouble: trouble for their careers, trouble for their sanity, and trouble with beings that have powers that are not phenomenal in the Kantian sense but all too phenomenal (in the general English usage sense). Why get involved? Better to define the problem away, ignore the problem away, or if pushed, ridicule the problem away. This is the safe course of action, too, for unlike other scientific discoveries that were once defined away, ignored away, and ridiculed away, only to become accepted later on, there is

---

87. *Ibid.*, p. 3.

no *rival program of advancing knowledge* associated with UFO's. The stories never change, so the few scientists who do investigate these stories are never put into a position of being able to challenge their peers with new evidence, new interpretations, and most important of all, new scientific discoveries that will advance their own careers. Conventional science has nothing to fear from UFO's. Nothing scientific, anyway. And yet, how can "empirical" science retain its mythological position as being open-minded if it refuses to study these widespread phenomena?

If scientists could point to the evidence and tell people the following, they could solve their problems. "Look, these phenomena are familiar enough. They are the same sorts of demonic activity that accompany seances, paranormal phenomena, and other sorts of occult communication. These communications never tell us anything scientific. We don't learn a thing from them. They are confused messages, and they are often lies. There is nothing worth studying here because these are not true phenomena, but simply demonic trickery. Let's not waste our time or our money in further studies." But to make such a statement, they would have to abandon the reigning epistemological religion of the autonomy of man and the autonomy of the phenomenal realm. They refuse to make this break. They prefer to lie to the public, ridicule honest citizens, destroy evidence of the unusual, and attack their peers who are remaining faithful to science's legend of empirical open-mindedness. In short, they are making fools of themselves. Simple people know this, and no longer take scientific assurances as seriously as they take the stories of flying saucers.

The Possibility of Malevolence

The popular theology of the UFO cults is that these creatures are benevolent. They have mankind's best interests at heart. But Vallee's suspicion is exactly the opposite. These beings are not benevolent. On the contrary, they are a threat to mankind. But just how great a threat are they?

As invaders from outer space that possess vast and powerful technologies, they are not very relevant. They may be able to disrupt power lines temporarily, or disrupt radio communication, or even blow up missiles aimed at them. Occasionally, we hear of a jet fighter which disappears after having pursued or fired upon a UFO. But this is the risk of all demonism. Physical violence is rare, but it does happen. People also burst into flames from time to time. On the whole, however, the threat of UFO's is not technological. It is theological.

Vallee says that in recent years (as of 1975), the reports of paranormal events have accompanied the stories of close encounters with the inhabitants of UFO's. In fact, this correlation "seems to have become the rule rather than the exception, and most investigators have found it very difficult to deal with this aspect of the cases."[88] This is because the investigators are not well-informed Christians. Had such paranormal phenomena not accompanied these contacts, it would have been surprising. The contactees have dreams just before contact, or they hear voices inside their heads after contact. They may even receive eerie phone calls, with or without voices at the other "end." In short, they experience the same sorts of outside control that people described in earlier chapters experienced.

In many ways, the UFO phenomenon is analogous to Edgar Cayce's healing sessions. Vallee also makes the connection between Cayce and paranormal encounters,[89] but my assessment accentuates the sinister. For many years, Cayce believed that he was doing something religiously neutral. He continued to go to church and read his Bible. Similarly, for two decades, the UFO reports seemed to be mainly reports of odd phenomena, not theologically grounded encounters. But step by step, especially after 1965, the theology of the invaders has been made clear, and that theology is simply one or another version of New Age evolutionary humanism, meaning the old time occultism. There are even cases of healings associated with UFO sightings.[90]

Vallee correctly attributes malevolence to the creatures. He sees them as involved in a great deception, an attempt to implant deep within our society "far-reaching doubts concerning its basic philosophical tenets. . . ."[91] But he is still hypnotized by the "infinitely more complex nature of their technology that gives rise to the sightings."[92] The appearance of technology is the cutting edge of the invasion of a civilization that nearly worships technology. Vallee is only slightly beyond the average observer. He focuses on their presumed

---

88. Vallee, *Invisible College*, p. 17.
89. *Ibid.*, p. 25.
90. *Ibid.*, pp. 22-23.
91. *Ibid.*, p. 27.
92. *Ibid.*, p. 28.

higher level of technology, namely, the technology of psychological control, the technology of shifting men's consciousness. "We are faced with a *technology* that transcends the physical and is capable of manipulating our reality, generating a variety of altered states of consciousness and of emotional perceptions. The purpose of that technology may be to change our concepts of the universe."[93] They have fooled Vallee, too. Technology is their illusion; the reality is their theology: "Ye shall be as God."

The conventional scientists are in a jam—a jam created by the collapse of the Newtonian world view which they themselves have contributed to (quantum mechanics, light waves that are sometimes particles, etc.). Vallee asks rhetorically, "Why were the scientists remaining silent?" He criticizes them, quite correctly: ". . . by denying the existence of the mystery, the scientific community was taking serious chances with the belief system of the public. In my opinion, such attitudes have contributed to the long-term loss of popular support and popular respect for science."[94] But if they had seriously pursued the UFO "phenomena," they would have discovered a chink in the intellectual defensive armor against the invaders from the noumenal, invaders from hell. In either case, the public will lose respect for the autonomous science of humanistic man. They are damned methodologically if they seriously pursue the manifestations of the occult, and damned publicly if they don't. This is the fate of all autonomous thought: damnation. The same applies to political officials and other "agents of suppression." They simply cannot win, no matter what happens, unless the public manifestations of the occult should go away. In an age of transition in which millions have departed from traditional Christian faith, this reduction in public occultism is unlikely.

I agree entirely with Vallee, who italicizes these ideas: *"I think there is a general shifting of man's belief patterns, his entire relationship to the concept of the invisible. It is happening outside of any established structure, and science is not immune to it."*[95] I also agree with C. S. Lewis' prophetic demon, Screwtape: "Our policy, for the moment, is to conceal ourselves. Of course this has not always been so. We are really faced with a cruel dilemma. When the humans disbelieve in our existence we lose all the pleasing results of direct terrorism, and we make no

---

93. *Ibid.*, pp. 153-54.
94. *Ibid.*, p. 47.
95. *Ibid.*, p. 114.

magicians. On the other hand, when they believe in us, we cannot make them materialists and sceptics. At least, not yet. I have great hopes that we shall learn in due time how to emotionalise and mythologise their science to such an extent that what is, in effect, a belief in us (though not under that name) will creep in while the human mind remains closed to belief in the Enemy. The 'Life Force,' the worship of sex, and some aspects of Psychoanalysis may here prove useful. If once we can produce our perfect work—the Materialist Magician, the man, not using, but veritably worshipping, what he vaguely calls 'Forces' while denying the existence of 'spirits'—then the end of the war will be in sight."[96]

Conclusion

Jacques Vallee in 1975 predicted that industrial nations would soon have to put their best scientists on a program to study UFO's.[97] They haven't. He predicted that the next major religious revival could easily be centered around flying saucers.[98] It has yet to happen. The invisible college of UFO-oriented scientists is still as invisible as ever. If anything, interest in UFO's has declined. Perhaps too many people already believe. The shock value of UFO sightings is over. Most important, the visitors have always lied. They keep promising to show up. They do, too: in Kansas farm communities at 3 A.M. "Close Encounters of a Third Kind" became a Hollywood production. So did "E.T." Lots of fun, but not a new religion. Not yet.

Will the public's faith in UFO's continue? Probably. Will this make much difference? Probably not. Flying saucers are just one more manifestation of the ever-present religion of humanism: evolutionary, self-salvational, and gnostic. Flying saucerism's theology is not that unique. Its pseudo-technology is impressive to those who see it, but not many do see it up close, and in any case, major religious movements are not based on technology—influenced by it, yes, but not based on it. They are based on specific *presuppositional* views of God, man, law, and time. They are also based on a view, pro or con, of final judgment.

Men find many reasons to believe that they can escape the threat of final judgment. The doctrine of evolution is a major means of

96. C. S. Lewis, *The Screwtape Letters and Screwtape Proposes a Toast* (New York: Macmillan, [1961] 1969), Letter VII, pp. 32-33.

97. *Invisible College*, p. 200.

98. *Ibid.*, pp. 202-6.

escape for millions. So is the doctrine of reincarnation, a form of personal evolution. So is the doctrine of scientific man, the master of technology. The technological society is a Western development, and it grew out of biblical presuppositions. Its strength is also its weakness. Men believe in their own autonomy and forget about God and His law. But then they refuse to believe in demons. What Satan wants is the coming of the materialist magicians: people who believe in him but not in God.

This is the threat. The chariots of the gods from outer space replace the chariots of fire in the Bible. Men believe that they can preserve their metaphysical autonomy as sons of the ancient spacemen. No God created them or their world. (They never seem to ask themselves: "Who created the spacemen?") By preserving their metaphysical autonomy, people believe that they can safely preserve their *ethical* autonomy. They can safely continue to forget God. They adopt the ancient teachings of Eastern mysticism in the name of a coming higher technology. They use occult communications techniques in order to "keep the channels open" with high-tech space visitors: automatic writing, trances, ESP, clairvoyance, yogic meditation, and so forth.[99] You would think that these visitors could at least provide contactees with cheap transistor radios equal in efficiency to a Japanese $20 import! They don't.

For scientists, there is the time-worn Darwinian doctrine of evolution through natural selection, or the "new, improved" version offered by Harvard professor Stephen J. Gould, the "rapid, macroevolutionary leap" version.[100] For the less sophisticated, there are the popular science books on UFO's. And for the easily misled, there are books by contactees, with their messages of cosmic evolution and imminent leaps of being. The difference between Prof. Gould's vision of evolution and the First Intergalactic Church of Cosmic Vibrations' version has more to do with style than the reliability of evidence. The goal is the same: to evolve into God and out of eternal danger.

---

99. Wilson and Weldon, *Close Encounters*, pp. 180-81.

100. Stephen Jay Gould, "Evolution: Explosion, Not Ascent," *New York Times* (Jan. 22, 1979); Gould, *Ever Since Darwin* (New York: Norton, 1977); *The Panda's Thumb* (New York: Norton, 1980). Cf. Steven N. Stanley, *The New Evolutionary Timetable* (New York: Basic Books, 1982). An alternative explanation for these supposed "macro-evolutionary leaps" is found in Rupert Sheldrake, *The New Science of Life: The Hypothesis of Formative Causation* (Los Angeles: Tarcher, 1981).

10

ESCAPE FROM CREATUREHOOD

Therefore if any man be in Christ, he is a new creature: old things are passed away; behold, all things are become new.

II Corinthians 5:17

We come now to the heart of this book. By now the reader may be confused. What do all these things mean? Eyeless sight, auras photographed by Kirlian photography, spontaneous human combustion, psychic healing, knives in eyes, water witching, and other improbable facets of human life that the textbooks ignore. Dozens of books could be written and have been written on these topics, as well as thousands of books on similar weird events. There is far too much here for any one person to master. Yet we must not become like those described by St. Paul: "Ever learning, and never able to come to the knowledge of the truth" (II Tim. 3:7). There are fascinating aspects about the general subject of the occult, but books about the occult should not be written merely to satisfy the curious or the potential occult practitioner. Men and women should know of the existence of such phenomena in order to avoid them and give competent warnings to those who have not avoided them. We do not have any need for knowing everything about our spiritual opposition. We only need to know enough to recognize the danger and avoid it. The issue is *ethics*, not exhaustive knowledge. "And have no fellowship with the unfruitful works of darkness, but rather reprove them. For it is a shame even to speak of those things which are done of them in secret. But all things that are reproved are made manifest by the light: for whatsoever doth make manifest is light. Wherefore he saith, Awake thou that sleepest, and arise from the dead, and Christ shall give thee light. See then that ye walk circumspectly, not as fools, but as wise, redeeming the time, because the days are evil" (Eph. 5:11-16).

There are many other subjects that might have been covered: exorcism and demonic possession, ghosts, poltergeists, Fortean phenomena (the weird and unexplained), mediumship, Theosophy, spiritualism, secret societies, conspiracies, the history of witchcraft, vampirism, and on and on. What about the legendary Bigfoot?[1] What about the Loch Ness monster? What about myriads of other alien animals?[2] Are all these things real? Better put, are they part of the natural order? Are they part of that domain which God assigned mankind the responsibility of bringing under dominion (Gen. 1:28)? Can they be subdued to the glory of God by means of biblical law, or will they simply disappear, just as demons progressively disappear, in the face of man's extension of the dominion covenant?

We are back to my original premise: Satan and his supernatural host reveal themselves in any form which is acceptable to not-yet-fully-demonized mankind. Satan can throw as many strange phenomena at mankind as mankind is willing to fritter away his time investigating, in search of hidden meanings or messages of the coming self-transcendence. The endless quest of the true believers is matched by the endless skepticism of the nineteenth-century rationalist: neither is ever satisfied with the facts at his disposal. Both want more facts. Endless facts threaten to overwhelm the average reader. And as we read in the Bible, "of making many books there is no end; and much study is a weariness of the flesh" (Eccl. 12:12).

The thesis of this book is straightforward: there are unexplained events in this world. There are events that cannot, by their very nature, be explained by the standards of nineteenth-century rationalistic science. These events are real phenomena, and few men can simply push them aside by attributing their origin to the random events in a chance-created world. Finally, while some of these facts may be explained sometime in the future by science (Kirlian photography is the most obvious example), the best explanation is that supernatural and highly personal powers are involved. The events are too frequently associated with religious teachings that are at bottom demonic: reincarnation, self-transcendence, radical monism, the deification of man, the worship of evil, and the denial of the Creator-creature distinction. Especially the denial of the Creator-creature distinction.

---

1. Kenneth Wylie, *Bigfoot: A Personal Inquiry into a Phenomenon* (New York: Viking, 1980).

2. Janet and Colin Beard, *Alien Animals* (Harrisburg, Pennsylvania: Stackpole, 1981).

A corollary of the main thesis is that modern humanism, or logically permissable developments of the humanist tradition, are in accord with the premises of Satanism with regard to the definition of man. This is not to say that all humanists are demonists. But it does mean that *a commitment to the philosophy of humanism is no longer a reliable shield against the demonic*. Humanism does not prevent men from dabbling in the occult or even embracing it. It certainly does not prevent the sons and daughters of the humanists of the 1930's from experimenting with hallucinatory drugs. In fact, such experimentation is consistent with an overall philosophy, inherited from their humanistic parents, of total criticism, antinomian experimentation, and radical skepticism. As Screwtape wrote to Wormwood, when the materialists believe in demons but not in God, the battle is over.[3]

The first principle of humanism, from the Greeks to the Renaissance to the present, is that *man is the measure of all things*. The Roman poet, Terrence, said it best: "I am a man; and nothing human is foreign to me." This was one of Karl Marx's familiar phrases.[4] It undergirded the philosophy, writings, and practices of the Marquis de Sade. The problem is: that which is human can be utterly inhumane. There was a memorable exchange in a scene in a television movie about the life of Raoul Wallenberg, a Swede who saved many Rumanian Jews from the Nazi concentration camps. A group of Jews were being taken away to a camp. "How can you still believe in God?" wailed a young Jew to a rabbi. The rabbi's reply was appropriate: "How can you still believe in man?" Man as the measure of all things is a potentially terrifying guideline.

The Lure of Occultism

Why do men turn to the occult? There is no single answer. Different men have different motivations. The quest for power is common to all occultists who call upon the forces of nature, the forces of human intuition, or the demonic forces of the nether realm. But occult experimentation goes beyond the mere quest for power. If men wanted power, and only power, modern technology would provide them with abundant power. Colin Wilson, himself an occultist, has argued that men are trapped in the "triviality of everydayness,"

---

3. C. S. Lewis, *The Screwtape Letters and Screwtape Proposes a Toast* (New York: Macmillan, [1943] 1969), Letter #7, p. 33.

4. Franz Mehring, *Karl Marx: The Story of His Life* (Ann Arbor: University of Michigan Press, [1918] 1962), p. 290.

to use the phrase of the modern philosopher Heidegger. They have had their minds formed by the focused vision of rationalism, but as a result men have been cut off from the unseen realms around them.[5] It is more a quest for *meaning* than for power. In a crucially important passage, Wilson states that "Religion, mysticism and magic all spring from the same basic 'feeling' about the universe: a sudden feeling of *meaning*. . . ."[6] Magic is therefore the science of the future, not the past. The human mind is about to evolve to a new stage. For a thousand years, the unconscious powers of man were pushed underground by the development of the intellect. "Now the wheel has come full circle; intellect has reached certain limits, and it cannot advance beyond them until it recovers some of the lost powers."[7] Modern philosophy is rigid, narrow, and formal. It has failed in the quest for both meaning and power.

Why should the occult provide meaning? How can it provide power? These questions are seldom even asked by those who write about occultism. Why should the mere existence of personal powers that are outside the range of normal human experience testify to some higher meaning? Why is the world of the savage any more meaningful than the world of the physicist? Wilson asserts: "In a sense, the Indians and Peruvians were closer to the truth than modern man, for their intuition of 'unseen forces' kept them wide open to the vistas of meaning that surround us."[8] Those who buy Castaneda's books apparently believe this, but why is primitivism closer to truth — and what kind of truth does primitivism proclaim? Why does the ability to recognize the manifestations of occult power as the products of demonic interference with regular patterns of fixed law — or seemingly fixed law — entitle the savage to claim that he senses the true meaning of creation? Don Juan's explanation of the universe is strangely modern, almost Kantian. Familiarity with hallucinatory herbs and occult rituals may well open up one's mind to realms of the creation that Western men have learned to ignore, or in fact have actually overpowered temporarily, but why should there be more meaning associated with this form of perception and power than with the computer or the atomic bomb? Yet there is a growing body of occultists and mystics who are convinced that Wilson is correct

---

5. Colin Wilson, *The Occult: A History* (New York: Random House, 1971), p. 23.
6. *Ibid.*, p. 28.
7. *Ibid.*, p. 39.
8. *Ibid.*, p. 23.

and that the realm of the occult is a more meaningful realm.

No socially important movement survives without a philosophy of life and religious commitment to that philosophy on the part of its adherents. This is as true of the various forms of Satanism, occultism, mysticism, and paranormal phenomenalism as it is for the major religions in man's history. Men want to find both meaning and power in life. If they have abandoned this hope, then they will search for a means of escape. The fact that the major Eastern religions, Buddhism and Hinduism, are marked by magicians and mystics, power-seekers and monistic retreaters, should not surprise us. Those who have sought power and meaning apart from God have at times found power, both rational and occult, but their ultimate hope — that there is meaning in the world apart from that imposed on creation by a sovereign personal God — cannot be achieved. Power does not satisfy, and meaning does not stem from man, the hypothetical measure of all things.

Power Without Providence

The heart of occultism is its commitment to a universe devoid of an ultimate sovereign. Man may have power, individual men may have power, and demons may have power. Impersonal forces of the universe may have power. But there must not be an ultimate form of power which is absolutely sovereign. The universe is chance- or fate-created; it may or may not be illusion; but it is not controlled by providence. The universe may have meaning or it may not; in any case, its meaning or lack of meaning is autonomous.

> The world's a chance-determined thing,
> It's plain enough to see;
> Probably governed by the laws
> Of probability.

The religion of Satan offers self-determination to man, yet it simultaneously promises bondage. To take power over anything in the creation requires a source of power: law, demons, forces, God. Every man is under someone's yoke. The assertion of total autonomy is a fool's dream. There can be no order, no meaning, no existence apart from sovereign authority. But men persist in clinging to their claims of autonomy. When they look at themselves and their world, however, they see that imperfection is overwhelming. They want to escape from the imperfect universe around them if they cannot control it and purify it, yet they themselves are immersed in the creation, imperfect creatures that would not find peace if they could remake the universe in their own image. *The enemy of autonomous man is the creation itself*. It testifies to a holy God and a judgment to come (Romans 1:18-25).

Ethics or Metaphysics (Magic)

The response to the human condition that has been made by orthodox Christianity is to point to the source of the imperfection: man's ethical rebellion against God. It is a willful suppressing of the truth in unrighteousness that blinds man and condemns him. The curse of the universe is a response by God to man's ethical rebellion, and the promise of external restoration goes with the promise of internal regeneration (Romans 8:18-23). Men must be conformed ethically to the image of God's Son, who was perfectly human, but to achieve this goal, each man requires grace from God (Romans 8:29; Eph. 2:8-9). The heart of man's problem, therefore, is man's own heart. The grace of God involves the means of *progressive sanctification*: the step-by-step submission to the laws of God. St. Paul writes: "I press toward the mark for the prize of the high calling of God in Christ Jesus" (Phil. 3:14). The goal is therefore the ultimate (post-judgment) attainment of *perfect humanity*, not the attainment of full divinity. "For our conversation [citizenship] is in heaven; from whence also we look for the Saviour, the Lord Jesus Christ: who shall change our vile body, that it may be fashioned like unto his glorious body, according to the working whereby he is able even to subdue all things unto himself" (Phil. 3:20-21). The goal is not *metaphysical self-transcendence*; the goal is *ethical maturity*. The Fall of man was ethical; the restoration of man is ethical.

This is the Christian view. In contrast to it is the religion of Satan. The Satanic religion, whether occult, evolutionist, Marxist, environmentalist, or any other form of human autonomy, presents man's plight as essentially metaphysical. There was a flaw in the creation. Indeed, some systems (monistic Eastern philosophy) teach that the creation itself was the flaw. The Time before time, the Existence prior to existence, was the golden age. Whatever form of Satanic philosophy, it sets forth as the goal of man self-regeneration. It may be achieved by ritual, contemplation, asceticism, magic, drugs, lawlessness, revolution, economic planning, or whatever, but the source of the regenerating power is to be found in the creation.

Man must transcend himself. He must become a new creature. He must overcome the world. He must do all of these things by means of power which is immanent. In short, the very essence of Satanic religion is the call to *escape from finitude*. This means the *divinization of man*, and it very often includes the *abolition of time*. It requires a *higher consciousness*. It requires a *politics of humanistic self-transcendence*.

The Divinization of Man

In chapter eight, I cited the explicit statements of two modern satanists, Anton LaVey and Aleister Crowley, that affirm that man alone is sovereign because man alone is divine. Colin Wilson goes one step farther: "It is unnecessary to point out that all the great religions hold the view that the essence of man and the essence of God are one and the same."[9] He is incorrect; neither orthodox Judaism nor orthodox Christianity has ever affirmed such a doctrine, and the absence of just this doctrine made both religions unique in the ancient world.

In contrast, as Wilson correctly points out, is the philosophical principle of magic — a principle attributed to the mythical Hermes Trismegistus, the supposed writer of influential occult manuscripts that were revived during the Renaissance: "As above, so below."[10] The microcosm is the same as the macrocosm. As Crowley put it: "There is a single main definition of the object of all magical Ritual. It is the uniting of the Microcosm with the Macrocosm. The Supreme and Complete Ritual is therefore the Invocation of the Holy Guardian Angel; or, in the language of Mysticism, Union with God."[11] Furthermore, wrote Crowley: "This consists of a real identification of the magician and the god. Note that to do this in perfection involves the attainment of a species of Samadhi; and this fact alone suffices to link irrefragibly magick with mysticism."[12]

Union with God or even identification with God: here is the concept of the divinization of man. It is a denial of the Creator-creature distinction. The Fall of man was not the willful ethical rebellion against an absolutely sovereign God, nor shall restoration be the absolutely sovereign gift of a merciful God. Man shall save himself by becoming the saving God.

---

9. *Ibid.*, p. 103.
10. *Ibid.*, pp. 193, 232.
11. Aleister Crowley, *Magick in Theory and Practice* (New York: Castle, n.d.), p. 11.
12. *Ibid.*, p. 17.

Alchemy

Alchemists believed in such a self-transcendence. Alchemy was not simply limited to medieval Europe, but was a phenomenon also common to India, China, and Islamic cultures. It produced a huge and virtually unreadable body of esoteric literature. There is even a scholarly journal, *Ambix*, devoted to alchemy's history. The mental image of the alchemist in the minds of those who have even heard of it is that of a lonely investigator in his secret laboratory, painstakingly searching for the chemical formula which will allow him to turn lead into gold. Textbooks in European history may mention alchemy briefly as the forerunner to modern scientific chemistry. The textbook formula runs something like the following: take medieval alchemy, add to it the principles of Cartesian logic and mathematics, sprinkle in a bottle of Enlightenment philosophy, and shake gently for three centuries: out pops modern chemistry.

The textbook account is misleading. It was the Reformation, not the Enlightenment, that produced modern science.[13] More importantly, it was not the methodology of alchemy which made scientific investigation possible, but rather alchemy's opposite. However secretive scientists may be prior to publishing their findings, the methodology of science is based upon open knowledge, publication, repeatable experiments, the international division of intellectual labor, and the concept of regular law. In contrast, alchemy was above all the knowledge of the secret initiates, and its goal was secret, esoteric knowledge. It was the science of gnosticism.[14] Its technique was based on the idea that in the endless mixing of the same ingredients —chemical opposites— the chemicals would somehow transcend themselves after a hundred or a thousand identical operations. No one could know in advance when or how this transformation would take place. No one attempting to repeat this process could be assured of success. The discovery of the so-called Philosopher's Stone which would allow the alchemist to turn lead into gold was the product of the alchemist's very soul. The crucial fact to bear in mind is this: alchemy was fundamentally a religious procedure. Eliade, summarizing the findings of the psychologist C. G. Jung, writes: "The aim of

---

13. Robert K. Merton, *Social Theory and Social Structure* (New York: Free Press, 1969), ch. 18.

14. H. J. Shepard, "Gnosticism and Alchemy," *Ambix*, VI (1958), pp. 140-48; Shepard, "The Redemption Theme in Hellenistic Alchemy," *Ambix*, VII (1959), pp. 42-76.

the *opus magnum* [great work] was at once the freeing of the human soul and the healing of the cosmos. In this sense alchemy is a continuation of Christianity. In the eyes of the alchemists, observes Jung, Christianity saved man but not nature. It is the alchemist's dream to heal the world in its totality; the Philosopher's Stone is conceived as the *Filius Macrocosmi* who heals the world, whereas, according to the alchemists, Christ is the Saviour of the Microcosm, that is, of man only. The ultimate goal of the *opus* is Cosmic Salvation; for this reason, the *Lapis Philosophorum* is identified with Christ."[15]

Chinese alchemists searched for the "divine cinnabar," or drinkable gold, which would produce eternal life — the elixir of youth, in other words.[16] The Philosopher's Stone was seen as the elixir of immortality.[17] The alchemist was concerned with the transcending of time, and he was therefore the inheritor of ancient paganism, with its ritual attempts to return to the primordial chaos, the Time before time.[18]

Louis Pauwels and Jacques Bergier, the authors of the enormously successful book, *The Morning of the Magicians* (1960), believe in alchemy. Their book supposedly heralds a new dawning of an age of alchemy. They, too, agree with Jung about the religious impulse of alchemy. "For the alchemist, it must never be forgotten that power over matter and energy is only a secondary reality. The real aim of the alchemist's activities, which are perhaps the remains of a very old science belonging to a civilization long extinct, is the transformation of the alchemist himself, his accession to a higher state of consciousness. The material results are only a pledge of the final result, which is spiritual. Everything is oriented towards the transmutation of man himself, towards his deification, his fusion with the divine energy, the fixed center from which all material energies emanate. The alchemist's is that science 'with a conscience' of which Rabelais speaks. It is a science which tends to exalt man rather than matter; as Teilhard de Chardin puts it: 'The real aim of physics should be to integrate Man as a totality in a coherent representation of the world.' "[19] Interestingly enough, they quote Teilhard, whose mon-

---

15. Mircea Eliade, *The Forge and the Crucible: The Origin and Structures of Alchemy* (New York: Harper Torchbooks, [1956] 1971), p. 225.

16. *Ibid.*, pp. 109-11.

17. *Ibid.*, pp. 124, 167.

18. *Ibid.*, pp. 174-75.

19. Louis Pauwels and Jacques Bergier, *The Morning of the Magicians* (New York: Avon, [1960] 1973), p. 118.

istic, evolutionary philosophy was condemned by the Roman Catholic Church. He was far more Buddhist or Hindu in his religious perspective than Christian.

The Coming "Leap of Being"

Alchemy follows the lead of magic, arguing for the principle that
"as above, so below." All being is at bottom one, or *monistic*. It is
therefore man's task to bridge the gap between his own temporarily
limited being and God's eternal being. (The fact that Luther was a
supporter of alchemy therefore comes as a shock, for his theology
mitigates against the monism that undergirds alchemy.[20]) With its
roots in gnosticism, alchemy was self-consciously committed to the
divinization of man.[21] Pauwels and Bergier wax eloquent about the
alchemist's quest: "The 'Great Work' is done. The alchemist himself
undergoes a transformation which the texts evoke, but which we are
unable to describe, having only the vaguest analogies to guide us.
This transformation, it seems, would be, as it were, a promise, or
foretaste, experienced by a privileged being, of what awaits humanity after attaining the very limits of its knowledge of the earth and its
elements: its fusion with the Supreme Being, its concentration on a
fixed spiritual goal, and its junction with other centers of intelligence
across the cosmic spaces. Gradually, or in a sudden flash of illumination, the alchemist, according to tradition, discovers the meaning of
his long labors. The secrets of energy and of matter are revealed to
him, and at the same time he glimpses the infinite perspectives of
Life. He possesses the key to the mechanics of the Universe. He es-
tablishes a new relationship between his own mind, which from now
on is *illuminated*, and the Universal Mind eternally deepening its
concentration."[22]

The manipulation of metals brings on the sudden flash of illumination, the *higher consciousness* which is the goal for all occult groups.
This key phrase — higher consciousness — serves as a kind of talisman
among radical humanist groups. Consciousness-raising within
Women's Liberation, the new consciousness of Esalen and the other

---

20. Eliade, *Forge*, pp. 190-91. Eliade relies on the study of Lutheran alchemy written by the Lutheran scholar, John Warwick Montgomery, "Cross, Constellation,
and Crucible: Lutheran Astrology and Alchemy in the Age of the Reformation,"
Transactions of the Royal Society of Canada, I Ser. 4 (June 1963), Sect. II, pp. 251-700.

21. It is the thesis of this book that man's self-deification is the very heart of the
religion of Satan — the temptation to be as God.

22. Pauwels and Bergier, *Morning*, p. 137.

mystical illuminist organizations, and the drug-induced consciousness—mind-expanding—of the counter-culture all reach out to the
void in search of a new creation. Such a hypothetical "leap of being"
is the very essence of gnosticism. Man is needed to complete the evolutionary development of the Universal Mind—God. Without man,
God could not complete His own being. This is not the God of
Christianity, but is instead the God of Hegel, as Prof. Molnar has
demonstrated so well in his book, *God and the Knowledge of Reality.*

Alchemy, like modern humanism, is based on a Pelagian view of
man. (Pelagius earned the wrath of Augustine fifteen centuries ago.)
Man is supposedly basically good. The possibility for perfection is
always present in life. Man's being is not flawed by the effects of ethical rebellion. Given this outlook, the self-transcendence of man becomes a sociological imperative: "At the stage we have reached in
scientific research our minds and intelligence will have to surpass
themselves and rise to transcendent heights; the human, all-too-
human, will no longer suffice."[23] Not only is this leap of being a sociological imperative, but it is also an ethical imperative: "If men have
in them the physical possibility of attaining one or other of these
states [of higher consciousness], the quest for the best means of doing so ought to be the principal aim of their lives."[24] This transformation is strictly a question of the proper *technique.* "If my brain is
equipped with the necessary machinery—if all this does not belong
exclusively to the domain of religion or mythology—if it is not all a
question of divine 'grace' or 'magical initiation' but depends upon
certain techniques and certain internal and external attitudes capable of setting this machinery in motion—then I am satisfied that my
only ambition and most urgent duty ought to be to reach this 'awakened state' and attain these heights at which the mind can soar."[25]

The techniques of two thousand five hundred years of alchemy
are a standing testimony to men's faith that the "if nots" of the cited
passage really *are* nots—that technique is superior to grace in the
quest for human self-transcendence.

Directed Evolution

Like the vast majority of the "higher consciousness" prophets today, the authors are totally committed to a theory of cosmic evolu-

---

23. *Ibid.*, pp. 60-61.
24. *Ibid.*, p. 357.
25. *Idem.*

tion. Not Darwin's antiseptic evolution of random mutations and randomly changing environments, but purposeful evolution. We are headed for Teilhard's "omega point," that Hegelian monist resolution point of all progress. A new stage in man's evolutionary process is dawning: "A revolution is taking place before our eyes—the unexpected remarriage of reason, at the summit of its victories, and intuition. For the really attentive observer the problems facing contemporary intelligence are no longer problems of progress. The concept of progress has been dead for some years now. Today it is a question of a change of state, of a transmutation. From this point of view those concerned with the domain of the interior life and its realities are in step with the pioneering savants who are preparing the birth of a world that will have nothing in common with our present world of laborious transition in which we have to live for just a little while longer."[26]

What these defenders of alchemy are saying is significant. They are focusing their attention not on the everyday labors of the common man, nor on the steady accumulation of scientific knowledge, but rather on the *radically discontinuous event which will bring forth a new world*. They have abandoned the idea of progress, as have so many of the intellectuals of our day, especially the younger men whose careers were closely linked with the occult explosion and Vietnam protests of the post-1965 era. Not progress but mutation. Yet not random mutation, either. Mutation which is directed by *a new elite of illuminated ones*.

Activism toward the world has no meaning for the authors; theirs is an interior world. The next stage of history will stem from the affairs of the psyche or the transcendent states of consciousness—beyond consciousness. The formal activism of the alchemist has once again become internalized and passive. Thus it must always be. *If men are not passive before God, then in principle they cannot be active toward the world*. Only for brief periods of time can they borrow or steal the spiritual capital of future-oriented Christianity. Modern autonomous man has killed the faith in progress, yet he is called upon to create a new world: "Man can have access to a secret world—*see* the Light, *see* Eternity, comprehend the Laws of Energy, integrate within himself the rhythm of the destiny of the Universe, consciously apprehend the ultimate concentration of forces and, like Teilhard de Chardin, live the incomprehensible life that starts from 'Point Omega,' in

---

26. *Ibid.*, pp. xxii-xxiii.

which the whole of creation, at the end of terrestrial time, will find its accomplishment, consummation and exaltation. Man is capable of anything. His intelligence, equipped from the very beginning, no doubt with a capacity for infinite knowledge, can in certain conditions apprehend the whole mechanism of life. The powers of human intelligence, if developed to their fullest extent, could probably cope with anything in the whole Universe. But these powers stop short at the point where the intelligence, having reached the end of its mission, senses that there is still 'something other' beyond the confines of the Universe. Here it is quite possible for an analogical consciousness to function. There are no models in the Universe of what may exist outside the Universe. The door through which none may pass is the gateway to the Kingdom of Heaven."[27]

In this universe, man can cope with anything it has to offer. Man, in good Kantian fashion, stands reverently at the door to the Kingdom of Heaven, making sure that nothing over there bothers us over here. If something there gets into the Universe, however, it can be coped with. The mind of man will see to that.

What we are witnessing is the coming of an elite corps of mutants. Some have come before us: Jesus, Confucius, Mohammed. An international secret society of these mutants now exists. Salvation is coming — metaphysical transformation through the techniques of applied mutation. Pauwels and Bergier are optimistic, for they promise gnostic salvation. Man's very mind is the agent of salvation; salvation comes through knowledge (Socrates's famous dictum): "We are on the side of the invaders, on the side of the life that is coming, on the side of a changing age and changing ways of thought. Error? Madness? A man's life is only justified by his efforts, however feeble, towards better understanding. And to understand better is to become more attached. The more I understand, the more I love; for everything that is understood is good."[28]

Gnostic Salvation

The ideal of exhaustive knowledge is placed before mankind. If mankind, or an elite secret society of mutants, can attain exhaustive understanding, sin and the effects of sin will be erased from the universe. Man will be lord of creation. Nothing human is foreign to the alchemist, and nothing understood can be evil. This is the ancient

---

27. *Ibid.*, p. 341.
28. *Ibid.*, p. 416.

gnostic heresy: salvation by knowledge. The leap of being is ultimately intellectual, not moral. The secret knowledge of the adepts
shall redeem mankind and cope with the universe. As Crowley
describes the process: "The adept should have realized that his Act of
Union with the angel implies (1) the death of his old mind save in so
far as his unconscious elements preserve its memory when they absorb it, and (2) the death of his unconscious elements themselves.
But their death is rather a going forth to renew their life through
love."[29] The mind dies in self-transcendence (as Crowley's seems to
have done from time to time); the adept transcends memory, logic,
and creaturehood. Beyond human limitations is love. But only
beyond human limitations, if Crowley's life is any indication.

Man becomes God. "By the use of this system," Crowley asserts,
"the magician is able ultimately to unify the whole of his knowledge
— to transmute, even on the Intellectual Plane, the Many into the
One."[30] Crowley knew the language of alchemy. It is the quest for
exhaustive knowledge which motivates Eliade, too: the triumphant
advent of the post-Christian era (and few men can claim the breadth
of knowledge that Eliade has). "Now an encounter with the 'totally
other,' whether conscious or unconscious, gives rise to an experience
of a religious nature. It is not impossible that our age may go down
to posterity as the first to rediscover those 'diffuse religious experiences' which were destroyed by the triumph of Christianity. It is
equally possible that the attraction of the unconscious and its activities, the interest in myths and symbols, the fascination of the exotic,
the primitive, the archaic, and encounters with 'others,' with all the
ambivalent feelings they imply — that all this may one day appear as
a new type of religious experience."[31]

What is coming is a *new form of humanism,* according to Eliade.
"Now we may anticipate that all these elements are preparing for the
growth of a new humanism, which will not be a replica of the old.
For what principally concerns us now is to integrate the researches
of orientalists, ethnologists, depth psychologists, and historians of
religion in order to arrive at a total knowledge of man."[32] Humanism
can have encounters with the "wholly other," Barthian style, or with

---

29. Crowley, *Magick*, p. 287.
30. *Ibid.*, p. 5.
31. Eliade, *The Two and the One* (New York: Harper Torchbooks, [1962] 1969), pp.
11-12.
32. *Ibid.*, p. 12.

"others," LaVey and Crowley style. We are about to arrive at the total knowledge of man, inaugurating a new religious era which will be a new humanistic era. The West is about to be swallowed up in universal world history.[33]

The Whole Earth Catalog was the 1970's Bible of the counter-culture, drop-outs, retreatists, dome-building, back-to-nature communalists. The *Catalog* proclaims in its introduction: "PURPOSE: We *are* as gods and might as well get good at it." This is humanism's religious first principle, and alchemists, magicians, and occultists of all kinds can co-operate in terms of it.

The Abolition of Time

Time is inexorable, merciless, and linear. This is the Western view of time. The rebellion of man brought forth the burden of time, so that the Book of Revelation promises a day when "there should be time no longer" (10:6). But that day is in the future, the culmination of world history. The day of judgment shall finally remove the burden of time for the godly, and death, the last enemy, shall be overcome (I Cor. 15:55).

This view of time clearly involves the belief in a *radically discontinuous event.* "Behold, I shew you a mystery; We shall not all sleep, but we shall all be changed, In a moment, in the twinkling of an eye, at the last trump: for the trumpet shall sound, and the dead shall be raised incorruptible, and we shall be changed" (I Cor. 15:51-52). But it is an event in which man's actions, ritually or otherwise, play no part. Jesus, speaking in his capacity as perfect humanity, admitted that He did not know when the day of judgment would come: "But of that day and hour knoweth no man, not the angels of heaven, but my Father only" (Matt. 24:36).

While Christians look forward to that day, the church has never institutionalized or ritualized the day of judgment, except insofar as the symbolism of baptism implicitly points to death and resurrection, and the burial formulas, especially for seamen, mention the final day. It is significant that the church has not ritualized either the beginning or the end, neither creation nor the day of judgment, for God and He alone is sovereign over these two events. Time is totally in the hands of God. It is the means by which His plan is unfolded.

---

33. *Ibid.*, pp. 13-14.

East vs. West

Such a view of linear time is not shared by all peoples of the world. Were it not for the distinctly Western ideologies and Christianity, the primitive countries and the Eastern cultures would not believe in it, and many of them still do not. Time is viewed as a metaphysical condition to be transcended, rather than cursed by God in response to an act of moral rebellion by man. The burden of time can therefore be thrown off, the non-Christian believes, by karmic evolution through innumerable lives, or by communal ritual, or by asceticism. If men can return to the Time before time, actually or ritually, this return symbolizes escape from time. In ritually participating in the creation event — when the god brought form out of the primeval chaos — the community can hope to escape time's bondage in the future. These cultures are therefore backward-looking; in the past is their hope of collective salvation. The future-orientation of the West, as well as the West's commitment to the irreversibility of time, is not present in pagan cultures.

Mircea Eliade's description of Indian thought indicates the extent of the difference between Western and Eastern approaches to the question of time. When we realize the startling growth of interest in Eastern philosophy and religion among the West's young, Eliade's summary takes on an increased importance. "According to the Buddha, as indeed in Indian thought as a whole, man's life is doomed to suffering by the very fact that it is lived in Time. Here we touch upon a vast question which could not be summarized in a few pages, but it may be said, as a simplification, that suffering in this world is based upon, and indefinitely prolonged by, *karma*, therefore by the temporal nature of existence. It is the law of *karma* which imposes the innumerable transmigrations, the eternal return to existence and therefore to suffering. To deliver oneself from the karmic law, to rend the veil of Maya [the illusion of existence — G.N.] — this is equivalent to spiritual 'cure.' The Buddha is 'the king of physicians' and his message is proclaimed as the 'new medicine.' The philosophies, the ascetic and contemplative techniques and the mystical systems of India are all directed to the same end: the cure of man of the pain of existence in Time. It is by 'burning up' even the very last germ of a future life that one finally breaks out of the karmic cycle and attains deliverance from Time."[34]

---

34. Eliade, *Myths, Dreams, and Mysteries* (New York: Harper Torchbooks, [1957] 1967), p. 49.

One of the techniques used by Indian mystics to escape time's bondage is an exploration by the mystic of his previous incarnations. In doing so, one "burns up" his karmic residual. Buddha and his contemporary sages practiced this technique and recommended it. The goal is to retrace time backwards to the point of time's origin, "the point where existence first 'burst' into the world and unleashed time. Then one rejoins that paradoxical instant before which Time was not, because nothing had been manifested." Further, "to re-live one's past lives would also be to understand them and, to a certain degree, 'burn up' one's 'sins'; that is, the sum of the deeds done in the state of ignorance and capitalised from one life to the next by the law of *karma*. But there is something of even greater importance: one attains to the beginning of Time and enters the Timeless — the eternal present which preceded the temporal existence inaugurated by the 'fall' into human existence. In other words, it is possible, starting from any moment of temporal duration, to exhaust that duration by retracing in course to the source and so to come out into the Timeless, into eternity. But that is to transcend the human condition and to regain the non-conditioned state, which preceded the fall into Time and the wheel of existences."[35]

Man's goal, in this perspective, is to transcend all created limits. The existence of such limits, manifested best by the existence of time, is an intolerable burden. Men are to seek the pre-creation state, which was non-conditioned. This can mean one of two states: either total union with the metaphysical One or total and perfect spiritual autonomy. There have been yogis pursuing each of these goals: the One (fusion with Oneness) or the Many (isolated autonomy).[36]

The primary difference between the Indian view of time and the view of other pagan cultures is that in Indian theory man plays no part in the periodic re-creation of the world. The goal of ritual regeneration of the cosmos, such as we find in the seasonal fertility festivals of most primitive cultures, is not pursued. Instead, the goal is escape from the cosmic cycle.[37] But the means is the same in each case: the attempted return to the Time before time.

The question of time is the question of mortality. Why do men die? By reconstructing the creation events, men hope to explain how

---

35. *Ibid.*, p. 12.

36. Eliade, *Rites and Symbols of Initiation: The Mysteries of Birth and Rebirth* (New York: Harper Torchbooks, [1958] 1965), p. 107.

37. Eliade, *Myth and Reality* (New York: Harper Torchbooks, [1963] 1968), p. 62.

death came into the world. But the history of the creation is a sacred history; the concern with these pre-time events is soteriological: men want salvation from imperfection, a release from the bondage of mortality. The concern with profane history is reduced accordingly. Written records of the actions of actual men, apart from the tales of heroes and demi-gods, are not crucially important. It was the coming of Christianity, with its commitment to God's actions in human history, which brought the triumph of the book over the oral tradition, especially the secret oral tradition of the initiated. A people without a written history is a people without a history today.[38] Only by a lifetime of incomparable scholarly labor can a book like Maenchen-Helfen's study of the Huns be produced, and he never did complete it in his lifetime. They left no written records; the details concerning them must be derived from artistic fragments and the records of those nations, predominantly Christian, that the Huns invaded.

Astral Projection

One of the techniques used by adepts to escape the restraints of time and space is astral projection. Castaneda said that he used such techniques during his initiation. The book and movie, *The Other*, has the young occultist-murderer develop his powers through this exercise. Thelma Moss, the UCLA parapsychological researcher, devotes a chapter of her book, *The Probability of the Impossible* (1974), to out-of-body experiences. But one of the most frightening cases took place in June of 1975. A yoga instructor, Robert Antoszczyk, told his associates that he was going into seclusion in his room to practice astral projection. On June 3, the UPI story says, "His lifeless body was found on the floor of the room, in a yoga position that is used for deep meditation. He was flat on his back with his thumbs between his index and middle fingers." His mother claimed that he was in perfect health and did not use drugs. Local yoga experts in Ann Arbor, where the incident took place, asserted that such practices are not recommended. As a revealing sidelight, the report said that he taught his yoga classes at the local YMCA.

Astral projection and reincarnation are taught by the Edgar Cayce movement—Cayce was an astral projectionist, or at least he diagnosed people from great distances and described their surround-

---

38. *Ibid.*, pp. 157-61.

ings — and by the Church of Scientology. An important part of the initiation of shamans (medicine men) in primitive cultures is the out-of-body experience of flight.[39] In short, however such experiences occur in the perception of the actors, astral projection is a traditional means of transcending both time and space. It is a denial of the binding nature of man's normal faculties. Where it exists, Western concepts of privacy are made most difficult. Nevertheless Western techniques of spying and electronic communication are a lot more reliable and in the long run, more of a threat to privacy. Technology has made possible the equivalent power of astral projection, but it has placed such power in the hands of third-level bureaucrats instead of an initiated elite of adepts. The West has democratized, or at least bureaucratized, the ecstatic dreams of the shamans of the world, and has added videotape recordings as well.

"Time Is Money"

The West is concerned with reducing the burden of time. The communications revolution, the computer revolution, the data-retrieval networks, the highway, the jet plane, and numerous other features of Western culture have provided men with savings in time undreamed of by the masses. But there has been a difference: the burden of time has been recognized as ultimately unyielding to the manipulations of men. Each saving of time has a cost; technology can reduce this cost, but it cannot reduce it to zero.

The quest for zero-cost reductions in time is demonic. It denies that man faces fundamental limits as a creature. Western man may not be satisfied with running a hundred meters in 9.9 seconds. He admits that he cannot safely predict how low this time restraint will fall. But he affirms what the occultist will not admit: that the time it takes a man to travel one hundred meters cannot and will not be reduced to zero. The fact that Western man counts the cost accurately, i.e., can calculate the weight of each burden, enables him to reduce the burden through effective planning, discipline, and above all, capital formation. The socialist or communist, who affirms the religion of the occult — that the limits of scarcity are not natural, but are man-created — is less rational, cannot calculate economically, and threatens economic productivity whenever he takes over the reigns of political power. Socialist economics is the demonic philosophy of

39. Eliade, *Shamanism* (Princeton: Princeton University Press/Bollingen, [1964] 1974), pp. 127-44.

"stones into bread."[40] It denies the limits imposed by man's finitude and man's ethically fallen nature. The yogi and the commissar are not so very different after all.

Time and Social Class

Where present-oriented men dominate, culture degenerates. If the future-orientation of the Christian West is not present in a society, that society will be essentially lower class and stagnant. Men get what they pay for. If they prefer instant gratification, then they will pay for it at the expense of capital formation and greater future output.

Prof. Edward Banfield's classic book, *The Unheavenly City* (1970), earned him the wrath of political liberals because he argued forcefully that the Negro ghetto is what it is because of the time preference, i.e., the view of the future, held by the majority of those who live there. One's class position is determined, not by income, but by one's view of the future. For arguing in this manner, radical students and many of his professorial peers pressured him to leave Harvard University. (He returned several years later.)

This kind of thinking was clearly apostate: it argued against the acceptable tenets of liberal environmentalism. It meant, as Banfield specifically said, that apart from a change in the time preference of those who lived in the ghetto, all the wealth redistribution in the world will not lift the ghetto dwellers out of poverty. At best, the redistributed wealth will enable some ghetto residents to move out. He writes: "At the present-oriented end of the scale, the lower-class individual lives from moment to moment. If he has any awareness of a future, it is of something fixed, fated, beyond his control: things happen *to* him, he does not *make* them happen. Impulse governs his behavior, either because he cannot discipline himself to sacrifice a present for a future satisfaction or because he has no sense of the future. He is therefore radically improvident: whatever he cannot consume immediately he considers valueless. His bodily needs (especially for sex) and his taste for 'action' take precedence over everything else — and certainly over any work routine. He works only as he must to stay alive, and drifts from one unskilled job to another, taking no interest in the work."[41]

---

40. Ludwig von Mises, "Stones into Bread, the Keynesian Miracle," in Henry Hazlitt (ed.), *Critics of Keynesian Economics* (Princeton: Van Nostrand, 1960).

41. Edward Banfield, *The Unheavenly City* (Boston: Little, Brown & Co., 1970), p. 53.

In the face of a lower-class time perspective, the liberal political remedies have failed, especially welfare programs. In St. Paul, Minnesota, 6 percent of the city's families absorbed 77 percent of its public assistance, 51 percent of its health services, and 56 percent of its mental health and correctional casework services.[42] Furthermore, "It is not at all unlikely that cultures (as opposed to individuals) change their time horizons so as to adapt to changes in environment, but any such change must occur very slowly: a certain stability over time is a defining characteristic of culture."[43] He fails to mention religious revival. What we have seen for over a decade in America is religious revival: the higher-class families have seen many of their children converted to the lower-class, present-oriented philosophies of the East. The denial of time's boundaries has economic and cultural consequences. These consequences are disastrous.

Altered Consciousness

It was in the mid-1960's that hallucinogenic drugs became known as mind-expanding drugs. Somehow, the public was expected to believe that the expansion of the mind which is produced by these drugs is beneficial. After all, isn't expansion like growth? Isn't it a good thing to have one's perspective broadened? Isn't one of the goals of higher education cultural and intellectual broadening? The doors of perception were to be swung open, and whole new worlds would be available for exploration. The narrow band of frequencies in which our eyes and ears operate was no longer sufficient; our "vibrations" had to be increased. Our narrow, Western, middle-class blinders had to be ripped from our foreheads by means of new chemical substances. It would be "better living through chemistry" for one and all.

There was a messianic enthusiasm about drugs in the very early stages of the counter culture. The introduction of the Beatles' "Rubber Soul" album was generally regarded as a first step. The "Yeah, Yeah, Yeah" days of wanting to hold hands were gone; the Beatles had entered a new, more creative phase. The source of the new creativity, so the rumor went, was marijuana or some other drug, such as LSD. As a matter of fact, Ringo Starr, the group's drummer, later admitted that they had been "fooling around" with drugs, but that they had stopped. In 1965, the year of "Rubber Soul," the euphoria had

---

42. *Ibid.*, p. 127.
43. *Ibid.*, p. 222.

not yet worn off. Over the next five years, risk-oriented members of
the counter-culture began a chemical quest for nirvana. The results
were predictable: burned-out minds, death from drug overdoses,
shattered reality, shattered dreams. By 1970, the Beatles were about
to break up. Reality had asserted itself once again.

By 1970, the word was also out on LSD: too dangerous. Yet in
the interim, marijuana had become middle-class, taken as seriously
by the general public as bathtub gin had been taken in 1930. There
were still the equivalent of the "dries," cautioning young people
about the marijuana-heroin link, but not even the police were using
that line any longer. Timothy Leary reversed himself a few years
into the 1970's, repudiating his slogan: "Tune in, turn on, drop out."
The counter culture had grown up bit. It had found jobs scarce and
stereophonic albums more expensive than in 1965. The days of grass
and roses were over.

Nevertheless, a profound change had taken place in the West, for
the counter-culture's influence had been international. There was a
new acceptance of altered states of consciousness by a significant
minority of the public, especially the intellectuals, the young, and
the growing legion of sideline occultists, so that by the early 1970's,
there was a lot of discussion about alternatives to drugs. The Jesus
Freaks advised people to "turn on to Jesus." The Hare Krishnas
recommended rhythmic chanting. Proponents of the new techniques
of bio-feedback (alpha-wave machines) had their alternative, in kit
form for the less affluent. The Beatles had gone on Transcendental
Meditation, or TM (and, since the words are trademarked, as any
good business name should be, it is advertised as TM™), and their
followers responded by the millions. The Beatles are gone, but TM
is going strong. ("Not a religion," the advertising says, just as yoga
techniques are only an old body-building program from India.)
Cheap California wines became popular after 1970, although the recession of 1974-75 has led to some bankruptcies in the California
wine grape business. Drunkenness, the world's ancient pastime, was
back in favor, but now there were a whole series of techniques and
substances to supplement man's old stand-by. Drunkenness might
still be regarded as gross though legitimate, but TM, yoga, alpha-
wave training, and chanting, while a bit odd, were baptized avant-
garde and were officially respectable.

Perception and Responsibility

The problem with drunkenness is the problem with pot is the problem with LSD: the deliberate altering of the human consciousness merely for the sake of alteration, or for psychological escape, is a form of cultural and religious rebellion. "And be not drunk with wine," St. Paul writes, "wherein is excess, but be filled with the Spirit" (Eph. 5:18). Paul could advise Timothy to "use wine for thy stomach's sake" (I Tim. 5:23), so he was not issuing a general prohibition on what we might call social drinking. But he did condemn drunkenness. Why? Because drunkenness is the deliberate distortion of a man's perception of God's created reality. It is a denial of the creation to be drunk — the twisting of God's revelation of Himself through his creation. In short, man is forbidden to indulge in the distortion of his mental faculties merely for the sake of escaping normal reality. (This is not to imply that anesthetics are illegitimate, for these make the physician's task easier in operating and increase the likelihood of a man's restoration to health. Health, after all, is normal for a godly, progressive society, i.e., normative: Ex. 23:25).

Each man is personally responsible for his actions. This is the starting point of all human action. Each man is responsible before a sovereign God who has created reality. Each man is therefore responsible in terms of his lawful sphere of influence. From him to whom much is given, much is expected (Luke 12:48). Therefore, for any person to assess his own gifts and responsibilities, he must strive to perceive reality accurately. One of the most important economic developments of all time is the double-entry bookkeeping ledger. It enables men to keep an accurate record of their liabilities and assets. Without a free market which can assess the economic value of scarce economic resources, there can be no rational economic calculation and therefore no rational economic planning. Unless men are trying to conceal something, they do not deliberately make false entries in their business ledgers. The use of hallucinogenic drugs, yoga techniques of meditation, and other self-transcendence devices is comparable to making deliberately false entries into a ledger. It reduces men's ability to make accurate assessments of their actions in relation to a real external reality.

That yoga techniques should be successful in altering men's perception should come as no surprise. The philosophy of Indian monism, like that of Zen Buddhism, is to deny all reality. Reality is an illusion; existence is maya. The first step at transcending reality is control of the body. Hatha yoga techniques are the outward form of an inner system of philosophy. The goal of yoga is the liberation of man from the illusion of existence, and physical culture is the first step in this "liberation." Mental purification and spiritual awakening come from the manipulation of the body. This, of course, is almost the mirror image of Christianity, which teaches that regeneration precedes the acts of men, for "the natural man receiveth not the things of the Spirit of God" (I Cor. 2:14). The Christian doctrine of the Fall of man is ethical; the Indian is metaphysical. The Christian responds outwardly to a change in his inward condition; the yogi attempts to change his inward perception of reality—illusion—by manipulating his body. The Indian mystic is trying to escape from created reality, and various methods are used: asceticism, libertinism, withdrawal from society, meditation, immersion in work. The goal, however, is the systematic distortion of perception.

One of the first things to be distorted, as mentioned earlier, is the sense of time. This is also equally true of the hallucinogenic drugs. Aldous Huxley, in his *Doors of Perception* (1954), comments on his altered sense of time:

And along with indifference to space there went an even more complete indifference to time.

"There seems to be plenty of it," was all I would answer, when the investigator asked me to say what I felt about time.

Plenty of it, but exactly how much was entirely irrelevant. I could, of course, have looked at my watch; but my watch, I knew, was in another universe. My experience had been, was still, of an indefinite duration or alternatively of a perpetual present made up of one continually changing apocalypse.[44]

Plenty of time: for the Eastern mystic, yes; for the Western thinker, no. "Time is money," wrote Ben Franklin. But even more to the point are St. Paul's words, just two sentences prior to his statement on drunkenness: "See then that ye walk circumspectly, not as fools, but as wise, Redeeming [buying back] the time, because the days are evil" (Eph. 5:15-16). Time is the one truly unrenewable resource in man's life, but *only in a world of linear time and without reincarnation*.

---

44. Aldous Huxley, *The Doors of Perception* (New York: Perennial Library, [1954] 1970), p. 21.

What Huxley found was *meaningful irrelevance*. "I looked down by chance, and went on passionately staring by choice, at my own crossed legs. Those folds in the trowsers—what a labyrinth of endlessly significant complexity! And the texture of the gray flannel—how rich, how deeply, mysteriously sumptuous!"[45] He stared, seemingly for an immensely long time, at a chair.[46] He had the sense of being separate from himself.[47] Yet for all of these mindless experiences, he calls for more of the same—or better. Alcohol and tobacco cannot be prohibited, but they are not safe. "The universal and everpresent urge to self-transcendence is not to be abolished by slamming the currently popular Doors in the Wall. The only reasonable policy is to open other, better doors in the hope of inducing men and women to exchange their old bad habits for new and less harmful ones. Some of these other, better doors will be social and technological in nature, others religious or psychological, others dietetic, educational, athletic. But the need for frequent chemical vacations from intolerable selfhood and repulsive surroundings will undoubtedly remain."[48]

We need a new, non-habit-forming drug, cheaply synthesizable, less toxic than present ones. "And, on the positive side, it should produce changes more interesting, more intrinsically valuable than mere sedation or dreaminess, delusions of omnipotence or release from inhibition."[49]

A well-known fact about the use of LSD is that the user needs someone "straight" in the same room with him, or at least someone who is chained to the perception of reality. Psychologist Paul Stern writes: "Ordinarily one does not trip alone, but needs at least one other person who officially functions as guide or as a sort of safety net."[50] In a philosophical sense, Huxley wants to find a new hallucinogen which can, in and of itself, serve as a rational, "straight" guide. No mere dreaminess for him. We need meaning—the educated, well-read man's kind of meaning. But this desire is absolutely impossible to fulfill.

"In general," writes Stern, "drug users tend to overestimate the stimulus value of hallucinogens. Drugs do not 'cause,' in any meaningful sense of the term, the so-called hallucinogenic experience, as

---

45. *Ibid.*, p. 30.
46. *Ibid.*, p. 53.
47. *Ibid.*, p. 60.
48. *Ibid.*, p. 64.
49. *Ibid.*, p. 65.
50. Paul J. Stern, *In Praise of Madness* (New York: Norton, 1972), p. 86.

the stylus of the stereo does not 'cause' the music filling our room. To the extent that hallucinogens are effective, they act as catalysts releasing latent images stored in the mind."[51] Huxley hopes for built-in restraints from chemistry. He cannot have them. All he can hope for is that other users of such drugs, even the "perfect drug," will have pleasant, uplifting, and even educational escapes from reality. It will be like a day in the countryside, assuming the users like and appreciate the countryside. But what if the users like and appreciate mass murder. What if the drug users are the members of Charles Manson's family? Who will serve as the straight man in a society of Mansons?

Cosmic Consciousness

The battle over consciousness is the supreme human battle. Karl Marx called for class consciousness. Women's Liberation groups call for consciousness raising. R. M. Bucke, in a mediocre turn-of-the-century book which has somehow become a kind of classic, calls for *Cosmic Consciousness* (1901). The Western occultists call for Christ consciousness. The doors of perception are governed by first principles of interpretation, and each religious or ideological group wants its first principles sovereign in regulating other men's conscious (or unconscious) perception.

"The Saviour of man is Cosmic Consciousness — in Paul's language — the Christ."[52] So writes R. M. Bucke, who has assembled selections from the more famous historic figures who believed in cosmic consciousness (or who Bucke thinks so believed). His is another version of monism, as are most of the systems of cosmic consciousness. Like so many late-nineteenth-century illuminists, Bucke believed fervently in evolutionary progress, socialism, and mystical illumination.[53] The goal of cosmic consciousness is self-deification: "Finally the basic fact in cosmic consciousness is implied in its name — that fact is consciousness of the cosmos — this is what is called in the East the 'Brahmic Splendor,' which is in Dante's phrase capable of transhumanizing a man into a god."[54] Clearly, Bucke's own brief experience of cosmic consciousness did nothing to improve his sentence structure. He quotes Walt Whitman: "Divine am I, inside and

---

51. *Idem.*
52. R. M. Bucke, *Cosmic Consciousness* (New York: Dover, [1901] 1969), p. 6.
53. *Ibid.*, pp. 4, 22.
54. *Ibid.*, p. 17.

out."[55] He quotes John Yepes (St. John of the Cross; d. 1591):

For the soul courageously resolved on passing, interiorly and exteriorly, beyond the limits of its own nature, enters illimitably within the supernatural, which has no measure, but contains all measure imminently within itself. To arrive there is to depart hence, going away, out of oneself, as far as possible from this vile state to that which is highest of all. Therefore, rising above all that may be known and understood, temporally and spiritually, the soul must earnestly desire to reach that which in this life cannot be known, and which the heart cannot conceive; and, leaving behind all actual and possible taste and feeling of sense and spirit, must desire earnestly to arrive at that which transcends all sense and all feeling. . . . The more the soul strives to become blind and annihilated as to all interior and exterior things, the more it will be filled with faith and love and hope.[56]

The Void

This distinctly Eastern view of reality — the void — is a common feature of all monistic systems of mysticism. Van Til calls the process the "integration into the void." With reference to modern psychology, he writes: "The real reason why modern psychology has left no room for responsibility is found in the fact that it has taken the whole of the human personality in all its aspects, self-conscious and subconscious, and immersed it in an ultimate metaphysical void. Man cannot be responsible to the void."[57] It should surprise no one to learn that the founders of modern psychology, Freud and Jung, were both keenly interested in occult subjects, that Freud once remarked that he regretted not having devoted more of his life's work to a study of ESP, and that Freud was convinced at one stage of his career that cocaine would be a wonder drug for psychological therapy.[58] Salvation is in the void, beyond the categories of rationality, beyond the pressures of created reality.

The void need not be empty to function as a void. It may not be Buddhist Nirvana — the abolition of all existence — but if it is devoid of structure or meaning, it is a void. The experiences of the so-called higher consciousness remove men from the realms of created reality

---

55. *Ibid.*, p. 194.
56. *Ibid.*, pp. 145-46.
57. Cornelius Van Til, *Psychology of Religion*, Volume IV of *In Defense of the Faith* (Phillipsburg, New Jersey: Presbyterian & Reformed, [1961] 1971), p. 73.
58. Nandor Fodor, *Freud, Jung, and Occultism* (New Hyde Park, New York: University Books, 1971).

in which the direct confrontation with structure and meaning are clear-cut. The observer may train himself to say "chaos" when he examines his surroundings, but no one, other than a lunatic, can convince himself of this for lengthy periods of time. Reality and time are burdens, for they are cursed. Those who are in ethical rebellion feel the weight of reality, and they seek to flee into a more chaotic realm. In chaos and meaningless they believe they can escape God, escape their own creaturehood, and escape final judgment. They are wrong, but this is their hope.

Another Dead End

Not all Eastern thinkers are committed to the cultivation of states of altered consciousness. One contemporary Zen Buddhist master has written: "An ancient Zen saying has it that to become attached to one's own enlightenment is as much a sickness as to exhibit a maddeningly active ego. Indeed, the profounder the enlightenment, the worse the illness. . . . My own sickness lasted ten years."[59] Krishnamurti, a modern Indian religious teacher, has said much the same thing: "Meditation is not the mere experiencing of something beyond everyday thought and feeling nor is it the pursuit of visions and delights. An immature and squalid little mind can and does have visions of expanding consciousness, and experiences which it recognizes according to its own conditioning. This immaturity may be greatly capable of making itself successful in this world and achieving fame and notoriety. The gurus whom it follows are of the same quality and state. Meditation does not belong to such as these."[60]

One of the significant aspects of Aldous Huxley's life was that he finally abandoned hope in mystical "higher" consciousness at the very end of his life. A week before he died, at a time when he believed that LSD could put a man in touch permanently with the Tibetan Buddhists' "Clear Light of the Void," he realized, as Zaehner puts it, "that this was probably a gross misrepresentation of what was actually happening." While he was under the influence of a sedative, his wife made a tape recording of his discussion. "The whole thing has been very strange because in a way it was very good —but in a way it was absolutely terrifying, showing that when one

---

59. R. C. Zaener, *Zen, Drugs and Mysticism* (New York: Pantheon, 1972), p. 98.
60. *Ibid.*, p. 115.

thinks one's got beyond oneself, one hasn't. . . . I began with this marvelous sense of this cosmic gift, and then ended up with a rueful sense that one can be deceived. . . . It was an insight, but at the same time the most dangerous of errors . . . inasmuch as one was worshipping oneself"[61] (author's italics omitted). There would be no salvation through *soma* drugs in some brave new world, no final creation of an electric Tibet.

Despite these protests, those who have promoted Eastern techniques of mystic illumination have unquestionably gained followers on the basis of a promised entry into "higher" consciousness. Western men want results, they want action, they want bright lights and communion with God. Furthermore, they want these things in no more than three easy lessons. Maturity is not what most of them are after, especially Eastern maturity. Why import a foreign maturity when Christianity at least delivers the compound growth rates? If Zen Buddhism requires hostility to all reality, including altered consciousness, then it is easier to flirt with a less consistent form of relativism and world-denial.

Elitism vs. Common Faith

A religion like Zen Buddhism is totally elitist. It is not simply that only a few people ever get involved. If that were all there were to it, Americans searching for avant-garde religious commitments would have far less trouble. The intensity of Zen Buddhism's training in total irrationalism necessarily limits its members. Abbot Zenkei Shibayama, a modern Zen master, has admitted this: "It may not be difficult to *talk about* the experience of awakening to 'Self-nature' or 'True Self' which we have deep at the bottom of our personalities, but to come to this realization experientially as the fact of one's own actual experience, is not easy at all. It is so very difficult that it cannot be easily attained by ordinary people."[62] In short, "not everyone can be expected to have the training required for the attainment of the exquisite moment of *satori*."[63]

In contrast to these elitist religions, so obviously individualistic as far as the promised blessings are concerned, Christianity has always been a religion of the average man. We must become as little children, Christ said, to enter the kingdom of God (Matt. 18:3). The

---

61. *Ibid.*, p. 108.
62. *Ibid.*, p. 81.
63. *Ibid.*, p. 116.

breadth of membership in an open congregation has inevitably led to
the presence of hypocrites, immature beginners, and all sorts of weak
characters inside the membership, but that is the price of open doors.
The initiatory secret societies, the narrow membership of ascetic bro-
therhoods, the elitist access to altered consciousness may appeal to
true elitists and the temporary avant-garde hangers-on (before the
training takes up too much of their energy), but the exclusion of the
broad mass of humanity has confined these movements to groups of
monks or subsidized solitary adepts who contemplate their navels as a
technique for merging with the meaningless, monistic, divine void.
Societies are not constructed by the likes of these. Their productivity
is generally minimal, and very often they are subsidized by the "unwashed masses" who are willing to get dirty in order to be productive.
But it is this very element of elitism which has caught the attention of
the "hipsters, flipsters, and finger-poppin' daddies" (to quote "Lord"
Buckley, the 1950's cult figure) and the drifting young who want membership in groups sufficiently weird to shock their liberal parents.

The Politics of Self-Transcendence

Their parents, however, who are equally adrift, refuse to be ex-
cluded so easily. They, too, can wear bell-bottoms (which the U.S.
Navy finally abandoned in the 1970's), beads, and smoke marijuana.
They can also search for cosmic consciousness. And once they find
it, they will try to politicize it.

The International Cooperation Council

In *None Dare Call It Witchcraft*, I devoted considerable space to a
Southern California organization, the International Cooperation
Council (ICC). The ICC was a clearing house for every pseudo-Eastern
society, every higher consciousness club, every association of do-good-
ing, bead-wearing, middle-aged, swami-following ladies in the state. It
was the organization which can get members of the Lucis (formerly Lucifer) Trust and the Center for the Study of Democratic Institutions to
sit down and discuss the nature of the Good Society, and the bureaucratic World Constitution which will be necessary to impose vegetarian
ecstacy upon a thoughtless and underdeveloped world. Its slogan:

> Fostering the Emergence of a New Universal
> Man and Civilization Based on Unity in Diversity
> Among All Peoples

In 1979, the Unity-in-Diversity Council took over the ICC. We can still profit from a review of the older organization's activities, since it was an important clearing house in an important region in the period of the initial "coming of age" of New Age philosophy. In the mid-1970's, the ICC sponsored annual consciousness celebrations and other activities. It published a quarterly magazine, *The Cooperator*. It involved itself in educational activities, supplying any and all schools with materials. Its description of itself sounds quite progressive:

The International Cooperation Council (ICC) is a non-profit coordinating body of autonomous individuals and groups, each seeking in its own unique way to contribute constructively to the global transformation of our time. Based on the principle of "unity in diversity among all peoples," ICC is an experiment whose goal is to foster the emergence of a new universal man and civilization serving the well-being of all mankind. Utilizing the methods and knowledge of modern science in concert with valid insights of religion, philosophy, and the arts, the creative activities of ICC cover a spectrum from the search into man's inner nature to dynamic social action. More than one hundred and twenty-five groups are now cooperating with ICC.

What groups they are! Here is a partial listing:

> Army of Parapsychology and Medicine
> Ananda Meditation Retreat
> Aquarian Arcane College
> Association for Humanistic Psychology
> Astara, Inc.
> Astro Consciousness Institute for Self-Enlightenment and Peace
> Avatar Meher Baba Group
> The Boston Visionary Cell
> Buddhist Publication Society
> California Institute for Asian Studies
> Center for the Study of Democratic Institutions
> Center for the Study of Power
> Church of Essential Science
> Committee on Cosmic Humanism
> Esperanto League for North America
> Foundation for Universal Understanding
> Inner-Space Interpreters Service
> Institute of Human Engineering
> International Association of Educators for World Peace

Konko-Kyo Church of Izuo
The Love Project
The Mandala Society, Inc.
The New Age Press
Ontological Society
Rosicrucian Fellowship
Servers of the Great Ones
Sivananda Yoga Center
Sri Aurobindo Society
Technocracy, Inc.
Temple of Peace
Temple of Understanding
Theosophical Order of Service
Thomas Jefferson Research Center
United Nations Association
United World
Women's Universal Movement, Inc.
World Family
World Institute Council
World Union
You Institute

This list is taken from the *1974 Directory* (8th Annual Edition). Hopefully, it provides a general sense of what the ICC was really all about. Southern California is undoubtedly the congregating point in the United States for such groups as these, and it is nice to know that modern man's hunger for community is still alive. The problem for the rest of us is the kind of community these groups have in mind. In the Spring-Summer, 1973 issue of *The Coordinator*, the editorial, "A Model for Mankind," informs us:

Mankind is indeed being born and we of this time have the great privilege of being present at the creation. We must do everything we can to ensure that the new infant is not misshapen at birth but is well-formed and healthy so that it can have the maximum opportunity for surviving and growing to realize its full potential in the universe.

Mankind, it should be noted, is an androgynous being, having both male and female characteristics in one. It will grow both through an increasing complexity-consciousness of each cell and by individual cell multiplication. However, for Mankind to survive and flourish, a cure for the cancer of unlimited population growth must be found. When Mankind is ready to expand outward into space a new phase of growth can start, but that is primarily for coming generations. Our immediate task, in the child-hood of mankind, is to work for a universal consciousness.

This is a very revealing editorial statement. *First*, it displays the sense of drama: we are present at the creation of a new mankind. A great metaphysical event is about to take place: the autonomous self-liberation of Mankind. We are participating in the creation-event, just as pagan chaos festivals are supposed to allow men to do. *Second*, we are to see that the new infant is not misshapen. In other words, man is about to take control of man, or as C. S. Lewis has warned, some men are about to take control of all the others. This is a common theme in New Age groups: the need for the "illuminated ones" to take charge of the forces of mystical evolution. Evolution is not to be a democratic process. This is as true for the higher consciousness crowd as it is for the rationalistic central planners with their computers.

Third, the editor refers to society as an androgynous being, sim-ultaneously male and female. The image of the androgyne goes back to pagan religious symbolism. It is one of the most important ele-ments of alchemy, East and West. The unity of opposites will pro-duce the Philosopher's Stone, the transformation of man and nature. Prof. Molnar's discussion of this symbol is relevant to any discussion of the politics of transcendence: "In Theosophy, the androgyne figure is the symbol of the union of divine and human nature, and hence of the soul purified in view of ascent to unity in God. The androgyne is thus the archetype of man, symbolizing the end of passion, the final reabsorption of creation. . . . Through androgyne or other forms of Hermetic union the manipulator gains access to magic knowledge and power in order to contemplate nature's work and to complete it in a shorter time than nature would be able to do. Paracelsus was among those who assumed that nature has a certain direction not decipher-able except by the true knower, and that this direction pointed toward the primordial — undivided — state. The task of the Hermetic was to help nature achieve this end."[64] It also appeared from time to time in nineteenth-century revolutionary movements. Prof. Billington com-ments: "The idea that androgyny (the state of Adam before the fall) was the only truly liberated human condition had, since [Jacob] Boehme, been a central concept within the occult tradition."[65]

---

64. Thomas Molnar, *God and the Knowledge of Reality* (New York: Basic Books, 1972), pp. 89-90.

65. James Billington, *Fire in the Minds of Men: Origins of the Revolutionary Faith* (New York: Basic Books, 1980), p. 485.

Fourth, the myth of the population explosion is reaffirmed in order to call into question the legitimacy of one of man's primary means of subduing the earth to the glory of God (Gen. 1:28). Man is not to achieve his goal by means of procreation, but by higher consciousness techniques and social planning. *Fifth*, we must "work for a universal consciousness." In short, we must deny that there are fundamental distinctions between the saved and the lost, while affirming the universal consciousness of mankind.

The quest for the *spiritual unification of mankind* is the product of a distinctly religious impulse. Humanity is the God of the Enlightenment and post-Enlightenment humanism. The unity of the Godhead is an inescapable premise of all religious systems, and humanism's deity is man. Mankind must be forced to unite.[66] Yet at the same time, each man's full and absolute autonomy is the presupposition of man's rebellion. Thus, we find in *The Cooperator* a pair of essays, one calling for economic communism, and the other calling for the abolition of all hierarchical bureaucracies and the establishment of "The Horizontal Society," in which all previous guidelines and institutions in which "the future need not happen to us; we can make it happen."[67] In "The Two Forms of Communism," the author criticizes political Communism, which is not grounded on morality. The premise of this new communism is, of course, that there is no ultimate scarcity of goods and services, but that nature is totally bountiful: "But communism with a little 'c' greatly strengthens Western democracy. The technological resources of the West could be used to eliminate poverty, sickness and suffering to a near-utopian degree if the profit motive and the concept of private property—both of which are based on egoism—were abandoned and replaced with deep concern for human welfare instead of material goals. Eventually, of course, this would lead to the abandonment of money as the basis of our economy, and thereafter it would function on a good-will basis, using barter. In the meantime, every citizen could find his condition immensely improved through the provision of free necessities (food, clothing, shelter) while luxuries such as boats and cars and televisions might be sold at cost— not the inflated cost based on advertising, market research, wholesaler and retailer profit, and stockholding dividends, etc., but the real cost, which would be amazingly low."[68]

---

66. R. J. Rushdoony, *This Independent Republic* (Nutley, New Jersey: Craig Press, 1964), p. 142.

67. *The Cooperator*, V (Spring-Summer, 1973), p. 14.

68. *Ibid.*, p. 12.

In short, there is no curse on nature. Information is free (advertising must go). Capital equipment is free (no stockholder dividends needed). There is no need for an extensive and productive division of labor (no money needed). The planners are omniscient (no market research needed). Cars, boats, clothing, food, and shelter are not "material goals," but are obviously part of the "deep concern for human welfare." Such is the contemplated society in which cosmic consciousness shall reign supreme. This is the rationality of the politics of transcendence.

Predictably, the ICC was trying to take over the curriculum of the California government ("public") school system. Its bulletin, *New Consciousness Education* explicitly stated this as a goal. The reason for selecting the schools is simple: ". . . those participating in schooling are young, and their minds, during the elementary years, are relatively free from prejudice or harmful varieties of stereotypes commonly held by adults."[69] Of course, the curriculum designed by ICC adults would be free from prejudice or harmful varieties of stereotypes commonly held by adults. Besides, the churches are too diverse to organize successfully, and the civil government is too bureaucratic to move rapidly. Furthermore, every nation has a school system. It pays to take over the schools. The ICC gained the support of Assemblyman John Vasconcellos of California, who is the Chairman of the Joint Committee on the Master Plan of Higher Education for the state and Chairman of the Educational Goals Committee. Vasconcellos may be regarded as a bit of a weirdo by his colleagues, but that has not kept him from becoming very influential on the committees for education, where many of the major decisions are made.

My estimation of the ICC's influence is that it had very little. Nevertheless, it was another representative of a whole spectrum of occultist, higher consciousness, humanist organizations that are doing what they can when they can to reconstruct society along the lines of one world government. To try to find *the* central organization that is somehow directing all of the evil we see around us is futile. Besides, it gives too much credit to the organizational abilities of the Satanic opposition. But with multiple pressures politically and educationally from similarly minded groups like the ICC, the men become confused and their leaders can be swayed by organized, concentrated propaganda.

---

69. *New Consciousness Education*, I (Jan. 1973).

The Committee for the Future

The Committee for the Future, was an ICC-related organization, founded by Marx Toys fortune heiress, Barabra Marx Hubbard. It actually called for "the Politics of Transcendence." Its *New Worlds Newsletter* promises: "Estimates differ, but most knowledgeable observers agree that humanity has but a few decades—a cosmic blink of the eye—to alter our behavior and to coordinate our basic functions globally." The fusion of evolutionary humanism and evolutionary Eastern mysticism is striking:

The Politics of Transcendence grows out of new knowledge of the awesome history of our own genesis. With our young, but far-seeing, deep-seeing eyes of science we have caught a first glimpse of our own cosmic origins from a fiery star to our present condition as mankind in the 1970's A.D. From this "parental perspective" through which we view our own development, we appear to be a continuous, energetic process. Each stage of our evolution—the formation of the solar system, earth, life, animal, human—appears as a natural "discontinuity." This future condition, the future stage, the "next step," is as difficult for us to forecast as it would have been for a macro-module in the early seas to produce the cell, or for the single cell to imagine the fantasy of animals, or for those animals to foresee mankind.

The perspective of the Politics of Transcendence sees our present problems as dangerous but natural signals of an evolutionary shift which is occurring in every functional system within the body of mankind—economic, environmental, social, political, spiritual. From this perspective we appear to be making a birthliking transition from earth/only, scarcity systems toward universal, abundance systems.

The crucial action we will take during the period of transition will be profoundly affected by our image of the future—our idea of our "next step." If we see ourselves as a failing race, limited to one planet with finite resources, cursed with the original sin of irremediable selfishness, we shall surely fail. But, if we view ourselves as Universal Humanity, at the beginning of our emancipation from the brutalizing struggle for survival out of the animal world, born into a universe of process and pattern which appears conducive to ever-higher more coherent forms of life, if we see ourselves as capable of synthesizing our physical and psychic powers toward the transcendence of time/space. . . . why then, no one can predict our future. It is open, wide, far, outward, inward, toward a new dimension of being which now attracts millions to become the active constituency of the Politics of Transcendence.[70]

---

70. Barbara M. Hubbard, "The Politics of Transcendence," *New Worlds Newsletter*, Phase II, Vol. II (Jan. 1974), p. 2.

The Coming Paradigm Shift

It is one of those oddities of history that a decade after she wrote these words, Mrs. Hubbard met with me and two or three other men to discuss what she hoped would be a successful campaign to win her the Democratic Party's nomination for Vice President. This was in the fall of 1983. It was obvious to me at the time that she had not the foggiest notion of how politics works, or what it would take to get the nomination. You do not decide to run for Vice President overnight. Furthermore, if she was in a position even to get the nomination, she was wasting her time spending a day with me and the other two or three people, even if one of them did own a couple of local cable television stations. It was a preposterous scheme, but even if it had been successful at the nomination level, it would have produced the same results as Geraldine Ferraro's Vice Presidential nomination: a landslide for the opposition political party.

Mrs. Hubbard did not know who I was. Ironically, I had forgotten that I had included this preceding extract from her *New Worlds Newsletter* in *None Dare Call It Witchcraft*. I asked questions, and she must have thought that I was a good prospective convert to New Age thinking. She told me that I could get a better idea of what the "coming new wave" of political change is all about by reading a very special document. She then gave me a copy of a spiral-bound mimeographed manual entitled, *a proposal for an 18 month grant to establish an* EXPLORATORY PROJECT ON TRANSCENDENTAL POLITICS, submitted by Robert L. Olson, Marc David Sarkady, Clement Bezold, and James Turner, published by the New World Education Fund and the Institute for Alternative Futures. It was a collection of press clippings and extracts from New Age documents. The thing that still impresses me most about this uncopyrighted document is this: it has no date on it. Therefore, the groups' quest for funds can go on forever. It seemed to have been put together in 1981 or 1982. It announces a new, *decentralized* version of the New Age.

The advisory committee includes such luminaries as David Spangler (of Findhorn fame), John Naisbett (whose *Megatrends* had not yet been published but was scheduled for release), Willis Harmon (SRI International, formerly the Stanford Research Institute), California Assemblyman John 'Vasconcellos, Rick Carlson, author of *The End of Medicine* (the title tells all!), and Nancy Jack Todd, cofounder of the New Alchemy Institute (p. iv). It offers a recommended reading bibliography of "recent books that reflect a transformational view." Authors include Tom Hayden (Mr. Jane Fonda), Alvin Toffler, Marilyn Ferguson, Theodore Roszak, Abraham Maslow, Fritjof Capra, Jonas Salk, Mark Satin, Jeremy Rifkin, Gregory Bateson, Illa Prigogine, and Kirkpatrick Sale (p. iii). In short, we find many of the political figures whose names are found in Constance Cumbey's *Hidden Dangers of the Rainbow*, for which she has taken considerable criticism for over-emphasizing the *political* goals of New Age humanism.

Page one begins with a quotation from David Spangler: "Every culture is the product of a world view — a paradigm[71] — that represents that culture's understanding of the nature of reality. . . . We are witnessing the emergence of a new paradigm that radically redefines the nature of our world, the meaning of life, and the nature of the human being and his or her capabilities. As with similar shifts in the past, the result will be a restructuring of society. The nature of the politics that will guide such a society . . . is still unknown territory. What is clear, though, is that in the midst of this change, a different politics will emerge, either one that seeks to delay or prevent that paradigm shift through increasingly repressive policies or one that accepts the responsibility of a new vision and seeks to assist this transition to be as peaceful and skillful as possible."

This is a perceptive comment. Notice first that he openly admits that they have no blueprint for the political future. They reject the whole idea of blueprints. This was true of Marx and the revolutionary anarchist Bakunin in the middle of the nineteenth century. These people do not know what their world will be like, but they expect the rest of us to take it on their word of honor that it will be a marvelous place.

Second, he is correct in his assumption that any serious paradigm shift in a civilization will of necessity have political ramifications. It will affect every sphere of life. A true revolution begins in the minds of men, and it will restructure all areas of human thought: a culture's time perspective, legal order, concepts of political legitimacy, economics, and science. Without transformations in people's attitudes in these areas, no revolution can accurately be said to have taken place.

What Spangler and the New Age proponents do not choose to

---

71. This is the word which was brought into general use by Thomas Kuhn's book, *The Structure of Scientific Revolutions,* published first in 1962, and which gained prominence only after the counter-culture period began in 1965.

discuss, and what I was not yet confident about when I finished *None Dare Call It Witchcraft* in 1976, is this: there is another paradigm shift going on. (There may be dozens; in eras in which major religious transformation takes place, there are always many competing world views.) The crucial though quiet one is the shift of bright, young Christian leaders out of pietistic fundamentalism and into a dominion theology. Christian reconstructionism is one aspect of this shift. It offers the central intellectual and philosophical paradigms of this shift because of the self-consciousness of its adherents and because it is over two decades old as a definable, independent viewpoint. No other Protestant, Bible-believing, dominion-oriented world view is. Christian reconstructionists believe in Bible-based blueprints.

Spangler's main point is correct, however: we *are* seeing the break-up and breakdown of the older humanisms. The nineteenth-century's mechanistic vision has long since faded as an agreed-upon world view; indeterminacy has replaced it. The New Deal's economic solutions, as well as its political coalition, are also just about gone, which is also true of its ideological first-cousins in Europe. Top-down socialist economic planning has produced economic chaos everywhere, as Prof. Mises predicted as early as the 1920's.[72] The public is not sure about what should replace the present economic, religious, and political order, and so long as the system holds together economically, not many people will abandon it. But when the economic crisis comes — and both the reconstructionists and the New Agers believe that it is coming — today's political order which has "bet the farm" on the pragmatic success of government central planning will be on the defensive. Major changes are coming — changes of a magnitude greater than any we have seen since World War II, and perhaps since the late-eighteenth century.

Decentralism

The language of the New Agers today is decentralist. This language is misleading. The program of decentralized economics and localism has been the "property" and heritage of Christian conservatism since at least the days of Edmund Burke's *Reflections on the Revolution in France* (1790). The humanists have been tied to top-down rationalism

---

72. Ludwig von Mises, *Planned Chaos* (Irvington-on-Hudson, New York: Foundation for Economic Education, 1947). This essay is reprinted in his book, *Socialism: An Economic and Sociological Analysis* (Indianapolis, Indiana: Liberty Classics, [1922] 1981), Epilogue.

politically since at least Thomas Hobbes' *Leviathan* (1651). The French Enlightenment simply transferred Hobbes' vision of the king's sovereign central power to the democratic State's sovereign central power. The French Revolution was the result of this vision. So was the Russian Revolution.

Since 1900, Darwinian evolution has also led straight into the arms of the central planners. People want someone or some institution to guarantee the existence of meaning, progress, and success. In earlier centuries, they trusted the king and the church to provide such institutional confirmation of God's providence. This faith began to wane in the latter years of the nineteenth century. What institution would replace king and church? What sovereign force would replace God? The free market was the answer of late-nineteenth-century Social Darwinists: the eternal "law of competition."[73] This faith never became widespread. People have not trusted the hypothetically autonomous free market to give them what they want.

What finally replaced decentralized thinking was a new faith, a faith in the ability of scientists to work with politicians and professionally trained (and screened) bureaucrats to create a scientific program of central planning. The "laws of social evolution" and the "laws of economics" could be applied to society as a whole in order to produce social progress.[74] Since 1900, virtually everything that the leading humanist thinkers have officially promoted has led to centralization. Independent, market-produced technology has offered a tremendous potential for decentralization, but not the politics of humanism. The New Agers operate with the paradigm of evolution. It is central to their world view. This humanism is not necessarily Darwinian. It is not strictly scientific. It is closer to the evolutionism of alchemy than it is to the evolutionism of chemistry. Nevertheless, it is an evolutionary process which is being heralded by a self-conscious elite, whether "Tibetan masters," or "avatars," or just plain New Age members of one or another "inner circle." By necessity, the proposed evolutionary "leap of consciousness" begins with a minority of "aware" or "enlightened" or "illuminated" ones, who in turn spread the message and the various recommended techniques of enlightenment. The circles of initiation grow wider, but they remain circles of

---

73. Richard Hofstadter, *Social Darwinism in American Thought* (rev. ed.; New York: Braziller, 1959).

74. Gary North, *The Dominion Covenant: Genesis* (Tyler, Texas: Institute for Christian Economics, 1982), Appendix A and Appendix B.

initiation. The system is inherently elitist and centralized.

The New Age politics of self-transcendence may promote decentralization officially, but this commitment is an illusion, though perhaps based on self-delusion rather than outright deception. They are offering a self-conscious alternative to Christian civilization. At bottom, this is just another of Satan's alternatives to freedom and responsibility under God and before men. He has not changed. The only way Satan can challenge God's absolute sovereignty is to imitate Him; this means centralization, not decentralization. It means the quest for empire, not localism.

Christian conservatives can trust the decentralized free market because they trust a sovereign God. They can trust localism because they do not need to trust a sovereign central government. They can have faith in progress because they are members of a covenanted family, church, and (where the covenant is reaffirmed by citizens and their representatives) the civil government. The law-bound, grace-filled *covenant* between God and redeemed mankind—not a hypothetical leap of being, leap of consciousness, or leap of political community—is their presupposition.[75] There will be a change in politics which reflects a change in modern man's first principles (paradigm), but it will not be the politics of self-transcendence. It will be the politics of God's transcendence and man's ethical, covenantal subordination.

Lunatic Fringe Groups

What are we to make of the politics of self-transcendence? More to the point, what are we to make of the political feasibility of their program? When Tom Hayden and John Vasconcellos become two of the "major" political figures of a movement, can this movement be very big? Are two of California's oddest of odd-ball politicians—a state noted for its odd-balls—truly representative of "the wave of the future"?

We cannot be sure yet. Clearly, it does no good to apply standards of one era to the operations of those of the next. The next revolution always begins on the fringe. Had anyone in the British Parliament in 1765, the year the Stamp Act was first imposed in the North American colonies, ever heard of Thomas Jefferson (age 22) or John Adams (age 30), or George Washington (age 33)? The "old

---

75. Ray Sutton, *That You May Prosper: Dominion By Covenant* (Ft. Worth, Texas: Dominion Press, 1986).

man" of the American Revolution who was probably most responsible for getting it started with his agitation in Boston and his creation the Committees of Correspondence was Sam Adams, who was 43 in 1765. These men were unknown to the political leaders of Britain, and certainly unknown to King George III, yet they changed the course of history. In 1788, the same could have been said of Robespierre, Danton, Marat, and the other obscure men of the French Revolution, yet within a year, they had begun the process which was to overthrow European civilization by 1815.

Igor Shafarevich is a human rights protester in the Soviet Union. He is a well-known mathematician, and he contributed an essay to Alexander Solzhenitsyn's collection of essays, *From Under the Rubble* (1974). In his brilliant history of socialism, he points out: "At the moment of their inception, socialist movements often strike one by their helplessness, their isolation from reality, their naïvely adventuristic character and their comic, 'Golgolian' features (as Berdyaev put it). One gets the impression that these hopeless failures haven't a chance of success, and that in fact they do everything in their power to compromise the ideas they are proclaiming. However, they are merely biding their time. At some point, almost unexpectedly, these ideas find a broad popular reception, and become the forces that determine the course of history, while the leaders of these movements come to rule the destiny of nations."[76] What he writes concerning early socialist sects can be applied quite well to all successful revolutionary groups: they begin small, they look foolish, and eventually they take over society. Most fail; some win.

Satan Can't Go Home Again

The question is, which of today's "fringe groups" will win? Here I must indulge in a bit of prophecy. Prophecy is the proper application of fixed biblical principles to future situations. Time will tell if my prophecy is correct. I begin with the biblical presupposition that *history is linear*. Time does not go back. History does not repeat itself, although historians repeat each other. Whether we are talking about God's kingdom or Satan's attempted kingdom, the church or the satanic host, they do not go backwards. They may attempt it. Christians may join self-proclaimed "primitive" churches, or "first-century" churches, but they are fooling themselves. Time marches on. God's

---

76. Igor Shafarevich, *The Socialist Phenomenon* (New York: Harper and Row, [1975] 1980), p. 129.

providence is progressively manifested in history. Thus, any attempt by occultists to revive the primitive, pre-Christian past is doomed. Christ is no longer on the cross; He is risen. The church has come; and the old pre-Christian world is forever gone. A brief attempt can be made, of course: the Renaissance's attempt to revive the pagan institutions of classical antiquity; Hitler's attempt to revive the religion and symbols of ancient Norse mythology (combined with Eastern mysticism and magic) was futile, although it cost millions of lives to overcome it. But there is no going back.

The New Age mystics are equally doomed. They are proclaiming a very old religious view in the name of the next evolutionary leap forward. It is a leap backward. Combining computers and magic, science and higher consciousness, will not work. It is being attempted, but God will not allow it to be successful. This is the message of C. S. Lewis' novel, *That Hideous Strength*, and it is correct.

The New Agers appear ridiculous at times, and they are. They appear politically impotent, and they are. The extent to which they are successful today is based on the agreement on first principles that New Agers share with the older humanism—indeed, original Satanism: "Ye shall be as gods" (Gen. 3:5). They are attempting to break the mold of both Christian civilization and nineteenth-century rationalism. While they can successfully appeal to the younger, more consistent humanists—those who have already adopted the religious premises of "the leap of being" mystics—the world which they want to create cannot be sustained. They cannot overcome the intellectual, institutional, and religious failures of the old humanism, and still maintain the economic productivity of capitalism. They say they are opposed to socialism. But the choice is between top-down central planning or decentralized Christian capitalism. The in-between solutions cannot survive in the long run. They cannot operate.

In the seventeenth century, the socialists made a fundamental switch in their strategy: from heretical Christianity and mysticism to rationalism. They cannot go back. Shafarevich describes this transformation. They adopted a new organizational structure—initiatory centralization—and dropped the older religious underpinnings. "A new organizational structure is evolved, as well; socialist ideas develop within it and attempts are made to implement them. This is a sect with the standard 'concentric' structure—a narrow circle of leaders who are initiated into all aspects of the doctrine and a wide circle of sympathizers who are acquainted only with some of its aspects. The latter group tends to be linked with the sect by ties of an emotional character which are difficult to describe precisely. The leading role in the development of socialism passes to a new type of individual. The hermetic [magical] thinker and philosopher is replaced by the fervent and tireless publicist and organizer, an expert in the theory and practice of destruction."[77]

The New Agers represent an attempted return to the older tradition, that of the hermetical philosopher, the alchemist. Gone are the tireless publicists. The New Agers are attempting to return to Renaissance magic and Renaissance philosophy. Their program is initiatory. They no longer appeal to a broad base of potential converts. Their elitism is inescapable, despite their talk of decentralization. Their attempt will not be successful, although it may cause a lot of damage. They cannot revive a world that Christianity has already overcome. They cannot combine Darwinism and alchemy.

The Judgment of God

The subtitle of Constance Cumbey's *Hidden Dangers of the Rainbow* is incorrect: "The New Age Movement and Our Coming Age of Barbarism." If they should win, the subtitle would be correct. They are not necessarily going to win, even temporarily, and they are categorically not going to win permanently, meaning before Jesus comes again to judge the world. Contrary to the "pessimillennialism" of several critics of the New Age movement—explicit in the case of Dave Hunt[78] and implicit in the case of Mrs. Cumbey—the Bible does *not* teach that there is necessarily (prophetically) going to be a coming age of humanistic barbarism in which the New Agers will triumph over the church, or over the world from which the church has been "raptured." Christian people, not the New Age mystics, could be the ones to replace the humanists who are presently in authority in the United States. It depends entirely on the movement of God's Spirit.

---

77. *Ibid.*, pp. 78-79.

78. Dave Hunt, *Peace Prosperity and the Coming Holocaust* (Eugene, Oregon: Harvest House, 1983); Dave Hunt and T. A. McMahon, *The Seduction of Christianity: Spiritual Discernment in the Last Days* (Eugene, Oregon: Harvest House, 1985), ch. 14. While the analysis of Dave Hunt and Mrs. Cumbey concerning what New Agers believe, and the threat they pose to human freedom, is correct, their *predictions* have been colored by their pessimistic dispensational theory of the inevitable defeat of the church prior to the "Rapture." Readers should exercise great care and discernment in separating their analysis from their predictions, either explicit or implicit.

This does not mean that there will not be competition and even social conflict among the various groups that seek control. No doubt there will be. This also does not mean that the United States is not going to suffer judgment. It may have to suffer judgment as a prelude to national repentance, if it is to play a positive role in the process of worldwide Christian reconstruction. But we need to recognize that there are two kinds of judgment in the Bible: judgment unto *restoration* and judgment unto *destruction*. With respect to God's covenanted people, the Bible *always* speaks of the first form of judgment, unto restoration. It *never* speaks of judgment unto historic oblivion when it speaks of the remnant of the faithful. Read Isaiah chapters one and two for the outline of prophetic preaching concerning judgment. "And I will restore thy judges as at the first, and thy counsellors as at the beginning: afterward thou shalt be called, The city of righteousness, the faithful city. Zion shall be redeemed with judgment, and her converts with righteousness" (Isa. 1:26-27). Could anything be plainer? "Restore," "redeemed": Isaiah's language is crystal clear. Isaiah then goes on in the second chapter to describe this spiritual restoration. *The church of Jesus Christ is the lawful inheritor of these promises*, for Paul calls the church "the Israel of God." "And as many as walk according to this rule, peace be on them, and mercy, and upon the Israel of God" (Gal. 6:16).

To put it as clearly as I can: *Armageddon happens to the enemies of Christ's church, not to the faithful*. The conquest of "Canaan" is what God's people accomplish, by means of the gracious intervention of God, not by His physical presence, but spiritually, as His people work out their salvation with fear and trembling (Phil. 2:12). In short, God-fearing people conquer the world by preaching the gospel, exercising discipline under God in terms of His law, and redeeming — buying back — modern civilization. It takes time, but time is on our side. It is not on Satan's side. God owns the world, not Satan.

This leads us to the question of competence. Whose world- and-life view is more oriented toward dominion? Whose tool of dominion — whose law-order — has greater authority, God's revealed law or the "zero-blueprint" program of the New Agers? Whose kingdom is promised in the Bible to be the victorious one, in time and on earth, *before* Christ returns visibly to execute final judgment? The answer, contrary to those who preach "eat, meet, retreat, and wait for the

Rapture," is *the kingdom of God*.[79] On earth. Before Christ returns physically to judge the world.

Christian Reconstruction

Another "fringe group" in the land is an even tinier one: the "Christian Reconstructionists." They are even less well-known than the New Agers. Their influence is even more indirect. Their strength lies in their ability to speak to a new generation of conservative, Bible-believing Christians who have at last discovered that retreat, mysticism, pietism, and cultural irrelevance are not a valid program for serious Christians. While this shift in perception has only begun since about 1976, and has accelerated since 1980, it is still not widespread in the churches. The older pietism still prevails. But the pace of growth of these newer "dominion-oriented" Christian groups is much greater than the pietists, the media humanists, or the mystic humanists could have imagined as recently as 1978. It is much greater than even the "reconstructionists" guessed.

Their ideas have spread into fundamentalist and charismatic Christian circles by several roads. Some fundamentalists have been outraged by abortion and humanism in the schools. They have become active politically to help change things. The reconstructionists have provided a theological basis for getting involved in politics, which the fundamentalists had been out of since the mid-1920's.[80] Some of the charismatic groups believe in tightly knit church covenants. The reconstructionists have been the major theologians of the biblical covenant.[81] Other charismatics have preached personal financial victory and health through prayer and by obeying God's "principles." The reconstructionists have been the major defenders of the continuing legitimacy of God's law in New Testament times.[82] Some of these "positive confession" charismatics (also called "word of faith") have begun to preach that the optimism which God offers to individuals also applies to God's other covenanted associations:

---

79. David Chilton, *Paradise Restored: A Biblical Theology of Dominion* (Tyler, Texas: Reconstruction Press, 1985).

80. George Marsden, *Fundamentalism and American Culture: The Shaping of Twentieth-Century Evangelicalism, 1870-1925* (New York: Oxford University Press, 1980).

81. Ray Sutton, *That You May Prosper: Dominion By Covenant*.

82. R. J. Rushdoony, *Institutes of Biblical Law* (Nutley, New Jersey: Craig Press, 1973); Greg L. Bahnsen, *By This Standard: The Authority of God's Law Today* (Tyler, Texas: Institute for Christian Economics, 1985); Greg L. Bahnsen, *Theonomy in Christian Ethics* (2nd ed.; Phillipsburg, New Jersey: Presbyterian & Reformed, 1984).

families, churches, and civil governments. This represents a major break with the traditional pessimistic eschatology of fundamentalism, called dispensationalism. These charismatic leaders have not self-consciously made the break from premillennialism to postmillennial optimism, but the term "dominion" implies it. Again, the reconstructionists are the only Protestant theologians to have forthrightly preached postmillennialism after 1965. (R. J. Rushdoony was the pioneer here.)[83] Thus, the ideas of the reconstructionists have penetrated into Protestant circles that for the most part are unaware of the original source of the theological ideas that are beginning to transform them.

The Christian reconstructionists are still on the fringe. Indeed, they are on the fringe of a fringe (politically self-conscious conservative church members). Though it is difficult to trace their influence, their ideas are spreading. They are the ones who have blueprints.[84] They are the ones who have based their case on the Bible, which orthodox Christians claim to honor. They have available to them a broad base of tens of millions of registered voters in the United States who are confessed Christians.

The New Agers have a toehold in the public schools — a fading institution — and also in certain areas of the media. Occultism is unquestionably spreading. But they are facing an unprecedented political and cultural *backlash* of conservative people who are darkly tolerant of today's humanism, and who have been seriously compromised by it, but who will react negatively and rapidly, once the economic and political order built by the humanists begins to crumble. The New Agers, like the Christian reconstructionists, are predicting just such a crumbling. The New Agers believe that they will *permanently* "pick up the pieces." Some of those fundamentalist Christians who hold to a pessimistic eschatology also think the New Agers will pick up the pieces, at least until Jesus returns physically to establish His millennial kingdom. This prediction is not going to come true. Christians *eventually* are going to pick up the pieces, before Jesus returns physically, just as they picked up the pieces of the Roman Empire, when that "eternal" institution crumbled.

The top-down vision of the traditional power religionists is fad-

---

83. R. J. Rushdoony, *Thy Kingdom Come: Studies in Daniel and Revelation* (Fairfax, Virginia: Thoburn Press, [1971] 1978); cf. Chilton, *Paradise Restored*.

84. For example, the ten-volume "Biblical Blueprints" series published by Dominion Press in 1986.

ing. The next paradigm shift will be in the direction of decentralization. A strategy of victory must be built in terms of a new paradigm:
decentralization. The question is, whose version will win out: the "networkers' " (New Agers) or the "covenanters' " (Christians)? In the
competition between the two strategies, "networking" vs. "covenant-
ing," the covenanters will eventually win out, perhaps sooner than
anyone expects.

Why am I so confident? Because the "networkers" have no God
to guarantee the success of their decentralized attempt to integrate
mankind, nor do they have a tool of dominion comparable to the
power of fixed, unchanging, revealed legal standards—biblical
law.[85] The "networkers" will eventually disappear, either into the
radical individualism of mystical escape (the escape religion) or back
into the power religion. But make no mistake about it: the primary
competition is between these two strategies, however obscure the
leaders of both groups appear today.

Conclusion

Man is finite, and man is operating under a curse because of his
ethical rebellion. The best and the most that man can and should
hope for is the abolition of the effects of his rebellion. He can legitimately hope to become perfectly human after the day of judgment,
when the manifestation of the New Heavens and the New Earth is
made complete. But until then, he must content himself with the
working out in daily life of the principles of biblical law. He must
content himself with being finite. He must understand that he can
never be more than human, although the progressive sanctifying of
regenerated men and the society that they gradually construct is
God's down payment (earnest) of the coming day of restoration. In
short, man is human, his world is under limits, and finitude is with
us forever. The foundation of restoration is therefore ethical
regeneration—the new heart which God promises His people (Jer.
31:31-34; Hebrews 8:10-11; 10:15-17). Our problem as men is not our
finitude, for we are created beings. Our problem is moral, for we are
rebellious creatures.

The society of Satan promises self-transcendence in every area of
life. It calls for a new age, an Aquarian age, a proletarian age, an
Aryan age, a millennium of humanistic peace. Men are to transcend

---

85. Greg L. Bahnsen, *By This Standard: The Authority of God's Law Today* (Tyler,
Texas: Institute for Christian Economics, 1985).

all limits, becoming gods, determining good and evil. Men are to stand in judgment over God's word. Men are to build a paradise on earth, but without a blueprint, for in a world of evolutionary process, whirl is king.

The universe of humanism is theoretically an open universe — open, that is, to everyone but God. By closing the universe to God, humanistic man opens the door to the Moloch State. Rushdoony's words should stand as a perpetual warning: "Humanistic law, moreover, is inescapably totalitarian law. Humanism, as a logical development of evolutionary theory, holds fundamentally to a concept of an evolving universe. This is held to be an 'open universe,' whereas Biblical Christianity, because of its faith in the triune God and His eternal decree, is said to be a faith in a 'closed universe.' This terminology not only intends to prejudice the case; it reverses reality. The universe of evolution and humanism is a closed universe. There is no law, no appeal, no higher order, beyond and above the universe. Instead of an open window upwards, there is a closed cosmos. There is thus no ultimate law and decree beyond man and the universe. In practice, this means that the positive law of the state is absolute law. The state is the most powerful and most highly organized expression of humanistic law. There is no appeal beyond it. Man has no 'right,' no realm of justice, no source of law beyond the state, to which he can appeal against the state. Humanism therefore imprisons man within the closed world of the state and the closed universe of the evolutionary scheme."[86]

We are indeed called to create a politics of transcendence, but not a politics of self-transcendence. We are called to execute godly justice as laid down by God. We are called to work out our salvation with fear and trembling (Phil. 2:12). What we are *not* called to do is to regenerate our world, ourselves, or our institutions. Man is not ultimately creative; he is only subordinately creative. When he attempts to be ultimately creative, man becomes subordinately destructive, bringing death and mayhem to himself and his environment. The society of Satan is therefore doomed to failure in the long run, but it can create havoc for Christian culture in the meantime.

---

86. R. J. Rushdoony, "Humanistic Law," introduction to E. L. Hebden Taylor, *The New Legality* (Nutley, New Jersey: Craig Press, 1967), pp. vi-vii. This passage was updated by Rev. Rushdoony and appears in Gary North, *Marx's Religion of Revolution* (Nutley, New Jersey: Craig Press, 1968), pp. 118f.

11

IS THIS THE END OF THE WORLD?

And ye shall hear of wars and rumours of wars: see that ye be not trou-
bled: for all these things must come to pass, but the end is not yet.

Matthew 24:6

Do we hear of wars and rumors of wars? Constantly. Then be not
troubled, *for the end is not yet*. The words of Christ could not be
plainer. The time to start thinking about the possibility that the
world is coming to an end is when we stop hearing of wars and
rumors of wars. The return of Christ in final judgment will not come
while there are wars and rumors of wars. We must first beat our
swords into ploughshares.

No, it is not the end of the world. It is far more likely that it is the
end of *their* world. The revival of occultism in this century, and especially since 1965, is not the sign of the end of the world, the triumph
of Satan, the second coming of Christ, or any other apocalyptic
event. There have been outbreaks of demonism before. The Roman
Empire suffered such a plague after the first century, A.D. There was
renewed interest in witchcraft and magic in Western Europe in the
late-medieval period. The Renaissance was marked by magicians
and astrologers, and to a lesser degree, so was the Reformation. But
as Protestant Christianity grew in authority and influence, these
manifestations of the occult faded.[1] Occultism marked the end of the
medieval world; it marked the unsuccessful attempt of self-conscious
pagans to revive the dead classical world during the Renaissance. It
did not mark the modern world until quite recently. We have lived in
a Christian era, for modern rationalism has grown up in a culture in
which the logic of autonomous man has had restraints from Christian theology, or at least the cultural residue of that theology. In our

---

1. Keith Thomas, *Religion and the Decline of Magic* (New York: Scribner's, 1971).

378

day, however, the residue has been eroded away to a great extent. This humanist civilization has spent its spiritual capital, and its checks are bouncing. The decay of humanism has led to the revival of occultism. What we are witnessing is *occult revival and cultural disintegration*. What we may very well be witnessing is *humanist civilization's dying gasp*.

The Christian answer is not terror, retreat, and hopelessness. It is not a program of "eat, meet, and retreat." It is not waiting for the Rapture. The answer is a systematic, well-financed, decentralized program of comprehensive Christian reconstruction. Every area of life must be called back from the rot of humanism and the acids of occultism. *The possession and long-term maintenance of authority in this world must be seen by Christians as the product of regenerate men's self-confidence under God and in conformity to His moral and civil laws, as revealed in the Bible.* Confidence in the earthly victory of God's people is our motivation;[2] biblical law is our tool of dominion;[3] profitable service is our program. Reason flourishes in a framework of biblical revelation. It disintegrates when men attempt to operate in terms of their own hypothetical neutrality and autonomy.

We see before us the poison fruits of a self-professed autonomous Western rationalism which is running wild. The sons and daughters of twentieth-century rationalism have become, if not occultists, then certainly people who tolerate the world of occultism and who are incapable of successfully challenging it. The thin cord of Western rationalism cannot, apart from Christian values, support the weight of today's occult-laden civilization. If men insist on power apart from God-ordained meaning, then they will seek power any way they can. If rationalism works, fine; if occultism works, fine; if a fusion of the two works, fine. But ultimately, the Bible informs us, none of this works. Power cannot be attained in the long run by those who seek it and it alone.[4]

This has not been understood by twentieth-century fundamentalists. They saw the power of "the power religion," and they

---

2. David Chilton, *Paradise Restored: A Biblical Theology of Dominion* (Tyler, Texas: Reconstruction Press, 1985).

3. Greg L. Bahnsen, *By This Standard: The Authority of God's Law Today* (Tyler, Texas: Institute for Christian Economics, 1985); R. J. Rushdoony, *Institutes of Biblical Law* (Nutley, New Jersey: Craig Press, 1973).

4. Gary North, *Moses and Pharaoh: Dominion Religion versus Power Religion* (Tyler, Texas: Institute for Christian Economics, 1985).

mistakenly joined the ranks of "the escapist religion,"[5] thinking that it is the only alternative to the power religion.[6] The biblical alternative is not the escapist religion; it is the dominion religion. It involves optimism concerning the future, faith in the infallibility of the Bible, recognition that God's required tool of dominion is biblical law, and that God has ordained the victory of His people.[7]

Communists have adopted a secular version of this four-part outlook: confidence in their religion, scientific Marxism; confidence in the future (the victory of the proletariat); confidence in socialist law; and confidence in historic inevitability. Revolutionary Moslems have an analogous faith. So did late-nineteenth-century science.

This four-part theology has been absent from Western Christianity for over a century. Few denominations, even Bible-believing ones, profess more than one of these points. No denomination professes all four. Yet without all four, the ability of Christians to challenge the humanist world is drastically weakened.[8] It has only been since 1980 that a growing number of charismatic ("tongues-speaking") ministries have at least unofficially adopted three of the four: the self-attesting authority of the Bible (anti-"natural law"), the reliability of "biblical principles" (they are still afraid to say "Old Testament biblical law"), and optimism concerning the future, "dominion" (they are not yet ready to call themselves postmillennialists).

Eschatology

This vision of eschatological victory has been called historic postmillennialism. There is a major revival of this eschatological viewpoint taking place in the United States, especially in several charismatic Pentecostal circles. It is not being widely publicized, but hostile critics from the dispensational camp have recognized it.

It is necessary here to survey briefly the four major eschatological positions. ("Eschatology" = the doctrine of last things.) They are:

---

5. *Ibid.*, Introduction.

6. A good account of this retreat is found in George Marsden's book, *Fundamentalism and American Culture: The Shaping of Twentieth-Century Evangelicalism, 1870-1925* (New York: Oxford University Press, 1980).

7. Gary North, *Unconditional Surrender: God's Program for Victory* (2nd ed.; Tyler, Texas: Geneva Divinity School Press, 1983).

8. Gary North and David Chilton, "Apologetics and Strategy," *Christianity and Civilization*, 3 (1983).

1. Postmillennialism
2. Amillennialism
3. Historic premillennialism
4. Dispensationalism
   a. Pre-tribulational
   b. Mid-tribulational
   c. Post-tribulational

The prefixes "pre," "post," and "a" that are attached to "millennial" refer to the temporal placement of Christ's physical return to earth to begin the final judgment. Will this take place *after* ("post") the millennium (the reign of peace on earth), *before* ("pre") the millennium, or after no earthly millennium ("a")? Historically, the church has had defenders of all three positions. The early church fathers were mainly premillennial or postmillennial. The Roman Catholics after Augustine (early fifth century) became mainly amillennial, although there were occasional postmillennial revivals. Lutherans have always been amillennial. Calvin's eschatology was a mixture of amillennialism and postmillennialism.[9] The early Puritans were mainly postmillennial. Charles Haddon Spurgeon was postmillennial.

Dispensationalism is a late development. The original formulation, pretribulational, can be traced back no earlier than 1830 in Scotland. The history of the origins of premillennial, pre-tribulational dispensationalism is not discussed by its present-day adherents, probably because of their understandable embarrassment.[10] In 1830, a 15-year-old girl began attending private prayer meetings at which the phenomenon of "tongues" speaking (glossalalia) took place. Members of Edward Irving's church attended these meetings. Many of them experienced tongues, but young Margaret Macdonald made the crucial prophetic announcement, that Jesus would return to carry His servants up into heaven (the "Rapture") *before* He would arrive physically to establish His earthly millennial reign of a thou-

---

9. Gary North, "The Economic Thought of Calvin and Luther," *The Journal of Christian Reconstruction*, II (Summer 1975), pp. 103-6. For the case for Calvin as a postmillennialist, see Greg L. Bahnsen, "The *Prima Facie* Acceptability of Postmillennialism," *ibid.*, III (Winter 1976- 77), pp. 69-76. For Calvin as an amillennialist, see Heinrich Quistorp, *Calvin's Doctrine of the Last Things* (Richmond, Virginia: John Knox Press, 1955) and T. F. Torrance, *Kingdom and Church* (1956), ch. 4.

10. Dave MacPherson, *The Unbelievable Pre-Trib Origin* (Kansas City, Missouri: Heart of America Bible Society, 1973).

sand years (pre-millennial).

A young man named John Nelson Darby attended some of these meetings, and he then developed the theological system known as pretribulational, premillennial dispensationalism. This form of pre-millennialism differed from historic premillennialism because it divided God's reign over man into seven (sometimes eight) different periods, rather than two: Old Covenant and New Covenant. This theology was picked up by numerous preachers in the United States after 1870, and popularized most effectively in the footnotes of C. I. Scofield's *Scofield Reference Bible* (first edition, 1909). It is one of those oddities of history that most of those fundamentalist Christians who hold to the pretribulation Rapture doctrine reject tongues-speaking as either a false phenomenon, or a phenomenon of Satan. They have no idea that the pretribulation Rapture doctrine was first announced by a teenage tongues-speaking girl. (The origins of the Rapture doctrine would not disturb modern Pentecostals, who speak in tongues, and most of whom still *officially* hold the dispensational theology. But this movement began no earlier than 1907. Besides, many of them are now *unofficially* adopting postmillennialism, which makes developments even more odd, since those who hold historic postmillennialism have almost to a man regarded tongues-speaking as a false gift. The last of the great postmillennialist theologians of the late-nineteenth and early twentieth centuries, B. B. Warfield, correctly identified the coming of tongues at the Irvingite church meetings in 1830, and he included a chapter on these events in his book, *Counterfeit Miracles*.[11])

In recent years, a "post-trib" view has become more acceptable. This view says that the church will not be "raptured" out of the world until after the great tribulation. A handful of dispensationalists hold to a "mid-trib" view, arguing that the church will be "raptured" out in the middle of the tribulation.[12] *The inescapable conclusion of all varieties of the dispensational system is that the world will continue to increase in evil, until Jesus comes to "rapture" His people out of it.* The pretribulation version ("yes, we'll get out before things get really terrible") was the message of Hal Lindsey's best-selling book, *The Late, Great Planet*

---

11. B. B. Warfield, *Counterfeit Miracles* (London: Banner of Truth Trust, [1918] 1972), ch. 4: "Irvingite Gifts."

12. Richard R. Reiter, Paul D. Feinberg, Gleason L. Archer, and Douglas J. Moo, *The Rapture: Pre-, Mid-, or Post-Tribulational?* (Grand Rapids, Michigan: Academie Books of Zondervan Press, 1984).

Earth (1970), which has sold 20 million copies. It is also the message of two books that appeared in 1985, which trumpet the traditional "Armageddon line," and both became minor best-sellers in Christian bookstores. It is my contention that they represent the last gasp of an older theology, not the wave of the future.

David Wilkerson's Doomsday Warning

David Wilkerson, author of *The Cross and the Switchblade* in the 1960's, and *The Vision* in the early 1970's, has now written a book against earthly optimism which prophesies God's imminent sweeping judgment of the United States, *Set the Trumpet to Thy Mouth*. The first chapter is entitled, "The Destruction of America." It even contains a prophetic subsection: "America Will Not Repent." To put it rather bluntly, how does *he* know? Repentance is always offered to any society, but especially to a *covenanted* society, and the United States has been a covenanted nation under God since its beginnings in the early seventeenth century. He correctly identifies many evils in the land, but he does not admit that this nation can be salvaged ("salve" = healing ointment) by means of external judgment and subsequent repentance.

He attacks preachers who preach the possibility of personal prosperity through faith and self-discipline under God. He calls them "pillow prophets" (chapter 6). He has not acknowledged that God can call an externally successful yet rebellious nation to repentance. This was Jonah's experience with Nineveh. He also does not understand that there are two kinds of judgment: judgment unto restoration and judgment unto destruction and historic oblivion. God *never* judges His covenanted people in the second manner. He *always* judges them in preparation for a return to authority under Him. This is what premillennial dispensationalists never admit. (It is also what amillennialists neglect to discuss.)

Think of the prison experiences of God's people: Joseph in Egypt, the three Hebrew young men in the court of Nebuchadnezzar (and his fiery furnace), Daniel in the lion's den, Jesus in the "prison" of the tomb, Paul before Felix. In each case, the prison experience led directly to a victory of God's people. *Prison led to resurrection*. The prison experience marks the beginning of restoration for Christians. It is judgment unto restoration.

His message is the Christian church's psychological need for fearlessness in the face of inescapable defeat and the threat of death. "No hiding! No mountain cabins of escape! No caves or shelters! No stockpiles of food or weapons or water. God's holy remnant can look death right in the face and say, 'I fear you not. There is no more sting, no more terror. I am ready to be offered!' "[13] (I gather that he is post-tribulational.)

Well, I'm not planning to be offered! I am ready to have *them* offered. God is the consuming fire, not Satan. Even in an interim period of judgment, God spares His remnant. Obadiah, the high official of evil king Ahab, kept fifty prophets hidden in a cave and fed them and fifty more with bread and water (I Kings 18:4). Obadiah was gracious, and the prophets were wise to avoid a suicidal, premature, head-on confrontation with the king. *Spiritual maturity involves a proper perception of the times.* There are times when hiding in caves is an appropriate Christian tactic.[14] Elijah did. It is only when men believe that they have no earthly hope, no more time, and no responsibilities to the earthly future, that they devise suicidal frontal assaults. Wiser men bide their time and plan to steadily replace the tyrants. They plan to rule the affairs of men after God graciously releases them from bondage or prison.

Rev. Wilkerson has adopted a pessimistic eschatology, and he has applied it inaccurately to our day, chastising by implication his fellow charismatic preachers who are at last rallying their followers to a vision of *personal* victory and external success. Rev. Wilkerson, as a self-proclaimed prophet, tells us that nuclear holocaust is inevitable. Nonsense. Nuclear holocaust is unlikely, though of course possible. Nuclear *blackmail* by the Soviet Union is increasingly likely, if God's people do not change their ways, change their minds, and stop preaching inevitable earthly defeat. What *is* inevitable, *prior to Christ's physical return*, is the earthly defeat of Christ's enemies.

Prophetic Activities

Rev. Wilkerson has written a real "fire and brimstone" book, a classic ranting and raving book. Everything in America is bad. The church is at ease. Judgment is coming. But not one word in the book about:

---

13. David Wilkerson, *Set the Trumpet to Thy Lips* (Lindale, Texas: World Challenge, 1985), p. 27.

14. Gary North, "Confirmation, Confrontation, and Caves," *Christianity and Civilization*, 2 (1983).

1. The Christian-led battle against abortion.
2. The sacrificial giving of Christians to create an alternative to the public schools with Christian day schools.
3. The return of Christians to the political arena after half a century of antinomian slumber.
4. The coming of the Christian television networks and popular Christian programs such as "The 700 Club."
5. The coming of decentralized publishing technology which is making possible a new Reformation by means of a "technological end-run" around the humanist Establishment's media monopoly.
6. The battle against local sales of pornography.

These are "prophetic" activities, just as surely as passing out tracts on street corners is prophetic. Furthermore, they involve a lot more Christian maturity, a lot more planning, better communications skills, and more money than passing out tracts on street corners. Is Rev. Wilkerson unimpressed by such "worldly" pursuits? Are they useless? Does God dismiss them automatically as "too little, too late"? Rev. Wilkerson certainly does not call his readers to get involved in any of these actions. He does not say that he is getting involved in such activities. What, then, is he doing about the sins of our day? "I intend to stay on the streets, preaching to junkies and harlots."[15]

He proved his commitment in this regard in 1980 by selling his ministry's magnificent ranch and buildings in Lindale, Texas, conservatively appraised at $4 million at the time, to Youth With A Mission, for ten cents on the dollar. (The real estate agent who had originally intended to handle the transaction told me that his normal commission would have been as much as Rev. Wilkerson got for the entire property.) This East Texas property is only one of many that YWAM operates throughout the world.

From 1960 until 1985, Youth With A Mission grew from nothing to become the largest Protestant missionary organization in the world, with some 5,000 full-time missionaries in the field. Its charismatic founders are holding the organization's 25th anniversary at the very time I am writing this chapter, planning for the next 25 years of missionary activity, in which they hope to grow to tens of

---

15. Wilkerson, *Set the Trumpet*, p. 28.

thousands. They are not planning for Armageddon. They are planning to roll back Satan's kingdom with the gospel. They are using their East Texas property to train people to go out and begin to take over the world.

I think there is a lesson to be found in Rev. Wilkerson's decision to sell that magnificent East Texas property for a fraction of its market value, in order to return to the city streets: "The wealth of the present-oriented is laid up for the future-oriented."

Dealing with street people is Rev. Wilkerson's calling before God, and it is a good and holy calling, but like generations of pietistic evangelists before him, he reveals no visible respect for other Christian men's so-called "worldly" callings — in politics, education, and the many activities that I call fulfilling the dominion covenant.[16] His books reveal a very narrow view of what Christ's people can accomplish, are called upon to accomplish, and will accomplish *before* Christ comes again in judgment. He sees tract-passing as the best thing — just about the *only* thing — that is really positive for the Lord.

A Question of Time

What is his book really all about? First, it is a shrill defense of the older "Armageddon Now" type of dispensationalism.[17] Second, Rev. Wilkerson has taken a growing dispute among charismatic Christians (he himself is a charismatic) over the question of whether God wants to bless His people with health and wealth, and has elevated this debate into some sort of prelude to Armageddon. He is really trying to embarrass the "positive confession" charismatics with his book. He resents their theological message and their recommended program for self-improvement, both of which are based on optimism. (More on this below.)

He is clinging to a worn-out view of what the gospel is all about, a view which did not become widespread in American Protestant circles until the turn of this century. By shortening their view of the time Jesus supposedly has given to His people to accomplish their comprehensive assignment, fundamentalists after 1900 chose to focus their concerns on preaching and tract-passing. These are necessary minimal activities, but they are only the beginning in God's

16. Gary North, *The Dominion Covenant: Genesis* (Tyler, Texas: Institute for Christian Economics, 1982).

17. Dwight Wilson, *Armageddon Now! The Premillenarian Response to Russia and Israel Since 1917* (Grand Rapids, Michigan: Baker Book House, 1977).

program of comprehensive redemption.[18] The dominion covenant requires men to subdue the earth to the glory of God (Gen. 1:28; 9:1-17). His people still must accomplish this task before He comes again to judge their success. They have been given *sufficient time*; they must redeem it.

"Sufficient time": it really *does* matter what eschatology a person holds. It colors what a man believes that God has called His people to do. Eventually, the question of eschatology makes itself felt, for better or worse. Though many Christians think the subject can be safely ignored, it cannot be. There is never a choice of "eschatology vs. no eschatology"; it is always a question of *which* eschatology.

Rev. Wilkerson is still proclaiming the older fundamentalist paradigm of the external historical defeat of Christians, a view which has hamstrung efforts at Christian dominion in the United States for almost a century. It is now being replaced by a new paradigm, the paradigm of dominion. The escapist religion is going down with the power religion's sinking ship. The dominion religion is in the early stages of replacing both.

Dave Hunt's Coming Holocaust

Dave Hunt is a careful student of the cults and the occult. He understands the very real threat which New Age philosophy poses. He also recognizes the extent to which Christian leaders have unthinkingly adopted New Age "possibility thinking" and "think and grow rich" techniques. But his analysis is colored from start to finish by his belief that we are nearing the end of the so-called "Church Age," that Jesus is about to call His people into heaven at the Rapture, and that today's visible apostasy is a nearly inescapable one-way street to judgment. He holds the premillennial-dispensational belief that the church of Jesus Christ will lose in its confrontation with Satan, until Jesus returns physically to run the whole show. In short, *he thinks we redeemed people are a bunch of losers and incompetents, and no match for Satan and his followers.* He regards Christians as people who were called by God to a world-conquering task (Mat. 28:18-20), who were given the Holy Spirit (Acts 2:1-21), and then were sent on a task which God knew from the beginning that they could not accomplish without Christ's presence in the flesh. Obviously, if you begin with a low view of the church, and a high view of Satanic

---

18. Gary North, "Comprehensive Redemption: A Theology for Social Action," *The Journal of Christian Reconstruction*, VIII (Summer 1981).

power, you will be skeptical—even hostile—to those Christians who preach victory prior to Christ's coming.

Mr. Hunt is not so outspoken as Rev. Wilkerson. He does not categorically announce as some sort of Spirit-filled prophet that America will not repent. He writes concerning his message of the coming Armageddon: "If the world would take these warnings seriously and repent, God might withold His judgment. He has done so in the past, as in the case of Nineveh, which repented when Jonah warned of coming destruction." But he reminds us that "Armageddon isn't going to go away just because we all determine to think positively."[19]

"Positive Confession" and Eschatology

He then attacks Robert Tilton, whose satellite television network is gaining the support of thousands of charismatic Christians. About 2,000 churches receive Rev. Tilton's broadcasts, and the number is growing rapidly. He started it in late 1982. As a member of the charismatic "positive confession" movement—sometimes called "name it and claim it"—Rev. Tilton's message is optimistic. God does not intend for His people to be poor and sick. (Rev. Tilton has therefore adopted the principle underlying one of the aphorisms that has governed my own life: "It is better to be rich and healthy than it is to be poor and sick.") Mr. Hunt points out that the language used by other "positive confession" ministers is similar to the man-deifying language of the New Age "positive thinking" theology. There is no doubt that his accusation can be documented, and that some of these leaders need to get clear the crucial distinction between the imputed *human* perfection of Jesus Christ and the non-communicable divinity of Jesus Christ. This Creator-creature distinction is the most important doctrine separating the New Agers and orthodox Christianity.

But then Mr. Hunt makes a very revealing statement. He implicitly associates New Age optimism with an optimistic eschatology. He recognizes (as few of the "positive confession" leaders have recognized) that they have become operational postmillennialists. They have abandoned the mind-set of premillennial, pre-tribulational dispensationalism, even though they have not made this shift known to their followers, who still profess faith in dispensationalism. He sees clearly that a new eschatology is involved in

---

19. Dave Hunt and T. A. McMahon, *The Seduction of Christianity: Spiritual Discernment in the Last Days* (Eugene, Oregon: Harvest House, 1985), p. 216.

"positive confession," a *dominion eschatology*. He includes a subsection, "An Emerging Eschatology," in his final chapter. He does not like what is emerging, but at least he recognizes it.

He calls the "positive confession" movement "a new gospel." But he calls it this in the subsection on eschatology. Why the section on eschatology? Is he calling into question the orthodoxy of historic postmillennialism? What he conveniently fails to mention is that historic postmillennial eschatology is in no way connected with "positive confession" doctrines. It is not a new gospel. It is about 1800 years older than the doctrine of the premillennial, pretribulation rapture which Mr. Hunt holds, which as we have seen was first announced by a 15-year-old girl, Margaret Macdonald, who did so during an ecstatic trance at a private prayer meeting in Scotland in 1830. Some of the greatest leaders and theologians of the Bible-believing church in the United States have been postmillennialists, including most of the theologians of Princeton Theological Seminary before the liberals captured it in 1929: Charles Hodge, A. A. Hodge, Archibald Alexander, B. B. Warfield, Oswald T. Allis, and J. Gresham Machen. Machen led the intellectual counter-offensive against modernism in the 1920's and 1930's.[20] Dispensational scholars also fail to remind their readers that Dr. Allis, who wrote what they acknowledge as probably the definitive defense of the Mosaic authorship of the Pentateuch, *The Five Books of Moses*, also wrote the definitive refutation of dispensationalism, *Prophecy and the Church*.

Mr. Hunt misleads his readers: first, by failing to mention the long tradition of postmillennial optimism in the history of Protestant orthodoxy, and second, by equating the optimism of historic postmillennialism with New Age optimism. How does he accomplish this? By placing the following paragraph immediately after his paragraph criticizing the humanistic gospel of self-esteem:

There are many groups representing seemingly widely divergent points of view about whether the world can be saved, and if so, how. There is one point, however, upon which even those who seem to be opposed to each other find agreement. This otherwise-surprising unity is expressed in the growing opposition from many quarters to the traditional fundamentalist view that the *only* hope for this world to be saved from destruction is miraculous intervention by Jesus Christ. Increasing numbers of Christian

20. J. Gresham Machen, *Christianity and Liberalism* (New York: Macmillan, 1923), reprinted by William B. Eerdmans, Grand Rapids, Michigan.

leaders and their followers are rejecting this view, and at the same time they are also rejecting the idea that Christians are really citizens of heaven, not of this world, and that Christ is going to "rapture" His church out of this world. The whole idea of the rise of Antichrist to rule the world during a tribulation period, and the rapture of the church, whether pre-, mid-, or post-trib is falling into disfavor. The views of many Christians concerning the future of the world are beginning to have more and more in common with the humanistic hope that mankind can really "find itself" and on the basis of a common brotherhood begin to love one another and live up to our potential of humanness and authentic personhood.[21]

Why can't Christians have legitimate earthly hope regarding the effects of their work on earth? Why should all the efforts of Christians come to nothing, culturally speaking? After all, wasn't all power given to Jesus Christ after His resurrection (Matt. 28:18)? Furthermore, why can't Christians be ethical citizens of heaven while simultaneously working to establish a program of parallel standards for earthly citizenship that are ethically comparable to heaven's standards? After all, we pray the Lord's prayer, which includes the request: "thy kingdom come, thy will be done, on earth as it is in heaven." (Actually, there are many dispensational churches that refuse to pray the Lord's prayer, since it was supposedly part of the "Jewish dispensation" of the ministry of Jesus, not part of the "Church Age.") Why must we draw an absolute ethical distinction between heavenly citizenship and earthly citizenship? The pagan is subject to this distinction, but why must Christians be subject to it? Why must we adopt a theology which leads to a psychological "otherworldliness" in terms of our work on earth, and pessimism concerning our work's earthly results — the theology I call pietism? *It is this radical distinction between heaven and earth in the theology of dispensationalism which has played into the hands of the humanists.* Fundamentalists have been content to let evil men run the world, since the Christian's citizenship supposedly is exclusively in heaven. This is the theological basis of the alliance between the escapist religion and the power religion.

A Paradigm Shift

He is quite correct on one point, however. Dispensational eschatology is increasingly falling into disfavor. This is why he is worried, not just because a few charismatic preachers who are sloppy in their

---

21. Hunt and McMahon, pp. 215.

wording *appear* to have adopted New Age theology, lock, stock, and barrel. They have no more self-consciously adopted New Age theology than they have self-consciously adopted historic postmillennialism. It is not that they are drifting toward New Age religion; they are drifting instead toward historic postmillennialism. (I am probably the person most responsible for devising a strategy for speeding up this drift toward postmillennialism, which I think Mr. Hunt is aware of.)[22] But he is correct about the emerging paradigm shift from dispensationalism to postmillennialism, even if he is not correct about the coming holocaust:

> Two factions are now emerging within the church. One side adheres to the belief that an apostasy is coming for the church in the last days, and with it a great tribulation and God's judgment for the world. We are to rescue as many as we can before it is too late, calling them to citizenship in heaven. On the other side are those, equally sincere, who see the primary call of the church as solving social, economic, and political problems. Although they are also concerned to see souls saved, the conversion of the masses provides the means for taking over the world for Christ, taking dominion back from Satan, and thereby establishing the kingdom in order that Christ might return as king to reign at last. . . . There is a growing rejection within the church of this [first] fundamentalist scenario as negative, "gloom-and-doom" eschatology.[23]

This paragraph is accurate and very important. Mr. Hunt sees what all but one or two "positive confession" preachers have not even recognized in their own preaching and ministries: *they have become operational postmillennialists.* They have unquestionably broken psychologically with the older fundamentalism. They are returning, in short, to a historic Protestant eschatology, and are abandoning the Margaret Macdonald-John Nelson Darby-C. I. Scofield innovation of the nineteenth century.

Is he correct in his assessment that this shift represents a new commonality with New Agers who believe in "a common brotherhood" or the achievement of "authentic personhood"? I do not think so. If some "positive confession" preachers do pursue this New Age line, then they will eventually separate themselves from their former theological colleagues. They will begin to align themselves with

---

22. Gary North, "A Letter to Charismatics," *Christian Reconstruction*, IX (July/Aug. 1985).

23. Hunt and McMahon, pp. 215-16.

Robert Schuller and Norman Vincent Peale. There is no doubt that some of them have not come to grips with the Bible's teaching on Christology: that Jesus Christ in His incarnation was alone fully God and perfectly human.[24] Some of them have verbally equated Christian conversion with becoming divine. This is unquestionably incorrect. At conversion the Christian *definitively* has imputed to him Christ's *perfect humanity* (not His divinity), which he then *progressively* manifests through his earthly lifetime by means of his progressive ethical sanctification. But their confusion of language is a testimony to their lack of theological understanding; they *mean* "Christ's perfect humanity" when they say "Christ's divinity." Those who don't mean this will eventually drift away from the orthodox faith.

Unquestionably, getting one's doctrine of Christology straight ("ortho") is more important than getting the doctrine of eschatology straight. Postmillennialism with a false Christology is as perverse as dispensationalism with a false Christology. But a false Christology is independent of eschatology. Mr. Hunt implies that the poor wording of the "positive confession" charismatics' Christology reflects their eschatology. It doesn't. It simply reflects their sloppy wording and their lack of systematic study of theology and its implications, at least at this relatively early point in the development of the "positive confession" movement's history.

Mr. Hunt is well-read. He understands theology. This is why I find it very difficult to believe that Mr. Hunt really believes that a Robert Schuller-Robert Tilton sort of alliance is likely. Mr. Hunt understands far better than most observers what is *really* taking place. Indeed, it has already begun: bringing together the postmillennial Christian reconstructionists and the "positive confession" charismatics, with the former providing the footnotes, theology, and political action skills, and the latter providing the money, the audience, and the satellite technology.[25] It began when Robert Tilton's wife read Gary DeMar's *God and Government* in late 1983, and then persuaded her husband to invite a group of reconstructionists to speak before 1,000 "positive confession" pastors and their wives at a January 1984 rally sponsored by Rev. Tilton's church. The all-day

---

24. For the political implications of this creed, see R. J. Rushdoony, *The Foundations of Social Order: Studies in the Creeds and Councils of the Early Church* (Fairfax, Virginia: Thoburn Press, [1968] 1978), ch. 7: "The Council of Chalcedon: Foundation of Western Liberty."

25. Gary North, *Backward, Christian Soldiers?* (Tyler, Texas: Institute for Christian Economics, 1984), ch. 16: "The Three Legs of Christian Reconstruction's Stool."

panel was very well received.[26] DeMar subsequently taught a course on the Christian basis of civil government on Rev. Tilton's satellite network. It, too, was well received.

Mr. Hunt sees that if this fusion of theological interests takes place, then the day of unchallenged dominance by the old-time dispensational eschatology is about to come to an end. A new fundamentalism is appearing.[27] If the New Agers and New Dealers also recognized what Mr. Hunt has seen, they would be even more concerned than he is. The implicit and 60-year-old alliance between fundamentalism's escapist religion and the humanists' power religion is about to break up. The dominion religion of orthodox Christianity is going to challenge both of them. The false peace of this collapsing alliance, whose cornerstone has been the public school system, is being shattered by hard-core Christian activists who are tired of sitting in the back of humanism's bus.

It is not that the "positive confession" charismatics may be about to become New Age humanists; it is that they may be about to become Christian reconstructionists and postmillennialists. It is not simply Robert Tilton who constitutes Mr. Hunt's problem. It is also David Chilton.[28]

Conclusion

A paradigm shift is in progress inside American Protestant fundamentalism. It is a paradigm shift which above all involves the rethinking of the concept of dominion. Second, it involves a lengthening of the time perspective of Christians. Third, it involves a rethinking of the present-day authority of biblical law. This paradigm shift is not yet recognized, except by those who are self-consciously

26. To give a picture of what the new technology offers "the little guy," Rev. Robert Thoburn was one of the panel members. He was a former delegate to the House of Delegates in Virginia, and the founder of the most financially successful for-profit Christian school in America. Thirty days before the conference, he decided to write a paperback book, *The Christian in Politics.* He sat down in front of an IBM PC computer, wrote several chapters a day, and his son, a professional typesetter, typeset it from this computer's disks. The book was sent to the printers 10 days after he began, and 3,500 copies were available at the conference. The total investment was under $5,000, not counting the equipment. He sold the books and had his money back before the printer even sent the bill.

27. *Backward, Christian Soldiers?*, ch. 4: "Fundamentalism: Old and New."

28. David Chilton, *Paradise Restored: A Biblical Theology of Dominion* (Tyler, Texas: Reconstruction Press, 1985); *Days of Vengeance: A Commentary on the Book of Revelation* (Ft. Worth, Texas: Dominion Press, 1986).

pulling it off (the reconstructionists) and those whose paradigm is being threatened (the older fundamentalists).

The familiar refrain in dispensational circles has always been, "The end draweth nigh." This was as true in the 1830's as it is today. The end has not yet arrived. David Chilton's books make it clear that all the uproar about "the coming Armageddon" is based on a misinterpretation of what the Bible teaches. He revives the older Puritan view of eschatology, the view which was almost universally accepted in the mid-seventeenth century when the North American Protestant colonies were first colonized, and which motivated them in their efforts to turn a howling wilderness into a subdued garden.[29] Chilton shows why the supposed "old-time religion" of fundamentalism is, in fact, a recent theological development, and also why its interpretation of "the last days" is exegetically incorrect.

This gives Christians legitimate biblical reasons for earthly hope. It also gives us biblical reasons to get back in the comprehensive battle against the old enemy. Satan has been aided by the "old-time religion" of fundamentalism in his defensive attempts to maintain control of the institutions of power and influence. Fundamentalism's escapist theology was a way to defuse the eschatological time bomb of postmillennial victory. The eschatology of dominion has once again revived, as it has not since the period of the American Revolution. The defenders of the escapist religion do not appreciate what is happening—indeed, they are increasingly outraged—but they will be the beneficiaries anyway. They will lose their followers, but they will become residents of a Christian republic—or their heirs will, if we do not see it in our lifetimes.

This is not the end of the world. The church is not about to be raptured. The humanists, occultists, and New Agers are about to see their world ruptured. This process could be delayed by God's external judgment on the West, but it cannot be delayed until Christ's return in final judgment. It will happen long before Christ returns in glory.

In the meantime, God-fearing people must do their best to overcome the forces of evil, in time and on earth. Our citizenship is in heaven, and therefore we have a responsibility to do whatever we can to make this fallen world *progressively* resemble the sin-free world to come, just as we are to do in our personal lives, our families, and

---

29. *The Journal of Christian Reconstruction*, VI (Summer 1979): "Symposium on Puritanism and Progress."

our churches. Christ's kingdom is not *of* this world — its *place of origin* is in heaven — but it certainly is *in* this world, and has been from the beginning of His ministry.[30] It is the responsibility of Christians to make manifest on earth the kingdom which *in principle* has already come — manifest it in their personal ethics, and in civil, ecclesiastical, and every other kind of ethics.

God has regenerated people out of sin and into eternal life (John 3); He has also given these regenerate people the power to become sons of god (John 1:12). To say that He will not give them the ethical authority and ability to work out their salvation with fear and trembling (Phil. 2:12), *in every area of life*, is a counsel of despair, a message of defeat. It is also a message which is fading in popularity among younger Christians who will no longer tolerate the dispensational retreatism of their fathers. Best-selling author Hal Lindsey was wrong in the 1970's. It is not the late, great planet earth where we live; it is the world which we were called upon by God to subdue to His glory. Satan may be alive on planet earth, but he is not well; since Calvary, he has been mortally wounded. Let us suffer no longer the trembling shakes of Rapture fever. Let us get to work.

---

30. Gary North, *Backward Christian Soldiers?*, p. 4.

CONCLUSION

When spirits begin to speak with a man, he must beware that he believe nothing that they say. For nearly everything they say is fabricated by them, and they lie: for if they are permitted to narrate anything, as what heaven is and how things in the heavens are to be understood, they would tell so many lies that a man would be astonished.

Emanuel Swedenborg[1]

Secret knowledge revealed by secret sources inside secret societies is ultimately destructive knowledge. It results in the destruction of those who seek it and who think they have found it. The sources of the secret knowledge are liars, whether human or occult. If Swedenborg, who has been called the first spiritualist,[2] recognized this, how much more should the followers of Christ recognize it!

What we have surveyed so far is only the tip of the iceberg, if that. Occultism has been treated in detail in countless books in recent years: animal sacrifice, covens, human sacrifice, trances, spells, and so forth. What I have attempted to demonstrate is that the philosophy of occultism undergirds many movements that are not openly allied with the ancient arts of *wicca* (witchcraft). Occult forces exist that are not generally classified as witchcraft. In the case of Arigo, for example, the authorities could not prove that he prescribed potions or herbs. The Roman Catholic church did attempt to exorcise him, but having failed, the church's authorities steadily reclassified

---

1. Cited by Jacques Vallee, *The Invisible College* (New York: Dutton, 1975), p. 179.

2. "In a conscious state he wandered in the spirit world and conversed with the inhabitants as freely as with living men. He was in a sense the first spiritualist. Those who went before him did not commune with the spirits of departed men. Spirits were considered a different order of beings. The great principle of continuity was not known. It was he who bridged the gulf between life and death." Nandor Fodor, *The Encyclopaedia of Psychic Sciences* (New Hyde Park, New York: University Books, [1934] 1966), p. 373. He had been one of Sweden's greatest scientists, studying with Newton. At age 55, he retired and became a full-time mystic.

his powers as being simply *parapsychological*, which added an element of legitimacy to his healing. He himself distinguished between those of his patients who were genuinely ill and those who were under some sort of hex. (His vomiting occurred in the latter cases.)

The heart of the appeal of witchcraft is its promise of occult power. But this quest is supported by a philosophy of life. Man is to become God. Man's powers flow from the beyond, but not a God-controlled beyond. The restraints of biblical law are not acknowledged by practitioners of the occult arts. Some may acknowledge spirits as the source of their power; others, like LaVey, believe that the powers of witchcraft stem directly from man's link to impersonal forces of the universe. But all hold to *a view of man as a being wholly autonomous from the God of the Bible*. When they speak of God, it is not the God who prohibits occultism and warns men to test both prophets and spirits for their orthodoxy.

There is always a great temptation to investigate occultism for the sake of mere curiosity. It is exciting to be exposed to a world that is denied by one's former teachers. We are all subject to the "secret garden" syndrome, which is why most occult groups are so heavily immersed in mysteries, secret signs, oaths, and other such baggage. The Bible, in contrast, tells men to let their lights shine, not to hide their lights under a basket. Christians are to act like the city on a hill, illuminating all others with the wisdom of God. Secrecy may be a temporary measure in times of widespread persecution, but it is not the standard for the churches. But this lacks the excitement of belonging to a secret inner circle, or a supposed inner circle. The cell system of the Communist Party is efficient, no doubt, in keeping out spies, but it is not the ideal form of organization, for it cannot successfully resist conspiratorial, systematic, top-down evil.[3] One never knows just who is in control of such a cell system, and the structure leads to a kind of moral blindness — a blind following of orders from above and a stifling of those beneath.

C. S. Lewis warned against seeking to join any inner circle except one based on open principles of competence and service. "The lust for the esoteric, the longing to be inside, take[s] many forms which are not easily recognisable as Ambition. We hope, no doubt, for tangible profits from every Inner Ring we penetrate: power, money, liberty to break rules, avoidance of routine duties, evasion of disci-

---

3. Gary North, *Conspiracy: A Biblical View* (Ft. Worth, Texas: Dominion Press, 1986).

pline. But all these would not satisfy us if we did not get in addition the delicious sense of secret intimacy."[4] Being a member of some inner ring allows us to use the word "we" in contrast to "them," the outsiders. As he says, "your genuine Inner Ring exists for exclusion. There'd be no fun if there were no outsiders."[5]

The only inner circles worth joining are the church or professional associations. Membership is based on shared beliefs, open entry, and public standards. Pass a test, and you get in. Make a public profession of faith, and you get in. This is not the "inner ring" that Lewis talks about. These rings are open to the public; they increase the reign of morality and public service. He was speaking rather of the inner ring which draws you away from the rules that govern the outside world. Year by year, your loyalty shifts to members of the ring rather than to general principles of righteousness. "Of all passions the passion for the Inner Ring is most skillful in making a man who is not yet a very bad man do very bad things."[6] This is a major theme in his novel, *That Hideous Strength*. To save your integrity, you must get out.

The quest of the Inner Ring will break your hearts unless you break it. But if you break it, a surprising result will follow. If in your working hours you make the work your end, you will presently find yourself all unawares inside the only circle in your profession that really matters. You will be one of the sound craftsmen, and other sound craftsmen will know it. This group of craftsmen will by no means coincide with the Inner Ring or the Important People or the People in the Know. It will not shape that professional policy or work up that professional influence which fights for the profession as a whole against the public, nor will it lead to those periodic scandals and crises which the Inner Ring produces. But it will do those things which that profession exists to do and will in the long run be responsible for all the respect which that profession in fact enjoys and which the speeches and advertisements cannot maintain. And if in your spare time you consort simply with the people you like, you will again find that you have come unawares to a real inside, that you are indeed snug and safe at the centre of something which, seen from without, would look exactly like an Inner Ring. But the difference is that its secrecy is accidental, and its exclusiveness a by-product, and no one was led thither by the lure of the esoteric, for it is only four or five people who like one another meeting to do

---

4. C. S. Lewis, "The Inner Ring," in Lewis, *The Weight of Glory and Other Addresses* (New York: Macmillan, 1980), p. 100.

5. *Ibid.*, p. 104.

6. *Ibid.*, p. 103.

the things they like. This is friendship. Aristotle placed it among the virtues. It causes perhaps half of all the happiness in the world, and no Inner Ringer can ever have it.[7]

The only valid inner ring is the inner ring of *service*. It is the inner ring of those whose self-discipline makes them competent, people who enjoy the company of other competent people. It is the inner ring analogous to the one which the Apostles joined who followed Jesus. They sacrificed their jobs and at least temporarily their families also, but they were being trained to establish a worldwide service organization which would eventually spread across the face of the earth. It was not an inner ring based on secret signs, rituals, and doctrines; it was an inner ring of public preaching and, initially, public persecution by the established authorities. It was anti-Establishment because the Establishment was corrupt. It triumphed over the Roman Empire in the early fourth century, when there was no longer any other organized group with the numbers, the respect, the competence, the reliability, the institutional discipline, and the moral virtue necessary to pull together Rome's disintegrating civilization. Christ conquered Caesar by means of His service (and His followers' service) to God and man, not secrecy; by ethics, not power.

Curiosity Killed the Cat

Occultism is curious. It is fascinating. But it is not to be studied for its own sake. When the newly freed Israelites were being prepared for entrance into the promised land, which at the time was inhabited by numerous Canaanitic peoples, they were told to "make no mention of the name of other gods, neither let it be heard out of thy mouth" (Exodus 23:13). The temptation to delight in ghost stories is always present, and we should take care to guard ourselves from this temptation. Most of the stories are false, but some are true, and it is the true story which is believed that can harm men most.

We must always ask why we are investigating a topic, whether it be UFO's, Soviet prison camps, psychic healing, or whatever. Horror should not be indulged in for its own sake. The 1932 movie *Dracula* is not a horror film, but amusing, almost "camp," as they say. But *The Night of the Living Dead* and the various movies about a "bestial human who stalks unprotected young women, slaying

---

7. *Ibid.*, pp. 104-5.

several of them and their helpless boyfriends before being killed accidentally" are truly horrifying, and a person would be wise to avoid them. The same is true of most of the oddities described in this book. They are presented in order to instruct, not to invite imitation or endless research into the demonic.

The goal of this book is to present evidence of a set of phenomena that cannot be explained by the canons of Western rationalism. Some of them may be explainable, but not all. And even if there can conceivably be a post-Kantian explanation for a Ted Serios (which I doubt) or an Arigo (which I strongly doubt), this does not mean that the "rational" answer is, in fact, the accurate one. Ockham's epistemological razor—that the acceptable answer is always the simplest, that is, the one in closet conformity to the known laws of the universe—was devised by a radical religious skeptic who was self-consciously trying to push the signs of the supernatural out of the universe. Ockham's razor is not a neutral tool, and in times of growing irrationalism, occultism, and demonic activity, it is less and less useful in describing certain kinds of facts. Ockham's razor is best suited for a Christian culture which is not subjected to daily manifestations of occult power. When the rationalist culture which has abandoned the God of the Bible for Ockham's razor—a neutralist, rationalist conception of the autonomous universe—is invaded by the very supernatural, personal forces that rationalism denies, the exclusive use of Ockham's razor is suicidal.

This book is not to be used by men to achieve Screwtape's goal: persuading materialists to believe in demons but not in God. The demonic forces discussed in this book are powerful. We are wise to recall the second half of the first stanza of Martin Luther's most famous hymn, "A Mighty Fortress Is Our God":

"For still our ancient foe
Doth seek to work us woe;
His craft and power are great;
And, armed with cruel hate,
On earth is not his equal."

This hymn is a reminder of the power of God and His victory over the devil. Men who really do take its words seriously are not supposed to concentrate on the idea of Satan's power. They are to be reminded of the might of God's fortress.

"The prince of darkness grim,
We tremble not for him;
His rage we can endure,
For lo his doom is sure;
One little word shall fell him."

Conclusion

We must understand the kinds of enemies we face. A traditional rationalist who is tied to his nineteenth-century mechanistic world view does not recognize the dangers of real, existing, active, personal occult forces. The modern rationalist who simultaneously worships randomness and the laws of probability cannot recognize these dangers either. (He may, however, acknowledge that the manifestations of such power cannot be explained, on principle, unlike his nineteenth-century cousin, who believes that anything can be explained, given enough data and an appropriate theory.) We must recognize that the categories of humanistic reason have their limits, and he who is "purely rational" is blind to existing forces that can literally kill.

Occult revival and cultural disintegration can be reversed, but they can be reversed only by men who recognize their responsibilities under God to subdue the earth for the glory of God (Genesis 1:28). If those who call themselves Christians continue to ignore the cause of both occult revival and cultural disintegration, namely, the defection of Christians from the battlefields of life — social, intellectual, political, economic, artistic, educational — then the crises will only intensify. We are like stubborn mules; God has to hit us in the head several times before He catches our attention. I, for one, am tired of being hit over the head. I get the picture. It is time to go to work.[8]

---

8. Gary North, *Unconditional Surrender: God's Program for Victory* (2nd ed.; Tyler, Texas: Geneva Divinity School Press, 1983), Part III.

SCRIPTURE INDEX

OLD TESTAMENT

403

NEW TESTAMENT

INDEX

movies, 245, 257, 260
multiverse, 150-52
multiversity, 20, 25
Mumler, William, 108
Münsterberg, Hugo, 195-96
music, 6-7, 8-9, 11, 19, 103
mutants, 341
mutation, 340
Myers, John, 109
mysteries, 48, 62
mystery, 40, 41, 76, 146
mysticism, 27, 60-61, 335
myth, 50

nagual, 145-46, 149-50, 152-53
Naisbett, John, 365
Napoleon, 7
nature
    autonomy, 76
    conquest of, 37, 130-31
    Hall vs. Watson, 75-77
    laws of, 33
    magic, 282
    man over, 285-86
    oneness with, 115
nature/freedom, 33-34, 37-8, 130-31,
    142, 297
nature/grace, 30-33
Nautilus, 88
Nebel, Long John, 193
necromancy, 65
neo-evangelicals, 12-13
Netherlands, 174-80
networking, 376
neutrality, 60
New Age
    bureaucratized, 10
    elitism, 372
    evolution, 86n
    evolutionists, 368
    higher consciousness, 318
    key doctrine, 133
    leap of being, 318
    old view, 371
    optimism, 388-89
    philosophy, 359
    politics, 366, 369

"possibility thinking," 387
    Renaissance, 372
    revival, 6
    science, 82-87
    socialism &, 371
    West vs., 26
    world view, 5
New Alchemy Institute, 365
New Christian Right, 12, 14
New Deal, 11, 367
New Heavens, 376
New Left, 14
New World Education Fund, 365
New World Order, 189, 191-92, 340
new year, 276
New York City, 299
New York Times, 194, 201, 240-41,
    257, 289
newspapers, 257
Newton, Isaac, 22, 27, 45
Newtonianism, 28, 33, 41-3, 144,
    304, 310, 311
nihilism, 61
Nikolaiev, Karl, 90-91
1965
    Brazil, 244
    Castaneda's change, 137
    cute witches, 66
    inflation, 7
    Jeane Dixon, 184
    loss of faith, 156
    new beliefs, 223
    paranormal science, 82
    Project Blue Book, 303
    rise of counter-culture, 3
    rise of occultism, 3
    "Rubber Soul," 6, 249
    Soviet science, 88
    Soviet telepathy, 90
    Velikovsky, Immanuel, 246
    Watts riot, 7
Nisbet, Robert, 5, 14, 258
Nirvana, 355
Nixon, Richard, 9, 188, 197n, 240
noise, 50
nominalism, 35

The Dominion Covenant: Genesis

GARY NORTH

This is the first volume of a multi-volume commentary on the Bible. It is specifically an *economic* commentary — the first one ever published. What does the Bible require of men in the area of economics and business? What does the Bible have to say about economic theory? Does it teach the free market, or socialism, or a mixture of the two, or something completely different? Is there really an exclusively Christian approach to economics?

The Dominion Covenant: Genesis answers these questions, and many others, by setting forth the biblical foundations of economics. It offers the basis of a total reconstruction of economic theory and practice. It specifically abandons the universal presupposition of all modern schools of economics: Darwinian evolution. *Economics must begin with the doctrine of creation.*

The Dominion Covenant: Genesis represents a self-conscious effort to rethink the oldest and most rigorous social science in terms of the doctrine of creation. Every social science requires such a reconstruction. The "baptized humanism" of the modern Christian college classroom must be abandoned by all those who take seriously God's command that Christians go forth and subdue the earth (Gen. 1:28).

The message of this groundbreaking work is that God has given us clear, infallible standards of righteousness — practical guidelines by which Christians are to reconstruct civilization.

496 pp., indexed, bibliography, hb., $14.95
Dominion Press
P.O. Box 8204, Ft. Worth, TX 76124

Moses and Pharaoh: Dominion Religion Versus Power Religion

GARY NORTH

In the fifteenth century before the birth of Jesus, Moses came before Pharaoh and made what seemed to be a minor request: Pharaoh should allow the Israelites to make a three-day journey in order to sacrifice to their God. But this was not a minor request; given the theology of Egypt, *it was the announcement of a revolution* — an anti-humanist revolution.

The conflict between Moses and Pharaoh was a conflict between the religion of the Bible and its rival, the religion of humanism. It is not common for scholars to identify Egypt's polytheism with modern humanism, but the two theologies share their most fundamental doctrines: the irrelevance of the God of the Bible for the affairs of men; the evolution of man into God; the impossibility of an infallible word of God; the nonexistence of permanent laws of God; the impossibility of temporal judgment by God; and a belief in the power of man.

What Bible commentators have failed to understand is that the conflict between Moses and Pharaoh was at heart a conflict between the two major religions in man's history, *dominion religion* and *power religion*, with the third major religion — *escapist religion* — represented by the Hebrew slaves. What they have also failed to point out is that *there is an implicit alliance between the power religion and the escapist religion*. This alliance still exists.

This book is a detailed study of the conflict between Moses and Pharaoh. It discusses the implications of this conflict in several areas: theology, politics, sociology, and especially economics. This book is Part One of the second volume of a multi-volume set, *An Economic Commentary on the Bible*. The first volume, *The Dominion Covenant: Genesis*, was published in 1982.

432 pp., indexed, pb., $12.50
Dominion Press
P.O. Box 8204, Ft. Worth, TX 76124

The Sinai Strategy: Economics and the Ten Commandments

GARY NORTH

There can be little doubt that the Ten Commandments made possible the development of Western Civilization. There is almost equally little doubt that Western Civilization made possible the development of free market capitalism. The question must then be raised: What was it about the Ten Commandments which made possible the development of capitalism in the West, and nowhere else (except in cultures influenced by an already capitalistic West)?

It was not some hypothetical (and non-existent) universal natural law, or "natural law rightly understood," which made possible the development of the free market, but rather biblical law and a biblical concept of linear time. It was Western man's confidence in the validity of the Ten Commandments which alone created free market institutions in world history.

Is it therefore not sufficient to ask: Is capitalism Christian? It is not sufficient to appeal to natural law in the Christian West as the foundation of capitalism. What must be asked is a far more controversial question: Is orthodox, Bible-based Christianity inherently capitalistic? In other words, in cultures where the Bible is preached from Genesis to Revelation, will there be an innate tendency for that culture to adopt a free market economy? Therefore, is socialism inherently heretical biblically? Gary North answers "yes."

As secular humanism has steadily expanded its influence over the thinking of the West, especially the thinking of the intellectuals, the assault on free market capitalism has escalated. Humanism's denial of God's providence, God's law, and God's redeeming grace has created faith in a New World Order, a world in which elite central planners will direct a world-wide economic system. This is the society of Satan.

The Sinai Strategy is a detailed look at the Ten Commandments and their social, political, and, especially, economic implications. These commandments set forth a strategy of dominion. The war between capitalism and socialism is ultimately a war between God and Satan. Far too many compromised Christians have not recognized the nature of this ethical and institutional war, and they have sided with the socialists. Dr. North has drawn the dividing line between the humanists and the Christians themselves. Will it be God's law or Satan's, Christ's New World Order (inaugurated at Calvary) or Satan's New World Order (scheduled for the year 2000)?

396 pp., indexed, pb., $12.50
Dominion Press, P.O. Box 8204, Ft. Worth, TX 76124

Unconditional Surrender: God's Program for Victory

GARY NORTH

There is a war on. The war is between God and Satan. In our day, we see it most clearly in the conflicts between Christian institutions and the institutions of secular humanism. It is a war that is not going to go away. There will be a winner.

Unconditional Surrender is an introduction to this conflict. It covers the fundamental issues of the war: 1) What is the nature of *God*? 2) What is the nature of *man*? 3) What is the nature of *law*? If we can begin to answer these questions, then we will be able to recognize the nature of the battle.

Does Christianity make a difference in life? Does Christianity offer real-life solutions to the basic issues of life? Unquestionably, the answer is *yes*. But if we answer in the affirmative, then we have to start getting specific. Exactly how does Christianity make a difference? What kind of society would Christianity bring forth? In what ways would such a society be different from the society we live in today, the society of humanism? Is there a specifically biblical system of social ethics? What *practical* difference should Christianity make in the life of a ruler, businessman, judge, teacher, or scientist?

This book introduces people to the fundamentals of Christianity, including *applied* Christianity. It is thoroughly biblical. It provides evidence taken directly from the Scriptures. It offers suggestions for further reading, as well as the names and addresses of independent Christian organizations that are equipping Christians for the battles they face today.

264 pp., indexed, bibliography, pb., $9.95
Dominion Press
P.O. Box 8204, Ft. Worth, TX 76124

Backward, Christian Soldiers?
An Action Manual for
Christian Reconstruction

GARY NORTH

Jesus said to "Occupy till I come." But if Christians don't control the territory, they can't occupy it. They get tossed out into cultural "outer darkness," which is just exactly what the secular humanists have done to Christians in the 20th century: in education, in the arts, in entertainment, in politics, and certainly in the mainline churches and seminaries. Today, the humanists are "occupying." But they won't be for long. This book shows why.

For the first time in over a century, Christians are beginning to proclaim a seemingly new doctrine, yet the original doctrine was given to man by God: *dominion* (Genesis 1:28). But this doctrine implies another: *victory*. That's what this book is all about: *a strategy for victory*.

Satan may be alive on planet earth, but he's not well. He's in the biggest trouble he's been in since Calvary. If Christians adopt a *vision of victory* and a *program of Christian reconstruction*, we will see the beginning of a new era on earth: the kingdom of God manifested in every area of life. When Christ returns, Christians will be occupying, not hiding in the shadows, not sitting in the back of humanism's bus.

This book shows where to begin.

320 pp., indexed, pb., $5.95
Dominion Press
P.O. Box 8204, Ft. Worth, TX 76124

Conspiracy:
A Biblical View

GARY NORTH

Does the Council on Foreign Relations run America? No, God runs America!

Does the Council on Foreign Relations have more political influence than 50 million born-again Christians? You'd better believe it!

How can this be?

Conspiracy: A Biblical View introduces Christians to one of the most controversial topics today. What is the evidence for the conspiracy view of history? What is the theology which motivates conspirators? What are their tactics? Have they taken control over media, including higher education? What can Christians do to recapture America? These and many other questions are discussed in Dr. Gary North's latest work.

186 pp., indexed, pb., $6.95
Dominion Press
P.O. Box 8204, Ft. Worth, TX 76124

Paradise Restored: A Biblical Theology of Dominion

DAVID CHILTON

In recent years many Christians have begun to realize a long forgotten truth: God wants us to have dominion over the earth, just as He originally commanded Adam and Eve. By His atonement, Jesus Christ has restored us to Adam's lost position, guaranteeing that God's original plan will be fulfilled. God will be glorified throughout the world: *"The earth shall be full of the knowledge of the LORD, as the waters cover the sea." Isaiah 11:9.*

In order to demonstrate this truth from Scripture, David Chilton begins at the beginning, in the Garden of Eden. He shows how God established basic patterns in the first few chapters of Genesis — patterns which form the structure of later Biblical revelation. In the course of this book on eschatology, the reader is treated to an exciting, refreshingly *Biblical* way of reading the Bible. Avoiding the pitfalls of speculation, Chilton shows how even the most obscure prophecies can suddenly come alive with meaning to those who have grasped the Paradise Theme.

Building on a solid foundation of New Testament eschatology, the author deals at length with the message of the Book of Revelation — often with surprising results. Throughout the volume, the reader is confronted with the fact that our view of the *future* is inescapably bound up with our view of *Jesus Christ*. According to the author, the fact that Jesus is *now* King of kings and Lord of lords means that His Gospel must be victorious: the Holy Spirit will bring the water of life to the ends of the earth. The Christian message is one of Hope. Christ has defeated the devil, and we can look forward to increasing triumphs for His Kingdom in this age. Pentecost was just the beginning.

352 pp., indexed, bibliography, pb., $9.95
Dominion Press
P.O. Box 8204, Ft. Worth, TX 76124

The Days of Vengeance: An Exposition of the Book of Revelation

DAVID CHILTON

From the very beginning, cranks and crackpots have attempted to use Revelation to advocate some new twist on the Chicken Little Doctrine: *The Sky Is Falling!* But, as David Chilton shows in this careful, detailed exposition, St. John's Apocalypse teaches instead that Christians will overcome all opposition through the work of Jesus Christ. Most of the confusion over the meaning of the prophecy has resulted from a failure to apply five crucial interpretive keys to the Book of Revelation:

1. *Revelation is the most "Biblical" book in the Bible.* St. John quotes hundreds of passages from the Old Testament, often with subtle allusions to little-known rituals of the Ancient Near East. In order to understand Revelation, we need to know our Bibles backward and forward (or, at least, own a commentary that explains it!).

2. *Revelation is a prophecy about imminent events* — events that were about to break loose on the world of the first century. Revelation is not about nuclear warfare, space travel, or the end of the world. Again and again it specifically warns that "the time is near!" Revelation cannot be understood unless this fundamental fact is taken seriously.

3. *Revelation has a system of symbolism.* Everyone recognizes that St. John wrote his message in symbols. But the meaning of those symbols is not up for grabs. There is a systematic structure in Biblical symbolism. In order to understand Revelation properly, we must become familiar with the "language" in which it is written.

4. *Revelation is a worship service.* St. John did not write a textbook on prophecy. Instead, he recorded a heavenly worship service in progress. One of his major concerns, in fact, is that the worship of God is central to everything in life. It is the most important thing we do.

5. *Revelation is a book about dominion.* Revelation is not a book about how terrible the Antichrist is, or how powerful the devil is. It is, as the very first verse says, *The Revelation of Jesus Christ*. It tells us about His lordship over all; it tells us about our salvation and victory in the New Covenant, God's "wonderful plan for our life"; it tells us that the kingdom of the world has become the Kingdom of our God, and of His Christ; and it tells us that He shall reign forever and ever.

748 pp., indexed, bibliography, hb., $24.95
Dominion Press, P.O. Box 8204, Ft. Worth, TX 76124

Productive Christians in an Age of Guilt-Manipulators

David Chilton

One of the most insidious attacks upon orthodox Christianity has come from the so-called "Christian Left." This book answers the "bible" of that movement, *Rich Christians in an Age of Hunger*, by Ronald Sider.

David Chilton demonstrates that the "Christian Socialism" advocated by Sider is nothing more than baptized humanism—the goal of which is not charity, but raw, police-state power.

The debate between Sider and Chilton centers on one central issue: *Does the Bible have clear guidelines for every area of life?* Sider claims that the Bible does not contain "blueprints" for a social and economic order. The catch, of course, is that Sider then provides *his own* "blueprints" for society, calling for a taxation system which is completely condemned by God's infallible word. Chilton answers that the socialist "cure" is worse than the disease, for socialism actually *increases* poverty. Even when motivated by good intentions, unbiblical "charity" programs will damage the very people they seek to help.

Combining incisive satire with hard-hitting argumentation and extensive biblical references, Chilton shows that the Bible *does* have clear, forthright, and workable answers to the problem of poverty. *Productive Christians* is most importantly a major introduction to the system of Christian Economics, with chapters on biblical law, welfare, poverty, the third world, overpopulation, foreign aid, advertising, profits, and economic growth.

458 pp., indexed, bibliography, pb., $12.50
Dominion Press
P.O. Box 8204, Ft. Worth, TX 76124

You can purchase these and other
Dominion Press titles from your
local bookstore. If they are not in stock,
your bookstore may order them from:

Dominion Press
P.O. Box 8204
Ft. Worth, TX 76124

Is Someone You Love Involved with "Dungeons & Dragons"?

For a special report on this and other psychological fantasy games, send $2 to:

Fantasy Games Report
P.O. Box 8204
Ft. Worth, Texas 76124

_____
name

_____
address

_____
city, state, zip

WHY IS THIS
TEAR-OUT SHEET
STILL IN THIS BOOK?

Tear-out sheets are supposed
to be torn out and mailed in.

STOP
PROCRASTINATING!

Dr. Gary North
Institute for Christian Economics
P.O. Box 8000
Tyler, TX 75711

Dear Dr. North:

I read about your organization in your book, *Unholy Spirits*. I understand that you publish several newsletters that are sent out for six months free of charge. I would be interested in receiving them:

☐ *Biblical Economics Today*
    Dominion Strategies
    Christian Reconstruction
    and *Preface*

Please send any other information you have concerning your program.

_____
name

_____
address

_____
city, state, zip

☐ Enclosed is a tax-deductible donation to help meet expenses.

WHY IS THIS
TEAR-OUT SHEET
STILL IN THIS BOOK?

Tear-out sheets are supposed
to be torn out and mailed in.

STOP
PROCRASTINATING!